Governors State University
Library
Hours:
Monday thru Thursday 8:30 to 10:30
Friday and Saturday 8:30 to 5:00
Sunday 1:00 to 5:00 (Fall and Winter Trimester Only)

DEMCO

INFORMATION
SECURITY

INFORMATION SECURITY
PRINCIPLES AND PRACTICE

Mark Stamp
San Jose State University

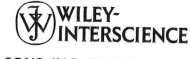

WILEY-
INTERSCIENCE

A JOHN WILEY & SONS, INC., PUBLICATION

Library of Congress Cataloging-in-Publication Data:

Stamp, Mark.
    Information security: principles and practice / Mark Stamp.
        p. cm.
    Includes bibliographical references and index.
    ISBN-10 0-471-73848-4 (cloth)
    ISBN-13 978-0-471-73848-0
    1. Computer security. I. Title.
    QA76.9.A25S69 2005
    005.8--dc22

                                        2005005152

Printed in the United States of America

10 9 8 7 6 5 4 3 2 1

To Melody, Austin, and Miles.

CONTENTS

3 SYMMETRIC KEY CRYPTO 33

4 PUBLIC KEY CRYPTO 61

III PROTOCOLS   207

9 SIMPLE AUTHENTICATION PROTOCOLS 209

10 REAL-WORLD SECURITY PROTOCOLS 235

PREFACE

I hate black boxes. One of my goals in writing this book was to illuminate some of those black boxes that are so popular in information security books today. On the other hand, I don't want to bore readers to death with trivial details (if that's what you want, go read some RFCs). As a result, I sometimes ignore details that I deem irrelevant to the topic at hand. You can judge whether I've struck the proper balance between these two competing goals.

Another goal of mine was to present the topic in a lively and interesting way. If any computing subject should be exciting and fun, it's information security. Security is happening now, it's in the news; it's clearly alive and kicking.

Some security textbooks offer a large dollop of dry useless theory. Reading one of these books is about as exciting as reading a calculus textbook. Other security books offer nothing but a collection of apparently unrelated facts, giving the impression that security is not really a coherent subject at all. Then there are books that present the topic as a collection of high-level managerial platitudes. These books may have a place, but if your goal is to design and build secure systems, you'd better understand something about the underlying technology. Finally, some security books focus on the human factors in security. While it is certainly critical to understand the role that human nature plays in security, I would argue that a security engineer must have a solid understanding of the inherent strengths and weaknesses of the technology before the human factors can be fully appreciated.

Information security is a huge topic, and unlike more established fields, it's not clear what material should be included in a book like this, or how best to organize the selected material. I've chosen to organize this book around the following four major themes.

- Cryptography
- Access Control
- Protocols
- Software

These themes are fairly elastic so that I can include what I consider to be the most significant material. For example, in my usage, access control includes the traditional topics of authentication and authorization, along with such nontraditional topics as firewalls and CAPTCHAs. The software theme is particularly flexible, including such diverse topics as secure software development, computer viruses, software reverse engineering, and operating systems.

I've strived to keep the presentation moving along in order to cover a reasonable selection of the most significant material. My goal is to cover each topic in just enough detail so that a reader can appreciate the basic security issue at hand and to avoid getting bogged down in trivia. I also attempt to regularly emphasize and reiterate the main points so that a significant point doesn't slip past the radar screen undetected.

Although this book is focused on practical issues, I've tried to cover enough of the fundamental principles so that the reader will be prepared for further study in the field. In addition, I've strived to minimize the required background knowledge as much as possible. In particular, the mathematical formalism has been kept to a bare minimum (the Appendix contains a review of all necessary math topics). Despite this self-imposed limitation, this book contains more substantive cryptography than most other security books. The required computer science background is also minimal—an introductory computer organization course (or comparable experience) is more than sufficient. Some programming experience and a rudimentary knowledge of assembly language would be helpful in a couple of sections, but it's not mandatory. Networking basics arise in a few sections. The Appendix contains a brief overview of networking that provides sufficient background material.

If you are an information technology professional who's trying to learn more about security, I would suggest that you read the entire book. Actually, that's my suggestion to everyone. But if you want to avoid the material that's most likely to slow you down and is not critical to the overall flow of the book, you can safely skip Section 4.5, all of Chapter 6 (though Section 6.3 is highly recommended), and Section 8.3.

If you are teaching a security class, it's important to realize that this book has more material than can be covered in a one semester course. The schedule that I generally follow in my undergraduate security class appears in the table below. This schedule allows ample time to cover a few of the optional topics.

Chapter	Hours	Comments
1. Introduction	1	Cover all.
2. Classic Cryptography	3	Sections 2.3.6 and 2.3.8 are optional.
3. Symmetric Key Crypto	4	Section 3.3.5 is optional.
4. Public Key Crypto	4	Omit 4.5; section 4.8 is optional.
5. Hash Functions	3	Cover 5.1 through 5.6 and 5.7.2. The remainder of 5.7 is optional.
6. Advanced Cryptanalysis	0	Omit entire chapter.
7. Authentication	4	Cover all.
8. Authorization	2	Cover 8.1 and 8.2. Sections 8.3 through 8.9 are optional (though 8.7 is recommended).
9. Authentication Protocols	4	Sections 9.4 and 9.5 are optional (9.5 is mentioned in Chapter 13).
10. Real-World Protocols	4	Cover all.
11. Software Flaws and Malware	4	Cover all.
12. Insecurity in Software	4	Sections 12.3 and 12.4 are optional. Recommended to cover part of 12.4.
13. OS and Security	3	Cover all.
Total	40	

Many variations on the outline above are possible. For example,

- For a greater emphasis on network security, cover the networking material in the Appendix and Sections 8.7 through 8.9. Then cover only the bare minimum of crypto and software topics.
- For a heavier crypto emphasis, cover all of Chapters 2 through 6 and Chapters 9 and 10 (where the crypto is applied) with selected additional topics as time permits. Although Chapter 6 is somewhat more technical than other chapters, it provides a solid introduction to cryptanalysis, a topic that is usually not treated in any substantive way, even in crypto books.
- If you prefer slightly more theory, cover security modeling in Sections 8.3 through 8.6, which can be supplemented by [212]. To stay within the time constraints, you can de-emphasize the software topics.

In any incarnation, a security course based on this book is an ideal venue for individual or group projects. The annotated bibliography provides an excellent starting point to search for suitable projects. In addition, many topics and problems lend themselves well to class discussions or in-class assignments (see, for example, Problem 13 in Chapter 10 or Problem 11 in Chapter 11).

If I were teaching this class for the first time, I would appreciate the PowerPoint slides that are available at the textbook website. These slides have all been thoroughly "battle tested" in a classroom setting and improved over several iterations. In addition, a solutions manual is available to instructors (sorry students) from the publisher.

It is also worth noting how the Appendices fit into the flow of the text. Appendix A-1, Network Security Basics, does not play a significant role until Part III. Even if you (or your students) have a solid foundation in networking, it's probably worthwhile to review this material, since networking terminology is not always consistent, and since the focus here is on security.

The Math Essentials of Appendix A-2 are required in various places. Elementary modular arithmetic (A-2.1) arises in a few sections of Chapter 3 and Chapter 5, while some of the more advanced concepts are required in Chapter 4 and Section 9.5. Permutations (A-2.2) are most prominent in Chapter 3, while elementary discrete probability (A-2.3) appears in several places. The elementary linear algebra in A-2.4 is only required in Section 6.4. Appendix A-3 is only used as a reference for problems in Chapter 3.

Just as any large and complex piece of software must have bugs, this book inevitably has errors. I would like to hear about any errors that you find. I will try to maintain a reasonably up-to-data errata on the textbook website. Also, I would appreciate a copy of any software that you develop that is related to the topics in this book. Applets that illustrate algorithms and protocols would be especially nice. And I'd appreciate problems or exercises that you develop and would be willing to share. Finally, don't hesitate to provide any suggestions you might have for future editions of this book.

ftp://ftp.wiley.com/public/sci_tech_med/information_security/

ABOUT THE AUTHOR

I've got more than a dozen years of experience in information security, including extensive work in industry and government. My work experience includes seven years at the National Security Agency followed by two years at a Silicon Valley startup company where I helped design and develop a digital rights management security product. This real-world work was sandwiched between academic jobs. While in academia, my research interests have included a wide variety of security topics.

With my return to academia in 2002, I quickly realized that none of the available security textbooks had much connection with the real world. I felt that I could write an information security book that would fill this gap, while also containing information that is vital to the working professional. I've honed the material by using the manuscript and notes as the basis for several information security classes I've taught over the past three years. As a result, I'm confident that the book succeeds as a textbook.

I also believe that this book will be valuable to working professionals, but then, I'm biased. I can say that many of my former students who are now at leading Silicon Valley companies tell me that the information they learned in my course has proved useful in the real world. And I certainly wish that a book like this had been available when I worked in industry, since my colleagues and I would have benefitted greatly from it.

I do have a life outside of information security. My family includes my lovely wife, Melody, and two great sons, Austin, whose initials are AES, and Miles, whose initials are not DES (thanks to Melody). We enjoy the outdoors, with frequent local trips involving such activities as bicycling, hiking, camping and fishing. I also spend too much time watching cartoons. Another favorite activity of mine is complaining about the absurd price of housing in the San Francisco Bay Area.

ACKNOWLEDGMENTS

My work in information security began when I was in graduate school. I want to thank my thesis advisor, Clyde F. Martin for introducing me to this fascinating subject.

In my seven years at NSA, I learned more about security than I could have learned in a lifetime anywhere else. Unfortunately, the people who taught me so much must remain anonymous.

At my ill-fated startup company, MediaSnap, Inc., I witnessed firsthand the commercial pressures that all-too-often lead to bad security. In spite of these pressures, we produced a high-quality digital rights management product that was far ahead of its time. I want to thank all at MediaSnap, and especially Joe Pasqua and Paul Clarke, for giving me the chance to work on such a fascinating and challenging project.

This book would not have been possible without the students here at San Jose State University who helped me to refine my notes over the past three years. Some of the students who deserve special mention for going above and beyond the call of duty include Wing Wong, Martina Simova, Deepali Holankar, Xufen Gao, Neerja Bhatnager, Amit Mathur, Ali Hushyar, Smita Thaker, Subha Rajagopalan, Puneet Mishra, Jianning Yang, Konstantin Skachkov, Jian Dai, Thomas Nikl, Ikai Lan, Thu Nguyen, Samuel Reed, Yue Wang, David Stillion, Edward Yin, and Randy Fort.

Richard Low, a colleague here at SJSU, provided helpful feedback on an early version of the manuscript. David Blockus deserves special mention for giving me detailed comments on each chapter at a particularly critical juncture in the writing of this book.

I want to thank all of the people at Wiley who applied their vast expertise to make the book writing process as painless as possible. In particular, Val Moliere, Emily Simmons, and Christine Punzo were all extremely helpful.

Of course, all remaining flaws are my responsibility alone.

1

INTRODUCTION

"Begin at the beginning," the King said, very gravely,
"and go on till you come to the end: then stop."
—Lewis Carroll, *Alice in Wonderland*

1.1 THE CAST OF CHARACTERS

Following tradition, Alice and Bob are the good guys. Occasionally we'll require additional good guys, such as Charlie.

Trudy is a generic bad guy who is trying to attack the system in some way. Some authors employ a team of bad guys where the name implies the particular nefarious activity. In this usage, Trudy is an "intruder" and Eve is an "eavesdropper" and so on. Trudy will be our all-purpose bad guy.

Alice, Bob, Trudy and the rest of the gang need not be humans. For example, one possible scenario would be that Alice is a laptop, Bob a server, and Trudy a human.

1.2 ALICE'S ONLINE BANK

Suppose that Alice starts an online banking business, appropriately named Alice's Online Bank[1], or AOB. What are Alice's information security concerns? If Bob is Alice's customer, what are his information security concerns? Are Bob's concerns the same as Alice's? If we look at AOB from Trudy's perspective, what security vulnerabilities might we see?

---

[1]Not to be confused with "Alice's Restaurant" [100].

Information Security: Principles and Practice, by Mark Stamp
Copyright © 2006 John Wiley & Sons, Inc.

First, let's consider the traditional triumvirate of confidentiality, integrity, and availability in the context of Alice's Bank. Then we'll point out some of the many other security concerns.

1.2.1 Confidentiality, Integrity, and Availability

Confidentiality aims to prevent unauthorized reading of information. AOB probably wouldn't care much about the confidentiality of the information it deals with, except for the fact that its customers certainly do. Bob doesn't want Trudy to know how much money he has in his savings account. Alice's Bank would also face legal problems if it failed to protect the confidentiality of such information.

Information has *integrity* if unauthorized writing is prohibited. Alice's Bank must protect the integrity of account information to prevent Trudy from, say, increasing the balance in her account or changing the balance in Bob's account.

Denial of service, or DoS, attacks are a relatively recent concern. Such attacks try to reduce access to information. As a result of the rise in DoS attacks, data *availability* has become a fundamental issue in information security. Availability is a concern for both Alice's Bank and Bob. If AOB's website is unavailable, then Alice can't make money from customer transactions and Bob can't get his business done. Bob might then take his business elsewhere. If Trudy has a grudge against Alice—or if she just wants to be malicious—she might attempt a denial of service attack on Alice's Online Bank.

1.2.2 Beyond CIA

Confidentiality, integrity, and availability (CIA) are only the beginning of the information security story. When Bob logs on to his computer, how does Bob's computer determine that "Bob" is really Bob and not Trudy? And when Bob logs into his account at Alice's Online Bank, how does AOB know that "Bob" is really Bob and not Trudy? Although these two authentication problems look similar on the surface, under the surface they are completely different. Authentication on a stand-alone system requires that Bob's password be verified. To do this securely, some clever techniques from the field of *cryptography* are required.

Authentication over a network is open to many kinds of attacks. The messages sent over a network can be viewed by Trudy. To make matters worse, Trudy can not only intercept messages, she can alter messages and insert messages of her own making. She can also replay old messages in an effort to, say, convince AOB that she is really Bob. Authentication in such a situation requires careful attention to the *protocols* that are used. Cryptography also has an important role to play in security protocols.

Once Bob has been authenticated by Alice's Bank, then Alice must enforce restrictions on Bob's actions. For example, Bob can't look at Charlie's account balance or install new accounting software on the system. However, Sam, the system administrator, can install new accounting software on AOB's system. Enforcing such restrictions is the domain of authorization. Note that authorization places restrictions on the actions of authenticated users. Since authentication and authorization both deal with issues of access to resources, we'll lump them together under the heading of *access control*.

All of the information security mechanisms discussed so far are implemented in *software*. Modern software systems tend to be large, complex, and rife with bugs. These bugs often lead to security flaws. What are these flaws and how are they exploited? How can AOB be sure that its software is behaving correctly? How can AOB's software developers limit the number of security flaws in the software they develop? We'll examine these software development related questions (and much more) when we discuss software.

Although bugs can (and do) give rise to security flaws, these security flaws are created unintentionally. On the other hand, some software is written with the intent of doing evil. Such malicious software, or malware, includes the all-too-familiar computer viruses and worms that plague the Internet today. How do these nasty beasts do what they do, and what can Alice's Bank do to limit their damage? What can Trudy do to increase the nastiness of such pests? We'll consider these and similar questions when we study software.

Bob also has many software concerns. For example, when Bob enters his password on his computer, how does he know that his password has not been captured and sent to Trudy? If Bob conducts a transaction at www.alicesonlinebank.com, how does he know that the transaction he sees on his screen is the same transaction that actually goes to the bank? In general, how can Bob be confident that his software is behaving as it should, instead of as Trudy would like it to behave? We'll consider these questions as well.

When discussing software and security, we'll need to consider operating system, or OS, topics. Operating systems are themselves large and complex pieces of software. OSs also enforce much of the security in any system, so some knowledge of OSs is necessary in order to more fully appreciate the challenges of information security.

1.3 ABOUT THIS BOOK

Lampson [139] states that real-world security depends on the following three things

- Specification/policy: What is the system supposed to do?
- Implementation/mechanism: How does it do it?
- Correctness/assurance: Does it really work?

I would add a fourth

- Human nature: Can the system survive "clever" users?

The focus of this book is primarily on the implementation/mechanism front. I believe this is appropriate, since the strengths, weaknesses, and inherent limitations of the mechanisms directly affect all of the other critical aspects of security. In other words, without a reasonable understanding of the mechanisms, it is not possible to have an informed discussion of any of the other three issues.

I've categorized the topics covered in this book into four major parts. The first part deals with cryptography, and the next two parts cover access control and protocols, respectively. The final part deals with the vast topic of software.

1.3.1   Cryptography

Cryptography or "secret codes" are a fundamental information security tool. Cryptography has many uses, including the protection of confidentiality and integrity, among many other vital information security functions. We'll discuss cryptography in detail, since this is essential background for much of the remainder of the book.

We'll begin our discussion of cryptography with a look at a handful of classic cipher systems. These classic systems illustrate fundamental principles that are employed in modern digital cipher systems, but in a more user-friendly format.

With this background, we'll be prepared to study modern cryptography. Symmetric key cryptography and public key cryptography both play major roles in information security, and we'll spend an entire chapter on each of these topics. We'll then turn our attention to hash functions, which are another fundamental security tool. Hash functions are used in many different contexts in information security. Some of these uses are quite surprising and not always intuitive. We'll discuss applications of hash functions to online bidding and spam reduction.

We'll also briefly consider a few special topics that are related to cryptography. For example, we'll discuss information hiding, where the goal is for Alice and Bob to communicate information without Trudy even knowing that any information has been passed. This is closely related to the concept of digital watermarking, which we also cover briefly.

The final chapter on cryptography deals with modern cryptanalysis, that is, the methods used to break modern cipher systems. Although this is relatively technical and specialized information, it's necessary to appreciate the attack methods in order to understand the design principles behind modern cryptographic systems.

1.3.2   Access Control

Access control deals with authentication and authorization. In the area of authentication, we'll consider many issues related to passwords. Passwords are the most often used form of authentication today, but this is primarily because passwords are free and definitely not because they are secure.

We'll consider how to securely store passwords. Then we'll delve into the issues surrounding secure password selection. Although it is possible to select strong passwords that are relatively easy to remember, it's difficult to enforce such policies on users. In fact, weak passwords present a major security weakness in most systems.

The alternatives to passwords include biometrics and smartcards. We'll consider some of the security benefits of these forms of authentication. In particular, we'll discuss the details of several biometric authentication methods.

Authorization deals with restrictions placed on authenticated users. Once Alice's Bank is convinced that Bob is really Bob, it must to enforce restrictions on Bob's actions.

The two classic methods for enforcing such restrictions are access control lists and capabilities. We'll look at the pluses and minuses of each of these authorization methods.

Authorization leads naturally to a few relatively specialized topics. We'll discuss multilevel security (and the related topic of multilateral security). For example, the military has TOP SECRET and SECRET information. Some users can see both types of information, while other users can only see the SECRET information. If both types of information are on a single system, how can we enforce such restrictions? This is an authorization issue that has potential implications far beyond classified military and government systems.

Multilevel security leads naturally into the rarified air of security modeling. The idea behind such modeling is to lay out the essential security requirements of a system. Ideally, by verifying a few simply properties, we would know that a particular system satisfies a particular security model. If so, the system would automatically inherit all of the security properties that are known to hold for such a model. We'll only present two of the simplest security models, both of which arise in the context of multilevel security.

Multilevel security also provides an opportunity to discuss covert channels and inference control. Covert channels are unintended channels of communication. Such channels are common and create potential security problems. Inference control attempts to limit the information that can unintentionally leak out of a database due to legitimate user queries. Both covert channels and inference control are difficult problems to deal with effectively in real-world systems.

Since firewalls act as a form of access control for the network, we stretch the usual definition of access control to include firewalls. Regardless of the type of access control employed, attacks are bound to occur. An intrusion detection system (IDS) is designed to detect attacks in progress. So we include a discussion of IDS techniques after our discussion of firewalls.

1.3.3 Protocols

We'll then cover security protocols. First, we'll consider the general problem of authentication over a network. Many examples will be provided, each of which illustrates a particular security pitfall. For example, replay is a critical problem, and we'll consider ways to prevent such an attack.

Cryptography will prove useful in authentication protocols. We'll give example of protocols that use symmetric cryptography, as well as examples that rely on public key cryptography. Hash functions also have an important role to play in security protocols.

Our study of simple authentication protocols will illustrate some of the subtleties that can arise in the field of security protocols. A seemingly insignificant change to a protocol can completely change its security. We'll also highlight several specific techniques that are commonly used in real-world security protocols.

Then we'll move on to study four specific security protocols. The first of these is the Secure Socket Layer, or SSL, which is used extensively to secure e-commerce on the Internet today. SSL is an elegant and efficient protocol.

We'll then discuss IPSec, which is another Internet security protocol. Conceptually, SSL and IPSec share many similarities, but the implementations differ greatly. In contrast to SSL, IPSec is complex and "over-engineered." Apparently due to its complexity, several security flaws are present in IPSec—despite a lengthy and open development process. This nicely illustrates the challenges inherent in developing security protocols.

The third real-world protocol that we'll consider is Kerberos, which is an authentication system based on symmetric cryptography. Kerberos follows an approach much different from either SSL or IPSec.

We'll also discuss the security mechanisms employed in GSM, a cellular phone system. Although the GSM security protocol is fairly simple, it's an interesting case study due to the large number of known attacks. These attacks include various combinations of attacks on the protocol itself, as well as the underlying cryptography.

1.3.4   Software

In the final part of the book, we'll take a look at some aspects of security and software. This is a huge topic, and we can only cover selected issues. We'll discuss security flaws and malware, which we've mentioned above.

We'll also consider software reverse engineering in order to illustrate how a dedicated attacker can deconstruct software, even without access to the source code. We then apply our newfound hacker's knowledge to the problem of digital rights management, which provides an excellent example of the limits of security in software—particularly when that software must execute in a hostile environment.

Our final software-related topic is operating systems (OSs). The OS is the arbiter of most security operations, so it's important to understand how the OS enforces security.

We then consider the requirements of a so-called trusted OS. A trusted OS provides strong assurances that the OS is performing properly. After this background, we consider a recent attempt by Microsoft to implement a trusted OS for the PC platform. This discussion further illustrates the challenges inherent in implementing security in software.

1.4   THE PEOPLE PROBLEM

Clever users have the ability to destroy the best laid security plans. For example, suppose that Bob wants to purchase an item from Amazon.com. Bob can use his Web browser to securely contact Amazon using the SSL protocol (discussed in Part III), which relies on cryptographic techniques (as discussed in Part I). Various access control issues arise in such a transaction (Part II), and all of these security mechanisms are enforced in software (Part IV). We'll see in Chapter 10, that a particular attack on this transaction will cause Bob's Web browser to issue a warning. Unfortunately, if Bob is a typical user, he will simply ignore the warning, which has the effect of defeating the security—regardless of how secure the cryptography, how well-designed the protocols and access control mechanisms, and how flawless the software.

To take just one more example, a great deal of security today rests on passwords. Users want to choose easy to remember passwords, but this makes it easier for Trudy to guess passwords—as discussed in Chapter 7. An obvious solution is to assign strong passwords to users. However, this is almost certain to result in passwords written on post-it notes and posted in prominent locations, making the system less secure than if users were allowed to choose their own (relatively weak) passwords.

The primary focus of this book is on understanding security mechanisms—the nuts and bolts of information security. In a few places, the "people problem" is discussed, but it would be possible to write several volumes on this topic. For more information on the role that humans play in information security, perhaps the best source is Ross Anderson's excellent book [14], which is filled with case studies of security failures, most of which have their roots firmly in human nature.

1.5 PRINCIPLES AND PRACTICE

This book is not a theory book. I've consciously tried to keep the focus on practical issues, and where some theory is required, I've strived to keep it to a minimum. My goal is to present just enough of the theory so that the reader can grasp the fundamental principles. For a more theoretical treatment of many of the topics discussed in this book, Bishop's book [27] is the obvious choice.

1.6 PROBLEMS

> *The problem is not that there are problems. The problem is*
> *expecting otherwise and thinking that having problems is a problem.*
> —Theodore I. Rubin

1. Among the fundamental challenges in information security are confidentiality, integrity, and availability, or CIA. Give an example where confidentiality is required, but not integrity. Give an example where integrity is required, but not confidentiality. Give an example where availability is the overriding concern.

2. RFID tags are extremely small devices capable of broadcasting a number over the air that can be read by a nearby sensor. It is predicted that RFID tags will soon be found in all sorts of products, including paper money, clothing items, and so on. If this occurs, a person could be surrounded by a "cloud" of RFID number that would provide a great deal of information about the person. Discuss some privacy and other security concerns that this might raise.

3. From a bank's perspective, which is usually more important, the integrity of its customer's data or the confidentiality of the data? From the perspective of the bank's customer, which is more important?

4. Some authors distinguish between secrecy, privacy, and confidentiality. In this usage, secrecy is equivalent to our use of the term confidentiality, whereas privacy is secrecy applied to personal data and confidentiality refers to an obligation not to divulge certain information. Discuss an example where privacy is required. Discuss an example where confidentiality (in this sense) is required.

5. Read the article [126] on Byzantine failure. Describe the problem and explain why the problem cannot occur if there are four generals, only one of which is a traitor. Why is this problem relevant to information security?

Part I

CRYPTO

2

CRYPTO BASICS

MXDXBVTZWVMXNSPBQXLIMSCCSGXSCJXBOVQXCJZMOJZCVC
TVWJCZAAXZBCSSCJXBQCJZCOJZCNSPOXBXSBTVWJC
JZDXGXXMOZQMSCSCJXBOVQXCJZMOJZCNSPJZHGXXMOSPLH
JZDXZAAXZBXHCSCJXTCSGXSCJXBOVQX

—plaintext from Lewis Carroll, *Alice in Wonderland*

The solution is by no means so difficult as you might
be led to imagine from the first hasty inspection of the characters.
These characters, as any one might readily guess,
form a cipher—that is to say, they convey a meaning...
—Edgar Allan Poe, *The Gold Bug*

2.1 INTRODUCTION

In this chapter, we'll discuss some of the basic elements of cryptography. This chapter will lay the foundation for the remaining crypto chapters, which, in turn, underpin much of the remainder of the book. We'll avoid mathematical rigor as much as possible, but we'll attempt to provide enough of the details so that you not only understand the "what" but can also appreciate the "why." ' After this introductory chapter, the focus of the remaining crypto chapters are the four major topics of

- symmetric key cryptography,
- public key cryptography,
- hash functions, and

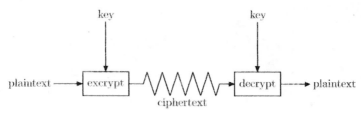

Figure 2.1. Crypto as a black box.

- advanced cryptanalysis.

A handful of special topics are also covered.

2.2 HOW TO SPEAK CRYPTO

The basic terminology of crypto includes the following.

- *Cryptology* is the art and science of making and breaking "secret codes."
- *Cryptography* is the making of "secret codes."
- *Cryptanalysis* is the breaking of "secret codes."
- *Crypto* is a synonym for any or all of the above (and more). The precise meaning should be clear from context.

A *cipher* or *cryptosystem* is used to *encrypt* data. The original data is known as *plaintext*, and the result of encryption is *ciphertext*. We *decrypt* the ciphertext to recover the original plaintext. A *key* is used to configure a cryptosystem for encryption and decryption. In a *symmetric* cipher, the same key is used to encrypt and to decrypt, as illustrated in the "black box" cryptosystem in Figure 2.1.[1]

There is also a concept of *public key* cryptography where the encryption and decryption keys are different. Since different keys are used, it's possible to make the encryption key public. In public key crypto, the encryption key is appropriately known as the *public key*, whereas the decryption key, which must remain secret, is the *private key*. In symmetric key crypto, the key is known as a *symmetric key*. We'll avoid the ambiguous term "secret key."

With any cipher, the goal is to have a system where the key is necessary in order to recover the plaintext from the ciphertext. That is, even if the attacker, Trudy, has complete knowledge of the algorithms used and lots of other information (to be made more precise later), she can't recover the plaintext without the key. That's the goal, although reality sometimes differs significantly.

A fundamental tenet of cryptography is that the inner workings of the cryptosystem are completely known to the attacker, Trudy, and the only secret is a key. This is known

---

[1]This is the only black box you'll find in this book.

as *Kerckhoffs Principle*, named after its originator, who in [125] laid out six principles of cipher design and use. The principle that now bears Kerckhoffs' name states that a cipher "must not be required to be secret, and it must be able to fall into the hands of the enemy without inconvenience" [124], that is, the design of the cipher is not secret.

What is the point of Kerckhoffs Principle? After all, life must certainly be more difficult for Trudy if she doesn't know how a cipher works. While this may be true, it's also true that the details of cryptosystems seldom remain secret for long. Reverse engineering efforts can easily recover algorithms from software, and algorithms embedded in tamper-resistant hardware are susceptible to similar attacks. And even more to the point, secret crypto-algorithms have a long history of failing to be secure once the algorithm has been exposed to public scrutiny—see [23] for a timely example. For these reasons, the cryptographic community will not accept an algorithm as secure until it has withstood extensive analyses by many cryptographers over an extended period of time. The bottom line is that any cryptosystem that does not satisfy Kerckhoffs Principle must be assumed flawed. That is, a cipher is "guilty until proven innocent."

Kerckhoffs Principle can be extended to cover aspects of security other than cryptography. In other contexts, Kerckhoffs Principle is taken to mean that the security design itself is open. The belief is that "more eyeballs" are more likely to expose security flaws. Although Kerckhoffs Principle (in both forms) is widely accepted in principle, there are many real-world temptations to violate this fundamental tenet, almost invariably with disastrous consequences for security. We'll see several examples of this throughout the book.

In the next section, we'll look briefly at a few classic cryptosystems. Although the history of crypto is a fascinating topic [119], the purpose of this material is simply to provide an elementary introduction to some of the crucial concepts that arise in modern cryptography.

2.3 CLASSIC CRYPTO

We'll examine four classic cryptosystems, each of which illustrates some particularly relevant feature. First on our agenda is the simple substitution, which is one of the oldest cipher systems—dating back at least 2,000 years—and one that is ideal for illustrating basic attacks. We then turn our attention to a double transposition cipher, which includes important concepts that are used in modern ciphers. We also discuss classic codebooks, since many modern ciphers can be viewed as the "electronic" equivalent of codebooks. Finally, we consider the only practical cryptosystem that is provably secure—the one-time pad.

2.3.1 Simple Substitution Cipher

In a particularly simple implementation of a simple substitution cipher, the message is encrypted by substituting the letter of the alphabet n places ahead of the current letter.

For example, with $n = 3$, the substitution—which acts as the key—is

```
plaintext:  a b c d e f g h i j k l m n o p q r s t u v w x y z
ciphertext: D E F G H I J K L M N O P Q R S T U V W X Y Z A B C
```

where we've followed the convention that the plaintext is lowercase and the ciphertext is uppercase. In this example, the key could be stated more succinctly as "3" since the amount of the shift is the key.

Using the key of 3, we can encrypt the plaintext message

```
fourscoreandsevenyearsago
```

by looking up each letter in the plaintext row and substituting the corresponding letter in the ciphertext row or by simply replacing each letter by the letter that is three positions ahead of it in the alphabet. In this particular example, the resulting ciphertext is

```
IRXUVFRUHDAGVHYHABHDUVDIR
```

It should be clear why this cipher is known as a simple substitution.

To decrypt, we simply look up the ciphertext letter in the ciphertext row and replace it with the corresponding letter in the plaintext row, or simply shift each ciphertext letter backward by three. The simple substitution with a shift of three is known as the Caesar's cipher because it was reputedly used with success by Julius Caesar.

If we limit the simple substitution to shifts, then the possible keys are $n \in \{0, 1, 2, \ldots, 25\}$. Suppose Trudy intercepts the ciphertext message

```
CSYEVIXIVQMREXIH
```

and she suspect that it was encrypted with a simple substitution cipher of the "shift by n" variety. Then she can try each of the 26 possible keys, decrypting the message with each putative key and checking whether the resulting putative plaintext looks like sensible plaintext. If the message really was encrypted via a shift by n, Trudy can expect to find the true plaintext—and thereby recover the key—after 13 tries, on average.

The brute force approach of trying all possible keys until we stumble across the correct one is known as an *exhaustive key search*. Since this attack is always an option, it's necessary (although far from sufficient) that the number of possible keys be too large for Trudy to simply try them all in any reasonable amount of time.

How large of a keyspace is large enough? Suppose Trudy has an incredibly fast computer that's able to test 2^{40} keys each second.[2] Then a keyspace of size 2^{56} can be

---

[2] In 1998 the Electronic Frontier Foundation (EFF) built a special-purpose key cracking machine for attacking the Data Encryption Standard (DES, which we'll discuss in the next chapter). This machine, which cost $220,000, consisted of about 43,200 processors, each of which ran at 40 MHz and was capable of testing about 2.5 million keys per second [116]. Extrapolating this to a state-of-the-art PC with a single 4 GHz processor, Trudy could test fewer than 2^{30} keys per second on one such machine.

exhausted in 2^{16} seconds or about 18 hours, whereas a keyspace of size 2^{64} would take more than half a year to exhaust.

The simple substitution cipher need not be limited to shifting by n. Any permutation of the 26 letters will suffice as a key. For example, the following key, which is not a shift of the alphabet, defines a simple substitution cipher

```
plaintext:  a b c d e f g h i j k l m n o p q r s t u v w x y z
ciphertext: Z P B Y J R G K F L X Q N W V D H M S U T O I A E C
```

If a simple substitution cipher can employ any permutation as a key, then there are 26! $\approx 2^{88}$ possible keys. With our superfast computer that tests 2^{40} keys per second, a keyspace of size 2^{88} would take more than 8900 millennia to exhaust. Of course, we'd expect to find the correct key half that time, or "just" 4450 millennia! Since 2^{88} keys is far more than Trudy can try in any reasonable amount of time, this cipher passes our first requirement, namely, that the keyspace is big enough to make an exhaustive key search infeasible.

Does this mean that a simple substitution cipher is secure? The answer is no, as the attack described in the next section illustrates.

2.3.2 Cryptanalysis of a Simple Substitution

Suppose Trudy intercepts the following ciphertext, which she suspects was produced by a simple substitution cipher—though not necessarily a shift by n.

```
PBFPVYFBQXZTYFPBFEQJHDXXQVAPTPQJKTOYQWIPBVWLXTOXBTFXQWAXBVCXQWAXFQ
JVWLEQNTOZQGGQLFXQWAKVWLXQWAEBIPBFXFQVXGTVJVWLBTPQWAEBFPBFHCVLXBQU
FEVWLXGDPEQVPQGVPPBFTIXPFHXZHVFAGFOTHFEFBQUFTDHZBQPOTHXTYFTODXQHFT
DPTOGHFQPBQWAQJJTODXQHFOQPWTBDHHIXQVAPBFZQHCFWPFHPBFIPBQWKFABVYYDZ
BOTHPBQPQJTQOTOGHFQAPBFEQJHDXXQVAVXEBQPEFZBVFOJIWFFACFCCFHQWAUVWFL
QHGFXVAFXQHFUFHILTTAVWAFFAWTEVOITDHFHFQAITIXPFHXAFQHEFZQWGFLVWWPTOFFA
```

(2.1)

Since it's too much work for Trudy to try all 2^{88} possible keys, can she be more clever? Assuming the underlying message is English, Trudy can make use of the English letter frequency counts in Figure 2.2 together with the frequency counts for the *ciphertext 2.1*, which appear in Figure 2.3.

From the ciphertext frequency counts, Trudy can see that "F" is the most common letter in the ciphertext message, whereas, according to Figure 2.2, "E" is the most common letter in the English language. Trudy therefore surmises that it's likely that "F" has been substituted for "E." Continuing in this manner, Trudy can try likely substitutions until she recognizes words, at which point she can be confident in her assumptions.

Initially, the easiest word to determine might be the first word, since Trudy doesn't know where the spaces belong in the text. Since the third letter is "e," and given the high frequency counts of the first two letter, Trudy might reasonably guess (correctly, as it turns out) that the first word of the plaintext is "the." Making these substitutions into the remaining ciphertext, she will be able to guess more letters and the puzzle will quickly unravel. Trudy will likely make some missteps along the way, but with sensible

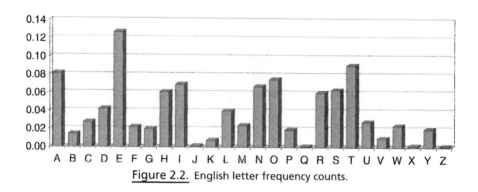

Figure 2.2. English letter frequency counts.

use of the statistical information available, she will find the plaintext in far less than 4450 millennia!

This attack on the simple substitution cipher shows that a large keyspace is not sufficient to ensure security. This attack also shows that cipher designers must guard against clever attacks. But how can we protect against all such attacks, since clever new attacks are developed all the time? The answer is that we can't. As a result, a cipher can only be considered secure as long as no attack against it has yet been found. And the more skilled cryptographers who have tried to break a cipher and failed, the more confidence we can have in the system.

2.3.3 Definition of Secure

There are several reasonable definitions of a secure cipher. Ideally, we would like to have mathematical proof that there is no feasible attack on the system. However, there is only one cipher system that comes with such a proof, and it's impractical for most uses.

Lacking a proof of the strength of a cipher, we could require that the best-known attack on the system is impractical. While this would seem to be the most desirable property, we'll choose a slightly different definition. We'll say that a cryptosystem is *secure* if the best-known attack requires as much work as an exhaustive key search, that

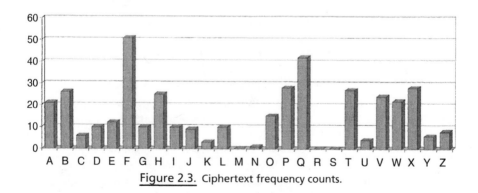

Figure 2.3. Ciphertext frequency counts.

is, there is no short-cut attack. By this definition, a secure cryptosystem with a small number of keys could be easier to break than an insecure cryptosystem with a large number of keys. The rationale for our definition is that, if a shortcut attack is known, the algorithm fails to provide its "advertised" level of security, as indicated by the key length. Such a shortcut attack indicates that the cipher has a design flaw.

In practice, we must select a cipher that is secure (in the sense of our definition) and has a large enough key space so that an exhaustive key search is impractical. Both factors are necessary.

2.3.4 Double Transposition Cipher

To encrypt with a double transposition cipher, we first write the plaintext into an array of a given size and then permute the rows and columns according to specified permutations. For example, suppose we write the plaintext attackatdawn into a 3×4 array

$$\begin{bmatrix} a & t & t & a \\ c & k & a & t \\ d & a & w & n \end{bmatrix}$$

Now if we transpose (or permute) the rows according to $(1, 2, 3) \rightarrow (3, 2, 1)$ and then transpose the columns according to $(1, 2, 3, 4) \rightarrow (4, 2, 1, 3)$, we obtain

$$\begin{bmatrix} a & t & t & a \\ c & k & a & t \\ d & a & w & n \end{bmatrix} \longrightarrow \begin{bmatrix} d & a & w & n \\ c & k & a & t \\ a & t & t & a \end{bmatrix} \longrightarrow \begin{bmatrix} n & a & d & w \\ t & k & c & a \\ a & t & a & t \end{bmatrix}$$

The ciphertext is then read from the final array:

NADWTKCAATAT   (2.2)

For the double transposition, the key consists of the size of the matrix and the row and column permutations. The recipient who knows the key can simply put the ciphertext into the appropriate sized matrix and undo the permutations to recover the plaintext.

For example, to decrypt *ciphertext 2.2*, the ciphertext is first put into a 3×4 array. Then the columns are numbered as $(4, 2, 1, 3)$ and rearranged to $(1, 2, 3, 4)$. Then the rows are numbered $(3, 2, 1)$ and rearranged into $(1, 2, 3)$, as illustrated below

$$\begin{bmatrix} N & A & D & W \\ T & K & C & A \\ A & T & A & T \end{bmatrix} \longrightarrow \begin{bmatrix} D & A & W & N \\ C & K & A & T \\ A & T & T & A \end{bmatrix} \longrightarrow \begin{bmatrix} A & T & T & A \\ C & K & A & T \\ D & A & W & N \end{bmatrix}$$

and we have recovered the plaintext, attackatdawn.

Unlike a simple substitution, the double transposition does nothing to disguise the letters that appear in the message. But it does appear to thwart an attack that relies on

TABLE 2.1. Abbreviated Alphabet.

letter	e	h	i	k	l	r	s	t
binary	000	001	010	011	100	101	110	111

the statistical information contained in the plaintext, since the plaintext statistics are disbursed throughout the ciphertext.

The double transposition is not a trivial cipher to break. The idea of "smearing" plaintext information through the ciphertext is so useful that it is employed by modern block ciphers.

2.3.5 One-Time Pad

The Vernam cipher, or one-time pad, is a provably secure cryptosystem. Historically it has been used at various times, but it's not very practical for most situations. However, it does nicely illustrate some important concepts that we'll see again later.

For simplicity, let's consider an alphabet with only eight letters. Our alphabet and the corresponding binary representation of letters are given in Table 2.1. It is important to note that the mapping between letters and bits is not secret. This mapping serves a similar purpose as the ASCII code, which is not secret either.

Suppose a spy named Alice wants to encrypt the plaintext message

```
heilhitler
```

using a one-time pad. She first consults Table 2.1 to convert the letters to the bit string

001 000 010 100 001 010 111 100 000 101.

The one-time pad requires a key consisting of a randomly selected string of bits that is the same length as the message. The key is then XORed with the plaintext to yield the ciphertext. A fancier way to say this is that we add the plaintext and key bits modulo 2.

We denote the XOR of bit x with bit y as $x \oplus y$. Since $x \oplus y \oplus y = x$, decryption is accomplished by XORing the same key with the ciphertext.

Suppose the spy Alice has the key

111 101 110 101 111 100 000 101 110 000

which is of the proper length to encrypt the message above. Then to encrypt, Alice computes

	h	e	i	l	h	i	t	l	e	r
plaintext:	001	000	010	100	001	010	111	100	000	101
key:	111	101	110	101	111	100	000	101	110	000
ciphertext:	110	101	100	001	110	110	111	001	110	101
	s	r	l	h	s	s	t	h	s	r

Converting the ciphertext bits back into letters, the ciphertext message to be transmitted is srlhssthsr.

When fellow spy Bob receives Alice's message, he decrypts it using the same key,

	s	r	l	h	s	s	t	h	s	r
ciphertext:	110	101	100	001	110	110	111	001	110	101
key:	111	101	110	101	111	100	000	101	110	000
plaintext:	001	000	010	100	001	010	111	100	000	101
	h	e	i	l	h	i	t	l	e	r

and thereby recovers the original plaintext.

Let's consider a couple of scenarios. First, suppose that Alice has an enemy, Charlie, within her spy organization. Charlie claims that the actual key used to encrypt Alice's message is

101 111 000 101 111 100 000 101 110 000 .

When Bob decrypts the ciphertext using this key, he find

	s	r	l	h	s	s	t	h	s	r
ciphertext:	110	101	100	001	110	110	111	001	110	101
"key":	101	111	000	101	111	100	000	101	110	000
"plaintext":	011	010	100	100	001	010	111	100	000	101
	k	i	l	l	h	i	t	l	e	r

Bob, who doesn't really understand crypto, orders that Alice be brought in for questioning.

Now let's consider a different scenario. Suppose that Alice is captured by her enemies, who have also intercepted the ciphertext. The captors are eager to read the message, and Alice is encouraged to provide the key for this super-secret message. Alice claims that she is actually a double-agent and to prove it she claims that the key is

111 101 000 011 101 110 001 011 101 101 .

When Alice's captors "decrypt" the ciphertext using this key, they find

	s	r	l	h	s	s	t	h	s	r
ciphertext:	110	101	100	001	110	110	111	001	110	101
"key":	111	101	000	011	101	110	001	011	101	101
"plaintext":	001	000	100	010	011	000	110	010	011	000
	h	e	l	i	k	e	s	i	k	e

Alice's captors, who are not very knowledgeable about crypto, congratulate Alice for her patriotism and release her.

These examples indicate why the one-time pad is provably secure. If the key is chosen at random, then an attacker who sees the ciphertext has no information about the message other than its length. That is, given the ciphertext, any "plaintext" of the same length can be generated by a suitable choice of "key," and all possible plaintexts are equally likely. And since we could pad the message with any number of random letters before encryption, the length is of no use either. So the ciphertext provides no information at all about the plaintext. This is the sense in which the one-time pad is provably secure.

Of course, this assumes that the cipher is used correctly. The pad, or key, must be chosen at random, used only once, and must be known only by the sender and receiver.

We can't do better than a provably secure cipher, so perhaps we should always use the one-time pad. However, there is one serious drawback to the one-time pad: the pad is the same length as the message and the pad—which is the key—must be securely transmitted to the recipient before the ciphertext can be decrypted. If we can securely transmit the pad, why not simply transmit the plaintext by the same means and do away with the encryption? Below, we'll see an historical example where it actually did make sense to use a one-time pad, in spite of this serious limitation. However, for modern high data-rate systems, a one-time pad cipher is totally impractical.

Why is it that the one-time pad can only be used once? Suppose we have two plaintext messages P_1 and P_2, encrypted as $C_1 = P_1 \oplus K$ and $C_2 = P_2 \oplus K$; that is, we have two messages encrypted with the same "one-time" pad K. In the cryptanalysis business, this is known as a *depth*. In the case of a one-time pad in depth,

$$C_1 \oplus C_2 = P_1 \oplus K \oplus P_2 \oplus K = P_1 \oplus P_2$$

and the key has disappeared from the problem. This cannot be good for anyone except for Trudy, the cryptanalyst.

Let's consider a specific example of a one-time pad in depth. Using the same bit encoding as in Table 2.1, suppose we have

$$P_1 = \texttt{like} = 100\,010\,011\,000 \quad \text{and} \quad P_2 = \texttt{kite} = 011\,010\,111\,000$$

and both are encrypted with the same key $K = 110\,011\,101\,111$. Then

	l	i	k	e
P_1:	100	010	011	000
K:	110	011	101	111
C_1:	010	001	110	111
	i	h	s	t

and

	k	i	t	e
P_2:	011	010	111	000
K:	110	011	101	111
C_2:	101	001	010	111
	r	h	i	t

If Trudy the cryptanalyst knows that the messages are in depth, she immediately sees that the second and fourth letters of P_1 and P_2 are the same, since the corresponding ciphertext letters are identical. But far more devastating is the fact that Trudy can now guess a putative message P_1 and check her results using P_2. Suppose that Trudy—who only has C_1 and C_2—suspects that

putative $P_1 = \texttt{kill} = 011\,010\,100\,100$.

Then she can find the corresponding putative key

	k	i	l	l
putative P_1:	011	010	100	100
C_1:	010	001	110	111
putative K:	001	011	010	011

and she can then use this K to "decrypt" C_2 and obtain

C_2:	101	001	010	111
putative K:	001	011	010	011
putative P_2:	100	010	000	100
	l	i	e	l

Since this K does not yield a sensible decryption for P_2, Trudy assumes that her guess for P_1 was incorrect. When Trudy eventually guesses $P_1 = \texttt{like}$ she will obtain the correct key K and decrypt $P_2 = \texttt{kite}$, thereby confirming the correctness of the key and the correctness of both decryptions.

2.3.6 Project VENONA

The VENONA project [239] is an interesting example of a real-world use of a one-time pad. In the 1930s and 1940s, Soviet spies entering the United States brought one-time pad keys with them. The spies used these keys to encrypt important messages, which were then sent back to Moscow. These messages dealt with the most sensitive spy operations of the time. In particular, the secret development of the first atomic bomb was a focus of much of the spying. The Rosenberg's, Alger Hiss, and many other identified spies—and many never identified spies—figure prominently in VENONA.

TABLE 2.2. VENONA Decrypt of message of September 21, 1944.

```
[C% Ruth] learned that her husband [v] was called up
by the army but he was not sent to the front. He is a
mechanical engineer and is now working at the ENORMOUS
[ENORMOZ] [vi] plant in SANTA FE, New Mexico.

[45 groups unrecoverable]

detain VOLOK [vii] who is working in a plant on ENORMOUS.
He is a FELLOWCOUNTRYMAN [ZEMLYaK] [viii]. Yesterday he
learned that they had dismissed him from his work. His
active work in progressive organizations in the past was
cause of his dismissal.
In the FELLOWCOUNTRYMAN line LIBERAL is in touch with
CHESTER [ix]. They meet once a month for the payment of
dues. CHESTER is interested in whether we are satisfied
with the collaboration and whether there are not any
misunderstandings. He does not inquire about specific
items of work [KONKRETNAYa RABOTA]. In as much as CHESTER
knows about the role of LIBERAL's group we beg consent to
ask C through LIBERAL about leads from among people who
are working on ENOURMOUS and in other technical fields.
```

The Soviet spies were well trained and never reused the key, yet many of the intercepted ciphertext messages were eventually decrypted by American cryptanalysts. How can that be, given that the one-time pad is provably secure? In fact, there was a flaw in the method used to generate the pads, so that there were repeats. As a result, many messages were in depth, which enabled the cryptanalysis of these messages.

Part of a VENONA decrypt is given in Table 2.2. This message refers to David Greenglass and his wife Ruth. LIBERAL is Julius Rosenberg who, along with his wife Ethyl, was eventually executed for his role in nuclear espionage.[3] The Soviet codename for the atomic bomb was, appropriately, ENORMOUS. The VENONA decrypts at [239] make for interesting reading.

2.3.7 Codebook Cipher

A classic codebook cipher is, literally, a dictionary-like book containing words and their corresponding codewords. Table 2.3 contains an excerpt from a famous codebook used by Germany during World War I.

For example, to encrypt the German word Februar, the entire word was replaced with the 5-digit "codeword" 13605. The codebook in Table 2.3 was used for encryption, while a corresponding codebook, arranged with the 5-digit codewords in numerical order, was used for decryption. A codebook is a substitution cipher, but the substitutions are far from simple, since substitutions are for entire words—or even phrases.

The codebook illustrated in Table 2.3 was used to encrypt the famous Zimmermann telegram. In 1917, German Foreign Minister Arthur Zimmermann sent an encrypted

---

[3] In a travesty of justice, David Greenglass never served any jail time.

TABLE 2.3. Excerpt from a German codebook.

Plaintext	Ciphertext
Februar	13605
fest	13732
finanzielle	13850
folgender	13918
Frieden	17142
Friedenschluss	17149
⋮	⋮

telegram to the German ambassador in Mexico City. The ciphertext message, as shown in Figure 2.4 [171], was intercepted by the British. At the time, the British and French were at war with Germany and its allies, but the United States was neutral [236].

The Russians had recovered a damaged version of the German codebook, and the partial codebook had been passed on to the British. Through painstaking analyses, the

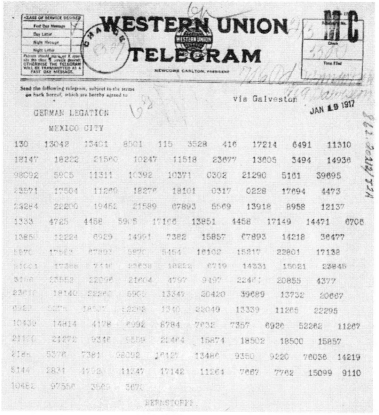

Figure 2.4. The Zimmermann telegram.

British were able to recover enough of the codebook to decrypt the Zimmermann telegram [61]. The telegram stated that the German government was planning to begin "unrestricted submarine warfare" and had concluded that this would likely lead to war with the United States. As a result, Zimmermann had decided that Germany should try to recruit Mexico as an ally to fight against the United States. The incentive for Mexico was that it would "reconquer the lost territory in Texas, New Mexico, and Arizona." When the decrypted Zimmermann telegram was released in the United States, public opinion turned against Germany and, after the sinking of the passenger liner Lusitania, the United States declared war on Germany.

The British were initially hesitant to release the Zimmermann telegram since they feared that the Germans would realize that their cipher was broken and, presumably, stop using it. However, in sifting through other cabled messages that had been sent at about the same time as the Zimmermann telegram, British analysts found that a variant of the telegram had been sent unencrypted. The version of the Zimmermann telegram that the British subsequently released closely matched the unencrypted version of the telegram. The German's concluded that their codebook had not been compromised and continued to use it for sensitive messages throughout the war.

Modern block ciphers use complex algorithms to generate ciphertext from plaintext (and vice versa) but at a higher level, a block cipher can be viewed as a codebook, where each key determines a distinct codebook.

2.3.8   Ciphers of the Election of 1876

The U.S. presidential election of 1876 was a virtual dead heat. At the time, the Civil War was still fresh in people's minds, "radical" Reconstruction was ongoing in the former Confederacy, and the nation was, in many ways, still bitterly divided.

The contestants in the election were Republican Rutherford B. Hayes and Democrat Samuel J. Tilden. Tilden had obtained a slight plurality of the popular vote, but it is the electoral college that determines the presidency. In the electoral college, each state sends a delegation and the entire delegation is supposed to vote for the candidate who received the largest number of votes in that particular state (though there is no legal requirement for a delegate to vote for a particular candidate, and on rare occasion a delegate will vote for another candidate).

In 1876, the electoral college delegations of four states were in dispute, and these held the balance. A commission of 15 members was appointed to determine which state delegations were legitimate—and thus determine the presidency. The commission decided that all four states should go to Hayes and he became president of the United States. Tilden's supporters immediately charged that Hayes' people had bribed officials to turn the vote in his favor, but no evidence was forthcoming.

Some months after the election, reporters discovered a large number of encrypted messages that had been sent from Tilden's supporters to officials in the disputed states. One of the ciphers used was a partial codebook together with a transposition on the words. The codebook was only applied to "important" words and the transposition was a fixed permutation for a message of a given length. The allowed message lengths were

TABLE 2.4. Election of 1876 codebook.

Plaintext	Ciphertext
Greenbacks	Copenhagen
Hayes	Greece
votes	Rochester
Tilden	Russia
telegram	Warsaw
⋮	⋮

10, 15, 20, 25, and 30 words, with all messages padded to one of these lengths. A snippet of the codebook appears in Table 2.4.

The permutation used for a message of 10 words was

9, 3, 6, 1, 10, 5, 2, 7, 4, 8.

One actual ciphertext message was

```
Warsaw they read all unchanged last are idiots can't situation
```

which was decrypted by undoing the permutation and substituting `telegram` for `Warsaw` to obtain

```
Can't read last telegram. Situation unchanged. They are all idiots.
```

The cryptanalysis of this weak cipher was relatively easy to accomplish [93]. Since a permutation of a given length was used repeatedly, many messages of particular length were in depth—with respect to permutation as well as the codebook. A cryptanalyst could therefore compare all messages of the same length, making it relatively easy to discover the fixed permutation, even without knowledge of the partial codebook. The analyst had to be clever enough to consider the possibility that all messages of a given length were using the same permutation, but, with this insight, the permutations were easily recovered. The codebook was then deduced from context and also with the aid of some unencrypted messages that provided clues as to the substance of the ciphertext messages.

And what did these decrypted messages reveal? The reporters were amused to discover that Tilden's supporters had tried to bribe officials in the disputed states. The irony was that Tilden's people were guilty of precisely what they had accused Hayes' people of doing!

By any measure, this cipher was poorly designed and weak. One lesson here is that the reuse (or overuse) of keys can be an exploitable flaw. In this case, each time a permutation was reused, it gave the cryptanalyst more information that could be collated to recover the permutation. In modern cipher systems, we try to limit the use of a single key so that we do not allow a cryptanalyst to accumulate too much information about a particular key—and to limit the damage if a key is discovered.

2.4 MODERN CRYPTO HISTORY

Don't let yesterday take up too much of today.
—Abraham Lincoln

Throughout the 20th century, cryptography played an important role in major world events. Late in the 20th century, cryptography became a critical technology for commercial and business communications as well. The Zimmermann telegram is one of the first examples from the last century of the role that cryptanalysis has had in political and military affairs. In this section, we mention a few other historical highlights from the past century. For more on the history of cryptography, the best source is Kahn's fascinating book [119].

In 1929, Secretary of State Henry L. Stimson ended the U.S. government's official cryptanalytic activity, justifying his actions with the immortal line, "Gentlemen do not read each other's mail" [224]. This would prove to be a costly mistake in the run up to the Japanese attack on Pearl Harbor.

Shortly after the attack of December 7, 1941, the United States restarted its cryptanalytic program in earnest. The successes of allied cryptanalysts during the World War II era were remarkable, and this period is often seen as the "golden age" of cryptanalysis. Virtually all significant axis cryptosystems were broken and the value of the intelligence obtained from these systems is difficult to overestimate.

In the Pacific theatre, the so-called Purple cipher was used for high level Japanese government communication. This cipher was broken by American cryptanalysts before the attack on Pearl Harbor, but the intelligence gained (code named Magic) provided no clear indication of the impending attack [61]. The Japanese Imperial Navy used a cipher known as JN-25, which was also broken by the Americans. The intelligence from JN-25 was almost certainly decisive in the extended battle of Coral Sea and Midway, where an inferior American force was able to halt the advance of the Japanese in the Pacific for the first time. The Japanese Navy was never able to recover from the losses inflicted during this battle.

In Europe, the breaking of the Enigma cipher (code named ULTRA) was also a crucial aid to the allies during the war [59, 87]. It is often claimed that the ULTRA intelligence was so valuable that in November of 1940, Churchill decided not to inform the British city of Coventry of an impending attack by the German Luftwaffe, since the primary source of information on the attack came from Enigma decrypts [229]. Churchill was supposedly concerned that a warning might tip off the Germans that their cipher had been broken.

The Enigma was initially broken by the Poles. After the fall of Poland, the Polish cryptanalysts escaped to France. Shortly thereafter, France fell to the Nazis and the Polish cryptanalysts escaped to England, where they provided their knowledge to British cryptanalysts. Remarkably, the Polish cryptanalysts were not allowed to continue their work on the Enigma. However, the British team—including the computing pioneer,

Alan Turing—developed an improved attack [59]. A picture of the Enigma appears in Figure 2.5, and the inner workings of the guts of the Enigma are presented in Problem 12 of Chapter 6.

In the post World War II era, cryptography finally moved from a "black art" into the realm of science. The publication of Claude Shannon's seminal 1949 paper *Information Theory of Secrecy Systems* [207] marks the turning point. Shannon's paper proved that the one-time pad is secure and also offered two fundamental cipher design principles: *confusion* and *diffusion*.

Confusion is designed to obscure the relationship between the plaintext and cipher-text, while diffusion is supposed to spread the plaintext statistics through the ciphertext. A simple substitution cipher and a one-time pad employ only confusion, whereas a double transposition is a diffusion-only cipher. Since the one-time pad is provably secure, evidently confusion alone is "enough," while, apparently, diffusion alone is not.

Figure 2.5. The Enigma cipher (Courtesy of T.B. Perera and the Enigma Museum).

These two concepts—confusion and diffusion—are still the guiding principles in cipher design today. In subsequent chapters, it will become clear how crucial these concepts are to modern block cipher design.

Until recently, cryptography remained primarily the domain of governments. That changed dramatically in the 1970s, primarily due to the computer revolution, which led to the need to protect large amounts of electronic data. By the mid-1970s, even the U.S. government realized that there was a legitimate commercial need for secure cryptography, and it was clear that the commercial products of the day were lacking. The National Bureau of Standards, or NBS[4], issued a request for cryptographic algorithms. The ultimate result of this process was a cipher known as the Data Encryption Standard, or DES, which became an official U.S. government standard.

It's impossible to overemphasize the role that DES has played in the modern history of cryptography. We'll have much more to say about DES in the next chapter.

After DES, academic interest in cryptography grew rapidly. Public key cryptography was discovered (or, more precisely, rediscovered) shortly after the arrival of DES. By the 1980s, there were annual CRYPTO conferences, which have consistently displayed high-quality work in the field. In the 1990s, the Clipper Chip and the development of a replacement for the aging DES were two of the many crypto highlights.

Governments continue to fund major organizations that work in crypto and related fields. However, it's clear that the crypto genie has escaped from its government bottle, never to be put back.

2.5 A TAXONOMY OF CRYPTOGRAPHY

In the next three chapters, we'll consider three categories of ciphers: *symmetric* ciphers, *public key* cryptosystems, and *hash functions*. Here, we'll give a very brief overview of these different categories.

While the distinction between public keys and symmetric keys might seem minor, it turns out that public key crypto can do some useful things that are impossible to achieve with symmetric ciphers.

In public key cryptography, the encryption keys can be made public. If, for example, you post your public key on the Internet, anyone with an Internet connection can encrypt a message for you, without any prior arrangement regarding the key. This is in stark contrast to a symmetric cipher, where the participants must agree on a key in advance. Prior to the adoption of public key crypto, secure delivery of symmetric keys was the Achilles heel of modern cryptography. A spectacular case of a failed symmetric key distribution system can be seen in the exploits of the Walker family spy ring. The Walker family sold cryptographic keys used by the U.S. military to the Soviet Union for nearly two decades before being discovered [60, 71].

---

[4]NBS has since been rechristened as the National Institute of Standards and Technology, or NIST, perhaps in an effort to recycle three-letter acronyms and thereby delay their eventual exhaustion by U.S. government agencies.

Public key cryptography has another somewhat surprising and extremely useful feature, for which there is no parallel in the symmetric key world. Suppose a message is "encrypted" with the private key instead of the public key. Since the public key is public, anyone can decrypt this message. At first glance such encryption might seem pointless. However, it can be used as a digital form of a handwritten signature—anyone can read the signature, but only the signer could have created the signature. As with all of these topics, we'll have much more to say about *digital signatures* in a later chapter.

Anything we can do with a symmetric cipher we can also accomplish with a public key cryptosystem. Public key crypto also enables us to do things that cannot be accomplished with a symmetric cipher. So why not use public key crypto for everything? The primary reason is speed. Symmetric key crypto is orders of magnitude faster than public key crypto. As a result, symmetric key crypto is used to encrypt the vast majority of data today. Yet public key crypto has a critical role to play in modern information security.

Each of the classic ciphers discussed above is a symmetric cipher. Modern symmetric ciphers can be subdivided into *stream ciphers* and *block ciphers*. Stream ciphers generalize the one-time pad approach, sacrificing provable security for a key that is of a reasonable length. A block cipher is, in a sense, the generalization of a codebook. In a block cipher, the key determines the codebook, and as long as the key remains fixed, the same codebook is used. Conversely, when the key changes, a different codebook is selected.

While stream ciphers dominated in the post-World War II era, today block ciphers are the kings of symmetric key crypto—with a few notable exceptions. Generally speaking, block ciphers are easier to optimize for software implementations, while stream ciphers are usually most efficient in hardware.

The third major crypto category we'll consider is hash functions. These functions take an input of any size and produce an output of a fixed size that satisfies some very special properties. For example, if the input changes in one or more bits, the output should change in about half of its bits. For another, it must be infeasible to find any two inputs that produce the same output. It may not be obvious that such a function is useful—or that such functions actually exist—but we'll see that they do exist and that they turn out to be extremely useful for a surprisingly wide array of problems.

2.6 A TAXONOMY OF CRYPTANALYSIS

The goal of cryptanalysis is to recover the plaintext, the key, or both. By Kerckhoffs Principle, we assume that Trudy the cryptanalyst has complete knowledge of the inner workings of the algorithm. Another basic assumption is that Trudy has access to the ciphertext—otherwise, why bother to encrypt? If Trudy only knows the algorithms and the ciphertext, then she must conduct a *ciphertext only* attack. This is the most disadvantageous possible scenario from Trudy's perspective.

Trudy's chances of success might improve if she has access to *known plaintext*. That is, Trudy might know some of the plaintext and observe the corresponding ciphertext. These matched plaintext-ciphertext pairs might provide information about the key. If all of the plaintext were known, there would be little point in recovering the key. But it's often the case that Trudy has access to (or can guess) some of the plaintext. For example, many kinds of data include stereotypical headers—e-mail being a good example. If such data is encrypted, the attacker can likely guess some of the plaintext and view the corresponding ciphertext.

Often, Trudy can actually choose the plaintext to be encrypted and see the corresponding ciphertext. Not surprisingly, this goes by the name of *chosen plaintext* attack. How is it possible for Trudy to choose the plaintext? We'll see that some protocols encrypt anything that is sent and return the corresponding ciphertext. It's also possible that Trudy could have limited access to a cryptosystem, allowing her to encrypt plaintext of her choice. For example, Alice might forget to log out of her computer when she takes her lunch break. Trudy could then encrypt some selected messages before Alice returns. This type of "lunchtime attack" takes many forms.

Potentially more advantageous for the attacker is an *adaptively chosen plaintext* attack. In this scenario, Trudy chooses the plaintext, views the resulting ciphertext, and chooses the next plaintext based on the observed ciphertext. In some cases, this can make Trudy's job significantly easier. *Related key* attacks are also significant in some applications. The idea here is to look for a weakness in the system when the keys are related in some special way.

There are other types of attacks that cryptographers occasionally worry about—mostly when they feel the need to publish another academic paper. In any case, a cipher can only be considered secure if no successful attack is known. We'll define "successful" more precisely in the next chapter.

Finally, there is one particular attack scenario that only applies to public key cryptography. Suppose Trudy intercepts a ciphertext that was encrypted with Alice's public key. If Trudy suspects that the plaintext message was either "yes" or "no," then she can encrypt both of these putative plaintexts with Alice's public key. If either matches the ciphertext, then the message has been broken. This is known as a *forward search*. Although a forward search will not succeed against a symmetric cipher, we'll see that this approach can be used to attack hash functions in some applications.

We've previously seen that the size of the keyspace must be large enough to prevent an attacker from trying all possible keys. The forward search attack implies that in public key crypto, we must also ensure that the size of the plaintext message space is large enough that the attacker cannot simply encrypt all possible plaintext messages.

2.7 SUMMARY

In this chapter we covered several classic cryptosystems, including the simple substitution, the double transposition, codebooks, and the one-time pad. Each of these illustrates some important points that we'll return to again in later chapters. We also discussed some elementary aspects of cryptanalysis.

In the next chapter we'll turn our attention to modern symmetric key ciphers. The following chapters cover public key cryptography, hash functions, and cryptanalysis. Cryptography will appear again in later parts of the book. In particular, cryptography is a crucial ingredient in the chapters on security protocols.

2.8 PROBLEMS

1. Given that the Caesar's cipher is used, find the plaintext from the ciphertext

   VSRQJHEREVTXDUHSDQWU

2. Find the plaintext and the key from the ciphertext

   CSYEVIXIVQMREXIH

   given that the cipher is a simple substitution of the shift-by-n variety.

3. If we have a computer that can test 2^{40} keys each second, what is the expected time to find a key by exhaustive key search if the keyspace is of size 2^{128}? Give your answer in years.

4. How does the Vigenere cipher work? Give an example. Use your knowledge of the statistical attack on the simple substitution cipher to devise an attack on the Vigenere cipher.

5. The weak ciphers used during the election of 1876 employed a fixed permutation of the words for a given length sentence. To see that this is weak, find the permutation of $(1, 2, 3, \ldots, 10)$ that was used to produce the scrambled sentences below, where "San Francisco" is treated as a single word. Note that the same permutation was used for all three sentences.

   first try try if you and don't again at succeed
   only you you you as believe old are are as
   winter was in the I summer ever San Francisco coldest spent

6. The weak ciphers of the election of 1876 used a partial codebook and a permutation of the words. Design a more secure version of this cipher.

7. Define the terms confusion and diffusion in the context of cryptology. Discuss a classic cipher that employs only confusion and also discuss a classic cipher that employs only diffusion. Which cipher discussed in this chapter employs both confusion and diffusion?

8. Decrypt the simple substitution example in *ciphertext 2.1*.

9. Decrypt the ciphertext that appears in the *Alice in Wonderland* quote at the beginning of the chapter.

10. Decrypt the following message that was encrypted using a simple substitution cipher:

    GBSXUCGSZQGKGSQPKQKGLSKASPCGBGBKGUKGCEUKUZKGGBSQEICA
    CGKGCEUERWKLKUPKQQGCIICUAEUVSHQKGCEUPCGBCGQOEVSHUNSU
    GKUZCGQSNLSHEHIEEDCUOGEPKHZGBSNKCUGSUKUASERLSKASCUGB
    SLKACRCACUZSSZEUSBEXHKRGSHWKLKUSQSKCHQTXKZHEUQBKZAEN
    NSUASZFENFCUOCUEKBXGBSWKLKUSQSKNFKQQKZEHGEGBSXUCGSZQ
    GKGSQPKUZBCQAEIISKOXSZSICVSHSHZGEGBSQSKKHSGKHMERQGKSKR
    EHNKIHSLIMGEKHSASUGKNSHCAKUNSQQKOSPBCISGBCQHSLIMQGKG
    SZGBKGCGQSSNSZXQSISQQGEAEUGCUXSGBSSJCQGCUOZCLIENKGCA
    USOEGCKGCEUQCGAEUGKCUSZUEGBSKGEHBCUGERPKHEHKHNSZKGGKD

11. Write a program to help an analyst decrypt a simple substitution cipher. Your program should take the ciphertext as input, compute letter frequency counts, and display these for the analyst. The program should then allow the analyst to guess the key and display the results of "decryption" with the putative key.

12. Extend the program developed in Problem 11 so that it initially tries to decrypt the message. Here is one sensible way to proceed. Use the computed letter frequencies and the known frequencies of English for an initial guess at the key. Then from the resulting putative decryption, count the number of dictionary words that appear and use this as a "score." Next, for each letter in the key, try swapping it with a letter that is adjacent (with respect to frequency counts) and recompute the score. If the score improves, update the key; if not, don't update the key. Iterate this process until the score does not improve for an entire pass through the alphabet. At this point you will pass your putative decryption to the analyst. In order to aid the analyst in the manual phase, your program should maintain all of the functionality of the program for Problem 11.

13. Encrypt the message

$$\text{we are all together}$$

using a double transposition cipher with 4 rows and 4 columns, using the row permutation

$$(1, 2, 3, 4) \longrightarrow (2, 4, 1, 3)$$

and the column permutation

$$(1, 2, 3, 4) \longrightarrow (3, 1, 2, 4).$$

14. Decrypt the ciphertext

`IAUTMOCSMNIMREBOTNELSTRHEREOAEVMWIHTSEEATMAEOHWHSYCEELTTEOHMUOUFEHTRFT`

This message was encrypted with a double transposition using a matrix of 7 rows and 10 columns. Hint: The first word is "there."

15. Outline an automated attack on a double transposition cipher, assuming that the size of the matrix is known.

16. Using the letter encodings in Table 2.1, the following two ciphertext messages were encrypted with the same one-time pad

`KHHLTK`   and   `KTHLLE`.

Find possible plaintexts for each message and the corresponding one-time pad.

17. Using the letter encodings in Table 2.1, the following ciphertext message was encrypted with a one-time pad

`KITLKE`.

If the plaintext is "thrill," what is the key? If the plaintext is "tiller," what is the key?

18. Suppose that you have a message consisting of 1024 bits. Design a method that will extend a key that is 64 bits long into a string of 1024 bits. Then this 1024 bits will be XORed with the message, just like a one-time pad. Is the resulting cipher as secure as a one-time pad? Is it possible for any such cipher to be as secure as a one-time pad?

19. Design a computerized version of a codebook cipher. Your cipher should include many possible codebooks, with the key used to determine the codebook that will be employed to encrypt (or decrypt) a particular message.

20. In the text, we described how a forward search attack can work against a public key cryptosystem. Why can't the same approach be used to break a symmetric cipher?

3

SYMMETRIC KEY CRYPTO

"You boil it in sawdust: you salt it in glue:
You condense it with locusts and tape:
Still keeping one principal object in view—
To preserve its symmetrical shape."
—Lewis Carroll, *The Hunting of the Snark*

The chief forms of beauty are order and symmetry...
—Aristotle

3.1 INTRODUCTION

In this chapter, we discuss the two branches of symmetric key cryptography: stream ciphers and block ciphers. Stream ciphers are like a one-time pad, except that we trade provable security for a relatively small (and manageable) key. The key is "stretched" into a long stream of bits, which is then used just like a one-time pad. Like their one-time pad brethren, stream ciphers employ—in Shannon's terminology—confusion only.

Block ciphers are based on the concept of a codebook, where the key determines the codebook. The internal workings of block cipher algorithms can be fairly intimidating, so it may be useful to keep in mind that a block cipher is really just an "electronic" codebook. Internally, block ciphers employ both confusion and diffusion.

We'll take a fairly close look at two stream cipher algorithms, A5/1 and RC4. Both of these algorithms are widely used today, with A5/1 being employed in GSM cell phones. The A5/1 algorithm is representative of a large class of stream ciphers that are based

Information Security: Principles and Practice, by Mark Stamp
Copyright © 2006 John Wiley & Sons, Inc.

in hardware. RC4 is used many places, including in the Secure Socket Layer, or SSL, protocol. RC4 is almost unique among stream ciphers since it is efficiently implemented in software.

In the block cipher realm, we'll look closely at DES, since it's relatively simple (by block cipher standards) and it's the block cipher to which all others must be compared. We'll also take a brief look at a few other popular block ciphers. Then we'll examine the various modes of operation of block ciphers and we'll consider the role of block ciphers in the area of data integrity, as opposed to confidentiality.

Our goal in this section is to introduce symmetric key ciphers and gain some understanding of their inner workings and their uses. That is, we'll focus more on the "how" than the "why." To understand why block ciphers are designed the way they are, some aspects of advanced cryptanalysis are essential. We've deferred the study of advanced cryptanalysis to Chapter 6.

3.2 STREAM CIPHERS

A stream cipher takes a key K of n bits in length and stretches it into a long *keystream*. This keystream is then XORed with the plaintext P to produce ciphertext C. The use of the keystream is identical to the use of the key in a one-time pad cipher. To decrypt with a stream cipher, the same keystream is generated and XORed with the ciphertext. An excellent introduction to stream ciphers can be found in Rueppel's book [194]; for leads into some aspects of the most challenging research problems in the field, see [114].

The function of a stream cipher can be viewed simply as

StreamCipher$(K) = S$

where K is the key and S is the keystream that we'll use like a one-time pad. The encryption formula is

$$c_0 = p_0 \oplus s_0, c_1 = p_1 \oplus s_1, c_2 = p_2 \oplus s_2, \ldots$$

where $P = p_0 p_1 p_2 \ldots$ is the plaintext, $S = s_0 s_1 s_2 \ldots$ is the keystream and $C = c_0 c_1 c_2 \ldots$ is the ciphertext. To decrypt ciphertext C, the keystream S is again used

$$p_0 = c_0 \oplus s_0, p_1 = c_1 \oplus s_1, p_2 = c_2 \oplus s_2, \ldots.$$

Provided that both the sender and receiver have the same stream cipher algorithm and that both know the key K, this system is a practical generalization of the one-time pad—although not provably secure in the sense of the one-time pad.

3.2.1 A5/1

The first stream cipher that we'll examine is A5/1, which is used by GSM cell phones for confidentiality. This algorithm has an algebraic description, but it also can be illustrated via a relatively simple picture. We'll give both descriptions here.

A5/1 employs three linear feedback *shift registers* [95], or LFSRs, which we'll label X, Y, and Z. Register X holds 19 bits, which we label $(x_0, x_1, \ldots, x_{18})$. The register Y holds 22 bits $(y_0, y_1, \ldots, y_{21})$, and Z holds 23 bits $(z_0, z_1, \ldots, z_{22})$. It's no accident that the three LFSRs hold a total of 64 bits.

Not coincidentally, the key K is 64 bits. The key is used as the *initial fill* of the three registers. After these three registers are filled with the key, we are ready to generate the keystream. But before we can describe the keystream, we need to discuss the registers X, Y, and Z in more detail.

When register X *steps*, the following occur

$$t = x_{13} \oplus x_{16} \oplus x_{17} \oplus x_{18}$$

$$x_i = x_{i-1} \quad \text{for } i = 18, 17, 16, \ldots, 1$$

$$x_0 = t$$

Similarly, for registers Y and Z, each step consists of

$$t = y_{20} \oplus y_{21}$$

$$y_i = y_{i-1} \quad \text{for } i = 21, 20, 19, \ldots, 1$$

$$y_0 = t$$

and

$$t = z_7 \oplus z_{20} \oplus z_{21} \oplus z_{22}$$

$$z_i = z_{i-1} \quad \text{for } i = 22, 21, 20, \ldots, 1$$

$$z_0 = t$$

respectively.

Given three bits x, y, and z, define maj(x, y, z) to be the "majority vote" function; that is, if the majority of x, y, and z are 0, then the function returns 0, otherwise it returns 1.

A5/1 is implemented in hardware, and at each clock pulse the value

$$m = \text{maj}(x_8, y_{10}, z_{10})$$

is computed. Then the registers X, Y, and Z step according to the following rules:

$$\text{If } x_8 = m \text{ then } X \text{ steps}$$

$$\text{If } y_{10} = m \text{ then } Y \text{ steps}$$

$$\text{If } z_{10} = m \text{ then } Z \text{ steps}$$

Finally, a keystream bit s is generated as

$$s = x_{18} \oplus y_{21} \oplus z_{22}$$

which is then XORed with the plaintext (if encrypting) or XORed with the ciphertext (if decrypting).

Although this may seem like a complicated way to generate a single keystream bit, A5/1 is easily implemented in hardware and can generate bits at a rate proportional to the clock speed. Also, the number of keystream bits that can be generated from a single 64-bit key is virtually unlimited—though eventually the keystream will repeat. The A5/1 algorithm has a simple "wiring diagram" representation, as illustrated in Figure 3.1. See [26] for more discussion of A5/1.

The A5/1 algorithm is representative of a large class of ciphers that are based on shift registers and implemented in hardware. These systems were once the kings of symmetric key crypto, but in recent years the block cipher has clearly taken over that title. And where a stream cipher is used today, it is likely to be RC4, which we'll discuss next.

Historically, shift register based stream ciphers were needed in order to keep pace with bit streams (such as audio) that are produced at a relatively high data rate. In the past, software-based crypto could not generate bits fast enough for such applications. Today, however, there are few applications for which software-based crypto is not appropriate. This is one of the primary reasons why block ciphers are on the ascendancy.

3.2.2 RC4

RC4 is a stream cipher, but it's a much different beast from A5/1. The algorithm in RC4 is optimized for software implementation, whereas A5/1 is designed for hardware, and RC4 produces a keystream byte at each step, whereas A5/1 only produces a single keystream bit. The RC4 algorithm is remarkably simple, because it is essentially just a lookup table containing a permutation of the 256-byte values. Each time a byte of keystream is produced, the lookup table is modified in such a way that the table always contains a permutation of $\{0, 1, 2, \ldots, 255\}$.

The entire RC4 algorithm is byte based. The first phase of the algorithm initializes the lookup table using the key. We'll denote the key as $key[i]$ for $i = 0, 1, \ldots, N - 1$,

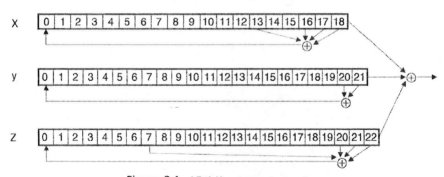

Figure 3.1. A5/1 Keystream generator.

TABLE 3.1. RC4 initialization.

```
for i = 0 to 255
    S[i] = i
    K[i] = key[i mod N]
next i
j = 0
for i = 0 to 255
    j = (j + S[i] + K[i]) mod 256
    swap(S[i],S[j])
next i
i = j = 0
```

where each key[i] is a byte, and the lookup table as $S[i]$, where each $S[i]$ is also a byte. Pseudo-code for the initialization of the permutation S appears in Table 3.1. One interesting feature of RC4 is that the key can be of any length from 0 to 256 bytes. The key is only used to initialize the permutation S.

After the initialization phase, each keystream byte is generated according to the algorithm in Table 3.2. The output, which we've denoted `keystreamByte`, is a single byte that can be XORed with plaintext (if encrypting) or XORed with ciphertext (if decrypting). RC4 output can also be used as a pseudo-random number generator for applications that require "cryptographic" (that is, unpredictable) pseudo-random numbers. We'll briefly discuss such applications in Chapter 5.

The RC4 algorithm—which can be viewed as a self-modifying lookup table—is elegant, simple, and efficient in software. However, there is an attack that is feasible against certain uses of RC4 [80, 150, 225], but the attack is infeasible if we simply discard the first 256 keystream bytes that are generated. This could be implemented by adding an extra 256 steps to the initialization phase, where each additional step generates—and discards—a keystream byte following the algorithm in Table 3.2.

RC4 is used in many applications, including SSL. However, the algorithm is fairly old and is not optimized for 32-bit processors (in fact, it's optimized for ancient 8-bit processors).

There seems to have been little effort to develop new stream ciphers in recent years. In fact, the "death of stream ciphers" was recently announced at a major conference by none other than Shamir [53]. Although this may be a slight exaggeration, it is clear that block ciphers are in the ascendency today.

TABLE 3.2. RC4 keystream byte.

```
i = (i + 1) mod 256
j = (j + S[i]) mod 256
swap(S[i], S[j])
t = (S[i] + S[j]) mod 256
keystreamByte = S[t]
```

3.3 BLOCK CIPHERS

An iterated block cipher splits the plaintext into fixed sized blocks and generates fixed sized blocks of ciphertext. The ciphertext is obtained from the plaintext by iterating a function F over some number of *rounds*. The function F, which depends on the output of the previous round and the key K, is known as a *round function*, not because of its shape, but because it is applied at each round.

The design goals for block ciphers are security and efficiency. It's not too difficult to develop either a secure block cipher or an efficient algorithm, but it's surprisingly tricky to design a secure block cipher that is highly efficient.

3.3.1 Feistel Cipher

A *Feistel cipher*, named after block cipher pioneer Horst Feistel, is a general cipher design principle, not a specific cipher. In a Feistel cipher, the plaintext P is split into left and right halves,

$$P = (L_0, R_0),$$

and for each round $i = 1, 2, \ldots, n$ new left and right halves are computed according to the rule

$$L_i = R_{i-1} \tag{3.1}$$

$$R_i = L_{i-1} \oplus F(R_{i-1}, K_i) \tag{3.2}$$

where K_i is the *subkey* for round i. The subkey is derived from the key K according to a *key schedule* algorithm. Finally, the ciphertext C is the output of the final round,

$$C = (L_n, R_n).$$

Of course, it's nice to be able to decrypt. The beauty of a Feistel cipher is that we can decrypt, regardless of the particular round function F. To do so, we simply solve *equations 3.1* and *3.2* for R_{i-1} and L_{i-1}, respectively, which allows us to run the process backward. For $i = n, n-1, \ldots, 1$, the decryption rule is

$$R_{i-1} = L_i$$

$$L_{i-1} = R_i \oplus F(R_{i-1}, K_i)$$

and the final result is the original plaintext $P = (L_0, R_0)$.

Any round function F will work in a Feistel cipher, provided that the output of F produces the correct number of bits. In particular, there is no requirement that the function F be invertible. However, a Feistel cipher will not be secure for every possible F. For example, the round function

$$F(R_{i-1}, K_i) = 0 \quad \text{for all } R_{i-1} \text{ and } K_i$$

is a legitimate round function in that we can "encrypt" and "decrypt" with this F, but the cipher is certainly not secure. One benefit of a Feistel cipher is that all questions of security become questions about the round function, so the analysis can be focused on F.

3.3.2 DES

We sent the [DES] S-boxes off to Washington. They came back and were all different.
—Alan Konheim, *one of the designers of DES*

I would say that, contrary to what some people believe, there is no evidence of tampering with the DES so that the basic design was weakened.
—Adi Shamir

The Data Encryption Standard, affectionately known as DES—which rhymes with "fez" and "pez"—was developed way back in the 1970s. The design is based on the Lucifer cipher, a Feistel cipher developed by IBM. DES is a surprisingly simple block cipher, but the story of how Lucifer became DES is anything but simple.

By the mid 1970s, it was clear even to U.S. government bureaucrats that there was a legitimate commercial need for secure crypto. At the time, the computer revolution was underway, and the amount—and sensitivity—of digital data was rapidly increasing.

In the mid 1970s, crypto was poorly understood outside of classified military and government circles, and they weren't talking (and, for the most part, they still aren't). The upshot was that businesses had no way to judge the merits of a crypto product and the quality of most such products was very poor.

Into this environment, the National Bureau of Standards, or NBS (now known as NIST) issued a request for cipher proposals. The winning submission would become a U.S. government standard and almost certainly a *de facto* industrial standard. Very few reasonable submissions were received, and it quickly became apparent that IBM's Lucifer cipher was the only serious contender.

At this point, NBS had a problem. There was little crypto expertise at NBS, so they turned to the government's crypto experts, the super-secret National Security Agency, or NSA.[1] The NSA designs and builds the crypto that is used by the U.S. military and government for highly sensitive information. The NSA also conducts "signals intelligence," or SIGINT, where it tries to obtain intelligence information.

The NSA was apparently reluctant to get involved with DES but eventually agreed to study the Lucifer design and offer an opinion. This all happened in secret, and when the information later came to public light [212] (as is inevitable in the United States) many were suspicious that NSA had placed a "backdoor" into DES so that it alone could easily break the cipher. Certainly, the SIGINT mission of NSA and a general climate of distrust of government fueled such fears. But it's worth noting that 30 years of intense

---

[1]NSA is so super-secret that its employees often joke that the acronym NSA stands for "No Such Agency" or "Never Say Anything."

cryptanalysis has revealed no backdoor in DES. Nevertheless, this suspicion tainted DES from its inception.

Lucifer eventually became DES, but not before a few subtle—and a few not so subtle—changes were made. The most obvious change was that the key length had been reduced from 128 bits to 64 bits. However, 8 of the 64 key bits were discarded, so the actual key length is a mere 56 bits. As a result of these modifications, the expected work required for a brute force exhaustive key search was reduced from 2^{127} to 2^{55}. By this measure, DES is 2^{72} times easier to break than Lucifer! Understandably, the suspicion was that NSA had had a hand in this. However, subsequent cryptanalysis of the DES algorithm has revealed attacks that require slightly less work than trying 2^{55} keys. As a result, DES is probably about as strong with a key of 56 bits as it would have been with the longer key.

The subtle changes to Lucifer involved the substitution boxes, or *S-boxes*, which are described below. These changes in particular fueled the suspicion of a backdoor. But it has become clear over time, that the modifications to the S-boxes actually strengthened the algorithm by offering protection against cryptanalytic techniques that were unknown (at least outside of NSA, and they're not talking) until many years later. The bottom line is that whoever modified the Lucifer algorithm (NSA, that is) knew what they were doing and, in fact, significantly strengthened the algorithm. See [164, 212] for more information on the role of NSA in the development of DES.

To summarize,

- DES is a Feistel cipher with 16 rounds;
- DES has a 64-bit block length;
- DES uses a 56-bit key;
- each round of DES uses a 48-bit subkey and each subkey consists of a 48-bit subset of the 56-bit key.

Each round of DES is relatively simple—at least by the standards of block cipher design. The DES S-boxes are one of its most important security features. We'll see that S-boxes are a common feature of most modern block cipher designs. In DES, each S-box maps 6 bits to 4 bits, and DES employs eight distinct S-boxes. The S-boxes, taken together, map 48 bits to 32 bits. The same S-boxes are used at each round of DES.

Since DES is a Feistel cipher, encryption follows the formulas given in *equations 3.1* and *3.2*. A single round of DES is illustrated in the wiring diagram in Figure 3.2, where the numbers are the number of bits that follow that particular "wire."

Unravelling the diagram in Figure 3.2, we see that the DES round function F can be written as

$$F(R_{i-1}, K_i) = \text{P-box}(\text{S-boxes}(\text{Expand}(R_{i-1}) \oplus K_i)). \qquad (3.3)$$

With this round function, DES is seen to be a Feistel cipher as defined in *equations 3.1* and *3.2*.

Since the DES block size is 64 bits, each L_i and R_i is 32 bits. As required by *equation 3.1*, the new left half is simply the old right half. The round function F is the

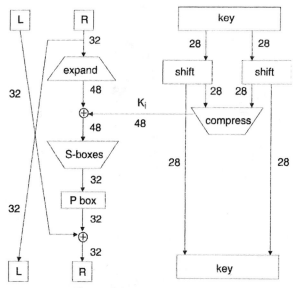

Figure 3.2. One round of DES.

composition of the expansion permutation, addition of subkey, S-boxes, and P-box, as given in *equation 3.3*.

The expansion permutation expands its input from 32 to 48 bits, and the 48 bit subkey is XORed with the result. The S-boxes then compress these 48 bits down to 32 bits before the result is passed through the P-box. The P-box output is then XORed with the old left half to obtain the new right half.

Next, we'll describe each of the components of F, as well as the calculation of the subkey K_i. But it's important to keep the big picture in mind, and to realize that the overall structure of DES is actually very simple. In fact, some of these operations are of no security benefit whatsoever, and, when these are stripped away, the algorithm is even simpler.

We'll follow the convention that bits are numbered from left to right, beginning with 0. The 48-bit result of the DES expansion permutation consists of the bits

31	0	1	2	3	4	3	4	5	6	7	8
7	8	9	10	11	12	11	12	13	14	15	16
15	16	17	18	19	20	19	20	21	22	23	24
23	24	25	26	27	28	27	28	29	30	31	0

where the 32-bit input is, according to our convention, numbered as

0	1	2	3	4	5	6	7	8	9	10	11	12	13	14	15
16	17	18	19	20	21	22	23	24	25	26	27	28	29	30	31.

Each of the eight DES S-boxes maps 6 bits to 4 bits, and, consequently, each can be viewed as an array of 4 rows and 16 columns, with one "nibble" (4-bit value) stored in each of the 64 positions. Each S-box is constructed so that each of its four rows is a permutation of the hexadecimal digits $\{0, 1, 2, \ldots, E, F\}$. We give S-box number 1 below, where the input to the S-box is denoted $b_0 b_1 b_2 b_3 b_4 b_5$. Note that the first and last input bits are used to index the row, while the middle four bits index the column.

$b_0 b_5$	\multicolumn{16}{c}{$b_1 b_2 b_3 b_4$}

	0000	0001	0010	0011	0100	0101	0110	0111	1000	1001	1010	1011	1100	1101	1110	1111
00	1110	0100	1101	0001	0010	1111	1011	1000	0011	1010	0110	1100	0101	1001	0000	0111
01	0000	1111	0111	0100	1110	0010	1101	0001	1010	0110	1100	1011	1001	0101	0011	1000
10	0100	0001	1110	1000	1101	0110	0010	1011	1111	1100	1001	0111	0011	1010	0101	0000
11	1111	1100	1000	0010	0100	1001	0001	0111	0101	1011	0011	1110	1010	0000	0110	1101

The permutation structure of S-box 1 is easier to see if we rewrite the bits in hexadecimal:

$b_0 b_5$	\multicolumn{16}{c}{$b_1 b_2 b_3 b_4$}

	0	1	2	3	4	5	6	7	8	9	A	B	C	D	E	F
0	E	4	D	1	2	F	B	8	3	A	6	C	5	9	0	7
1	0	F	7	4	E	2	D	1	A	6	C	B	9	5	3	8
2	4	1	E	8	D	6	2	B	F	C	9	7	3	A	5	0
3	F	C	8	2	4	9	1	7	5	B	3	E	A	0	6	D

All eight DES S-boxes are listed in the Appendix.

The DES "permutation box," or P-box, serves no security purpose, and its real purpose seems to have been lost to the mists of history. One plausible explanation is that the designers wanted to make DES more difficult to implement in software since the original design called for special hardware. It was apparently hoped that DES would remain a hardware-only algorithm. In fact, the S-boxes were originally classified, so the hardware-only approach might have been aimed at keeping these secret. Predictably, the DES S-boxes became public knowledge almost immediately.

For the record, the P-box permutation is

15	6	19	20	28	11	27	16	0	14	22	25	4	17	30	9
1	7	23	13	31	26	2	8	18	12	29	5	21	10	3	24.

The only significant remaining part of DES is the subkey generation, or key schedule algorithm. This is a somewhat convoluted process, but the ultimate result is simply that 48 of the 56 bits of key are selected at each round. However, the details are security-critical, since block ciphers have been attacked via flawed key schedule algorithms.

As usual, we'll number the 56-bit DES key from left-to-right, beginning with 0. We first extract 28 of the DES key bits, permute them, and call the result LK. The DES key bits of LK are the following bits of the original key

49	42	35	28	21	14	7
0	50	43	36	29	22	15
8	1	51	44	37	30	23
16	9	2	52	45	38	31

Similarly, the remaining 28 bits of the DES key are known as RK, which is given by the key bits

```
55  48  41  34  27  20  13
 6  54  47  40  33  26  19
12   5  53  46  39  32  25
18  11   4  24  17  10   3
```

Before we can describe the key schedule algorithm, we need a few more items. Define the permutation LP as

```
13  16  10  23   0   4   2  27  14   5  20   9
22  18  11   3  25   7  15   6  26  19  12   1
```

and the permutation RP as

```
12  23   2   8  18  26   1  11  22  16   4  19
15  20  10  27   5  24  17  13  21   7   0   3
```

Finally, define

$$r_i = \begin{cases} 1 & \text{if } i \in \{1, 2, 9, 16\} \\ 2 & \text{otherwise.} \end{cases}$$

The DES key schedule algorithm for generating the 48-bit subkey K_i for round i can now be described as in Table 3.3.

For completeness, there are two other features of DES that we must mention. An initial permutation is applied to the plaintext before round one, and its inverse is applied after the final round. Also, when encrypting, the halves are swapped after last round, so the actual ciphertext is (R_{16}, L_{16}) instead of (L_{16}, R_{16}). Neither of these serves any security purpose, and we'll ignore them in the remaining discussion.

A few words on the security of DES may be useful. First, mathematicians are very good at solving linear equations, and the only part of DES that is not linear is the S-boxes. As a result, the S-boxes are crucial to the security of DES. Actually, the

TABLE 3.3. DES key schedule algorithm.

for each round $i = 1, 2, \ldots, n$
    LK = cyclically left shift LK by r_i bits
    RK = cyclically left shift RK by r_i bits
    The left half of subkey K_i consists of bits LP of LK
    The right half of subkey K_i consists of bits RP of RK
next i

expansion permutation has an important security role to play and, to a lesser extent, so does the key schedule. All of this will become much clearer after we discuss linear and differential cryptanalysis in a later chapter. For more details on the design of DES, see [203].

Despite the concern over the design of DES—particularly the role of NSA in the process—DES has clearly stood the test of time [141]. Today, DES is vulnerable simply because the key is too small, not because of any noteworthy shortcut attack. Although some attacks have been developed that, in theory, require slightly less work than an exhaustive key search, all practical DES crackers built to date simply try all keys until they stumble across the correct one. The inescapable conclusion is that the designers of DES knew what they were doing.

We'll have more to say about DES when we study advanced cryptanalysis in a later chapter. In fact, DES was the impetus for many recent developments in the field of cryptanalysis.

Next, we describe triple DES, which is often used to effectively extend the key length of DES. We'll follow this with a quick overview of a few other block ciphers. Then we discuss one truly simple block cipher in more detail.

3.3.3 Triple DES

Before moving on to other ciphers, we must discuss a popular variant of DES known as triple DES, or 3DES. But before that, we need some notation. Let P be a block of plaintext, K a key, and C the corresponding block of ciphertext. For DES, C and P are each 64 bits, while K is 56 bits. The notation that we'll adopt for the encryption of P with key K is

$$C = E(P, K)$$

while the corresponding decryption is denoted

$$P = D(C, K).$$

DES is nearly ubiquitous, but its key length is insufficient today. It turns out that there is a clever way to use DES with a larger key length. Intuitively, it seems that "double" DES might be the thing to do,

$$C = E(E(P, K_1), K_2). \qquad (3.4)$$

This would seem to offer the benefits of a 112 bit key, with the only drawback being a loss of efficiency due to the two DES operations.

However, there is an attack on double DES that renders it more-or-less equivalent to single DES. Although the attack is somewhat impractical, it's close enough to being practical, that it is cause for concern. This attack is a chosen plaintext attack. We select a particular plaintext P and obtain the corresponding ciphertext C. Our goal is to find the keys K_1 and K_2 in *equation 3.4*. First we precompute a table of size 2^{56} containing the pairs $E(P, K)$ and K for all possible key values K. We sort this table on the values $E(P, K)$. Now given this table and the ciphertext value C corresponding to the chosen P, we decrypt C with keys $\tilde{K}$ until we find a value $D(C, \tilde{K})$ that is in table. The value that we find in the table will be $E(P, K)$ for some K and we have

$$D(C, \tilde{K}) = E(P, K)$$

where $\tilde{K}$ and K are known. That we have found the 112-bit key can be seen by encrypting both sides with $\tilde{K}$, which gives

$$C = E(E(P, K), \tilde{K}),$$

that is, $K_1 = K$ and $K_2 = \tilde{K}$ in *equation 3.4.*

This attack on double DES requires that we pre-compute and store an enormous table of 2^{56} elements. But the table computation is one-time work, so if we use this table many times (by attacking double DES many times) the work for computing the table can be amortized over the number of attacks. Neglecting the work needed to precompute the table, the work consists of computing $D(C, K)$ until we find a match in the table. This has an expected work of 2^{55}, just as in an exhaustive key search attack on single DES.

Since double DES isn't secure, will triple DES fare any better? At least we can say that a meet-in-the-middle attack similar to the attack on double DES is impractical since the table pre-computation is infeasible—or the per attack work is infeasible if we reduce the table to a practical size.

It seems that the logical approach to triple DES would be

$$C = E(E(E(P, K_1), K_2), K_3)$$

but this is not the way it's done. Instead, triple DES is defined as

$$C = E(D(E(P, K_1), K_2), K_1).$$

Notice that triple DES only uses two keys, and encrypt-decrypt-encrypt, or EDE, is used instead of EEE. The reason for only using two keys is that 112 bits is sufficient, but why EDE? Surprisingly, the answer is backwards compatibility with single DES. If 3DES is used with $K_1 = K_2 = K$ then it collapses to single DES

$$C = E(D(E(P, K), K), K) = E(P, K).$$

Triple DES is popular today. But with the coming of the Advanced Encryption Standard, triple DES should fade from use over time.

3.3.4 AES

By the 1990s it was apparent everyone—even the U.S. government—that DES had outlived its usefulness. The crucial problem with DES is that the key length of 56 bits is susceptible to an exhaustive key search. Special-purpose DES crackers have been built that can recover DES keys in a matter of hours, and distributed attacks using volunteer computers on the Internet have succeeded in finding DES keys [70].

In the early 1990s, the National Institute of Standards and Technology (NIST), which is the present incarnation of NBS, issued a call for crypto proposals for the Advanced Encryption Standard or AES. Unlike the DES call for proposals of 20 years earlier, NIST was inundated with quality proposals. The field was eventually narrowed down to a handful of finalists, and an algorithm known a Rijndael (pronounced something like "rain doll") was ultimately selected. See [140] for information on the AES competition and [54] for the details on the Rijndael algorithm.

The AES competition was conducted in a completely open manner and, unlike the DES competition, the NSA was openly involved as one of the judges. As a result, there are no plausible claims of a backdoor having been inserted into AES. In fact, AES is highly regarded in the cryptographic community. Shamir has stated that he believes data encrypted with a 256-bit AES key will be "secure forever," regardless of any conceivable advances in computing technology [52].

Like DES, the AES is an iterated block cipher. Unlike DES, the AES algorithm is not a Feistel cipher. The major implication of this is that, in order to decrypt, the AES operations must be invertible. Also unlike DES, the AES algorithm has a highly mathematical structure. We'll only give a quick overview of the algorithm—large volumes of information on all aspects of AES are readily available. No crypto algorithm in history has received as much scrutiny in as short of a period of time as the AES. See [5, 187] for more information on the Rijndael algorithm.

Some of the pertinent facts of AES are as follows.

- Three block sizes are available: 128, 192, or 256 bits.
- Three key lengths are available (independent of selected block length): 128, 192, or 256 bits.
- The number of rounds varies from 10 to 14, depending on the key length.
- Each round consists of four functions, which are in three "layers." The functions are listed below, with the layer in parentheses.

    —ByteSub (nonlinear layer)

    —ShiftRow (linear mixing layer)

    —MixColumn (nonlinear layer)

    —AddRoundKey (key addition layer)

Assuming a 192-bit block size, AES treats the data as a 4×6 byte array

$$\begin{bmatrix} a_{00} & a_{01} & a_{02} & a_{03} & a_{04} & a_{05} \\ a_{10} & a_{11} & a_{12} & a_{13} & a_{14} & a_{15} \\ a_{20} & a_{21} & a_{22} & a_{23} & a_{24} & a_{25} \\ a_{30} & a_{31} & a_{32} & a_{33} & a_{34} & a_{35} \end{bmatrix}$$

The `ByteSub` operation is applied to each byte a_{ij}, that is, $b_{ij} = \texttt{ByteSub}(a_{ij})$. The result is the array of b_{ij} as illustrated below:

$$
\begin{bmatrix}
a_{00} & a_{01} & a_{02} & a_{03} & a_{04} & a_{05} \\
a_{10} & a_{11} & a_{12} & a_{13} & a_{14} & a_{15} \\
a_{20} & a_{21} & a_{22} & a_{23} & a_{24} & a_{25} \\
a_{30} & a_{31} & a_{32} & a_{33} & a_{34} & a_{35}
\end{bmatrix}
\longrightarrow \texttt{ByteSub} \longrightarrow
\begin{bmatrix}
b_{00} & b_{01} & b_{02} & b_{03} & b_{04} & b_{05} \\
b_{10} & b_{11} & b_{12} & b_{13} & b_{14} & b_{15} \\
b_{20} & b_{21} & b_{22} & b_{23} & b_{24} & b_{25} \\
b_{30} & b_{31} & b_{32} & b_{33} & b_{34} & b_{35}
\end{bmatrix}
$$

`ByteSub`, which is roughly the EAS equivalent of the DES S-boxes, can be viewed as a nonlinear—but invertible—composition of two mathematical functions, or it can be viewed simply as a lookup table. We'll take the latter view. The `ByteSub` lookup table appears in Table 3.4. For example, `ByteSub(3c)` = eb since eb appears in row 3 and column c of Table 3.4.

The `ShiftRow` operation is a simple cyclic shift of the bytes in each row of the 4×6 byte array. This operation is given by

$$
\begin{bmatrix}
a_{00} & a_{01} & a_{02} & a_{03} & a_{04} & a_{05} \\
a_{10} & a_{11} & a_{12} & a_{13} & a_{14} & a_{15} \\
a_{20} & a_{21} & a_{22} & a_{23} & a_{24} & a_{25} \\
a_{30} & a_{31} & a_{32} & a_{33} & a_{34} & a_{35}
\end{bmatrix}
\longrightarrow \texttt{ShiftRow} \longrightarrow
\begin{bmatrix}
a_{00} & a_{01} & a_{02} & a_{03} & a_{04} & a_{05} \\
a_{11} & a_{12} & a_{13} & a_{14} & a_{15} & a_{10} \\
a_{22} & a_{23} & a_{24} & a_{25} & a_{20} & a_{21} \\
a_{33} & a_{34} & a_{35} & a_{30} & a_{31} & a_{32}
\end{bmatrix},
$$

that is, the first row doesn't shift, the second row right-shifts five bytes, the third row right-shifts four bytes, and the last row right-shifts three bytes. Note that `ShiftRow` is inverted by simply shifting in the opposite direction.

TABLE 3.4. AES ByteSub.

	0	1	2	3	4	5	6	7	8	9	a	b	c	d	e	f
0	63	7c	77	7b	f2	6b	6f	c5	30	01	67	2b	fe	d7	ab	76
1	ca	82	c9	7d	fa	59	47	f0	ad	d4	a2	af	9c	a4	72	c0
2	b7	fd	93	26	36	3f	f7	cc	34	a5	e5	f1	71	d8	31	15
3	04	c7	23	c3	18	96	05	9a	07	12	80	e2	eb	27	b2	75
4	09	83	2c	1a	1b	6e	5a	a0	52	3b	d6	b3	29	e3	2f	84
5	53	d1	00	ed	20	fc	b1	5b	6a	cb	be	39	4a	4c	58	cf
6	d0	ef	aa	fb	43	4d	33	85	45	f9	02	7f	50	3c	9f	a8
7	51	a3	40	8f	92	9d	38	f5	bc	b6	da	21	10	ff	f3	d2
8	cd	0c	13	ec	5f	97	44	17	c4	a7	7e	3d	64	5d	19	73
9	60	81	4f	dc	22	2a	90	88	46	ee	b8	14	de	5e	0b	db
a	e0	32	3a	0a	49	06	24	5c	c2	d3	ac	62	91	95	e4	79
b	e7	c8	37	6d	8d	d5	4e	a9	6c	56	f4	ea	65	7a	ae	08
c	ba	78	25	2e	1c	a6	b4	c6	e8	dd	74	1f	4b	bd	8b	8a
d	70	3e	b5	66	48	03	f6	0e	61	35	57	b9	86	c1	1d	9e
e	e1	f8	98	11	69	d9	8e	94	9b	1e	87	e9	ce	55	28	df
f	8c	a1	89	0d	bf	e6	42	68	41	99	2d	0f	b0	54	bb	16

Next, the `MixColumn` operation is applied to each column of the current 4×6 byte array as indicated below:

$$
\begin{bmatrix} a_{0i} \\ a_{1i} \\ a_{2i} \\ a_{3i} \end{bmatrix} \longrightarrow \texttt{MixColumn} \longrightarrow \begin{bmatrix} b_{0i} \\ b_{1i} \\ b_{2i} \\ b_{3i} \end{bmatrix} \text{ for } i = 0, 1, 2, \ldots, 5.
$$

`MixColumn` consists of shift and XOR operations, and it's most efficiently implemented as a lookup table. The overall operation is nonlinear but invertible, and, as with `ByteSub`, it serves a similar purpose as the DES S-boxes.

The `AddRoundKey` operation is straightforward. Similar to DES, a key schedule algorithm is used to generate a subkey for each round. Let k_{ij} be the 4×6 subkey array for a particular round. Then the subkey is XORed with the current 4×6 byte array a_{ij} as illustrated below:

$$
\begin{bmatrix} a_{00} & a_{01} & a_{02} & a_{03} & a_{04} & a_{05} \\ a_{10} & a_{11} & a_{12} & a_{13} & a_{14} & a_{15} \\ a_{20} & a_{21} & a_{22} & a_{23} & a_{24} & a_{25} \\ a_{30} & a_{31} & a_{32} & a_{33} & a_{34} & a_{35} \end{bmatrix} \oplus \begin{bmatrix} k_{00} & k_{01} & k_{02} & k_{03} & k_{04} & k_{05} \\ k_{10} & k_{11} & k_{12} & k_{13} & k_{14} & k_{15} \\ k_{20} & k_{21} & k_{22} & k_{23} & k_{24} & k_{25} \\ k_{30} & k_{31} & k_{32} & k_{33} & k_{34} & k_{35} \end{bmatrix}
$$

$$
= \begin{bmatrix} b_{00} & b_{01} & b_{02} & b_{03} & b_{04} & b_{05} \\ b_{10} & b_{11} & b_{12} & b_{13} & b_{14} & b_{15} \\ b_{20} & b_{21} & b_{22} & b_{23} & b_{24} & b_{25} \\ b_{30} & b_{31} & b_{32} & b_{33} & b_{34} & b_{35} \end{bmatrix}
$$

We'll ignore the AES key schedule, but it's a significant part of the security of the algorithm. Finally, as we noted above, each of the four functions, `ByteSub`, `ShiftRow`, `MixColumn`, and `AddRoundKey`, are invertible. As a result, the entire algorithm is invertible, and consequently AES can decrypt as well as encrypt.

3.3.5 Three More Block Ciphers

In this section, we briefly mention three block cipher algorithms, namely, the International Data Encryption Algorithm (IDEA), Blowfish, and RC6. Each of these has some particular noteworthy design feature. In the next section, we'll take a closer look at the Tiny Encryption Algorithm, or TEA [246].

IDEA is the handiwork of James L. Massey, one of the great—though lesser-known—cryptographers of modern times. The most innovative feature of IDEA is its use of *mixed mode arithmetic*. The algorithm combines addition modulo 2 (XOR) with addition modulo 2^{16} and the Lai-Massey multiplication, which is almost multiplication modulo 2^{16}. These operations together produce the necessary nonlinearity, and as a result no explicit S-box is required. Massey was the first to use this approach, which is in common usage today. See [156] for more details on the design of IDEA.

Blowfish is Bruce Schneier's favorite crypto algorithm, no doubt because he invented it. Schneier is a well-known cryptographer and a good writer on all things security related. The interesting quirk of Blowfish is its use of *key dependent S-boxes*. Instead of having fixed S-boxes, Blowfish generates its S-boxes based on the key. It can be shown that typical Blowfish S-boxes are secure. See [202] for more information on Blowfish.

RC6 is due to Ron Rivest, whose crypto accomplishments are truly remarkable, including the public key system RSA and the previously mentioned RC4 stream cipher, as well as one of the most popular hash functions, MD5. The unusual aspect of RC6 is its use of data-dependent rotations [188]. It is highly unusual to rely on the data as an essential part of the operation of a crypto algorithm. RC6 was one of the AES finalists, though it ultimately lost.

These three ciphers illustrate some of the many variations that have been used in the quest for the ideal balance between security and performance in block cipher design. In a later chapter we discuss linear and differential cryptanalysis, which makes the trade-offs inherent in block cipher design clearer.

3.3.6 TEA

The final block cipher that we'll consider is the Tiny Encryption Algorithm, or TEA. The wiring diagrams that we've displayed so far might lead you to conclude that block ciphers are necessarily complex. TEA nicely illustrates that such is not necessarily the case.

TEA uses a 64-bit block length and a 128-bit key. The algorithm assumes a computing architecture with 32-bit words, so all mathematical operations are implicitly modulo 2^{32}. The number of rounds is variable but must be relatively large compared with previous block ciphers that we've seen (32 rounds is considered secure).

In block cipher design, there is a trade-off between the complexity of each round and the number of rounds required. Ciphers such as DES try to strike a balance between these two, while AES reduces the number of rounds but has a more complex round function. TEA, on the other hand, uses a very simple round function; however, as a consequence, the number of rounds must be large to achieve a high level of security. Pseudo-code for TEA encryption—assuming 32 rounds are used—appears in Table 3.5, where "$\ll$" is the left shift and "$\gg$" is the right shift.

One thing to notice about TEA is that it's not a Feistel cipher, and so we need separate encryption and decryption routines. But TEA is "almost" a Feistel cipher in that it uses addition and subtraction instead of XOR. However, the need for separate

TABLE 3.5. TEA encryption.

```
(K[0], K[1], K[2], K[3]) = 128 bit key
(L, R) = plaintext (64-bit block)
delta = 0x9e3779b9
sum = 0
for i = 1 to 32
    sum = sum + delta
    L = L + (((R ≪ 4) + K[0]) ⊕ (R + sum) ⊕ ((R ≫ 5) + K[1]))
    R = R + (((L ≪ 4) + K[2]) ⊕ (L + sum) ⊕ ((L ≫ 5) + K[3]))
next i
ciphertext = (L, R)
```

encryption and decryption routines is a minor concern with TEA, since so few lines of code are required. The algorithm is also fairly efficient, even with the large number of rounds. The TEA decryption algorithm, assuming 32 rounds, appears in Table 3.6.

There is an obscure "related key" attack on TEA [123]. If a cryptanalyst knows that two TEA messages are encrypted with keys that are related to each other in a special way, then the plaintext can be recovered. This is a low-probability attack that in most circumstances can probably be ignored. But there is a slightly more complex variant of TEA, known as extended TEA, or XTEA [165] that overcomes this potential problem. There is also a simplified version of TEA, known as STEA, that is extremely weak, but is used to illustrate certain types of attacks [160].

3.3.7 Block Cipher Modes

Using a stream cipher is easy—you generate a keystream that is the same length as the plaintext and XOR. Using a block cipher is also easy, as long as you have exactly one block to encrypt. But how should multiple blocks be encrypted with a block cipher? And how should a partial block be encrypted? It turns out that the answers are not as simple as it might seem.

Suppose we have multiple plaintext blocks

$$P_0, P_1, P_2, \ldots$$

For a fixed key K, a block cipher is a codebook, since it creates a fixed mapping between plaintext and ciphertext blocks. Following the codebook idea, the obvious thing to do is to use a block cipher in so-called electronic codebook, or ECB, mode. In ECB mode, we encrypt using the formula

$$C_i = E(P_i, K) \quad \text{for } i = 0, 1, 2, \ldots$$

TABLE 3.6. TEA decryption.

```
(K[0], K[1], K[2], K[3]) = 128 bit key
(L, R) = ciphertext (64-bit block)
delta = 0x9e3779b9
sum = delta ≪ 5
for i = 1 to 32
    R = R − (((L ≪ 4) + K[2]) ⊕ (L + sum) ⊕ ((L ≫ 5) + K[3]))
    L = L − (((R ≪ 4) + K[0]) ⊕ (R + sum) ⊕ ((R ≫ 5) + K[1]))
    sum = sum − delta
next i
plaintext = (L, R)
```

Then we can decrypt according to

$$P_i = D(C_i, K) \quad \text{for } i = 0, 1, 2, \ldots$$

This approach works, but there are some security problems with ECB mode.

Suppose ECB mode is used, and an attacker observes that $C_i = C_j$. Then the attacker knows that $P_i = P_j$. Although this may seem innocent enough, there are cases where the attacker will know part of the plaintext, and any match with a known block reveals another block. But even if the attacker does not know P_i or P_j, some information has been revealed, namely, that these two plaintext blocks are the same, and we don't want to give the cryptanalyst anything for free—especially if there is a reasonable way to avoid it.

Massey [151] gives a dramatic illustration of this weakness of ECB mode. We give a similar example in Figure 3.3, which shows an (uncompressed) image of Alice next to the same image encrypted in ECB mode. While every block of the right-hand image in Figure 3.3 has been encrypted, the blocks that were the same in the original image are the same in the ECB-encrypted version. In this case, it's not difficult for Trudy to guess the plaintext from the ciphertext!

Fortunately, there are several solutions to this weakness of ECB mode. We'll discuss the most common method, cipher block chaining, or CBC, mode. In CBC mode, the ciphertext from a block is used to obscure the plaintext of the next block before it is encrypted. The encryption formula for CBC mode is

$$C_i = E(P_i \oplus C_{i-1}, K) \quad \text{for } i = 0, 1, 2, \ldots \tag{3.5}$$

Figure 3.3. Alice and ECB mode.

which is decrypted via

$$P_i = D(C_i, K) \oplus C_{i-1} \quad \text{for } i = 0, 1, 2, \ldots. \tag{3.6}$$

The first block requires special handling since there is no ciphertext block C_{-1}. An *initialization vector*, or IV, is used to take the place of C_{-1}. Since the ciphertext is not secret and since the IV plays the role of a ciphertext block, it need not be secret either. But the IV should be randomly selected. Using the IV, the first block is encrypted as

$$C_0 = E(P_0 \oplus \text{IV}, K)$$

with the formula in *equation 3.5* used for the remaining blocks. The first block is decrypted as

$$P_0 = D(C_0, K) \oplus \text{IV}$$

with the formula in *equation 3.6* used to decrypt all remaining blocks. Since the IV need not be secret, it's usually randomly generated by the sender and sent as the first "ciphertext" block. The recipient must know to treat the first block as the IV.

The benefit of CBC mode is that identical plaintext will not yield identical ciphertext. This is dramatically illustrated by comparing Alice's image encrypted using ECB mode—which appears in Figure 3.3—with the image of Alice encrypted in CBC mode, which appears in Figure 3.4.

A possible concern with CBC mode is the effect of errors. When the ciphertext is transmitted, garbles might occur—a 0 could become a 1 or vice versa. If a single

 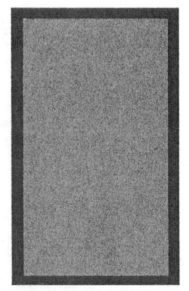

Figure 3.4. Alice prefers CBC mode.

transmission error makes the plaintext unrecoverable, then CBC would be useless in many applications. Fortunately, this is not the case.

Suppose the ciphertext block C_i is garbled to, say, G. Then

$$P_i \neq D(G, K) \oplus C_{i-1} \quad \text{and} \quad P_{i+1} \neq D(C_{i+1}, K) \oplus G$$

but

$$P_{i+2} = D(C_{i+2}, K) \oplus C_{i+1}$$

and all subsequent blocks are decrypted correctly. The fact that a single-bit error causes two entire blocks to be garbled could be a serious concern in high error rate environments such as wireless. Stream ciphers do not have this problem—a single garbled ciphertext bit results in a single garbled plaintext bit—and that is one reason why stream ciphers are sometimes preferred in wireless applications.

Another concern with a block cipher is a *cut-and-paste attack*. Suppose the plaintext

Money␣for␣Alice␣is␣$1000

Money␣for␣Trudy␣is␣$2␣␣␣

where "␣" is a blank space, is to be encrypted with a block cipher that has a 64-bit block size. Assuming that each character requires 8 bits, the plaintext blocks are

$P_0 = $ Money␣fo

$P_1 = $ r␣Alice␣

$P_2 = $ is␣$1000

$P_3 = $ Money␣fo

$P_4 = $ r␣Trudy␣

$P_5 = $ is␣$2␣␣␣

Suppose this data is encrypted using ECB mode. Then the ciphertext blocks are computed as $C_i = E(P_i, K)$ for $i = 0, 1, \ldots, 5$.

Now suppose that Trudy knows that ECB mode is used, she knows the general structure of the plaintext, and she knows that she will receive $10, but she doesn't know how much Alice will receive—though she suspects it's much more than $10. If Trudy can rearrange the order of the ciphertext blocks to

$$C_0, C_1, C_5, C_3, C_4, C_2 \qquad (3.7)$$

then Bob will decrypt this as

```
MoneyⓊforⓊAliceⓊisⓊ$2ⓊⓊⓊ
MoneyⓊforⓊTrudyⓊisⓊ$1000
```

which is clearly a preferable outcome for Trudy!

You might think that CBC mode would eliminate the cut-and-paste attack. If so, you'd be wrong. With CBC mode, a cut-and-paste attack is still possible, although it's slightly more difficult and some data will be corrupted. This is explored further in the problems in Section 3.6.

It is also possible to use a block cipher to generate a keystream, which can then be used just like a stream cipher keystream. There are several acceptable ways to accomplish this feat, but we'll only mention one, namely, counter mode, or CTR. As with CBC mode, CTR mode employs an initialization vector, or IV. The CTR mode encryption formula is

$$C_i = P_i \oplus E(\text{IV} + i, K)$$

and decryption is accomplished via

$$P_i = C_i \oplus E(\text{IV} + i, K).$$

CTR mode is often selected when random access is required. However, random access is also straightforward with CBC mode. There are many other block cipher modes; see [203] for descriptions of the more common ones.

3.4 INTEGRITY

Whereas confidentiality deals with preventing unauthorized reading, integrity is concerned with preventing unauthorized writing. For example, suppose that you electronically transfer funds from one account to another. You may not want others to know about this transaction, in which case encryption will effectively provide the desired confidential. Whether you are concerned about confidentiality or not, you certainly want the transaction that you submit to be accurately received. This is where integrity comes into the picture.

In the previous section, we studied the use of block ciphers for confidentiality. Here we show that block ciphers can also be used to provide data integrity.

It is important to realize that confidentiality and integrity are two very different concepts. Encryption with any cipher—from the one-time pad to block ciphers, in any of their modes—does not protect the data from malicious or inadvertent changes. If Trudy manipulates the ciphertext (say, by a cut-and-paste attack) or if garbles occur in transmission, the integrity of the data has been destroyed. We want to be able to automatically detect when the received data is not the same as the sent data. We've seen several examples—and you should be able to give several more—to show that encryption does not assure integrity.

A message authentication code, or MAC, uses a block cipher to ensure data integrity. The procedure is simply to encrypt the data in CBC mode, discarding all ciphertext blocks except the final block, which is the MAC. The formula, assuming N blocks of data, is

$$C_0 = E(P_0 \oplus \text{IV}, K), \quad C_1 = E(P_1 \oplus C_0, K), \dots,$$

$$C_{N-1} = E(P_{N-1} \oplus C_{N-2}, K) = \text{MAC}.$$

The MAC and the plaintext are then sent to the recipient who repeats the process and compares the computed "MAC" with the received MAC. If there is any difference, the receiver knows that the data (or MAC) has changed; however, if there is no difference, then the data is almost certainly correct. Note that, as in CBC mode, the sender and receiver must share a symmetric key K and a non-secret IV.

Why does the MAC work? Suppose Alice sends P_0, P_1, P_2, P_3 to Bob, along with a MAC. If Trudy changes plaintext block P_1 to, say, Q during transmission, then when Bob attempts to verify the MAC, he computes

$$C_0 = E(P_0 \oplus \text{IV}, K), \quad \tilde{C}_1 = E(Q \oplus C_0, K), \quad \tilde{C}_2 = E(P_2 \oplus \tilde{C}_1, K),$$

$$\tilde{C}_3 = E(P_3 \oplus \tilde{C}_2, K) = \text{"MAC"} \neq \text{MAC}.$$

Any change to a plaintext block propagate through the subsequent blocks to the computed MAC.

Recall that with CBC encryption, a change in a ciphertext block only affects two of the recovered plaintext blocks. In contrast, the example above shows that any change in the plaintext affects all subsequent blocks in CBC encryption. This is the crucial property that enables a MAC to provide integrity.

Often confidentiality and integrity are both required. In such cases, for efficiency it would be useful to obtain both with a single CBC "encryption" of the data. However, if we CBC encrypt the data and send the resulting ciphertext and the computed MAC, we would simply repeat the final ciphertext block twice. This cannot provide any additional security. Unfortunately, there is no obvious way to obtain both confidentiality and integrity in a single encryption of the data. This topic is explored in more detail in the problems at the end of the chapter.

Computing a MAC based on CBC encryption is not the only way to provide for data integrity. A hashed MAC, or HMAC, is another standard approach to integrity. We'll discuss HMAC in Chapter 5.

3.5 SUMMARY

In this chapter, we've covered a great deal of material on symmetric key cryptography. There are two distinct types of symmetric ciphers: stream ciphers and block ciphers. We briefly discussed two stream ciphers, A5/1 and RC4. Stream ciphers generalize the one-time pad, where provable security is traded for practicality.

Block ciphers, on the other hand, can be viewed as the "electronic" equivalent of a codebook. We discussed the block cipher DES in considerable detail and mentioned several other block ciphers briefly. We then considered various modes of using block ciphers. We also showed that block ciphers can be used for data integrity.

Symmetric key crypto is used for data confidentiality. There are two slightly different flavors of confidentiality. On the one hand, we can encrypt data that is to be transmitted over an insecure channel. On the other hand, we might encrypt data that is stored on an insecure media, such as a computer hard drive. Symmetric key crypto—in the form of a MAC—can also be used to ensure data integrity.

Symmetric ciphers are also useful in authentication protocols, as we'll see in a later chapter. It's also interesting to note that stream ciphers, block ciphers, and hash functions (to be discussed in a later chapter) are all equivalent in the sense that anything you can do with one, you can accomplish with the other two. For this reason, these three are often referred to as cryptographic "primitives."

Symmetric key cryptography is an enormous topic. We've only scratched the surface here; however, armed with the background from this chapter, we'll be prepared to tackle all of the issues concerning symmetric ciphers that arise in later chapters.

In order to really understand the reasoning behind block cipher design, it's necessary to delve more deeply into the field of cryptanalysis. Chapter 6, which deals with advanced cryptanalysis, is highly recommended for anyone who wants to gain a deeper understanding of block cipher design principles.

3.6 PROBLEMS

1. Let $K = (k_0 k_1 k_2 \ldots k_{55})$ be a 56-bit DES key. List the 48 bits of each DES subkey $K_1, K_2, \ldots, K_{16}$. Make a table that contains the number of subkeys in which each bit k_i is used. Can you design a DES key schedule algorithm in which each key bit is used an equal number of times?

2. Implement the Tiny Encryption Algorithm (TEA) and use it to encrypt the 64-bit block

   0x0123456789ABCDEF

   using the 128-bit key

   0xA56BABCD00000000FFFFFFFFABCDEF01.

   Decrypt the resulting ciphertext to obtain the original plaintext. Then encrypt and decrypt the message

   Four score and seven years ago our fathers brought forth on this continent, a new nation, conceived in Liberty, and dedicated to the proposition that all men are created equal.

   using each of the following three different modes: ECB mode, CBC mode, and CTR mode. In each case, use the key given above.

3. Draw diagrams to illustrate encryption and decryption in CBC mode.

4. The formula for counter mode encryption is
$$C_i = P_i \oplus E(\text{IV} + i, K).$$
Suppose instead we use the formula
$$C_i = P_i \oplus E(K, \text{IV} + i).$$
Is this secure? If so, why? If not, describe an attack.

5. AES consists of four functions in three layers. Which of the functions are primarily for confusion and which are primarily for diffusion? Which of the layers are for confusion and which are for diffusion? Justify your answers.

6. Implement the RC4 algorithm. Suppose the key consists of the following seven bytes:

key = (0x1A, 0x2B, 0x3C, 0x4D, 0x5E, 0x6F, 0x77).

List the permutation S after the initialization phase. List the permutation S after generating 100 bytes of the keystream. List the permutation S after generating 1000 bytes of the keystream.

7. For bits x, y, and z, the function maj(x, y, z) is the "majority vote" function, that is, if two or more of the three bits are 0, then the function returns 0; otherwise, it returns 1. Write the truth table for this function and derive the boolean function that is equivalent to maj(x, y, z).

8. Implement the A5/1 algorithm. Suppose that, after a particular step, the values in the registers are
$$X = (x_0, x_1, \ldots, x_{18}) = (1010101010101010101)$$
$$Y = (y_0, y_1, \ldots, y_{21}) = (1100110011001100110011)$$
$$Z = (z_0, z_1, \ldots, z_{22}) = (11100001111000011110000)$$
Generate and print the next 32 keystream bits. Print the contents of X, Y and Z after the 32 keystream bits have been generated.

9. What is a Feistel Cipher? Why is the Tiny Encryption Algorithm, TEA, not a Feistel Cipher? Why is TEA "almost" a Feistel Cipher?

10. Suppose that we use a block cipher to encrypt according to the rule
$$C_0 = \text{IV} \oplus E(P_0, K), \quad C_1 = C_0 \oplus E(P_1, K), \quad C_2 = C_1 \oplus E(P_2, K), \quad \ldots$$
What is the corresponding decryption rule? Give two security disadvantages to this mode compared with CBC mode.

11. A stream cipher can be viewed as a generalization of a one-time pad. Recall that the one-time pad is provably secure. Why can't we prove that a stream cipher is secure using the same argument that was used for the one-time pad?

12. For any stream cipher, why must the keystream eventually repeat?

13. For DES, how many bits are in the key, how many bits are in a plaintext block, how many bits are in each subkey, how many rounds, and how many S-boxes?

14. DES swaps the output of the final round, that is, the ciphertext is not $C = (L_{16}, R_{16})$ but instead is $C = (R_{16}, L_{16})$. What is the purpose of this swap? Hint: The swap serves no security purpose.

15. Recall the attack on double DES discussed in the text. Suppose that we instead define double DES as $C = D(E(P, K_1), K_2)$. Describe a "meet-in-the-middle" attack on this version of double DES.

16. An IV need not be secret, but does it need to be random? Are there any security disadvantages (or advantages) if IVs are selected in sequence instead of being generated at random?

17. Suppose that ciphertext blocks

$$C_0, C_1, C_2, \ldots, C_9$$

are encrypted in CBC mode. Show that a cut-and-paste attack is possible; that is, show that it is possible to rearrange the blocks so that some of the blocks decrypt correctly, even though they are not in the correct order.

18. Explain how to do random access on data encrypted using CBC mode. What is the disadvantage of using CBC for random access compared with CTR mode?

19. CTR mode generates a keystream using a block cipher. Give another method for using a block cipher as a stream cipher. Does your method support random access?

20. Suppose we encrypt in CBC mode using key K and we compute a MAC using the key $K \oplus X$, where X is a known constant. The ciphertext and the MAC are sent to the recipient. Show that the recipient will detect a cut-and-paste attack.

21. Suppose that we define triple DES with a 168-bit key as $C = E(E(E(P, K_1), K_2), K_3)$. Assuming that we can compute and store a table of size 2^{56}, show that this version of triple DES is no more secure than the usual 3DES, $C = E(D(E(P, K_1), K_2), K_1)$. Hint: Mimic the meet-in-the-middle attack for double DES discussed in the book.

22. Give two ways to encrypt a partial block using a block cipher. Your first method should result in ciphertext that is the size of a complete block, while your second method should not expand the data. Discuss any possible security concerns of your two methods.

23. Consider a Feistel cipher with four rounds and $P = (L_0, R_0)$. What is the ciphertext C if the round function is
   a. $F(R_{i-1}, K_i) = 0$.
   b. $F(R_{i-1}, K_i) = R_{i-1}$.
   c. $F(R_{i-1}, K_i) = K_i$.
   d. $F(R_{i-1}, K_i) = R_{i-1} \oplus K_i$.

24. Let X be data. Define $F(X)$ to be the MAC when X is CBC encrypted with key K and a given IV. Is F one-way; that is, given $F(X)$ is it possible to find X? Is F collision resistant; that is, given $F(X)$ is it possible to find a Y such that $F(Y) = F(X)$?

25. Suppose that the ciphertext in *equation 3.7* had been encrypted in CBC mode instead of ECB mode. If Trudy believes ECB mode is used and tries the same cut-and-paste attack, which blocks decrypt correctly?

26. Obtain the file `Alice.bmp` from the textbook website and use the TEA cipher to ECB encrypt the image, leaving the first 10 blocks unencrypted. View the encrypted image. What would happen if you were to try the same thing with a JPG file?

27. Suppose that Alice and Bob always choose the same IV.
    a. Discuss one security problem this creates if CBC mode is used.
    b. Discuss one security problem this creates if CTR mode is used.
    c. If the same IV is always used, which is more secure, CBC or CTR mode?

28. Suppose that Alice and Bob always use CBC mode encryption and they choose IVs in sequence. What are the security advantages and disadvantages of this approach compared with using a random IV?

29. Give a diagram analogous to that in Figure 3.2 for the TEA cipher.

30. Suppose Alice uses DES to compute a MAC. She then sends the plaintext and the corresponding MAC to Bob. If Trudy alters one block of plaintext before Bob receives it, what is the probability that Bob does not detect the change?

31. Alice has four blocks of plaintext, P_0, P_1, P_2, P_3, which she encrypts using CBC mode to obtain C_0, C_1, C_2, C_3. She then sends the IV and ciphertext to Bob. Upon receiving the ciphertext, Bob plans to verify the integrity as follows. He'll first decrypt to obtain the putative plaintext, and then he'll re-encrypt this plaintext using CBC mode and the received IV. If he obtains the same C_3 as the final ciphertext block, he will trust the integrity of the plaintext.
    a. Suppose that Trudy changes C_1 to a random value X (leaving all other blocks and the IV unchanged). Will Bob detect that the data lacks integrity?
    b. Suppose that Trudy changes C_3 to a random value Y (leaving all other blocks and the IV unchanged). Will Bob detect that the data lacks integrity?
    c. Is Bob's integrity checking method secure?

32. Using CBC mode, Alice encrypts four blocks of plaintext, P_0, P_1, P_2, P_3 and she sends the resulting ciphertext blocks, C_0, C_1, C_2, C_3 and the IV to Bob. Suppose that Trudy is able to change any of the ciphertext blocks before they are received by Bob. If Trudy knows P_1, show that she can "replace" P_1 with X; that is, when Bob decrypts C_1 he will obtain X instead of P_1.

33. Suppose Alice has four blocks of plaintext, P_0, P_1, P_2, P_3. She computes a MAC using key K_1, and then CBC encrypts the data using key K_2 to obtain C_0, C_1, C_2, C_3. Alice sends the IV, the ciphertext, and the MAC to Bob. However, Trudy intercepts the message and replaces C_1 with X so that Bob receives the IV, C_0, X, C_2, C_3, and the MAC. Bob attempts to verify the integrity of the data by decrypting (using key K_2) and then computing a MAC (using key K_1) on the putative plaintext.
    a. Show that Bob will detect Trudy's tampering.
    b. Suppose that Alice and Bob only share a single symmetric key K. They agree to let $K_1 = K$ and $K_2 = K \oplus Y$, where Y is known to Alice, Bob, and Trudy. Does this create any security problem?

4

PUBLIC KEY CRYPTO

You should not live one way in private, another in public.
—Publilius Syrus

Three may keep a secret, if two of them are dead.
—Ben Franklin

4.1 INTRODUCTION

In this chapter, we delve into the remarkable subject of public key cryptography. Public key crypto is sometimes know as "asymmetric" cryptography, "two key" cryptography, or even "non-secret key" cryptography, but we'll stick with public key cryptography.

In symmetric key cryptography, the same key is used to both encrypt and decrypt. In public key cryptography, one key is used to encrypt and a different key is used to decrypt. As a result, the encryption key can be made public. This solves one of the most vexing problems of symmetric key crypto, namely, how to securely distribute the symmetric key. Actually, public key cryptography is more broadly defined to include methods that don't conform to the "two key" model but do involve some crucial information being made public.

Public key crypto is a relative newcomer, having been invented by cryptographers working for GCHQ (the British equivalent of NSA) in the late 1960s and early 1970s and, independently, by academic researchers shortly thereafter [147]. The government cryptographers clearly did not grasp the full potential of their discovery, and it lay

Information Security: Principles and Practice, by Mark Stamp
Copyright © 2006 John Wiley & Sons, Inc.

dormant until the academicians pushed it into the limelight. The ultimate effect has been nothing short of a revolution in cryptography.

In this chapter, we'll examine some of the most important public key cryptosystems. There are nowhere near the number of public key cryptosystems as there are symmetric ciphers, since public key system are based on very special mathematical structures, whereas just about anyone can design a plausible symmetric cipher.

A public key cryptosystem is based on a "trap door one-way function," that is, a function that is easy to compute in one direction and hard to compute in other direction. The purpose of the trap door is to ensure that an attacker cannot use the public information to recover the secret information. For example, it is relatively easy to generate two prime numbers p and q and compute their product $N = pq$. But, given N, it is difficult (as far as is known) to find its factors p and q.

A warning on notation is required. In symmetric key crypto, the plaintext is P and the ciphertext is C. But in public key crypto, tradition has it that we encrypt a message M, although, strangely, the result is still ciphertext C. Below, we follow this tradition.

To do public key crypto, Bob must have a *key pair* consisting of a *public key* and a *private key*. Anyone can use Bob's public key to encrypt a message for Bob, but only Bob can decrypt the message, since only Bob has the private key.

Bob can also digitally *sign* a message M by "encrypting" it with his private key. Then anybody can "decrypt" the message using Bob's public key. You might reasonably wonder what possible use this could be. In fact, this is one of the most useful features of public key crypto. A digital signature is like a handwritten signature—only more so. Only Bob, the holder of the private key, can digitally sign, just as only Bob can write his handwritten signature. Anyone with Bob's public key can verify his digital signature, similar to the way that anyone can read Bob's non-digital signature. However, the digital signature has some significant advantages over a handwritten signature. For one thing, a digital signature is more firmly tied to the document itself. Whereas a handwritten signature can be photocopied onto another document, that's not possible with a digital signature. Even more significant is the fact that it's impossible to forge a digital signature without the private key. In the non-digital world, a forgery of Bob's signature might only be detectable by a trained expert. But a digital signature forgery can be detected by anyone.

Next, we'll discuss several public key cryptosystems. The first one that we'll consider is the knapsack cryptosystem. This is appropriate since the knapsack was one of the first proposed public key systems. Although the knapsack that we'll present is known to be insecure, it's an easily understood system. After the knapsack, we'll discuss the gold standard of public key crypto, RSA. We'll then look at the Diffie-Hellman key exchange, which, as with RSA, is widely used in practice.

We'll also discuss elliptic curve cryptography, or ECC. While ECC is not a cryptosystem *per se*, it does offer a different mathematical realm in which to do the math that arises in many public key systems. The advantage of ECC is that it's more efficient (in both time and space) and so it's favored in resource-constrained environments such as wireless and handheld devices.

If you have not yet done so, this would be a good place to review the information on modular arithmetic found in the Appendix.

4.2 KNAPSACK

In their seminal paper [67], Diffie and Hellman conjectured that public key cryptography was possible, though they offered no viable system. Shortly thereafter, the Merkle-Hellman knapsack cryptosystem was proposed by—believe it or not—Merkle and Hellman. We'll meet Hellman again later, but it is worth noting that Merkle was also one of the founders of public key cryptography. He wrote a groundbreaking paper [157] that also foreshadowed public key cryptography. Merkle's paper was submitted for publication at about the same time as Diffie and Hellman's paper, though it appeared much later. For some reason, Merkle's contribution never seems to receive the attention it deserves.

The Merkle-Hellman knapsack cryptosystem is based on a problem[1] that is known to be NP-complete [88]. This seems to make it an ideal candidate for a secure public key cryptosystem.

The knapsack problem can be stated as follows. Given a set of n weights

$$W_0, W_1, \ldots, W_{n-1}$$

and sum S, find $a_0, a_1, \ldots, a_{n-1}$, where each $a_i \in \{0, 1\}$, so that

$$S = a_0 W_0 + a_1 W_1 + \cdots + a_{n-1} W_{n-1}$$

provided this is possible. For example, suppose the weights are

$$85, 13, 9, 7, 47, 27, 99, 86$$

and the desired sum is $S = 172$. Then a solution to the problem exists and is given by

$$a = (a_0, a_1, a_2, a_3, a_4, a_5, a_6, a_7) = (11001100)$$

since $85 + 13 + 47 + 27 = 172$. Although the general knapsack problem is known to be NP-complete, there is a special case that can be solved in linear time.

A *superincreasing knapsack*, is similar to the general knapsack except that when the weights are arranged from least to greatest, each weight is greater than sum of all previous weights. For example,

$$3, 6, 11, 25, 46, 95, 200, 411 \tag{4.1}$$

is a superincreasing knapsack. Solving a superincreasing knapsack problem is easy. Suppose we are given the set of weights in *equation 4.1* and the sum $S = 309$.

---

[1] Ironically, the knapsack cryptosystem is not based on the knapsack problem. Instead it's based on a more restricted problem, known as subset sum. Nevertheless, the cryptosystem is universally known as the knapsack. Eschewing our usual pedantic nature, we'll refer to both the cryptosystem and the underlying problem as knapsacks.

To solve this, we simply start with the largest weight and work toward the smallest to recover the a_i in linear time. Since $S < 411$, we have $a_7 = 0$. Then since $S > 200$, we have $a_6 = 1$ and we let $S = S - 200 = 109$. Then since $S > 95$, we have $a_5 = 1$ and we let $S = S - 95 = 14$. Continuing in this manner, we find $a = 10100110$, which we can easily verify solves the problem since $3 + 11 + 95 + 200 = 309$.

Next, we'll list the steps in the procedure used to construct a knapsack cryptosystem. We'll then illustrate each of these steps with a specific example.

1. Generate a superincreasing knapsack.
2. Convert the superincreasing knapsack into a general knapsack.
3. The public key is the general knapsack.
4. The private key is the superincreasing knapsack together with the conversion factors.

Below, we'll see that it's easy to encrypt using the general knapsack and, with the private key, that it's easy to decrypt the ciphertext. Without the private key, it appears that a very difficult problem must be solved to recover the plaintext from the ciphertext.

Now we'll present a specific example. For this example, we'll follow the numbering in the outline above.

1. We'll choose the superincreasing knapsack

$$(2, 3, 7, 14, 30, 57, 120, 251).$$

2. To convert the superincreasing knapsack into a general knapsack, we choose a multiplier m and a modulus n so that m and n are relatively prime and n is greater than the sum of all elements in the superincreasing knapsack. For this example, we choose $m = 41$ and $n = 491$. Then the general knapsack is computed from the superincreasing knapsack by modular multiplication:

$$2m = 2 \cdot 41 = 82 \bmod 491$$
$$3m = 3 \cdot 41 = 123 \bmod 491$$
$$7m = 7 \cdot 41 = 287 \bmod 491$$
$$14m = 14 \cdot 41 = 83 \bmod 491$$
$$30m = 30 \cdot 41 = 248 \bmod 491$$
$$57m = 57 \cdot 41 = 373 \bmod 491$$
$$120m = 120 \cdot 41 = 10 \bmod 491$$
$$251m = 251 \cdot 41 = 471 \bmod 491.$$

The resulting general knapsack is $(82, 123, 287, 83, 248, 373, 10, 471)$, which appears to be a general (non-superincreasing) knapsack.

3. The public key is the general knapsack

Public key: $(82, 123, 287, 83, 248, 373, 10, 471)$.

4. The private key is the superincreasing knapsack together with the modular inverse of the conversion factor m, that is,

Private key: $(2, 3, 7, 14, 30, 57, 120, 251)$ and

$$m^{-1} \bmod n = 41^{-1} \bmod 491 = 12.$$

Suppose Bob's public and private key pair are given in *step* 3 and *step* 4, above. Then if Alice wants to encrypt the message $M = 150$ for Bob, she first converts 150 to binary, that is, 10010110. Then she uses the 1 bits to select the elements of the general knapsack that are summed to give the ciphertext. In this case, Alice finds

$$C = 82 + 83 + 373 + 10 = 548.$$

To decrypt this ciphertext, Bob uses his private key to find

$$Cm^{-1} \bmod n = 548 \cdot 12 \bmod 491 = 193$$

Bob then solves the superincreasing knapsack for 193. This is an easy (linear time) problem from which Bob recovers the message in binary 10010110 or, in decimal, $M = 150$.

Only elementary properties of modular arithmetic are required to verify that the decryption formula works. In this example, we have

$$
\begin{aligned}
548m^{-1} &= 82m^{-1} + 83m^{-1} + 373m^{-1} + 10m^{-1} \\
&= 2mm^{-1} + 14mm^{-1} + 57mm^{-1} + 120mm^{-1} \\
&= 2 + 14 + 57 + 120 \\
&= 193 \bmod 491.
\end{aligned}
$$

In words, multiplying by m^{-1} transforms the problem into the superincreasing realm, where it's easy to solve for the weights. Proving that the decryption formula works in general is equally straightforward.

Without the private key, it appears that the attacker, Trudy, must find a subset of the elements of the public key that sum to the ciphertext value C. In this example, Trudy must find a subset of $(82, 123, 287, 83, 248, 373, 10, 471)$ that sums precisely to 548. This appears to be a general knapsack problem, which is known to be a very difficult problem.

The trapdoor in the knapsack occurs when we convert the superincreasing knapsack into the general knapsack using modular arithmetic. The conversion factors are unavailable to an attacker. The one-way feature results from the fact that it is easy to encrypt with the general knapsack, but it's apparently hard to decrypt without the private key.

But with the private key, we can convert the problem into a superincreasing knapsack problem, which is easy to solve.

Unfortunately, this clever knapsack public key cryptosystem is insecure. It was broken (by Shamir) in 1983 using an Apple II computer [205]. The attack relies on a technique known as "lattice reduction" that we'll discuss in detail in the cryptanalysis chapter. The bottom line is that the "general knapsack" that is derived from the superincreasing knapsack is not really a general knapsack. In fact, it's a very special and highly structured case of the knapsack, and the lattice reduction attack is able to take advantage of this structure to easily solve for the plaintext (with a high probability).

Much research has been done on the knapsack problem since the Merkle-Hellman knapsack was broken. Today, there are knapsack variants that appear to be secure, but people are reluctant to use them since the name "knapsack" is forever tainted. For more information on the knapsack cryptosystem, see [65, 138, 169].

4.3 RSA

Like any worthwhile public key cryptosystem, RSA is named after its putative inventors, Rivest, Shamir, and Adleman. We've met Rivest and Shamir previously, and we'll hear from both again. In fact, Rivest and Shamir are two of the giants of modern crypto. However, the RSA concept was actually invented by Cliff Cocks of GCHQ a few years before R, S, and A reinvented it [147]. This does not in any way diminish the achievement of Rivest, Shamir, and Adleman, since the GCHQ work was classified and was not even widely known within the classified crypto community.

If you've ever wondered why there is so much interest in factoring large numbers, it's because the security of RSA is based on the fact that factoring appears to be difficult. However, it's not known that factoring is difficult in the sense that, say, the traveling salesman problem is difficult. That is, factoring is not known to be NP-complete.

To generate an RSA public and private key pair, choose two large prime numbers p and q and form their product $N = pq$. Next, choose e relatively prime to $(p - 1)(q - 1)$ and find the multiplicative inverse of e modulo $(p - 1)(q - 1)$. Denote this inverse of e by d. At this point, we have $N = pq$, as well as e and d, which satisfy $ed = 1 \bmod (p - 1)(q - 1)$. Now forget the factors p and q.

The number N is the *modulus*, whereas e is the *encryption exponent* and d is the *decryption exponent*. The RSA key pair consists of

$$\text{Public key: } (N, e)$$

and

$$\text{Private key: } d.$$

In RSA, encryption and decryption are accomplished via modular exponentiation. To encrypt with RSA, we raise the message M to the encryption exponent e, modulo N, that is,

$$C = M^e \bmod N.$$

To decrypt C, modular exponentiation with the decryption exponent d is used

$$M = C^d \bmod N.$$

It's probably not obvious that this decryption actually works—we'll prove that it does shortly. Assume for a moment that it does work. If Trudy can factor N to find p and q then she can use the public value e to easily find the private value d since $ed = 1 \bmod (p - 1)$ $(q - 1)$. In other words, factoring the modulus breaks RSA. However, it is not known whether factoring is the only way to break RSA.

Why does RSA work? Given $C = M^e \bmod N$, we must verify that

$$M = C^d \bmod N = M^{ed} \bmod N. \qquad (4.2)$$

To do so, we need the following standard result from number theory [34].

Euler's Theorem: If x is relatively prime to n then $x^{\phi(n)} = 1 \bmod n$.

Recall that

$$ed = 1 \bmod (p - 1)(q - 1)$$

and

$$\phi(N) = (p - 1)(q - 1).$$

These two facts together imply that

$$ed - 1 = k\phi(N)$$

for some integer k.

Now we have all of the necessary pieces of the puzzle to verify that RSA decryption works. We have

$$C^d = M^{ed} = M^{(ed-1)+1} = M \cdot M^{ed-1} = M \cdot M^{k\phi(N)} = M \cdot 1^k = M \bmod N \quad (4.3)$$

where we have used Euler's Theorem to eliminate the ominous looking term $M^{\phi(N)}$. This confirms that the RSA decryption exponent does, in fact, decrypt the ciphertext C.

4.3.1 RSA Example

Let's consider a simple RSA example. To generate, say, Alice's keypair, we select the two "large" primes, $p = 11$ and $q = 3$. Then the modulus $N = pq = 33$ and $(p - 1)(q - 1) = 20$. Next, we choose the encryption exponent $e = 3$, which, as required, is relatively prime to $(p - 1)(q - 1)$. We then compute the corresponding decryption exponent, which is $d = 7$, since $ed = 3 \cdot 7 = 1 \bmod 20$. We have

$$\text{Public key: } (N, e) = (33, 3)$$

and

Private key: $d = 7$.

Now suppose Bob wants to send Alice the message is $M = 15$. Bob looks up Alice's public key $(N, e) = (33, 3)$ and computes the ciphertext C as

$$C = M^e \bmod N = 15^3 = 3375 = 9 \bmod 33$$

which he then sends to Alice. To decrypt the ciphertext $C = 9$, Alice uses her private key $d = 7$ to find

$$M = C^d \bmod N = 9^7 = 4{,}782{,}969 = 144{,}938 \cdot 33 + 15 = 15 \bmod 33$$

and Alice has recovered the original message M from the ciphertext C.

4.3.2 Repeated Squaring

Modular exponentiation of large numbers with large exponents is an expensive proposition. To make this more manageable (and thereby make RSA more efficient), several tricks are commonly used. One such trick is the method of *repeated squaring* for modular exponentiation.

Suppose we want to compute 5^{20}. Naïvely, we would simply multiply 5 by itself 20 times and reduce the result mod 35, that is

$$5^{20} = 95{,}367{,}431{,}640{,}625 = 25 \bmod 35. \tag{4.4}$$

However, this method results in an enormous intermediate value, even though the final answer is restricted to the range 0 to 34.

Now suppose we want to do an RSA encryption $M^e \bmod N$. In a secure implementation of RSA, the modulus N is at least 1024 bits. As a result, for a typical value of e, the numbers involved will be so large that it is impractical to compute $M^e \bmod N$ by the naïve approach as in *equation 4.4*. Fortunately, the method of repeated squaring allows us to compute such an exponentiation without creating extremely large numbers at any intermediate step.

Repeated squaring works by building up the exponent e one bit at a time. At each step we double the current exponent and if the binary expansion of e has a 1 in the corresponding position, we also add one to the exponent.

How can we double (and add one) to an exponent? Basic properties of exponentiation tell us that if we square x^y, we obtain x^{2y} and that $x \cdot x^y = x^{y+1}$. Consequently, it's easy to double an exponent or add one to an exponent.

Using basic properties of modular arithmetic, we can reduce each of the intermediate results by the modulus, thereby avoiding any extremely large numbers. An example should clarify the process. Consider again 5^{20}. First, note that the exponent 20 is 10100 in binary. Now 10100 can be "built up" one bit at a time as

$$(0, 1, 10, 101, 1010, 10100) = (0, 1, 2, 5, 10, 20).$$

As a result, the exponent 20 can be constructed by a series of steps, where each step consists of doubling and, when the next bit in the binary expansion of 20 is 1, adding one, that is,

$$1 = 0 \cdot 2 + 1$$
$$2 = 1 \cdot 2$$
$$5 = 2 \cdot 2 + 1$$
$$10 = 5 \cdot 2$$
$$20 = 10 \cdot 2.$$

Now to compute 5^{20}, repeated squaring proceeds as

$$5^1 = (5^0)^2 \cdot 5^1 = 5 \bmod 35$$
$$5^2 = (5^1)^2 = 5^2 = 25 \bmod 35$$
$$5^5 = (5^2)^2 \cdot 5^1 = 25^2 \cdot 5 = 3125 = 10 \bmod 35$$
$$5^{10} = (5^5)^2 = 10^2 = 100 = 30 \bmod 35$$
$$5^{20} = (5^{10})^2 = 30^2 = 900 = 25 \bmod 35$$

Although there are many steps in the repeated squaring algorithm, each step is simple and, most importantly, we never have to deal with a number that is greater than the cube of the modulus. Compare this to *equation 4.4*, where we had to deal with an enormous intermediate value.

4.3.3   Speeding Up RSA

A clever trick that is employed to speed up RSA is to use the same encryption exponent e for all users. As far as anyone knows, this does not weaken RSA in any way. The decryption exponents (the private keys) of different users will be different, provided different p and q are chosen for each key pair.

Amazingly, a suitable choice for the common encryption exponent is $e = 3$. With this choice of e, each public key encryption only requires two multiplications. However, the private key operations remain expensive since there is no special structure for d. This is often desirable since all of the encryption may be done by a central server, while the decryption is effectively distributed among the clients. Of course, if the server needs to sign, then a small e does not reduce its workload. In any case, it would certainly be a bad idea to choose the same d for all users.

With $e = 3$, a *cube root attack* is possible. If $M < N^{1/3}$ then $C = M^e = M^3$; that is, the mod N operation has no effect. As a result, an attacker can simply compute the usual cube root of C to obtain M. In practice, this is easily avoided by padding M with enough bits so that $M > N^{1/3}$.

With $e = 3$, another type of the cube root attack exists. If the same message M is encrypted for three different users, yielding, say, ciphertext C_1, C_2, and C_3, then the

Chinese Remainder Theorem [34] can be used to recover the message M. This is also easily avoided in practice by randomly padding each message M or by including some user-specific information in each M.

Another popular common encryption exponents is $e = 2^{16} + 1$. With this e, each encryption requires only 17 steps of the repeated squaring algorithm. An advantage of $e = 2^{16} + 1$ is that the same encrypted message must be sent to $2^{16} + 1$ users before the Chinese Remainder Theorem attack can succeed.

Next, we'll examine the Diffie-Hellman key exchange algorithm, which is a very different sort of public key algorithm. Whereas RSA relies on the difficulty of factoring, Diffie-Hellman is based on the so-called discrete log problem.

4.4 DIFFIE-HELLMAN

The Diffie-Hellman key exchange algorithm, or DH for short, was invented by Malcolm Williamson of GCHQ and shortly thereafter it was independently reinvented by its namesakes, Whitfield Diffie and Martin Hellman [147].

DH is a "key exchange" algorithm because it can only be used to establish a shared secret, which is generally then used as a shared symmetric key. It's worth emphasizing that the words "Diffie-Hellman" and "key exchange" always go together—DH is not for encrypting or signing, but instead it allows users to establish a shared secret. This is no mean feat, since the key establishment problem is one of the fundamental pitfalls to symmetric key cryptography.

The security of DH relies on the computational difficulty of the *discrete log* problem. Suppose you are given g and $x = g^k$. Then to find k you would compute the usual logarithm $\log_g(x)$. Now given g, p, and $g^k \bmod p$, the problem of finding k is analogous to the logarithm problem, but in a discrete setting; thus this problem is known as the discrete log. It appears that the discrete log problem is very difficult to solve, although, as with factoring, it is not known to be, say, NP-complete.

The mathematical setup for DH is relatively simple. Let p be prime and let g be a generator, which is to say that for any $x \in \{1, 2, \ldots, p - 1\}$ we can find an exponent n such that $x = g^n \bmod p$.

The values p and the generator g are public. Now for the key exchange, Alice generates her secret exponent a and Bob generates his secret exponent b. Alice sends $g^a \bmod p$ to Bob and Bob sends $g^b \bmod p$ to Alice. Then Alice computes

$$(g^b)^a \bmod p = g^{ab} \bmod p$$

and Bob computes

$$(g^a)^b \bmod p = g^{ab} \bmod p$$

and $g^{ab} \bmod p$ is the shared secret, which is then typically used as a symmetric key. A DH key exchange is illustrated in Figure 4.1.

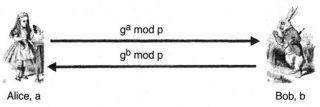

Figure 4.1. Diffie-Hellman key exchange.

An attacker Trudy can see g^a mod p and g^b mod p, and it seems that Trudy is tantalizingly close to knowing the secret g^{ab} mod p. But she's not since

$$g^a \cdot g^b = g^{a+b} \neq g^{ab} \text{ mod } p.$$

Apparently, Trudy needs to find either a or b, which appears to require that she solve the difficult discrete log problem. Of course, if Trudy can find a or b or g^{ab} mod p by any other means, the system is also broken. But as far as is known, the only way to break DH is to solve the discrete log problem.

The DH algorithm is susceptible to a man-in-the-middle, or MiM, attack.[2] This is an active attack where Trudy places herself between Alice and Bob and captures messages from Alice to Bob and vice versa. With Trudy thusly placed, the DH exchange between Alice and Bob can be subverted. Trudy simply establishes a shared secret, say, g^{at} mod p with Alice, and another shared secret g^{bt} mod p with Bob, as illustrated in Figure 4.2. Neither Alice nor Bob has any clue that anything is amiss, yet Trudy is able to read and change any messages passing between Alice and Bob.

The MiM attack in Figure 4.2 is a major concern when using DH. How can we prevent this MiM attack? There are several possibilities, including

1. encrypt the DH exchange with a shared symmetric key;
2. encrypt the DH exchange with public keys; and
3. sign the DH values with private keys.

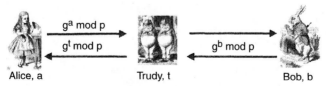

Figure 4.2. Diffie-Hellman man-in-the-middle attack.

---

[2]We'll avoid the annoying politically correct terminology "middleperson attack."

You may be wondering why we would use DH to establish a symmetric key if we already have a shared symmetric key (as in *1*) or a key pair (as in *2* and *3*). This is an excellent question to which we'll give an excellent answer when we discuss protocols in Chapters 9 and 10.

4.5 ELLIPTIC CURVE CRYPTOGRAPHY

"Elliptic curve" is not a particular cryptosystem. Instead, elliptic curves simply provide another way to perform the complex mathematical operations required in public key cryptography. For example, there is an elliptic curve version of Diffie-Hellman.

The advantage of elliptic curve cryptography (ECC) is that fewer bits are needed for the same level of security as in the non-elliptic curve case. On the down side, elliptic curves are more complex, and, as a result, mathematics on elliptic curves is somewhat more expensive. But overall, elliptic curves appear to offer a computational advantage. For this reason, ECC is particularly popular in resource-constrained environments such as handheld devices.

An elliptic curve E is the graph of a function of the form

$$E : \ y^2 = x^3 + ax + b$$

together with a special point at infinity, denoted ∞. The graph of a typical elliptic curve appears in Figure 4.3.

4.5.1 Elliptic Curve Math

Figure 4.3 also illustrates the method used to find the sum of two points on an elliptic curve. To add the points P_1 and P_2, a line is drawn through the two points. This line

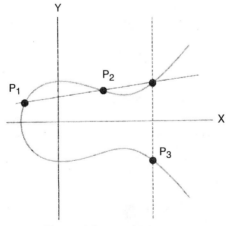

Figure 4.3. An elliptic curve.

TABLE 4.1. Points on the curve $y^2 = x^3 + 2x + 3$ (mod 5).

$x = 0$	$\implies$	$y^2 = 3 \implies$ no solution mod 5
$x = 1$	$\implies$	$y^2 = 6 = 1 \implies y = 1, 4$ mod 5
$x = 2$	$\implies$	$y^2 = 15 = 0 \implies y = 0$ mod 5
$x = 3$	$\implies$	$y^2 = 36 = 1 \implies y = 1, 4$ mod 5
$x = 4$	$\implies$	$y^2 = 75 = 0 \implies y = 0$ mod 5

usually intersects the curve in one other point. If so, this other point is reflected about the x-axis to obtain the sum,

$$P_3 = P_1 + P_2$$

as illustrated in Figure 4.3. Addition is the only mathematical operation on elliptic curves that we'll require.

For cryptography, we require a discrete set of points. This is easily accomplished by adding "mod p" to the generic elliptic curve equation, that is,

$$y^2 = x^3 + ax + b \text{ (mod } p).$$

For example, consider the elliptic curve

$$y^2 = x^3 + 2x + 3 \text{ (mod 5).} \tag{4.5}$$

We can list all of the points (x, y) on this curve by substituting for the possible values of x and solving for corresponding y value or values. Doing so, we obtain the results in Table 4.1.

Then the points on the elliptic curve in *equation 4.5* are

$$(1, 1) \ (1, 4) \ (2, 0) \ (3, 1) \ (3, 4) \ (4, 0) \text{ and } \infty. \tag{4.6}$$

The algorithm for adding two points on an elliptic curve appears in Table 4.2. Let's apply the algorithm in Table 4.2 to find the points $P_3 = (1, 4) + (3, 1)$ on the curve in *equation 4.5*. First, we compute

$$m = (1 - 4)/(3 - 1) = -3 \cdot 2^{-1} = -3 \cdot 3 = 1 \text{ mod 5.}$$

Then

$$x_3 = 1^2 - 1 - 3 = -3 = 2 \text{ mod 5}$$

and

$$y_3 = 1(1 - 2) - 4 = -5 = 0 \text{ mod 5.}$$

Therefore, on the curve $y^2 = x^3 + 2x + 3$ (mod 5), we have $(1, 4) + (3, 1) = (2, 0)$. Note that $(2, 0)$ is also on the on the curve in *equation 4.5*, as indicated in *equation 4.6*.

TABLE 4.2. Addition on an elliptic curve mod p.

Given: curve $E: y^2 = x^3 + ax + b \pmod{p}$
$\quad\quad P_1 = (x_1, y_1)$ and $P_2 = (x_2, y_2)$ on E
Find: $P_3 = (x_3, y_3) = P_1 + P_2$
Algorithm:
$x_3 = m^2 - x_1 - x_2 \pmod{p}$
$y_3 = m(x_1 - x_3) - y_1 \pmod{p}$
where $m = \begin{cases} (y_2 - y_1) \cdot (x_2 - x_1)^{-1} \bmod p & \text{if } P_1 \neq P_2 \\ (3x_1^2 + a) \cdot (2y_1)^{-1} \bmod p & \text{if } P_1 = P_2 \end{cases}$
Special case 1: If $m = \infty$ then $P_3 = \infty$
Special case 2: $\infty + P = P$ for all P

4.5.2 ECC Diffie-Hellman

Now that we can do addition on elliptic curves, let's consider the ECC version of Diffie-Hellman. The public information consists of a curve and a point on the curve. We'll select the curve

$$y^2 = x^3 + 11x + b \pmod{167} \tag{4.7}$$

leaving b to be determined momentarily. Next, we can select any point (x, y) and determine b so that this point lies on the resulting curve. In this case, we'll choose, say $(x, y) = (2, 7)$. Then substituting $x = 2$ and $y = 7$ into *equation 4.7*, we find $b = 19$. Now the public information is

$$\text{Public: Curve } y^2 = x^3 + 11x + 19 \pmod{167} \text{ and point } (2, 7) \tag{4.8}$$

Alice and Bob each must select their own secret multipliers.[3] Suppose Alice selects $A = 15$ and Bob selects $B = 22$. Then Alice computes

$$A(2, 7) = 15(2, 7) = (102, 88)$$

where all arithmetic is done on the curve in *equation 4.8*. Alice sends this result to Bob. Bob computes

$$B(2, 7) = 22(2, 7) = (9, 43)$$

which he sends to Alice. Now Alice multiplies the value she received from Bob by her secret A, that is,

$$A(9, 43) = 15(9, 43) = (131, 140).$$

---

[3]Because we know how to do addition on an elliptic curve, we can do multiplication as repeated addition.

Similarly, Bob computes

$$B(102, 88) = 22(102, 88) = (131, 140)$$

and Alice and Bob have established a shared secret, suitable for use as a symmetric key. Note that this works since $AB(2, 7) = BA(2, 7)$. The security of this method rests on the fact that, although Trudy can see $A(2, 7)$ and $B(2, 7)$, she (apparently) must find A or B before she can determine the shared secret. As far as is known, this elliptic curve version of DH is as difficult to break as the regular DH. Actually, for a given number of bits, the elliptic curve version is harder to break, which allows for the use of smaller values for an equivalent level of security.

All is not lost for Trudy. She can take some comfort in the fact that the ECC version of DH is just as susceptible to a MiM attack as the usual Diffie-Hellman key exchange.

There are many good sources of information on elliptic curves. See [192] for a readable treatment and [28] for more of the mathematical details.

4.6 PUBLIC KEY NOTATION

Before discussing the uses of public key crypto, we need to consider the issue of notation. Since public key crypto uses two keys per user, adapting the notation that we used for symmetric key crypto would be awkward. In addition, a digital signature is an encryption (with the private key), but the same operation is a decryption when applied to ciphertext.

We'll adopt the notation used in [122] for public key encryption, decryption, and signing:

- Encrypt message M with Alice's public key: $C = \{M\}_{\text{Alice}}$
- Decrypt ciphertext C with Alice's private key: $M = [C]_{\text{Alice}}$
- Signing is the same operation as decrypting, so the notation for Alice signing message M is $S = [M]_{\text{Alice}}$, where S is the signed message

Since encryption and decryption are inverse operations,

$$[\{M\}_{\text{Alice}}]_{\text{Alice}} = [[M]_{\text{Alice}}\}_{\text{Alice}} = M.$$

Never forget that the public key is public. As a result, anyone can compute $\{M\}_{\text{Alice}}$. On the other hand, the private key is private, so only Alice has access to her private key. As a result, only Alice can compute $[C]_{\text{Alice}}$ or $[M]_{\text{Alice}}$. The implication is that anyone can encrypt a message for Alice, but only Alice can decrypt the ciphertext. In terms of signing, only Alice can sign M, but, since the public key is public, anyone can verify the signature. We'll have more to say about signature verification after we discuss hash functions in the next chapter.

4.7 USES FOR PUBLIC KEY CRYPTO

You can do anything with a public key crypto algorithm that you can do with a symmetric key crypto algorithm, only slower. This includes confidentiality, in the form of transmitting data over an insecure channel or securely storing data on an insecure media. It also includes integrity, where public key signing plays the role of a symmetric key MAC.

But public key crypto offers two major advantages over symmetric key crypto. The first is that with public key crypto, we don't need to established a shared key in advance. The second major advantage is that digital signatures offer not only integrity but also non-repudiation. We'll look closer at these two advantages below.

4.7.1 Confidentiality in the Real World

The primary advantage of symmetric key cryptography is efficiency.[4] In the realm of confidentiality, the primary advantage of public key cryptography is the fact that no shared key is required.

Is there any way that we can get the best of both worlds? That is, can we have the efficiency of symmetric key crypto and yet not have to share a key in advance, as with public key crypto? The answer is an emphatic yes. The way to achieve this highly desirable result is with a *hybrid cryptosystem*, where public key crypto is used to establish a symmetric key, and the resulting symmetric key is then used to encrypt the data. A hybrid cryptosystem is illustrated in Figure 4.4.

The hybrid cryptosystem in Figure 4.4 is only for illustrative purposes. In fact, Bob has no way to know that he's talking to Alice—since anyone can do public key operations—so he would be foolish to encrypt sensitive data and send it to "Alice" following this protocol. We'll have much more to say about secure authentication and key establishment protocols in a later chapter.

4.7.2 Signatures and Non-repudiation

Public key crypto can be used for integrity. Recall that, with symmetric key crypto, a MAC provides for integrity. Public key signatures provide integrity, but they also provide

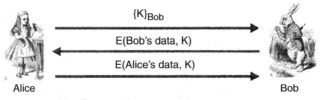

Figure 4.4. Hybrid cryptosystem.

---

[4]A secondary benefit is that no public key infrastructure, or PKI, is required. We'll discuss PKI below.

non-repudiation, which is something that symmetric keys by their very nature cannot provide.

To understand *non-repudiation*, let's first consider integrity in the symmetric key case. Suppose Alice orders 100 shares of stock from her favorite stockbroker, Bob. To ensure the integrity of her order, Alice computes a MAC using a shared symmetric key K_{AB}. Suppose that shortly after Alice places the order—and before she has paid any money to Bob—the stock loses 80% of its value. At this point Alice claims that she did not place the order, that is, she *repudiates* the transaction.

Can Bob prove that Alice placed the order? No, he cannot. Since Bob also knows the symmetric key K_{AB}, he could have forged the message in which Alice placed the order. So even though Bob knows that Alice placed the order, he can't prove it.

Now consider the same scenario, but with Alice using a digital signature in place of the MAC computation. As with the MAC computation, the signature provides integrity. Now suppose that Alice tries to repudiate the transaction. Can Bob prove that the order came from Alice? Yes he can, since only Alice has access to her private key. Digital signatures therefore provide integrity and non-repudiation. We'll have more to say about signatures and integrity in the next chapter.

4.7.3 Confidentiality and Non-repudiation

Suppose Alice wants to send a message M to Bob. For confidentiality, Alice can encrypt M with Bob's public key, and for integrity and non-repudiation, she can sign M with her private key. But suppose that Alice, who is very security conscious, wants both confidentiality and non-repudiation. Then she can't simply sign M as that will not provide confidentiality, and she can't simply encrypt M as that won't provide integrity. The solution seems straightforward enough—Alice can sign the message M and encrypt the result before sending it to Bob, that is,

$$\{[M]_{\text{Alice}}\}_{\text{Bob}}.$$

Or is it better for Alice to encrypt M first and then sign the result? In this case, Alice would compute

$$[\{M\}_{\text{Bob}}]_{\text{Alice}}.$$

Can the order possibly matter?

Let's consider a couple of different scenarios, similar to those in [56]. First, suppose that Alice and Bob are romantically involved. Alice decides to send the message

$$M = \text{``I love you''}$$

to Bob. So using sign and encrypt, she sends Bob

$$\{[M]_{\text{Alice}}\}_{\text{Bob}}.$$

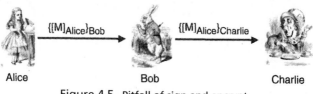

Figure 4.5. Pitfall of sign and encrypt.

Subsequently, Alice and Bob have a lovers tiff and Bob, in an act of spite, decrypts the signed message to obtain $[M]_{\text{Alice}}$ and re-encrypts it as

$$\{[M]_{\text{Alice}}\}_{\text{Charlie}}.$$

Bob then sends this message to Charlie, as illustrated in Figure 4.5. Charlie thinks that Alice is in love with him, which causes a great deal of embarrassment for both Alice and Charlie, much to Bob's delight.

Alice, having learned her lesson from this bitter experience, vows to never sign and encrypt again. When she wants confidentiality and non-repudiation, Alice will always encrypt then sign.

Some time later, after Alice and Bob have resolved their earlier dispute, Alice develops a great new theory that she wants to send to Bob. This time her message is [41]

$$M = \text{``Brontosauruses are thin at one end, much much thicker}$$

$$\text{in the middle, then thin again at the other end''}$$

which she dutifully encrypts then signs

$$[\{M\}_{\text{Bob}}]_{\text{Alice}}$$

before sending to Bob.

However, Charlie, who is still angry with both Bob and Alice, has set himself up as a man-in-the-middle who is able to intercept all traffic between Alice and Bob. Charlie has heard that Alice is working on a great new theory, and he suspects that this particular encrypted and signed message has something to do with it. So Charlie uses Alice's public key to compute $\{M\}_{\text{Bob}}$, which he signs before sending it on to Bob,

$$[\{M\}_{\text{Bob}}]_{\text{Charlie}}.$$

This scenario is illustrated in Figure 4.6.

When Bob receives the message from Charlie, he assumes that this great new theory is Charlie's, and he immediately gives Charlie a bonus. When Alice learns that Charlie has taken credit for her great new theory, she swears never to encrypt and sign again!

What is the problem here? In the first scenario, Charlie assumed that $\{[M]_{\text{Alice}}\}_{\text{Charlie}}$ must have been sent from Alice to Charlie. That's clearly not the case, since Charlie's

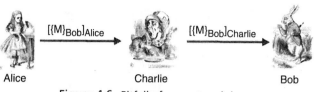

Figure 4.6. Pitfall of encrypt and sign.

public key is public. The problem in this case is that Charlie does not understand public key crypto.

In the second scenario, Bob assumed that $[\{M\}_{Bob}]_{Charlie}$ must have originated with Charlie, which is not the case, since Alice's public key—which was used by Charlie to effectively remove Alice's signature from the original message—is public. In this case, it is Bob who does not understand the limitations of public key crypto. In public key crypto, anyone can do the public key operations. That is, anyone can encrypt a message and anyone can verify a signature.

4.8 PUBLIC KEY INFRASTRUCTURE

A public key infrastructure, or PKI, is the sum total of everything required to securely use public key crypto. It's surprisingly difficult and involved to assemble all of the necessary pieces of a PKI into a working whole. Some significant PKI issues must be overcome before public key crypto is useful in most real world settings. For a discussion of some of the risks inherent in PKI, see [73].

A *digital certificate*, or public key certificate, or, simply, a certificate contains a user's name along with the user's public key. In most situations the certificate must be signed by a *certificate authority*, or CA, which acts as a *trusted third party*, or TTP. By signing the certificate, the CA is confirming that the identity stated in the certificate is that of the holder of the corresponding private key. Note that the CA is not vouching for the identity of the holder of the certificate, since the certificate is public. Today, the largest commercial source for certificates is VeriSign [240].

An important subtle point here is that verifying the signature does not verify the source of the certificate. Certificates are public knowledge, so, for example, Charlie could send Alice's certificate to Bob. Bob can't assume he's talking to Alice just because he received Alice's valid certificate.

When you receive a certificate, you must verify the signature. If the certificate is signed by a CA that you trust, then you would attempt to verify the signature using that CA's public key. Anyone can create a certificate and claim to be anyone else—only the verification of the signature can create trust in the validity of the certificate.

A certificate could contain just about any other information that is deemed of value to the participants. However, the more information, the more likely the certificate will become invalid. For example, it might be tempting for a corporation to include the employee's department in his certificate. But then any reorganization will invalidate the certificate.

If a CA makes a mistake, the consequences can be dire. For example, VeriSign once issued a signed certificate for Microsoft to someone else [101]; that is, VeriSign gave the corresponding private key to someone other than Microsoft. That someone else could then have acted (electronically, at least) as Microsoft. This particular error was quickly detected, and the certificate was revoked apparently before any damage was done.

This raises another PKI issue, namely, *certificate revocation*. Certificates are usually issued with an expiration date. But if a private key is compromised, or it is discovered that a certificate was issued in error, the certificate must be revoked immediately. Most PKI schemes require regular certificate revocation lists, or CRLs, which are supposed to be used to filter compromised certificates. In some situations, this could place a significant burden on users, which means that it is likely to lead to mistakes and security flaws.

To summarize, any PKI must deal with the following issues:

- Key generation and management
- Certificate authorities (CAs)
- Certificate revocation lists (CRLs)

Next, we'll briefly discuss a few of the many *trust models* that are used today. Ultimately, you must rely on a digital signature to decide whether to trust a certificate. A basic issue in public key cryptography is determining whose signature you are willing to trust. There are several possible trust models that can be employed. We'll follow the terminology in [122].

Perhaps the most obvious trust model is the *monopoly model*, where one universally trusted organization is the CA for the known universe. This approach is naturally favored by whoever happens to be the biggest commercial CA at the time (currently, VeriSign). Some have suggested that the government should play the role of the monopoly CA. However, many people don't trust the government.

One major drawback to the monopoly model is that it creates a very big target for attack. If the monopoly CA is ever compromised, the entire PKI system fails. Also, if you don't trust the monopoly CA, then the system is useless for you.

The *oligarchy model* is one step away from the monopoly model. In this model, there are multiple trusted CA. In fact, this is the approach that is used in Web browsers today—a Web browser might be configured with 80 or more CA certificates. The security-conscious user is free to decide which of the oligarchy CAs he is willing to trust and which he is not.

At the opposite extreme from the monopoly model is the *anarchy model*. In this model, anyone can be a CA, and it's up to the users to decide which "CAs" they want to trust. In fact, this approach is used in PGP, where it goes by the name of "web of trust."

The anarchy model can place a significant burden on users. For example, suppose you receive a certificate signed by Frank and you don't know Frank, but you do trust Bob and Bob says Alice is trustworthy and Alice vouches for Frank. Should you then trust Frank? This is clearly beyond the patience of the average user, who is likely to simply trust anybody or nobody in order to avoid headaches like this.

There are many other PKI trust models, most of which try to provide reasonable flexibility while putting a minimal burden on the end users. The fact that there is no agreed upon trust model is itself one of the major problems with PKI.

4.9 SUMMARY

In this chapter, we've covered most of the important public key crypto topics. We began with the knapsack, which has been broken, but provides a nice introductory example. We then discussed RSA and Diffie-Hellman in detail.

We also discussed elliptic curve cryptography (ECC) which promises to play a larger role in the future, particularly in resource-constrained devices. ECC is not a particular type of cryptosystem; instead, it offers another way to do the math in public key cryptography.

We then considered signing and non-repudiation, which are major benefits of public key cryptography. And we presented a hybrid cryptosystem, which is the way that public key crypto is used in the real world for confidentiality. We also discussed the challenge of PKI, which often proves a major roadblock to the deployment of public key crypto.

This concludes our overview of public key cryptography. But we will see many applications of public key crypto in later sections of the book. In particular, many of these topics will resurface when we discuss security protocols.

4.10 PROBLEMS

1. What information must a digital certificate contain? What additional information can a digital certificate contain?

2. Suppose Alice's RSA public key is (e, N) and her private key is d. Alice wants to sign message M, that is, $[M]_{\text{Alice}}$. Give the mathematical formula that will be used.

3. In *equation 4.3*, we proved that for RSA, encryption "works," that is, $[\{M\}_{\text{Alice}}]_{\text{Alice}} = M$. Prove that, for RSA, signature verification works, that is, $\{[M]_{\text{Alice}}\}_{\text{Alice}} = M$.

4. Alice's RSA public key is $(N, e) = (33, 3)$ and her private key is $d = 7$.

   a. If Bob encrypts the message $M = 19$ for Alice, what is the ciphertext C? Show that Alice can decrypt C to obtain M.

   b. Let S be the result when Alice digitally signs the message $M = 25$. What is S? If Bob receives M and S, explain the process Bob will use to verify the signature. Show that in this case the signature verification succeeds.

5. Why is it a bad idea to use the same RSA key pair for both signing and encryption?

6. To speed up RSA, we can require that $e = 3$ for all users. This creates the possibility of a cube root attack as discussed in the text. Explain this attack and how to prevent it. For $(N, e) = (33, 3)$ and $d = 7$, verify that the cube root attack works when $M = 3$ but not when $M = 4$.

7. On the diagram of the Diffie-Hellman key exchange in Figure 4.1, clearly indicate which information is public and which is private.

8. Suppose Bob and Alice share a symmetric key K. Draw a diagram to illustrate a variant of the Diffie-Hellman key exchange between Bob and Alice that prevents the man-in-the-middle attack.

9. A digital signature provides for data integrity and a MAC provides for data integrity. A signature also provides for non-repudiation, while a MAC does not. Why not?

10. A hybrid cryptosystem uses both public key and symmetric key cryptography in order to obtain the benefits of each. Illustrate such a system using Diffie-Hellman as the public key system and DES as the symmetric cipher. Illustrate such a system using RSA as the public key system and AES as the symmetric cipher.

11. Illustrate a man-in-the-middle attack on the ECC version of Diffie-Hellman.

12. Suppose that Alice signs the message M = "I love you" and then encrypts it with Bob's public key before sending it to Bob. As discussed in the text, Bob can decrypt this to obtain the signed message and then encrypt the signed message with Charlie's public key and forward the resulting ciphertext to Charlie. Can Alice prevent this attack by using symmetric key cryptography?

13. Suppose Alice and Bob use the following protocol when Alice sends a message M to Bob.

    a. Alice computes $S = [M]_{\text{Alice}}$
    b. Alice sends (M, S) to Bob
    c. Bob computes $V = \{S\}_{\text{Alice}}$
    d. Bob accepts the signature as valid provided $V = M$

    With this protocol, it's possible for Trudy to forge Alice's signature on a random "message" as follows. Trudy generates a value R. She then computes $N = \{R\}_{\text{Alice}}$ and sends (N, R) to Bob. Following the protocol above, Bob computes $V = \{R\}_{\text{Alice}}$. Since $V = N$, Bob accepts the signature and he believes Alice sent him the signed "message" N, which is almost certainly garbage. As a result, Bob gets very annoyed with Alice. Suppose we modify the protocol to

    a. Alice computes $S = [F(M)]_{\text{Alice}}$
    b. Alice sends (M, S) to Bob
    c. Bob computes $V = \{S\}_{\text{Alice}}$
    d. Bob accepts the signature as valid provided $V = F(M)$

    What conditions must the function F satisfy in order to prevent the annoying attack described above?

14. Suppose that Bob's knapsack private key is $(3, 5, 10, 23)$ and $m^{-1} = 6$, and that the modulus is $n = 47$.

    a. Find the plaintext for the ciphertext $C = 20$. Give your answer in binary.
    b. Find the plaintext for the ciphertext $C = 29$. Give your answer in binary.
    c. Find m and the public key.

15. Show that in the knapsack cryptosystem it is always possible to decrypt the ciphertext if you know the private key.

16. In the knapsack example in the text, the ciphertext was not reduced modulo n. Show that this particular example also works if the ciphertext is reduced modulo n. Show that this is always the case; that is, show that it makes no difference to the recipient whether the ciphertext was reduced modulo n or not. Is either case preferable from the attacker's perspective?

17. The man-in-the-middle attack on Diffie-Hellman is illustrated in Figure 4.2. Suppose that Trudy wants to establish a single Diffie-Hellman value, $g^{abt} \bmod p$, that she, Alice and Bob all share. Does the attack illustrated below accomplish this?

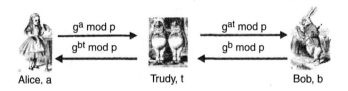

18. In RSA, a common encryption exponent of $e = 3$ or $e = 2^{16} + 1$ is sometime used. The RSA math also works if we use a common decryption exponent of, say, $d = 3$. Would it be a good idea to use $d = 3$ as a common decryption exponent? If so, why? If not, can you find a secure common decryption exponent d?

19. For RSA, we proved in *equation 4.3* that the private key d decrypts the ciphertext. Give the analogous proof that the the public key e can be used to verify signatures.

20. Why does a digital signature provide integrity?

21. How can you prevent a forward search attack on a public key cryptosystem?

22. Given the elliptic curve

$$E : \quad y^2 = x^3 + 7x + b \ (\bmod \ 11)$$

and the point $P = (4, 5)$, determine b so that P is on E. List all points on E and find the sum $(4, 5) + (5, 4)$ on E.

23. Consider the elliptic curve

$$E : \quad y^2 = x^3 + 11x + 19 \ (\bmod \ 167).$$

The points $P = (2, 7)$ is on E. Suppose this E and P are used in an ECC Diffie-Hellman key exchange, where Alice chooses the secret value $A = 12$ and Bob chooses the secret value $B = 31$. What value does Alice send to Bob? What does Bob send to Alice? What is the shared secret?

24. In the Elgamal digital signature scheme, the public key is the triple (y, p, g) and the private key is x, where these numbers satisfy

$$y = g^x \bmod p. \tag{4.9}$$

To sign a message M, choose a random number k such that k has no factor in common with $p - 1$ and compute

$$a = g^k \bmod p.$$

Then find a value s that satisfies

$$M = xa + ks \bmod (p - 1),$$

which is easy to do using the Euclidean Algorithm. The signature is verified provided that

$$y^a a^s = g^M \bmod p. \qquad (4.10)$$

a. Select values (y, p, g) and x that satisfy *equation 4.9*. Choose a message M, compute the signature, and verify that *equation 4.10* holds.

b. Prove that the math in Elgamal works; that is, prove that *equation 4.10* always holds. Hint: Use Fermat's Little Theorem: If p is prime and p does not divide z, then $z^{p-1} = 1 \bmod p$.

5

HASH FUNCTIONS AND OTHER TOPICS

"I'm sure [my memory] only works one way." Alice remarked.
"I can't remember things before they happen."
"It's a poor sort of memory that only works backwards," the Queen remarked.
"What sort of things do you remember best?" Alice ventured to ask.
"Oh, things that happened the week after next," the Queen replied in a careless tone.
—Lewis Carroll, *Through the Looking Glass*

He can compress the most words into the smallest ideas of any man I ever met.
—Abraham Lincoln

5.1 WHAT IS A HASH FUNCTION?

A cryptographic *hash function* $h(x)$ must provide the following.

- *Compression*: For any size of input x, the output length of $y = h(x)$ is small. In practice, cryptographic hash functions produce a fixed size output, regardless of the length of the input.
- *Efficiency*: It must be easy to compute $h(x)$ for any input x. The computational effort required to compute $h(x)$ will certainly grow with the length of x, but it should not grow too fast.
- *One-way*: Given any value y, it's computationally infeasible to find a value x such that $h(x) = y$. Another way to say this is that it is difficult to invert the hash.

Information Security: Principles and Practice, by Mark Stamp
Copyright © 2006 John Wiley & Sons, Inc.

- *Weak collision resistance*: Given x and $h(x)$, it's infeasible to find y, with $y \neq x$, such that $h(y) = h(x)$.
- *Strong collision resistance*: It's infeasible to find any x and y, with $x \neq y$, such that $h(x) = h(y)$.

Collisions must exist since the input space is much larger than the output space. For example, suppose a hash function generates a 128-bit output. If we consider, say, all possible 150-bit input values then, on average, 2^{22}, or more than 4,000,000, of these input values hash to each possible output value. And this is only counting the 150-bit inputs. The collision resistance properties require that all of these collisions (as well as all others) are hard to find. Remarkably, cryptographic hash functions do exist.

Hash functions are extremely useful in security. One important use of a hash function is in the computation of a digital signature. Recall that Alice signs a message M by using her private key to "encrypt," that is, she computes $S = [M]_{\text{Alice}}$. If Alice sends M and S to Bob, then Bob can verify the signature by verifying that $M = \{S\}_{\text{Alice}}$. However, if M is big, $[M]_{\text{Alice}}$ is costly to compute—not to mention the wasted bandwidth in sending M and S, which are the same size.

Suppose Alice has a cryptographic hash function h. Then $h(M)$ can be viewed as a "fingerprint" of the file M. That is, $h(M)$ is much smaller than M but it identifies M. And if M' differs from M in one or more bits, $h(M)$ and $h(M')$ can be expected to differ in about half of their bits. Given such a function h, Alice could sign M by computing $S = [h(M)]_{\text{Alice}}$ and sending Bob M and S. Then Bob would verify that $h(M) = \{S\}_{\text{Alice}}$.

What is the advantage of signing $h(M)$ instead of M? Assuming that $h(M)$ is efficient to compute, it's more efficient for Alice to sign $h(M)$ than M since the expensive private key operation only needs to be applied to the small fingerprint $h(M)$ instead of to the entire file M. The larger M and the more efficient $h(M)$, the greater the savings. In addition, bandwidth is conserved, as Alice sends few extra bits to Bob.

5.2 THE BIRTHDAY PROBLEM

The so-called birthday problem is a fundamental issue in many areas of cryptography. We present it here, since it's critical to understanding the security implications of hashing.

Suppose you are in a room with N other people. How large must N be before you expect to find at least one other person with the same birthday as you? An equivalent way to state this is, how large must N be before the probability that someone has the same birthday as you is greater than $1/2$? As with many probability calculations, it's easier to compute the probability of the complement, that is, the probability that none of the N people have the same birthday as you, and subtract the result from one.

Your birthday is on one particular day of the year. If a person does not have the same birthday as you, their birthday must be on one of the other 364 days. Assuming all birth dates are equally likely, the probability that a randomly selected person does not have the same birthday as you is $364/365$. Then the probability that none of N

people have the same birthday as you is $(364/365)^N$, and the probability that at least one person has the same birthday as you is

$$1 - (364/365)^N.$$

Setting this expression equal to $1/2$ and solving for N, we find $N = 253$. Since there are 365 days in a year, this seems about right.

Again, suppose there are N people in a room. But now we want to answer the question, how large must N be before the probability is greater than $1/2$ that any two or more people have same birthday? Again, it's easier to solve for the probability of the complement and subtract the result from one. In this case, the complement is that all N people have different birthdays.

Number the N people in the room $0, 1, 2, \ldots, N - 1$. Person 0 has a particular birthday. If all people have different birthdays, then person 1 must have a birthday that differs from person 0; that is, person 1 can have a birthday on any of the remaining 364 days. Similarly, person 2 can have a birthday on any of the remaining 363 days, and so on. Again, assuming that all birth dates are equally likely and taking the complement, the resulting probability is

$$1 - 365/365 \cdot 364/365 \cdot 363/365 \cdots (365 - N + 1)/365.$$

Setting this expression equal to $1/2$ we find $N = 23$. This is often referred to as the *birthday paradox*, and, at first glance, it does seem paradoxical that with only 23 people in a room, we expect to find two or more with the same birthday. However, a few moments thought makes the result much less paradoxical. In this problem, we are comparing the birthdays of all pairs of people. With N people in a room, the number of comparisons is $N(N - 1)/2 \approx N^2$. Since there are only 365 different birth dates, we should expect to find a match at about the point where $N^2 = 365$, or $N = \sqrt{365} \approx 19$. Viewed in this light, the birthday paradox is not so paradoxical.

What do birthdays have to do with cryptographic hash functions? Suppose a hash function $h(x)$ produces an output that is N bits long. Then there are 2^N different possible hash values. Suppose that all hash output values are equally likely. Since $\sqrt{2^N} = 2^{N/2}$, the birthday problem implies that if we hash about $2^{N/2}$ different inputs, we can expect to find a collision, that is, two inputs that hash to the same value. This method of "breaking" a hash function is analogous to an exhaustive key search attack on a symmetric cipher.

The implication here is that a secure hash that generates an N-bit output requires work of about $2^{N/2}$ to break, while a secure symmetric key cipher with a key of length N requires about 2^{N-1} work to break. The bottom line is that the output of a hash function must be about twice the number of bits as a symmetric cipher key for an equivalent amount of security—assuming no shortcut attack exists for either.

5.3 NON-CRYPTOGRAPHIC HASHES

Before discussing a specific cryptographic hash function, we'll first consider a few simple non-cryptographic hashes. Suppose the input data is

$$X = (X_0, X_1, X_2, \ldots, X_{n-1})$$

where each X_i is a byte. We can define a hash function $h(X)$ by

$$h(X) = (X_0 + X_1 + X_2 + \cdots + X_{n-1}) \bmod 256.$$

This certainly accomplishes compression, since any size of input is compressed to an 8-bit output. But this can't be secure, since the birthday problem tells us that, if we hash just $2^4 = 16$ randomly selected inputs, we can expect to find a collision. In fact, collisions are easy to construct directly. For example

$$h(10101010, 00001111) = h(00001111, 10101010) = 10111001.$$

Not only is the hash output length too short, but there is too much algebraic structure.
    As another non-cryptographic hash example, consider the following. Again, the data is written as bytes

$$X = (X_0, X_1, X_2, \ldots, X_{n-1}).$$

Here, we'll define the hash $h(X)$ as

$$h(X) = nX_0 + (n-1)X_1 + (n-2)X_2 + \cdots + 2X_{n-2} + X_{n-1} \bmod 256.$$

Is this hash secure? At least it gives different results when two bytes are swapped, for example,

$$h(10101010, 00001111) \neq h(00001111, 10101010).$$

But, again, we have the birthday problem issue, and it also happens to be relatively easy to construct collisions. For example

$$h(00000001, 00001111) = h(00000000, 00010001) = 00010001.$$

Despite the fact that this is not a secure cryptographic hash, it's used successfully in a particular non-cryptographic application [193].
    An example of a non-cryptographic "hash" that is is widely used is the cyclic redundancy check, or CRC [247]. This calculation is essentially long division, with the remainder acting as the CRC value. The difference with ordinary long division is that XOR is used in place of subtraction.

In a CRC calculation, the divisor is given. For example, suppose the divisor is 10011 and the data is 10101011. Then we append four 0s to the data and the CRC calculation is

$$
\begin{array}{r}
10110110 \\
10011 \overline{)101010110000} \\
10011 \\
\hline
11001 \\
10011 \\
\hline
10101 \\
10011 \\
\hline
11000 \\
10011 \\
\hline
10110 \\
10011 \\
\hline
1010
\end{array}
$$

and the CRC checksum is the remainder, 1010. With this choice of divisor, it's easy to find collisions, and, in fact, it's easy to construct collisions for any CRC system [8].

CRCs are sometimes (mistakenly) used in applications where cryptographic integrity is required. For example, WEP [30] uses a CRC checksum where a cryptographic hash would be more appropriate. CRCs and similar checksum methods are only designed to detect transmission errors—not to detect intentional tampering with the data.

5.4 TIGER HASH

Now we'll turn our attention to cryptographic hash functions. Two particular hash functions are the most popular today. One of these is MD5, where the "MD" is for "message digest." Amazingly, MD5 is the successor to MD4, which itself was the successor to MD2. The earlier MDs are no longer considered secure, due to the fact that collisions have been found. In fact, an MD5 collision was recently discovered as well [196]; see Problem 25. All of the MDs were invented by crypto guru Ron Rivest. MD5 produces a 128-bit output.

The other contender for title of "the world's most popular hash function" is SHA–1 which is a U.S. government standard. Being a government standard, SHA is, of course, a three-letter acronym. SHA stands for "secure hash algorithm." You might ask, why is it SHA–1 instead of SHA? In fact, there was a SHA (now known as SHA–0), but it apparently had a flaw, as SHA–1 came quickly on the heels of SHA, with some minor modifications but without explanation.

The SHA–1 algorithm is actually very similar to MD5. The major practical difference between the two is that SHA–1 generates a 180-bit output, which provides a significant margin of safety over MD5. Cryptographic hash functions such as MD5 and SHA–1 consist of a number of rounds. In this sense, they're reminiscent of block ciphers. For the details on these two hash functions, see Schneier [203].

A hash function is considered secure provided no collisions have been found. As with block ciphers, efficiency is a major concern in the design of hash functions. If, for example, it's more costly to compute the hash of M than to sign M, the hash function is not very useful, at least in the signing application discussed above.

A desirable property of any cryptographic hash function is the so-called *avalanche effect*, or strong avalanche effect. The goal is that any small change in the input should result in a large change in the output. Ideally, any change in the input will result in output values that are uncorrelated, and an attacker will then be forced to conduct an exhaustive search for collisions.

Ideally, the avalanche effect should occur after a few rounds, yet we would like the rounds to be as simple and efficient as possible. The designers of hash functions face similar trade-offs as the designers of iterated block ciphers.

The MD5 and SHA–1 algorithms are not particularly interesting, as they both seem to consist of a random collection of transformations. Instead of discussing either of these in detail, we'll look closely at the Tiger hash. Tiger, which was developed by Ross Anderson and Eli Biham, seems to have a more structured design than SHA–1 or MD5. In fact, Tiger can be given in a form that is very reminiscent of a block cipher [10].

Tiger was designed to be "fast and strong" and hence the name. It was also designed for optimal performance on 64-bit processors and to be a drop in replacement for MD5, SHA–1, or any other hash with an equal or smaller output.

Like MD5 and SHA–1, the input to Tiger is divided into 512-bit blocks, with the input padded to a multiple of 512 bits, if necessary. Unlike MD5 or SHA–1, the output of Tiger is 192 bits. The numerology behind the choice of 192 is that Tiger is designed for 64-bit processors and 192 bits is exactly three 64-bit words. In Tiger, all intermediate rounds also consist of 192 bit values.

Tiger's block cipher influence can be seen in the fact that it employs four S-boxes, each of which maps 8 bits to 64 bits. Tiger also employs a "key schedule" algorithm, which, since there is no key, is applied to the input block, as described below.

The input X is padded to a multiple of 512 bits and written as

$$X = (X_0, X_1, \ldots, X_{n-1}) \tag{5.1}$$

where each X_i is 512 bits. The Tiger algorithm employs one *outer round* for each X_i, for $i = 0, 1, 2, \ldots, n - 1$, where one such round is illustrated in Figure 5.1. Each of a, b, and c in Figure 5.1 is 64 bits and the initial values of (a, b, c) for the first round are

$a = $ 0x0123456789ABCDEF

$b = $ 0xFEDCBA9876543210

$c = $ 0xF096A5B4C3B2E187

while the final (a, b, c) from a round is the initial triple for the subsequent round. The final (a, b, c) from the final round is the 192-bit hash value. From this perspective, Tiger indeed looks very much like a block cipher.

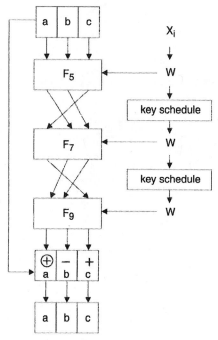

Figure 5.1. Tiger outer round.

Notice that the input to the outer round F_5, is (a, b, c). Labeling the output of F_5 as (a, b, c), the input to F_7 is (c, a, b) and, similarly, the input to F_9 is (b, c, a). Each function F_m in Figure 5.1 consists of eight *inner rounds* as illustrated in Figure 5.2. We write the 512 bit input W as

$$W = (w_0, w_1, \ldots, w_7)$$

where each w_i is 64 bits. Note that all lines in Figure 5.2 represent 64 bits.

The input values for the $f_{m,i}$, for $i = 0, 1, 2, \ldots, 7$, are

$$(a, b, c), (b, c, a), (c, a, b), (a, b, c), (b, c, a), (c, a, b), (a, b, c), (b, c, a),$$

respectively, where the output of $f_{m,i-1}$ is labeled (a, b, c). Each $f_{m,i}$ depends on a, b, c, w_i, and m, where w_i is the ith 64-bit sub-block of the 512-bit input W. The subscript m of $f_{m,i}$ is a multiplier, as defined below.

We write c as

$$c = (c_0, c_1, \ldots, c_7)$$

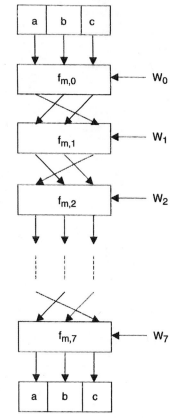

Figure 5.2. Tiger inner round for F_m.

where each c_i is a single byte. Then $f_{m,i}$ is given by

$$c = c \oplus w_i$$
$$a = a - (S_0[c_0] \oplus S_1[c_2] \oplus S_2[c_4] \oplus S_3[c_6])$$
$$b = b + (S_3[c_1] \oplus S_2[c_3] \oplus S_1[c_5] \oplus S_0[c_7])$$
$$b = b \cdot m$$

where each S_i is an S-box mapping 8 bits to 64 bits. These S-boxes are large, so we won't list them here. For more details on the S-boxes, see [10].

The only remaining item to discuss is the *key schedule*. Let W be the 512-bit input to the key schedule algorithm. As above, we write $W = (w_0, w_1, \ldots, w_7)$ where each w_i is 64 bits. Let $\bar{w}_i$ be the binary complement of w_i. Then the key schedule is given in Table 5.1, where the output is given by the final $W = (w_0, w_1, \ldots, w_7)$.

TABLE 5.1. Tiger key schedule.

$$w_0 = w_0 - (w_7 \oplus \texttt{0xA5A5A5A5A5A5A5A5})$$
$$w_1 = w_1 \oplus w_0$$
$$w_2 = x_2 + w_1$$
$$w_3 = w_3 - (w_2 \oplus (\bar{w}_1 \ll 19))$$
$$w_4 = w_4 \oplus w_3$$
$$w_5 = w_5 + w_4$$
$$w_6 = w_6 - (w_5 \oplus (\bar{w}_4 \gg 23))$$
$$w_7 = w_7 \oplus w_6$$
$$w_0 = w_0 + w_7$$
$$w_1 = w_1 - (w_0 \oplus (\bar{w}_7 \ll 19))$$
$$w_2 = w_2 \oplus w_1$$
$$w_3 = w_3 + w_2$$
$$w_4 = w_4 - (w_3 \oplus (\bar{w}_2 \gg 23))$$
$$w_5 = w_5 \oplus w_4$$
$$w_6 = w_6 + w_5$$
$$w_7 = w_7 - (w_6 \oplus \texttt{0x0123456789ABCDEF})$$

To summarize, the Tiger hash consists of 24 rounds, which can be viewed as three outer rounds, each of which has eight inner rounds. All intermediate hash values are 192 bits.

It's claimed that the S-boxes are designed so that each input bit affects each of a, b, and c after three rounds. Also, the key schedule algorithm is designed so that any small change in the message will affect many bits in the intermediate hash values. The multiplication in the final step of $f_{m,i}$ is also a critical feature of the design. Its purpose is to ensure that each input to an S-box in one round gets mixed into many S-boxes in the next round. Together, the S-boxes, key schedule, and multiply ensure the desired strong avalanche effect [10].

Tiger clearly borrows many ideas from block cipher design, including S-boxes, multiple rounds, mixed mode arithmetic, a key schedule, and so on. At a higher level, we can even say that Tiger employs Shannon's principles of confusion and diffusion.

5.5 HMAC

Recall that for message integrity we can compute a message authentication code, or MAC, using a block cipher in cipher block chaining (CBC) mode. The MAC is the final encrypted block, which is known as the CBC residue. Since a hash function yields a different value if the input changes, we should be able to use a hash to verify message integrity. But we can't send the message M along with its hash $h(M)$, since an attacker could simply replace M with M' and $h(M)$ with $h(M')$. However, if we make the hash depend on a symmetric key, then we can compute a *hashed MAC*, or HMAC.

How should we mix the key into the HMAC? Two obvious approaches are $h(K, M)$ and $h(M, K)$. Suppose we choose to compute the HMAC as $h(K, M)$. There is a potential problem with this approach. Most cryptographic hashes hash the message in blocks. For MD5, SHA–1, and Tiger, the block size used is 512 bits. As a result, if $M = (B_1, B_2)$, where each B_i is 512 bits, then

$$h(M) = F(F(A, B_1), B_2) = F(h(B_1), B_2) \tag{5.2}$$

for some function F, where A is a fixed initial constant. For example, in the Tiger hash, the function F consists of the outer round illustrated in Figure 5.1, with each B_i corresponding to a 512-bit block of the input and A corresponding to the 192-bit initial values of (a, b, c).

If $M' = (M, X)$, Trudy might be able to use *equation 5.2* to find $h(K, M')$ from $h(K, M)$ without knowing K, since, for K, M, and X of the appropriate size,

$$h(K, M') = h(K, M, X) = F(h(K, M), X) \tag{5.3}$$

where the function F is known.

Is $h(M, K)$ better? It does prevent the previous attack. However, if it should happen that there is a collision, that is, if there exists some M' with $h(M') = h(M)$, then by *equation 5.2*, we have

$$h(M, K) = F(h(M), K) = F(h(M'), K) = h(M', K) \tag{5.4}$$

provided that M and M' are each a multiple of the block size. This is certainly not as serious of a concern as the previous case, since if such a collision occurs, the hash function is insecure. But if we can eliminate this attack, then we should do so.

In fact, we can prevent both of these potential problems by slightly modifying the method used to mix the key into the hash. As described in RFC 2104 [133], the approved method for computing an HMAC is as follows. Let B be the block length of hash, in bytes. For MD5, SHA–1, and Tiger, $B = 64$. Next, define

$$\text{ipad} = \text{0x36 repeated } B \text{ times}$$

and

$$\text{opad} = \text{0x5C repeated } B \text{ times.}$$

Then the HMAC of M is

$$\text{HMAC}(M, K) = H(K \oplus \text{opad}, H(K \oplus \text{ipad}, M))$$

which thoroughly mixes the key into the resulting hash. An HMAC can be used in place of a MAC for message integrity. HMACs also have several other uses, some of which we'll see in later chapters.

5.6 USES OF HASH FUNCTIONS

Some of the standard applications that employ hash functions include authentication, message integrity (using an HMAC), message fingerprinting, data corruption detection, and digital signature efficiency. There are a large number of additional clever and sometimes surprising uses for secure hash functions. Below we'll consider two interesting examples where hash functions can be used to solve security-related problems. It also happens to be true that a hash function can be used to do anything that can be done with symmetric key cipher and vice versa.

First, briefly consider the use of hash functions to securely place online bids. Then we'll discuss an interesting approach to spam reduction that relies on hashing.

5.6.1 Online Bids

Suppose there is an online auction with three bidders, Alice, Bob, and Charlie. This auction uses "sealed bids"; that is, each bidder submits one secret bid, and only after all bids have been received are the bids revealed. As usual, the highest bidder wins.

Alice, Bob, and Charlie don't trust each other and, in particular, they don't trust that their bids will remain secret after having been submitted. For example, if Alice places a bid of $10.00 and Bob is able to learn of Alice's bid prior to placing his bid (and prior to the deadline for bidding), he could bid $10.01.

To allay these fears, the auction site proposes the following scheme. Each bidder will determine their bids, with bid A from Alice, bid B from Bob, and bid C from Charlie. Then Alice will submit $h(A)$, Bob will submit $h(B)$, and Charlie will submit $h(C)$. Only after all three hashed bids have been received and revealed to all three participants will the bidders submit their (unhashed) bids, A, B, and C. If the hash function is secure, it's one-way, so there is no disadvantage to submitting a hashed bid prior to a competitor. And since collisions are infeasible to find, no bidder can change their bid after submitting the hash value. Since there is no disadvantage in being the first to submit a hashed bid, and there is no way to change a bid once a hash value has been sent, this scheme prevents the cheating that could have resulted from a naïve bidding approach.

5.6.2 Spam Reduction

Another intriguing example of the value of hashing arises in the following proposed spam reduction technique. Spam is defined as unwanted and unsolicited bulk e-mail. In this scheme, Alice will refuse to accept an e-mail until she has proof that the sender expended a significant amount of "effort" to send the e-mail. Here, effort will be measured in terms of computing resources, in particular, CPU cycles. For this to be practical, it must be easy for Alice to verify that the sender did indeed do the work, yet it must not be possible for the sender to cheat and not do the required work. If we can design such a scheme, then we will have limited the amount of e-mail that any user can send by making it costly to send e-mail in bulk.

Let M be an e-mail message and let T be the current time. The sender of message M must find a value R such that

$$h(M, R, T) = (\underbrace{00\ldots0}_{N}, X), \qquad (5.5)$$

that is, the sender must find a value R so that the hash in *equation 5.5* has zeros in all of its first N output bits. Then the sender sends the triple (M, R, T). Before Alice accepts the e-mail, she needs to verify the time T and that $h(M, R, T)$ begins with N zeros.

The sender must find a hash that begins with N zeros; therefore, he will need to compute, on average, about 2^N hashes. On the other hand, the recipient can verify that $h(M, R, T)$ begins with N zeros by computing a single hash. So the work for the sender—measured in hashes—is about 2^N while the work for the recipient is always a single hash. The sender's work increases exponentially in N while the recipient's work is negligible, regardless of the value of N.

To make this scheme practical, we must to choose N so that the work level is acceptable for normal e-mail users but unacceptably high for spammers. With this scheme, it's also possible that users could select their own individual value of N in order to match their personal tolerance for spam. For example, if Alice hates spam, she could choose, say, $N = 40$. While this would likely deter spammers, it might also deter many legitimate e-mail senders.

Bob, on the other hand, doesn't mind receiving some spam and he never wants to miss a personal e-mail, so he might set his value to, say, $N = 10$. This might be enough to avoid some spam, and it will only place a negligible burden on any legitimate e-mail sender.

Spammers are sure to dislike such a scheme. Legitimate bulk e-mailers also might not like this scheme, since they would need to spend money in order to compute vast numbers of hashes quickly. But that is precisely the goal of this scheme—to increase the cost of sending bulk e-mail.

5.7 OTHER CRYPTO-RELATED TOPICS

In this section, we discuss three topics related to crypto that are interesting, but don't fit neatly into the categories of symmetric crypto, public key crypto, or hash functions. First, we'll consider Shamir's secret sharing scheme. This is a very simple procedure that can be used to split a secret among users. We'll also mention one application for this technique.

Then we'll discuss randomness. In crypto, we often need random keys, random large primes, and so on. We'll discuss some of the problems of actually generating random numbers and we'll present a fun example to illustrate the pitfalls of poor random number selection.

Finally, we'll briefly consider the topic of information hiding, where the goal is to hide information in other data, such as embedding secret information in a JPEG image. If an attacker does not know that information is present, the information can be passed without anyone but the participants knowing that communication has occurred. Information hiding is a large topic and we'll only scratch the surface.

5.7.1 Secret Sharing

Suppose we have a secret S and we would like Alice and Bob to share this secret in the sense that

- Neither Alice nor Bob alone (nor anyone else) can determine S with a probability better than guessing.
- Alice and Bob together can determine S.

At first glance, this seems to present a difficult problem. However, it's easily solved, and the solution essentially derives from the fact that "two points determine a line."

Given the secret S, draw a line L in the plane through the point $(0, S)$ and give Alice a point $A = (X_0, Y_0)$ on L and give Bob another point $B = (X_1, Y_1)$, also on the line L. Then neither Alice nor Bob individually has any information about S, since an infinite number of lines pass through a single point. But together, the two points A and B uniquely determine L, and therefore the point S. This example is illustrated in the "2 out of 2" illustration in Figure 5.3. We call this a secret sharing scheme, since there are two participants and both must cooperate in order to recover the secret S.

It's easy to extend this idea to an "m out of n" secret sharing scheme, for any $m \leq n$, where n is the number of participants, any m of which must cooperate in order to recover the secret. For $m = 2$, a line always works. For example, a 2 out of 3 scheme appears in Figure 5.3.

A line, which is a polynomial of degree one, is uniquely determined by two points, whereas a parabola, which is a polynomial of degree two, is uniquely determined by three points. In general, a polynomial of degree $m - 1$ is uniquely determined by m points. This elementary fact allows us to easily construct an m out of n secret sharing scheme for any $m \leq n$. For example, a 3 out of 3 scheme is illustrated in Figure 5.3.

Since the secret S is likely to be a key or some other digital quantity, it makes more sense to deal with discrete quantities instead of real numbers, and this secret sharing

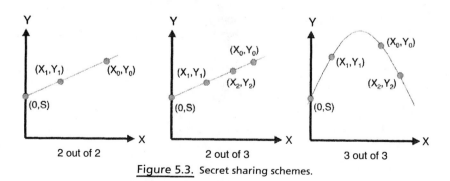

Figure 5.3. Secret sharing schemes.

scheme works equally well modulo p. This elegant and secure secret sharing concept is due to the "S" in RSA (Shamir, that is) [206].

5.7.1.1 *Key Escrow.*

One particular application where secret sharing would be useful is in the *key escrow* problem [63, 64]. Suppose that we require users to store their keys with an official escrow agency. The government could then—with a court order—get access to keys as an aid to criminal investigations. This would put crypto in a similar category as, say, traditional telephone lines, which can be tapped with a court order. At one time the U.S. government tried to promote key escrow and even went so far as to develop a system (Clipper and Capstone) that included key escrow as a feature. However, the key escrow idea was widely disparaged, and it was eventually abandoned; see [43] for a brief history of the Clipper chip.

One concern with key escrow is that the escrow agency might not be trustworthy. One way to ameliorate this concern is to have several escrow agencies and allow users to split the key among n of these, so that m of the n must cooperate in order to recover the key. Alice could then select the n escrow agencies that she considers most trustworthy and have her secret split among these using an m out of n secret sharing scheme.

Shamir's secret sharing scheme could be used to implement such a key escrow scheme. For example, suppose $n = 3$ and $m = 2$ and Alice's key is S. Then the "2 out of 3" scheme illustrated in Figure 5.3 could be used, where, for example, Alice might choose to have the Department of Justice hold the point (X_0, Y_0), the Department of Commerce hold (X_1, Y_1), and Fred's Key Escrow, Inc. hold (X_2, Y_2). Then any two of these three escrow agencies would need to cooperate in order to determine Alice's key S.

5.7.2   Random Numbers

We've seen that random numbers are required to generate symmetric keys as well as RSA key pairs and Diffie-Hellman exponents. In a later chapter, we'll see that random numbers have an important role to play in security protocols as well.

Random numbers are also used in many non-security applications such as simulations and statistics. In such applications, the random numbers usually only need to be "statistically" random; that is, they must pass certain statistical tests that show they are in some sense indistinguishable from random.

However, *cryptographic random numbers* must be statistically random and they must also satisfy the much more stringent requirement that they are unpredictable. Why must such numbers be unpredictable? Suppose, for example, that a server generates the following symmetric keys:

- K_A for Alice
- K_B for Bob
- K_C for Charlie
- K_D for Dave.

Alice, Bob, and Charlie don't like Dave, so they cooperate to see whether they can determine Dave's key. If Dave's key K_D can be predicted from knowledge of the keys K_A, K_B, and K_C, then the security of the system is broken.

5.7.2.1 Texas Hold 'em Poker.

Now let's consider a real-world example that nicely illustrates the wrong way to generate cryptographic random numbers. ASF Software, Inc., developed an online version of a card game known as Texas Hold 'em Poker [96]. In this game, several "community cards" are dealt face up, so that everyone can see these cards. Each player also receives some cards of his own, which only he can see. Each player uses his own cards together with the community cards to obtain the best hand possible. The game includes several rounds of betting as the community cards are revealed. The game is illustrated in Figure 5.4.

In the online version of the game, random numbers are used to shuffle a virtual deck of cards. The AFS software had a serious flaw in the way that the random numbers were used to shuffle the deck of cards. As a result, the program did not produce a truly random shuffle, and it was possible for a player to cheat by determining the entire deck in real time. The cheating player would then know all other players' hands.

How was this possible? First, note that there are $52! > 2^{225}$ possible shuffles of a deck of 52 cards. The AFS poker program used a "random" 32-bit integer to determine the shuffle. Consequently, the program could only generate at most 2^{32} different shuffles out of the 2^{225} possible.

To generate the "random" shuffle, the program used the built-in Pascal pseudo-random number generator, or PRNG. Furthermore, the PRNG was reseeded with each shuffle, with the seed value being a known function of the number of milliseconds since midnight. The number of milliseconds in a day is

$$24 \cdot 60 \cdot 60 \cdot 1000 < 2^{27}$$

and consequently, less than 2^{27} distinct shuffles were possible.

Trudy, the attacker, could do even better. If she synchronized her clock with the server, Trudy could reduce the number of shuffles that needed to be tested to less than 2^{18}. These 2^{18} possible shuffles could all be generated in real time and tested against the "up" cards to determine the actual shuffle for the hand currently in play. In fact, after the first (of five) rounds of betting, Trudy could determine the shuffle uniquely and she would then know the final hands of all other players—even before any player knew his own final hand.

Player's hand   Community cards in center of the table

Figure 5.4. Texas Hold 'em Poker.

The AFS Texas Hold 'em Poker program is an extreme example of the ill effects of using predictable random numbers where cryptographic random numbers are required. Although the shuffle could not be predicted exactly, the number of possible random shuffles was so small that it was possible to break the system.

Cryptographic random numbers are not predictable. For example, the keystream generated by any secure stream cipher must be unpredictable. Consequently, the keystream from RC4 cipher would be a good source of cryptographic random numbers. However, the selection of the key (which acts as the initial seed value for RC4 in this case) is still a critical issue.

5.7.2.2   *Generating Random Bits.*   True randomness is not only hard to find, it's hard to define. Perhaps the best we can do is the concept of *entropy*, as originated by Claude Shannon. Entropy can be used to measure the uncertainty or, conversely, the predictability of a sequence of bits. We won't go into the details here, but a good discussion of entropy can be found in [234].

Sources of true randomness do exist. For example, radioactive decay is such a source. However, nuclear computers are not very popular, so we'll need to find another source. Several hardware devices are available that can be used to gather some random bits based on various physical and thermal properties that are known to be highly unpredictable. Another popular source of randomness is an online lava lamp [155], which achieves its randomness from its inherently chaotic behavior.

Since software is deterministic, true random numbers must be generated external to the code. In addition to the special devices mentioned above, reasonable sources of randomness include mouse movements, keyboard dynamics, certain network activity, etc. It is possible to obtain some high-quality random bits by such methods, but the quantity of such bits is limited. For more information see [99].

Randomness is an important and often overlooked topic in security. It's always worth remembering that, "The use of pseudo-random processes to generate secret quantities can result in pseudo-security" [122].

5.7.3   Information Hiding

In this section we'll discuss two aspects of information hiding, namely, steganography and digital watermarking. Steganography, or "hidden writing," is the attempt to hide the fact that information is being transmitted. An example of a watermark is hiding identifying information in digital music in order to identify those responsible for illegal redistribution.

In a story related by Herodotus (circa 440 BC), a Greek general shaved the head of a slave and wrote a message on the slave's head warning of a Persian invasion. After the slave's hair had grown back sufficiently to cover the message, the slave was sent through enemy lines to deliver his hidden message to another general. Throughout military history, steganography has been used far more often than cryptography.

The modern version of steganography involves hiding information in media such as image files, audio data, or even software [218]. This type of information hiding can also be viewed as a form of covert channel—a topic we'll return to when we discuss multilevel security in Chapter 8.

Digital watermarking is information hiding for a somewhat different purpose. There are several varieties of watermarks; in one type, an "invisible" identifier is added to data. For example, an identifier could be added to digital music so that, in principle, if a pirated version of the music appears, the watermark could be read from it and the purchaser—and the presumed pirate—could be identified. Such techniques have been developed for virtually all types of digital media, as well as for software.

Digital watermarks come in many different flavors, including

- *Invisible watermarks*, which are not supposed to be perceptible in the media.
- *Visible watermarks*, which are meant to be observed. TOP SECRET stamped on a document is an example of such a watermark.

Watermarks can be further categorized as

- *Robust watermarks*, which are supposed to remain readable even if they are attacked.
- *Fragile watermarks*, which are designed to be destroyed or damaged if any tampering occurs.

For example, we could insert a robust invisible mark in digital music in the hope of detecting piracy. Then when pirated music appears on the Internet, perhaps we can trace it back to its source. Or we might insert a fragile invisible mark into an audio file. If the watermark is unreadable, the recipient knows that tampering has occurred. This latter approach is essential a form of integrity check. Various other combinations of watermarks can be used.

Many modern currencies include (non-digital) watermarks. Several current U.S. bills, including the $20 bill pictured in Figure 5.5, have visible watermarks. In the $20 bill, the image of President Jackson is embedded in the paper itself, in the right-hand part of the bill, and is visible when held up to a light. This visible watermark is designed to make counterfeiting more difficult, since special paper is required in order to duplicate this easily verified watermark.

Figure 5.5. Watermarked currency.

One watermarking scheme that has been proposed would insert information into a photograph in such a way that if the photo were damaged it would be possible to reconstruct the entire image from a small surviving piece of the original [129]. It has been claimed that one square inch of a photo can contain enough information to reconstruct entire photograph, without affecting the quality of the image.

Let's consider a very simple approach to steganography that is applicable to digital images. Images employ 24 bits for color—one byte each for red, green, and blue, denoted R, G, and B, respectively. For example, the color represented by $(R, G, B) =$ $(0x7E, 0x52, 0x90)$ is much different from $(R, G, B) = (0xFE, 0x52, 0x90)$, even though the colors only differ by one bit. On the other hand, the color represented by $(R, G, B) = (0xAB, 0x33, 0xF0)$ is indistinguishable from $(R, G, B) =$ $(0xAB, 0x33, 0xF1)$, which also differ by only a single bit. In fact, the low-order RGB bits are unimportant, since they represent imperceptible changes in color. Since the low-order bits don't matter, we can use these bits to "hide" information.

Consider the two images of Alice in Figure 5.6. The left-most Alice contains no hidden information, whereas the right-most Alice has the entire *Alice in Wonderland* book (in PDF format) embedded in the low-order RGB bits. To the human eye, the two images appear identical, regardless of the resolution. While this example is visually stunning, it's important to remember that if we compare the bits in these two images, we would see the differences. In particular, it's easy for an attacker to write a computer program to extract the low-order RGB bits—or to overwrite the bits with garbage—thereby destroying the hidden information, without doing any damage to the image.

Another simple steganography example might help to further demystify the process. Consider an HTML file that contains the text [38]

Figure 5.6. A tale of two Alices.

> "The time has come," the Walrus said,
> "To talk of many things:
> Of shoes and ships and sealing wax
> Of cabbages and kings
> And why the sea is boiling hot
> And whether pigs have wings."

In HTML, the RGB font colors are specified by a tag of the form

```
<font color="#rrggbb"> ... </font>
```

where `rr` is the value of R in hexadecimal, `gg` is G in hex, and `bb` is B in hex. For example, the color black is represented by `#000000`, whereas white is `#FFFFFF`.

Since the low-order bits of R, G, and B won't affect the perceived color, we can hide information in these bits, as shown in the HTML snippet in Table 5.2. Reading the low-order bits of the RGB colors yields the "hidden" information 110 010 110 011 000 101.

Hiding information in the low-order RGB bits of HTML color tags is obviously not very robust. For one thing, if an attacker knows the scheme, he can read the hidden information as easily as the recipient. Or an attacker could destroy the information by replacing the HTML file with another one that is identical, except that the low-order RGB bits are random garbage.

It is tempting to hide information in bits that don't matter, since doing so will be invisible, in the sense that the content will not be affected. But doing so also makes it easy for an attacker who knows the scheme to read or destroy the information. While the bits that don't matter in image files may not be as obvious to humans as low-order RGB bits in HTML tags, such bits are equally susceptible to attack by anyone who understands the image format.

The conclusion here is that, in order for information hiding to be robust, the information must reside in bits that do matter. But this creates a serious challenge, since any changes to bits that do matter must be done very carefully in order to remain "invisible."

As noted above, if Trudy knows the information hiding scheme, she can recover the hidden information as easily as the intended recipient. Watermarking schemes therefore generally encrypt the hidden data before embedding it in the object. But even so, if Trudy understands how the scheme works, she can almost certainly damage or destroy the information. This fact has driven developers to often rely on secret proprietary watermarking

TABLE 5.2. Simple steganography.

```
<font color="#010100">"The time has come," the Walrus said,</font><br>
<font color="#000100">"To talk of many things:</font><br>
<font color="#010100">Of shoes and ships and sealing wax</font><br>
<font color="#000101">Of cabbages and kings</font><br>
<font color="#000000">And why the sea is boiling hot</font><br>
<font color="#010001">And whether pigs have wings."</font><br>
```

schemes, which runs contrary to the spirit of Kerckhoffs Principle. This has, predictably, resulted in many approaches that fail badly when exposed to the light of day.

Further complicating the steganographer's life, an unknown watermarking scheme can almost certainly be diagnosed by a *collusion attack*. That is, the original object and a watermarked object (or just several different watermarked objects) can be compared to determine the bits that carry the information. As a result, watermarking schemes generally use spread spectrum techniques to better hide the information-carrying bits. Such approaches only make the attacker's job slightly more difficult. The challenges and perils of watermarking are nicely illustrated by the attacks on the SDMI scheme, as described in [51].

The bottom line is that digital information hiding is more difficult than it appears at first glance. Information hiding is an active research area, and, although none of the work to date has lived up to the promise of its proponents, the implications of robust schemes would be enormous. Although the field of information hiding is extremely old, the digital version is relatively young, so there may still be room for considerable progress.

5.8 SUMMARY

In this chapter, we discussed cryptographic hash functions, which are extremely useful in security, and we described the Tiger hash in detail. We then discussed HMAC and other interesting uses of hash functions, including a spam-prevention scheme.

We also discussed a few topics related to crypto that don't fit nicely into the other chapters. Shamir's secret sharing scheme offers a secure method for sharing a secret in any m out of n arrangement. We also discussed random numbers, a topic that is of critical security importance, since random numbers arise in many security contexts. We gave an example to illustrate the pitfalls of failing to use cryptographic random numbers where they are required.

We finished with a brief discussion of information hiding. Although neither steganography nor digital watermarking has yet proven robust in practice, it is an evolving field where substantial progress may yet occur.

5.9 PROBLEMS

1. How could you use the Advanced Encryption Standard (AES) as a secure hash function? Note that a hash function does not use a key. Hint: Consider the Tiger hash outer round.

2. At the start of this chapter, we listed several properties that a secure hash function must satisfy. Suppose that a hash function fails to provide compression but provides all of the other required properties. Give an application where a secure hash function is used, but where this hash function would fail to be useful. Repeat this for each of these properties:

   a. Efficiency

   b. One-way

   c. Collision resistance

3. Suppose that you want to encrypt a message that consists of three blocks of plaintext, P_0, P_1, and P_2. All you have available is a hash function and a symmetric key K. How would you securely encrypt and decrypt this message?

4. Suppose that a secure cryptographic hash function generates hash values that are n bits in length. How could an attacker break this hash function and what is the expected work factor?

5. Consider a CRC that uses the divisor 10011. Find two "collisions" with the data 10101011; that is, find two other data values that produce the same CRC checksum as 10101011.

6. Consider a CRC that uses the divisor 10011. Suppose the data value is 11010110. Trudy wants to change the data to 111***** where she doesn't care about the * positions, but she wants the resulting checksum to be the same as for the original data. Find all data values Trudy could choose.

7. Show that *equation 5.3* holds if K, M, and X are all multiples of the hash block length (usually, 64 bytes). For which other sizes of K, M, and X does *equation 5.3* hold? Show that *equation 5.4* holds for any size of M, M', and K, provided that $h(M) = h(M')$.

8. Alice's computer needs to have access to a symmetric key K_A. Consider the following two methods for deriving and storing the key K_A:

   (i) The key is $K_A = h(\text{Alice's password})$, and K_A is not stored on Alice's computer. Whenever K_A is required, Alice enters her password and the key is generated.

   (ii) The key K_A is initially generated at random, and it is stored as $E(K_A, K)$, where $K = h(\text{Alice's password})$. Whenever K_A is required, Alice enters her password, which is used to decrypt the key.

   Discuss one advantage of method (i) and one advantage of method (ii).

9. Suppose that Sally (a server) needs access to a symmetric key for user Alice and another symmetric key for Bob and another symmetric key for Charlie. Then Sally could generate symmetric keys K_A, K_B, and K_C and store these in a database. An alternative is *key diversification*, where Sally generates and stores a single key K_S. Then Sally generates the key K_A when required as $K_A = h(\text{Alice}, K_S)$, with keys K_B and K_C generated in a similar manner. Describe one advantage and one disadvantage of key diversification.

10. Recall the online bid method discussed in Section 5.6.1.

    a. What properties of the secure hash function h does this scheme rely on to prevent cheating?

    b. Suppose that Charlie is certain that Alice and Bob will both submit bids between $10,000 and $20,000. Describe an attack that Charlie can use to determine Alice's bid and Bob's bid from their respective hash values. How can the bidding procedure be modified to prevent this attack?

11. We say that a transformation T is *incremental* if it satisfies the following property: Having once applied T to M, the time to update the result upon modification of M is proportional to the amount of modification done to M. Suppose we have an incremental hash function H.

   a. Discuss one application where the incremental hash H is clearly superior to a (non-incremental) hash function.

   b. Suppose a message M can only be modified by appending more bits; that is, the modified message M' is $M' = (M, X)$, for some X. Given a secure hash function h, define an incremental hash function H using h.

12. Suppose Bob and Alice want to flip a coin over a network. Alice proposes the following procedure:

   (i) Alice selects a value $X \in \{0, 1\}$.

   (ii) Alice generates a 256-bit random symmetric key K.

   (iii) Using AES, Alice computes $Y = E(X, R, K)$, where R consists of 255 random bits.

   (iv) Alice sends Y to Bob.

   (v) Bob guesses a value $Z \in \{0, 1\}$ and tells Alice.

   (vi) Alice gives the key K to Bob who computes $(X, R) = D(Y, K)$.

   (vii) If $X = Z$ then Bob wins; otherwise Alice wins.

   Explain how Alice can cheat. Using a hash function, modify this protocol so that Alice can't cheat.

13. Suppose that a hash function generates a 12-bit output. If you hash 2^{10} randomly selected messages, how many collisions would you expect to find?

14. Suppose that h is a secure hash that generates an n-bit hash value.

   a. What is the expected number of hashes that must be computed to find one collision?

   b. What is the expected number of hashes that must be computed to find 10 collisions? That is, what is the expected number of hashes that must be computed in order to find pairs (x_i, z_i) such that $h(x_i) = h(z_i)$, for $i = 0, 1, 2, \ldots, 9$?

15. A k-way collision is a set of values $x_0, x_1, \ldots, x_{k-1}$ that all hash to the same value. Suppose that h is a secure hash that generates an n-bit hash value.

   a. What is the expected number of hashes that must be computed to find one k-way collision?

   b. What is the expected number of hashes that must be computed to find m k-way collisions?

16. A program implementing the author's "Bobcat" hash algorithm can be found on the textbook website. This hash is essentially a scaled down version of Tiger; however, whereas Tiger produces a 192-bit hash (three 64-bit words), Bobcat produces a 48-bit hash (three 16-bit words). With any hash function, a smaller hash value can be obtained by simply truncating the output.

   a. Find a collision for the 12-bit version of Bobcat. How many hashes did you compute before you found your first 12-bit collision?

   b. Find a collision for the full 48-bit Bobcat hash.

17. Verify that the RGB colors (0x7E, 0x52, 0x90) and (0x7E, 0x52, 0x10) are clearly different, and the colors (0xAB, 0x32, 0xF1) and (0xAB, 0x33, 0xF1) are indistinguishable.

18. Obtain the image file alice.bmp from the textbook website. Use a hex editor to hide the information "attack at dawn" in the file. Give a listing showing the bits that were modified and their location in the file, as well as the corresponding unmodified bits. Provide screen snapshots of the original BMP file, as well as the BMP file containing the hidden message.

19. Obtain the image files alice.bmp and aliceStego.bmp and the programs stego.c and stegoRead.c from the textbook website. Use stegoRead to extract the hidden PDF file contained in aliceStego.bmp. Use the programs to insert another file into a different (uncompressed) image file and extract the information. Provide screen snapshots of the image with and without the hidden information.

20. Write a program to hide information in an audio file and to extract the hidden information. Can you discern any difference in the quality of the audio?

21. Write a program to hide information in a video file and to extract the hidden information. Can you discern any difference in the quality of the video?

22. Fill in the number of bits on each line of the Tiger hash outer round in Figure 5.1.

23. Suppose that you have a text file and you plan to distribute it to several different people. Describe a simple non-digital watermarking method that you could use to place a distinct invisible watermark in each copy of the file. Note that "invisible" does not mean that the watermark is literally invisible; instead, it means that the watermark is not obvious to the reader.

24. Let h be the Tiger hash and let F the Tiger outer round in Figure 5.1. Then for $M = (B_1, B_2, B_3)$, where each B_i is 512 bits, give the analog of *equation 5.2*. Now suppose $M = (B_1, B_2, \ldots, B_n)$ where each B_i is 512 bits. Show that $h(M) = F(h(B_1, B_2, \ldots, B_{n-1}), B_n)$.

25. Recently, a collision was found in MD5 [196]. Find all bit positions where the following two messages (given in hexadecimal) differ and verify that their MD5 hash values are the same:

```
d1  31  dd  02  c5  e6  ee  c4    69  3d  9a  06  98  af  f9  5c
2f  ca  b5  87  12  46  7e  ab    40  04  58  3e  b8  fb  7f  89
55  ad  34  06  09  f4  b3  02    83  e4  88  83  25  71  41  5a
08  51  25  e8  f7  cd  c9  9f    d9  1d  bd  f2  80  37  3c  5b
96  0b  1d  d1  dc  41  7b  9c    e4  d8  97  f4  5a  65  55  d5
35  73  9a  c7  f0  eb  fd  0c    30  29  f1  66  d1  09  b1  8f
75  27  7f  79  30  d5  5c  eb    22  e8  ad  ba  79  cc  15  5c
ed  74  cb  dd  5f  c5  d3  6d    b1  9b  0a  d8  35  cc  a7  e3
```

and

```
d1  31  dd  02  c5  e6  ee  c4    69  3d  9a  06  98  af  f9  5c
2f  ca  b5  07  12  46  7e  ab    40  04  58  3e  b8  fb  7f  89
55  ad  34  06  09  f4  b3  02    83  e4  88  83  25  f1  41  5a
08  51  25  e8  f7  cd  c9  9f    d9  1d  bd  72  80  37  3c  5b
96  0b  1d  d1  dc  41  7b  9c    e4  d8  97  f4  5a  65  55  d5
35  73  9a  47  f0  eb  fd  0c    30  29  f1  66  d1  09  b1  8f
75  27  7f  79  30  d5  5c  eb    22  e8  ad  ba  79  4c  15  5c
ed  74  cb  dd  5f  c5  d3  6d    b1  9b  0a  58  35  cc  a7  e3
```

6

ADVANCED CRYPTANALYSIS

It is the glory of God to conceal a thing:
but the honor of kings is to search out a matter.
—Proverbs 25:2

The magic words are squeamish ossifrage
—Solution to RSA challenge problem
posed in 1977 by Ron Rivest, who
estimated that breaking the message
would require 40 quadrillion years.
It was broken in 1994.

6.1 INTRODUCTION

In this chapter we'll discuss the following advanced cryptanalytic techniques:

- Linear and differential cryptanalysis
- A side-channel attack on RSA
- The lattice reduction attack on the knapsack
- Hellman's time-memory trade-off attack on DES

These attacks represent only a small sample of the many cryptanalytic techniques that have been developed in recent years. But each is representative of a significant general cryptanalytic principle.

Information Security: Principles and Practice, by Mark Stamp
Copyright © 2006 John Wiley & Sons, Inc.

Linear and differential cryptanalysis are not used to attack cryptosystems directly. Instead, they are used to analyze block ciphers for design weaknesses. As a result, block ciphers are designed with these techniques in mind. In order to understand the design principles employed in block ciphers today, it is therefore necessary to have some understanding of linear and differential cryptanalysis.

A side channel is an unintended source of information. For example, power usage or careful timing might reveal information about an underlying computation. Timing attacks have been used successfully on several public key systems, and we'll discuss one such attack on RSA. Although side channel attacks are not classic cryptanalytic techniques, these attacks have recently been used to break many encryption schemes, so it is critical to understand the implications of such attacks.

In the chapter on public key cryptography, we mentioned the attack on the knapsack cryptosystem. In this section, we'll give more details on the attack. We do not present all of the mathematical nuances, but we provide sufficient information to understand the concept behind the attack and to write a program to implement the attack. It is a relatively simple attack that nicely illustrates the role that mathematics can play in breaking cryptosystems.

Finally, we'll discuss Hellman's time-memory trade-off attack on DES. This attack nicely illustrates the role that algorithms can play in cryptanalysis.

6.2 LINEAR AND DIFFERENTIAL CRYPTANALYSIS

The influence of the Data Encryption Standard (DES) on modern cryptography can't be overestimated. Both linear and differential cryptanalysis were developed to attack DES. As mentioned above, these techniques don't generally yield practical attacks. Instead, linear and differential "attacks" point to design weaknesses in block ciphers. These techniques have become basic analytic tools that are applied to the analysis of all block ciphers today.

Differential cryptanalysis is, in the unclassified world, due to Biham and Shamir (yes, that Shamir, yet again) who introduced the technique in 1990. Subsequently, it has become clear that someone involved in the design of DES (that is, NSA) was aware of differential cryptanalysis in the mid 1970s. Differential cryptanalysis is a chosen plaintext attack.

Linear cryptanalysis was apparently developed by Matsui in 1993. Since DES was not designed to offer optimal resistance to a sophisticated linear cryptanalysis attacks, either NSA did not know about the technique in the 1970s or they were not concerned about such an attack. Linear cryptanalysis is a slightly more realistic attack than differential cryptanalysis, primarily because it is a known plaintext attack instead of a chosen plaintext attack.

6.2.1 Quick Review of DES

We don't require all of the details of DES here, so we'll give a simplified overview that only includes the essential facts that we'll need below. DES has eight S-boxes, each of which maps six input bits, denoted $x_0x_1x_2x_3x_4x_5$, to four output bits, denoted $y_0y_1y_2y_3$. For example, DES S-box number one is, in hexadecimal notation,

x_0x_5	0	1	2	3	4	5	6	$x_1x_2x_3x_4$ 7	8	9	A	B	C	D	E	F
0	E	4	D	1	2	F	B	8	3	A	6	C	5	9	0	7
1	0	F	7	4	E	2	D	1	A	6	C	B	9	5	3	4
2	4	1	E	8	D	6	2	B	F	C	9	7	3	A	5	0
3	F	C	8	2	4	9	1	7	5	B	3	E	A	0	6	D

Figure 6.1 gives a much simplified view of DES, which is sufficient for the subsequent discussion. Below, we are most interested in analyzing the nonlinear parts of DES, so the diagram highlights the fact that the S-boxes are the only nonlinearity in DES. Figure 6.1 also illustrates the way that the subkey K_i enters into a DES round. This will also be important in the discussion to follow.

Next, we'll present a quick overview of differential cryptanalysis followed by a similar overview of linear cryptanalysis. We'll then present a simplified version of DES, which we've called Tiny DES, or TDES. We'll present both linear and differential attacks on TDES.

6.2.2   Overview of Differential Cryptanalysis

Since differential cryptanalysis was developed to analyze DES, let's discuss it in the context of DES. Recall that all of DES is linear except for the S-boxes. We'll see that the linear parts of DES play a significant role in its security; however, from a cryptanalytic point of view, the linear parts are easy. Mathematicians are good at solving linear

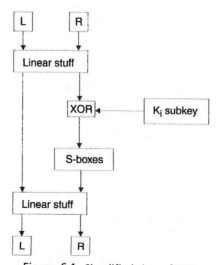

Figure 6.1. Simplified view of DES.

equations, so it is the nonlinear parts that represent the major cryptanalytic hurdles. As a result, both differential and linear cryptanalysis are focused on dealing with the nonlinear parts of DES, namely, the S-boxes.

The idea behind a differential attack is to compare input and output differences. For simplicity, we'll first consider a simplified S-box. Suppose that a DES-like cipher uses the 3-bit to 2-bit S-box

		column		
row	00	01	10	11
0	10	01	11	00
1	00	10	01	11

(6.1)

where, for input bits $x_0 x_1 x_2$, the bit x_0 indexes the row, while $x_1 x_2$ indexes the column. Then, for example, $\text{Sbox}(010) = 11$ since the bits in row 0 and column 10 are 11.

Consider the two inputs, $X_1 = 110$ and $X_2 = 010$, and suppose the key is $K = 011$. Then $X_1 \oplus K = 101$ and $X_2 \oplus K = 001$ and we have

$$\text{Sbox}(X_1 \oplus K) = 10 \quad \text{and} \quad \text{Sbox}(X_2 \oplus K) = 01. \qquad (6.2)$$

Now suppose that K in *equation 6.2* is unknown, but the inputs $X_1 = 110$ and $X_2 = 010$ are known as well as the corresponding outputs $\text{Sbox}(X_1 \oplus K) = 10$ and $\text{Sbox}(X_2 \oplus K) = 01$. Then from *S-box 6.1* we see that $X_1 \oplus K \in \{000, 101\}$ and $X_2 \oplus K \in \{001, 110\}$. Since X_1 and X_2 are known, we have

$$K \in \{110, 011\} \cap \{011, 100\}$$

which implies that $K = 011$. This "attack" is essentially a known plaintext attack on the single S-box (6.1) for the key K. The same approach will work on a single DES S-box.

However, attacking one S-box in one round of DES does not appear to be particularly useful. In addition, the attacker will not know the input to any round except for the first, and the attacker will not know the output of any round but the last. The intermediate rounds appear to be beyond the purview of the cryptanalyst.

For this approach to prove useful in analyzing DES, we must be able to extend the attack to one complete round; that is, we must take into account all eight S-boxes simultaneously. Once we have extended the attack to one round, we must then extend the attack to multiple rounds. On the surface, both of these appear to be daunting tasks.

However, we'll see that by focusing on input and output differences, it becomes easy to make some S-boxes "active" and others "inactive." As a result, we can, in some cases, extend the attack to a single round. To then extend the attack to multiple rounds, we must choose the input difference so that the output difference is in a useful form for the next round. This is challenging and depends on the specific properties of the S-boxes, as well as the linear mixing that occurs at each round.

The crucial point here is that we'll focus on input and output differences. Suppose we know inputs X_1 and X_2. Then, for input X_1, the actual input to the S-box is $X_1 \oplus K$ and for input X_2 the actual input to S-box is $X_2 \oplus K$, where the key K is unknown.

Differences are defined modulo 2, implying that the difference operation is the same as the sum operation, namely, XOR. Then the S-box input difference is

$$(X_1 \oplus K) \oplus (X_2 \oplus K) = X_1 \oplus X_2, \qquad (6.3)$$

that is, the input difference is independent of the key K. This is the fundamental observation that enables differential cryptanalysis to work.

Let $Y_1 = \text{Sbox}(X_1 \oplus K)$ and let $Y_2 = \text{Sbox}(X_2 \oplus K)$. Then the output difference $Y_1 \oplus Y_2$ is almost the input difference to next round. The goal is to carefully construct the input difference, so that we can "chain" differences through multiple rounds. Since the input difference is independent of the key—and since differential cryptanalysis is a chosen plaintext attack—we have the freedom to choose the inputs so that the output difference has any particular form that we desire.

Another crucial element of a differential attack is that an S-box input difference of zero always results in an output difference of zero. Why is this the case? An input difference of 0 simply means that the input values, say, X_1 and X_2, are the same, in which case the output values Y_1 and Y_2 must be the same, that is, $Y_1 \oplus Y_2 = 0$. The importance of this elementary observation is that we can make S-boxes "inactive" with respect to differential cryptanalysis by choosing their input differences to be zero.

A final observation is that it is not necessary that things happen with certainty. In other words, if an outcome only occurs with some nontrivial probability, then we may be able to develop a probabilistic attack that will still prove useful in recovering the key.

Given any S-box, we can analyze it for useful input differences as follows. For each possible input value X, find all pairs X_1 and X_2 such that $X = X_1 \oplus X_2$ and compute the corresponding output differences $Y = Y_1 \oplus Y_2$, where $Y_1 = \text{Sbox}(X_1)$ and $Y_2 = \text{Sbox}(X_1)$. By tabulating the resulting counts, we can find the most biased input values. For example for *S-box 6.1*, this analysis yields the results in Table 6.1.

For any S-box, an input difference of 000 is not interesting since this mean the input values are the same and the S-box is "inactive" (with respect to differences) since the output values must be the same. For the example in Table 6.1, an input difference of 010

TABLE 6.1. S-box difference analysis.

	$\text{Sbox}(X_1) \oplus \text{Sbox}(X_2)$			
$X_1 \oplus X_2$	00	01	10	11
000	8	0	0	0
001	0	0	4	4
010	0	8	0	0
011	0	0	4	4
100	0	0	4	4
101	4	4	0	0
110	0	0	4	4
111	4	4	0	0

always gives an output of 01, which is the most biased possible result. And, as noted in *equation 6.3*, by selecting, say, $X_1 \oplus X_2 = 010$, the actual input difference to the S-box would be 010 since the key K drops out of the difference.

Differential cryptanalysis of DES is fairly complex. To illustrate the technique more concretely, but without all of the complexity inherent in DES, we'll present a scaled-down version of DES that we'll call Tiny DES, or TDES. Then we'll perform differential and linear cryptanalysis on TDES. But first, we present a quick overview of linear cryptanalysis.

6.2.3   Overview of Linear Cryptanalysis

Ironically, linear cryptanalysis—like differential cryptanalysis—is focused on the non-linear part of a block cipher. Although linear cryptanalysis was developed a few years after differential cryptanalysis, it's conceptually simpler, it's more effective on DES, and it only requires known plaintext—as opposed to chosen plaintext.

In differential cryptanalysis, we focused on input and output differences. In linear cryptanalysis, the objective is to approximate the nonlinear part of a cipher with linear equations. Since mathematicians are good at solving linear equations, if we can find such approximations it stands to reason that we can use these to attack the cipher. Since the only nonlinear part of DES is its S-boxes, linear cryptanalysis will be focused on the S-boxes.

Consider again *S-box 6.1*. We'll denote the three input bits as $x_0 x_1 x_2$ and the two output bits as $y_0 y_1$. Then x_0 determines the row, and $x_1 x_2$ determines the column. In Table 6.2, we've tabulated the number of values for which each possible linear approximation holds. Since there are eight output values in each case, any number other than four indicates a nonrandom output.

The results in Table 6.2 show that, for example, $y_0 = x_0 \oplus x_2 \oplus 1$ with probability 1 and $y_0 \oplus y_1 = x_1 \oplus x_2$ with probability $3/4$. Using information such as this, in our analysis we can replace the S-boxes by linear functions. The result is that, in effect, we've traded the nonlinear S-boxes for linear equations, where the linear equations only hold with some probability.

TABLE 6.2.   S-box linear analysis.

Input Bits	Output Bits		
	y_0	y_1	$y_0 \oplus y_1$
0	4	4	4
x_0	4	4	4
x_1	4	6	2
x_2	4	4	4
$x_0 \oplus x_1$	4	2	2
$x_0 \oplus x_2$	0	4	4
$x_1 \oplus x_2$	4	6	6
$x_0 \oplus x_1 \oplus x_2$	4	6	2

For these linear approximations to be useful in attacking a block cipher such as DES, we'll try to extend this approach so that we can solve linear equations for the key. As with differential cryptanalysis, we must somehow "chain" these results through multiple rounds.

How well can we approximate a DES S-boxes with linear functions? Each DES S-box was designed so that no linear combination of inputs is a good approximation to a single output bit. However, there are linear combinations of output bits that can be approximated by linear combinations of input bits. As a result, there is potential for success in the linear cryptanalysis of DES.

As with differential cryptanalysis, the linear cryptanalysis of DES is complex. To illustrate a linear attack, we'll next describe TDES, a scaled-down DES-like cipher. Then we'll perform differential and linear cryptanalysis on TDES.

6.2.4 Tiny DES

Tiny DES, or TDES, is a DES-like cipher that is simpler and easier to analyze than DES. TDES was designed by the author to make linear and differential attacks relatively easy to implement. TDES is certainly a contrived cipher, and it would be trivial to break in practice. Yet it's similar enough to DES to illustrate the principles behind linear and differential cryptanalysis.

TDES is a much simplified version of DES that employs

- A 16-bit block size
- A 16-bit key size
- Four rounds
- Two S-boxes, each mapping 6 bits to 4 bits
- A 12-bit subkey in each round

TDES has no P-box, initial or final permutation. Essentially, we have eliminated all features of DES that contribute nothing to its security, while at the same time scaling down the block and key sizes.

Note that the small key and block sizes imply that TDES cannot offer any real security, regardless of the underlying algorithm. Nevertheless, TDES will be a useful tool in understanding linear and differential attacks, as well as the larger issues of block cipher design.

TDES is a Feistel cipher, and we denote the plaintext as (L_0, R_0). Then for $i = 1, 2, 3, 4$,

$$L_i = R_{i-1}$$
$$R_i = L_{i-1} \oplus F(R_{i-1}, K_i)$$

where the ciphertext is (L_4, R_4). A single round of TDES is illustrated in Figure 6.2, where the numbers of bits are indicated on each line. Next, we'll completely describe all of the pieces of the TDES algorithm.

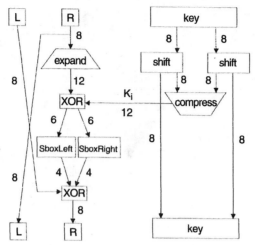

Figure 6.2. One round of Tiny DES.

TDES has two S-boxes, which we denote SboxLeft(X) and SboxRight(X). Both S-boxes map 6 bits to 4 bits, as in standard DES. The parts of TDES that we'll be most interested in are the S-boxes and their input. To simplify the notation, we'll define the function

$$F(R, K) = \mathrm{Sboxes}(\mathrm{expand}(R) \oplus K) \qquad (6.4)$$

where

$$\mathrm{Sboxes}(x_0x_1x_2 \ldots x_{11}) = (\mathrm{SboxLeft}(x_0x_1 \ldots x_5), \mathrm{SboxRight}(x_6x_7 \ldots x_{11})).$$

The expansion permutation is given by

$$\mathrm{expand}(R) = \mathrm{expand}(r_0r_1r_2r_3r_4r_5r_6r_7) = (r_4r_7r_2r_1r_5r_7r_0r_2r_6r_5r_0r_3). \qquad (6.5)$$

The left TDES S-box, which we denote by SboxLeft(X), is, in hexadecimal,

$$ (6.6) $$

x_0x_5	0	1	2	3	4	5	6	7	8	9	A	B	C	D	E	F
								$x_1x_2x_3x_4$								
0	6	9	A	3	4	D	7	8	E	1	2	B	5	C	F	0
1	9	E	B	A	4	5	0	7	8	6	3	2	C	D	1	F
2	8	1	C	2	D	3	E	F	0	9	5	A	4	B	6	7
3	9	0	2	5	A	D	6	E	1	8	B	C	3	4	7	F

whereas the right S-box, SboxRight(X), also in hex notation, is

		$x_1x_2x_3x_4$														
x_0x_5	0	1	2	3	4	5	6	7	8	9	A	B	C	D	E	F
0	C	5	0	A	E	7	2	8	D	4	3	9	6	F	1	B
1	1	C	9	6	3	E	B	2	F	8	4	5	D	A	0	7
2	F	A	E	6	D	8	2	4	1	7	9	0	3	5	B	C
3	0	A	3	C	8	2	1	E	9	7	F	6	B	5	D	4

$$(6.7)$$

As with DES, each row in a TDES S-box is a permutation of the hexadecimal digits $\{0, 1, 2, \ldots, E, F\}$.

The TDES key schedule is very simple. The 16-bit key is denoted

$$K = k_0k_1k_2k_3k_4k_5k_6k_7k_8k_9k_{10}k_{11}k_{12}k_{13}k_{14}k_{15}$$

and the subkey is generated as follows. Let

$$LK = k_0k_1 \ldots k_7$$
$$RK = k_8k_9 \ldots k_{15}.$$

Then for each round $i = 1, 2, 3, 4$,

$$LK = \text{rotate } LK \text{ left by } 2$$
$$RK = \text{rotate } RK \text{ left by } 1$$

and K_i is obtained by selecting bits 0, 2, 3, 4, 5, 7, 9, 10, 11, 13, 14, and 15 of (LK, RK). The subkeys K_i can be given explicitly as

$$K_1 = k_2k_4k_5k_6k_7k_1k_{10}k_{11}k_{12}k_{14}k_{15}k_8$$
$$K_2 = k_4k_6k_7k_0k_1k_3k_{11}k_{12}k_{13}k_{15}k_8k_9$$
$$K_3 = k_6k_0k_1k_2k_3k_5k_{12}k_{13}k_{14}k_8k_9k_{10}$$
$$K_4 = k_0k_2k_3k_4k_5k_7k_{13}k_{14}k_{15}k_9k_{10}k_{11}$$

In the next section, we'll describe a differential attack on TDES. After that, we'll describe a linear attack on TDES. These attacks illustrate the crucial principles that apply to differential and linear cryptanalysis of DES and other block ciphers.

6.2.5   Differential Cryptanalysis of TDES

Our differential attack on TDES will focus on the right S-box, which appears in *S-box 6.7*. Suppose that we tabulate SboxRight(X_1) $\oplus$ SboxRight(X_2) for all pairs X_1 and X_2 with $X_1 \oplus X_2 = 001000$. Then we find that

$$X_1 \oplus X_2 = 001000 \text{ implies } \text{SboxRight}(X_1) \oplus \text{SboxRight}(X_2) = 0010 \quad (6.8)$$

with probability 3/4. Recall that for any S-box,

$$X_1 \oplus X_2 = 000000 \text{ implies } \text{SboxRight}(X_1) \oplus \text{SboxRight}(X_2) = 0000. \quad (6.9)$$

Our goal is to make use of these observations to develop a viable differential attack on TDES.

Differential cryptanalysis is a chosen plaintext attack. Suppose we encrypt two chosen plaintext blocks, $P = (L, R)$ and $\tilde{P} = (\tilde{L}, \tilde{R})$ that satisfy

$$P \oplus \tilde{P} = (L, R) \oplus (\tilde{L}, \tilde{R}) = 0000\ 0000\ 0000\ 0010 = 0x0002. \qquad (6.10)$$

Then P and $\tilde{P}$ differ in one specific bit and agree in all other bit positions. Let's carefully analyze what happens to this difference as P and $\tilde{P}$ are encrypted with TDES.

First, consider

$$F(R, K) \oplus F(\tilde{R}, K) = \texttt{Sboxes}(\texttt{expand}(R) \oplus K) \oplus \texttt{Sboxes}(\texttt{expand}(\tilde{R}) \oplus K).$$

From the definition of $\texttt{expand}$ in *equation 6.5* we see that

$$\texttt{expand}(0000\ 0010) = 000000\ 001000.$$

Since $\texttt{expand}$ is linear, if $X_1 \oplus X_2 = 0000\ 0010$ then

$$\texttt{expand}(X_1) \oplus \texttt{expand}(X_2) = \texttt{expand}(X_1 \oplus X_2) = \texttt{expand}(0000\ 0010)$$
$$= 000000\ 001000. \qquad (6.11)$$

For the chosen plaintext in *equation 6.10* we have $R \oplus \tilde{R} = 0000\ 0010$. Then from the observation in *equation 6.11* it follows that

$$F(R, K) \oplus F(\tilde{R}, K) = \texttt{Sboxes}(\texttt{expand}(R) \oplus K) \oplus \texttt{Sboxes}(\texttt{expand}(\tilde{R}) \oplus K)$$
$$= (\texttt{SboxLeft}(A \oplus K), \texttt{SboxRight}(B \oplus K))$$
$$\oplus (\texttt{SboxLeft}(\tilde{A} \oplus K), \texttt{SboxRight}(\tilde{B} \oplus K))$$
$$= (\texttt{SboxLeft}(A \oplus K) \oplus \texttt{SboxLeft}(\tilde{A} \oplus K)),$$
$$(\texttt{SboxRight}(B \oplus K) \oplus \texttt{SboxRight}(\tilde{B} \oplus K))$$

where $A \oplus \tilde{A} = 000000$ and $B \oplus \tilde{B} = 001000$. This result, together with *equations 6.8* and *6.9* imply

$$F(R, K) \oplus F(\tilde{R}, K) = 0000\ 0010$$

with probability $3/4$.

In summary, if $R \oplus \tilde{R} = 0000\ 0010$, then for any (unknown) subkey K, we have

$$F(R, K) \oplus F(\tilde{R}, K) = 0000\ 0010 \qquad (6.12)$$

with probability $3/4$. In other words, for certain input values, the output difference of the round function is the same as the input difference, with a high probability. Next, we'll show that we can chain this results through multiple rounds of TDES.

TABLE 6.3. Differential cryptanalysis of TDES.

$(L_0, R_0) = P$	$(\tilde{L}_0, \tilde{R}_0) = \tilde{P}$	$P \oplus \tilde{P} = 0x0002$	Probability
$L_1 = R_0$	$\tilde{L}_1 = \tilde{R}_0$		
$R_1 = L_0 \oplus F(R_0, K_1)$	$\tilde{R}_1 = \tilde{L}_0 \oplus F(\tilde{R}_0, K_1)$	$(L_1, R_1) \oplus (\tilde{L}_1, \tilde{R}_1) = 0x0202$	$3/4$
$L_2 = R_1$	$\tilde{L}_2 = \tilde{R}_1$		
$R_2 = L_1 \oplus F(R_1, K_2)$	$\tilde{R}_2 = \tilde{L}_1 \oplus F(\tilde{R}_1, K_2)$	$(L_2, R_2) \oplus (\tilde{L}_2, \tilde{R}_2) = 0x0200$	$(3/4)^2$
$L_3 = R_2$	$\tilde{L}_3 = \tilde{R}_2$		
$R_3 = L_2 \oplus F(R_2, K_3)$	$\tilde{R}_3 = \tilde{L}_2 \oplus F(\tilde{R}_2, K_3)$	$(L_3, R_3) \oplus (\tilde{L}_3, \tilde{R}_3) = 0x0002$	$(3/4)^2$
$L_4 = R_3$	$\tilde{L}_4 = \tilde{R}_3$		
$R_4 = L_3 \oplus F(R_3, K_4)$	$\tilde{R}_4 = \tilde{L}_3 \oplus F(\tilde{R}_3, K_4)$	$(L_4, R_4) \oplus (\tilde{L}_4, \tilde{R}_4) = 0x0202$	$(3/4)^3$
$C = (L_4, R_4)$	$C = (\tilde{L}_4, \tilde{R}_4)$	$C \oplus \tilde{C} = 0x0202$	

Since differential cryptanalysis is a chosen plaintext attack, we'll choose P and $\tilde{P}$ to satisfy *equation 6.10*. In Table 6.3, we carefully analyze the TDES encryption of such plaintext values. By the choice of P and $\tilde{P}$, we have

$$R_0 \oplus \tilde{R}_0 = 0000\ 0010 \quad \text{and} \quad L_0 \oplus \tilde{L}_0 = 0000\ 0000.$$

Then from *equation 6.12*,

$$R_1 \oplus \tilde{R}_1 = 0000\ 0010$$

with probability $3/4$. From this result it follows that

$$\begin{aligned}
R_2 \oplus \tilde{R}_2 &= (L_1 \oplus F(R_1, K_2)) \oplus (\tilde{L}_1 \oplus F(\tilde{R}_1, K_2)) \\
&= (L_1 \oplus \tilde{L}_1) \oplus (F(R_1, K_2) \oplus F(\tilde{R}_1, K_2)) \\
&= (R_0 \oplus \tilde{R}_0) \oplus (F(R_1, K_2) \oplus F(\tilde{R}_1, K_2)) \\
&= 0000\ 0010 \oplus 0000\ 0010 \\
&= 0000\ 0000
\end{aligned}$$

with probability $(3/4)^2$. The results given in Table 6.3 for $R_3 \oplus \tilde{R}_3$ and $R_4 \oplus \tilde{R}_4$ are obtained in a similar manner.

We can derive an algorithm from Table 6.3 to recover some of the unknown key bits. We'll choose P and $\tilde{P}$ as in *equation 6.10* and find the corresponding ciphertext C and $\tilde{C}$. Since TDES is a Feistel cipher,

$$R_4 = L_3 \oplus F(R_3, K_4) \quad \text{and} \quad \tilde{R}_4 = \tilde{L}_3 \oplus F(\tilde{R}_3, K_4)$$

and $L_4 = R_3$ and $\tilde{L}_4 = \tilde{R}_3$. Consequently,

$$R_4 = L_3 \oplus F(L_4, K_4) \quad \text{and} \quad \tilde{R}_4 = \tilde{L}_3 \oplus F(\tilde{L}_4, K_4)$$

which can be rewritten as

$$L_3 = R_4 \oplus F(L_4, K_4) \quad \text{and} \quad \tilde{L}_3 = \tilde{R}_4 \oplus F(\tilde{L}_4, K_4).$$

Now if

$$C \oplus \tilde{C} = \texttt{0x0202} \qquad (6.13)$$

then from Table 6.3 we almost certainly have $L_3 \oplus \tilde{L}_3 = 0000\ 0000$, that is, $L_3 = \tilde{L}_3$. It follows that

$$R_4 \oplus F(L_4, K_4) = \tilde{R}_4 \oplus F(\tilde{L}_4, K_4)$$

which we rewrite as

$$R_4 \oplus \tilde{R}_4 = F(L_4, K_4) \oplus F(\tilde{L}_4, K_4). \qquad (6.14)$$

Note that in *equation 6.14*, the only unknown is the subkey K_4. Next, we show how to use this result to recover some of the bits of K_4.

For a chosen plaintext pair that satisfies *equation 6.10*, if the resulting ciphertext pairs satisfy *equation 6.13* then we know that *equation 6.14* holds. Then since

$$C \oplus \tilde{C} = (L_4, R_4) \oplus (\tilde{L}_4, \tilde{R}_4) = \texttt{0x0202},$$

we have

$$R_4 \oplus \tilde{R}_4 = 0000\ 0010 \qquad (6.15)$$

and we also have

$$L_4 \oplus \tilde{L}_4 = 0000\ 0010. \qquad (6.16)$$

Let

$$L_4 = \ell_0\ell_1\ell_2\ell_3\ell_4\ell_5\ell_6\ell_7 \quad \text{and} \quad \tilde{L}_4 = \tilde{\ell}_0\tilde{\ell}_1\tilde{\ell}_2\tilde{\ell}_3\tilde{\ell}_4\tilde{\ell}_5\tilde{\ell}_6\tilde{\ell}_7.$$

Then *equation 6.16* implies that $\ell_i = \tilde{\ell}_i$ for $i = 0, 1, 2, 3, 4, 5, 7$ and $\ell_6 \neq \tilde{\ell}_6$. Now substituting *equation 6.15* into *equation 6.14* and expanding the definition of F, we find

$$
\begin{aligned}
0000\ 0010 = &\Big(\texttt{SboxLeft}(\ell_4\ell_7\ell_2\ell_1\ell_5\ell_7 \oplus k_0k_2k_3k_4k_5k_7), \\
&\quad \texttt{SboxRight}(\ell_0\ell_2\ell_6\ell_5\ell_0\ell_3 \oplus k_{13}k_{14}k_{15}k_9k_{10}k_{11}) \Big) \\
&\oplus \Big(\texttt{SboxLeft}(\tilde{\ell}_4\tilde{\ell}_7\tilde{\ell}_2\tilde{\ell}_1\tilde{\ell}_5\tilde{\ell}_7 \oplus k_0k_2k_3k_4k_5k_7), \\
&\quad \texttt{SboxRight}(\tilde{\ell}_0\tilde{\ell}_2\tilde{\ell}_6\tilde{\ell}_5\tilde{\ell}_0\tilde{\ell}_3 \oplus k_{13}k_{14}k_{15}k_9k_{10}k_{11}) \Big).
\end{aligned}
\qquad (6.17)
$$

The left four bits of *equation 6.17* give us

$$
\begin{aligned}
0000 = &\texttt{SboxLeft}(\ell_4\ell_7\ell_2\ell_1\ell_5\ell_7 \oplus k_0k_2k_3k_4k_5k_7) \\
&\oplus \texttt{SboxLeft}(\tilde{\ell}_4\tilde{\ell}_7\tilde{\ell}_2\tilde{\ell}_1\tilde{\ell}_5\tilde{\ell}_7 \oplus k_0k_2k_3k_4k_5k_7)
\end{aligned}
$$

which holds for any choice of the bits $k_0 k_2 k_3 k_4 k_5 k_7$, since $\ell_i = \tilde{\ell}_i$ for all $i \neq 6$. Therefore, we gain no information about the subkey K_4 from the left S-box.

On the other hand, the right four bits of *equation 6.17* give us

$$0010 = \text{SboxRight}(\ell_0 \ell_2 \ell_6 \ell_5 \ell_0 \ell_3 \oplus k_{13} k_{14} k_{15} k_9 k_{10} k_{11})$$
$$\oplus \text{SboxRight}(\tilde{\ell}_0 \tilde{\ell}_2 \tilde{\ell}_6 \tilde{\ell}_5 \tilde{\ell}_0 \tilde{\ell}_3 \oplus k_{13} k_{14} k_{15} k_9 k_{10} k_{11}) \qquad (6.18)$$

which must hold for the correct choice of subkey bits $k_{13} k_{14} k_{15} k_9 k_{10} k_{11}$ and will only hold with some probability for an incorrect choice of these subkey bits. Since the right S-box and the bits of L_4 and $\tilde{L}_4$ are known, we can determine the unknown subkey bits that appear in *equation 6.18*. The algorithm for recovering these key bits is given in Table 6.4.

Each time the `for` loop in Table 6.4 is executed, count[K] will be incremented for the correct subkey bits, that is, for $K = k_{13} k_{14} k_{15} k_9 k_{10} k_{11}$, while for other indices K the count will be incremented with some probability. Consequently, the maximum counts indicate possible subkey values. There may be more than one such maximum count, but with a sufficient number of iterations, the number of such counts should be small.

In one particular test case of the algorithm in Table 6.4, we generated 100 pairs P and $\tilde{P}$ that satisfy $P \oplus \tilde{P} = 0\text{x}0002$. We found that 47 of the resulting ciphertext pairs satisfied $C \oplus \tilde{C} = 0\text{x}0202$ and for each of these we tried all 64 possible 6-bit subkeys as required by the algorithm in Table 6.4. In this experiment, we found that each of the four putative subkeys 000001, 001001, 110000, and 000111 had the maximum count of 47, while no other had a count greater than 39. We conclude that subkey K_4 must be one of these four values. Then from the definition of K_4 we have,

$$k_{13} k_{14} k_{15} k_9 k_{10} k_{11} \in \{000001, 001001, 110000, 111000\}$$

TABLE 6.4. Algorithm to recover subkey bits.

---

count[i] = 0, for $i = 0, 1, \ldots, 63$
for $i = 1$ to iterations
    Choose P and $\tilde{P}$ with $P \oplus \tilde{P} = 0\text{x}0002$
    Obtain corresponding $C = c_0 c_1 \ldots c_{15}$ and $\tilde{C} = \tilde{c}_0 \tilde{c}_1 \ldots \tilde{c}_{15}$
    if $C \oplus \tilde{C} = 0\text{x}0202$ then
        $\ell_i = c_i$ and $\tilde{\ell}_i = \tilde{c}_i$ for $i = 0, 1, \ldots, 7$
        for $K = 0$ to 63
            if $0010 ==$ (SboxRight$(\ell_0 \ell_2 \ell_6 \ell_5 \ell_0 \ell_3 \oplus K)$
                      $\oplus$SboxRight$(\tilde{\ell}_0 \tilde{\ell}_2 \tilde{\ell}_6 \tilde{\ell}_5 \tilde{\ell}_0 \tilde{\ell}_3 \oplus K))$ then
                increment count[K]
            end if
        next K
    end if
next i

---

which is equivalent to

$$k_{13}k_{14}k_9k_{10}k_{11} \in \{00001, 11000\}. \qquad (6.19)$$

In this case, the key is

$$K = 1010\ 1001\ 1000\ 0111$$

so that $k_{13}k_{14}k_9k_{10}k_{11} = 11000$ and we see that the results in *equation 6.19* are correct.

Of course, if we're the attacker, we don't know the key, so, to complete the recovery of K, we could exhaustively search over the remaining 2^{11} unknown key bits, and for each of these try both of the possibilities in *equation 6.19*. For each of these 2^{12} putative keys K, we would try to decrypt the ciphertext and for the correct key, we will recover the plaintext. We expect to try about half of the possibilities—about 2^{11} keys—before finding the correct key K.

The total expected work to recover the entire key K by this method is about 2^{11} encryptions, plus the work required for the differential attack, which is insignificant in comparison. As a result, we can recover the entire 16-bit key with a work factor of about 2^{11} encryptions, which is much better than an exhaustive key search, which has an expected work of 2^{15} encryptions. This shows that a shortcut attack exists, and as a result TDES is insecure.

6.2.6 Linear Cryptanalysis of TDES

The linear cryptanalysis of TDES is simpler than the differential cryptanalysis. Whereas the differential cryptanalysis of TDES focused on the right S-box, our linear cryptanalysis attack will focus on the left S-box, which appears in *S-box 6.6*.

With the notation

$$y_0y_1y_2y_3 = \texttt{SboxLeft}(x_0x_1x_2x_3x_4x_5),$$

it's easy to verify that, for the left S-box of TDES, the linear approximations

$$y_1 = x_2 \quad \text{and} \quad y_2 = x_3 \qquad (6.20)$$

each hold with probability 3/4. In order to construct a linear attack using these equations, we must be able to chain these results through multiple rounds.

Denote the plaintext by $P = (L_0, R_0)$ and let $R_0 = r_0r_1r_2r_3r_4r_5r_6r_7$. Then the expansion permutation is given by

$$\texttt{expand}(R_0) = \texttt{expand}(r_0r_1r_2r_3r_4r_5r_6r_7) = r_4r_7r_2r_1r_5r_7r_0r_2r_6r_5r_0r_3. \qquad (6.21)$$

From the definition of F in *equation 6.4*, we see that the input to the S-boxes in round one is given by $\texttt{expand}(R_0) \oplus K_1$. Then from *equation 6.21* and the definition of subkey K_1, we see that the input to the left S-box in round one is

$$r_4r_7r_2r_1r_5r_7 \oplus k_2k_4k_5k_6k_7k_1.$$

Let $y_0 y_1 y_2 y_3$ be the round one output of the left S-box. Then *equation 6.20* implies that

$$y_1 = r_2 \oplus k_5 \quad \text{and} \quad y_2 = r_1 \oplus k_6, \qquad (6.22)$$

where each equality holds with probability 3/4. In other words, for the left S-box, output bit number 1 is input bit number 2, XORed with a bit of key, and output bit number 2 is input bit number 1, XORed with a key bit, where each of these hold with probability 3/4.

In TDES—as in DES—the output of the S-boxes is XORed with the old left half bits. Let $L_0 = \ell_0 \ell_1 \ell_2 \ell_3 \ell_4 \ell_5 \ell_6 \ell_7$ and let $R_1 = \tilde{r}_0 \tilde{r}_1 \tilde{r}_2 \tilde{r}_3 \tilde{r}_4 \tilde{r}_5 \tilde{r}_6 \tilde{r}_7$. Then the the output of the left S-box from round one is XORed with $\ell_0 \ell_1 \ell_2 \ell_3$ to yield $\tilde{r}_0 \tilde{r}_1 \tilde{r}_2 \tilde{r}_3$. Combining this notation with *equation 6.22*, we have

$$\tilde{r}_1 = r_2 \oplus k_5 \oplus \ell_1 \quad \text{and} \quad \tilde{r}_2 = r_1 \oplus k_6 \oplus \ell_2 \qquad (6.23)$$

where each of these equations holds with probability 3/4. An analogous result holds for subsequent rounds, where the specific key bits depend on the subkey K_i.

As a result of *equation 6.23* we can chain the linear approximation in *equation 6.20* through multiple rounds. This is illustrated in Table 6.5. Since linear cryptanalysis is a known plaintext attack, the attacker knows the plaintext $P = p_0 p_1 p_2 \ldots p_{15}$ and the corresponding ciphertext $C = c_0 c_1 c_2 \ldots c_{15}$.

The final results in Table 6.5 follow from the fact that $L_4 = c_0 c_1 c_2 c_3 c_4 c_5 c_6 c_7$. We can rewrite these equations as

$$k_0 \oplus k_1 = c_1 \oplus p_{10} \qquad (6.24)$$

and

$$k_7 \oplus k_2 = c_2 \oplus p_9 \qquad (6.25)$$

where both hold with probability $(3/4)^3$. Since c_1, c_2, p_9, and p_{10} are all known, we have obtained some information about the key bits k_0, k_1, k_2, and k_7.

TABLE 6.5. Linear cryptanalysis of TDES.

$(L_0, R_0) = (p_0 \ldots p_7, p_8 \ldots p_{15})$	Bits 1 and 2 (numbered from 0)	Probability
$L_1 = R_0$	p_9, p_{10}	1
$R_1 = L_0 \oplus F(R_0, K_1)$	$p_1 \oplus p_{10} \oplus k_5, \quad p_2 \oplus p_9 \oplus k_6$	3/4
$L_2 = R_1$	$p_1 \oplus p_{10} \oplus k_5, \quad p_2 \oplus p_9 \oplus k_6$	3/4
$R_2 = L_1 \oplus F(R_1, K_2)$	$p_2 \oplus k_6 \oplus k_7, \quad p_1 \oplus k_5 \oplus k_0$	$(3/4)^2$
$L_3 = R_2$	$p_2 \oplus k_6 \oplus k_7, \quad p_1 \oplus k_5 \oplus k_0$	$(3/4)^2$
$R_3 = L_2 \oplus F(R_2, K_3)$	$p_{10} \oplus k_0 \oplus k_1, \quad p_9 \oplus k_7 \oplus k_2$	$(3/4)^3$
$L_4 = R_3$	$p_{10} \oplus k_0 \oplus k_1, \quad p_9 \oplus k_7 \oplus k_2$	$(3/4)^3$
$R_4 = L_3 \oplus F(R_3, K_4)$		
$C = (L_4, R_4)$	$c_1 = p_{10} \oplus k_0 \oplus k_1, \quad c_2 = p_9 \oplus k_7 \oplus k_2$	$(3/4)^3$

It's easy to implement a linear attack based on the results in Table 6.5. We are given the known plaintexts $P = p_0 p_1 p_2 \ldots p_{15}$ along with the corresponding ciphertext $C = c_0 c_1 c_2 \ldots c_{15}$. For each such pair, we increment a counter depending on whether

$$c_1 \oplus p_{10} = 0 \quad \text{or} \quad c_1 \oplus p_{10} = 1$$

and another counter depending on whether

$$c_2 \oplus p_9 = 0 \quad \text{or} \quad c_2 \oplus p_9 = 1.$$

For example, with 100 known plaintexts the following results were obtained

$$c_1 \oplus p_{10} = 0 \text{ occurred 38 times}$$
$$c_1 \oplus p_{10} = 1 \text{ occurred 62 times}$$
$$c_2 \oplus p_9 = 0 \text{ occurred 62 times}$$
$$c_2 \oplus p_9 = 1 \text{ occurred 38 times}$$

In this case, we conclude from *equation 6.24* that

$$k_0 \oplus k_1 = 1$$

and from *equation 6.25* that

$$k_7 \oplus k_2 = 0$$

In this example, the actual key is

$$K = 1010\ 0011\ 0101\ 0110$$

and we see that we've obtained correct results.

In this linear attack, we have only recovered the equivalent of two bits of information. To recover the entire key K, we could do an exhaustive key search for the remaining unknown bits. This would require an expected work of about 2^{13} encryptions, and the work for the linear attack is negligible in comparison. While this may not seem too significant, it is a shortcut attack, and so it shows that TDES is insecure, according to our definition.

6.2.7 Block Cipher Design

Since there is no way to prove that a practical cipher is secure and since it's difficult to protect against unknown attacks, cryptographers focus on preventing known attacks. For block ciphers, the known attacks are, primarily, linear and differential cryptanalysis— and variations on these approaches. Thus the primary goal in block cipher design is to make linear and differential attacks infeasible.

How can cryptographers make linear and differential attacks more difficult? For an iterated block ciphers, the crucial trade-offs are between the number of rounds, the degree of confusion, and the amount of diffusion.

In both linear and differential attacks, any one-round success probability that is less than 1 will almost certainly diminish with each subsequent round. Consequently, all else being equal, a block cipher with more rounds will be more secure from linear and differential attacks.

Another way to make linear and differential attacks more difficult is to have a high degree of confusion. That is, we can strive to reduce the success probability per round. For a DES-like cipher, this is equivalent to building better S-boxes. All else being equal, more confusion means more security.

On the other hand, better diffusion will also tend to make linear and differential attacks harder to mount. In both types of attacks, it is necessary to chain results through multiple rounds, and better diffusion will make it harder to connect one-round successes into usable chains.

In TDES, the number of rounds is small, and, as a result, the one-round success probabilities are not sufficiently diminished by encryption. Also, the TDES S-boxes are poorly designed, resulting in limited confusion. Finally, the TDES expand permutation—the only source of diffusion in the cipher—does a poor job of mixing the bits into the next round. All of these combine to yield a cipher that is highly susceptible to both linear and differential attacks.

To complicate the lives of block cipher designers, they must construct ciphers that are secure and efficient. One of the fundamental issues that block cipher designers face is the trade-off between the number of rounds and the complexity of each round. That is, a block cipher with a simple round structure will tend to provide limited mixing (diffusion) and limited nonlinearity (confusion), and consequently more rounds will be required. The Tiny Encryption Algorithm (TEA) is a good example of such a cipher. Each round of TEA is extremely simple, and as a result the confusion and diffusion properties are fairly weak, so a large number of rounds are required. At the other extreme, each round of the Advanced Encryption Standard (AES) has strong linear mixing and excellent nonlinear properties. So a relatively small number of AES rounds are needed, but each AES round is far more complex than each round of TEA.

6.3 SIDE CHANNEL ATTACK ON RSA

Often it's possible to attack a cipher without directly attacking the algorithm [66]. Many processes produce unintended "side channels" that leak information. This incidental information can arise due to the way that a computation is performed, the media used, the power consumed, electromagnetic emanations, and so on.

Paul Kocher is the leader in the field of side channel attacks [128]. Kocher's discovery of such attacks on smartcards delayed the widespread acceptance of smartcards by several years.

A large potential source of side channel information arises from so-called unintended emanations. There is an entire branch of security devoted to emissions security, or

TABLE 6.6. Repeated squaring.

```
x = M
for j = 1 to n
    x = mod(x², N)
    if dⱼ == 1 then
        x = mod(xM, N)
    end if
next j
return x
```

EMSEC, which is also goes by the name of TEMPEST [154]. For example, Anderson [14] describes how electromagnetic fields, or EMF, from a computer screen can allow the screen image to be reconstructed at a distance.

Smartcards have been attacked via their EMF emanations as well as by *differential power analysis*, or DPA, which exploits the fact that some computations require more energy consumption than others [127]. Attacks on EMF emissions and DPA attacks are passive. More active attacks often go by the name of *differential fault analysis* or DFA, where faults are induced with the goal of recovering information [11]. For example, excessive power may be put into a device in order to induce a fault. Such attacks may or may not be destructive. A smartcard used in some GSM cell phones could be attacked using DFA techniques [172].

In this section, we'll examine a timing attack on RSA. This attack exploits the fact that some computations in RSA take longer than others. By carefully measuring the time that an operation takes, we can determine the RSA private key [249]. A similar attack is robust enough that it has been successfully conducted against the RSA implementation in a version of openSSL over a network connection [33].

Let M be a message that Alice is to sign and let d be Alice's private key. Then Alice signs M by computing $M^d \bmod N$. Suppose that Trudy's goal is to find Alice's private key d. We'll assume that d is $n + 1$ bits in length and we'll denote the bits of d as

$$d = d_0 d_1 \ldots d_n \quad \text{where } d_0 = 1.$$

Recall that the method of repeated squaring provides an efficient means of computing modular exponentiation. Suppose repeated squaring is used to compute $M^d \bmod N$. The repeated squaring algorithm appears in Table 6.6.

Suppose that the $\text{mod}(x, N)$ in Table 6.6 is implemented as shown in Table 6.7. For efficiency, the expensive mod operation, denoted by "%," is only executed if a modular reduction is actually required.

Now consider the repeated squaring algorithm in Table 6.6. If $d_j = 0$ then $x = \text{mod}(x^2, N)$, but if $d_j = 1$ then two operations occur, namely, $x = \text{mod}(x^2, N)$ and $x = \text{mod}(xM, N)$. As a result, the computation time should differ when $d_j = 0$ compared with when $d_j = 1$. Can Trudy take advantage of this to recover Alice's private key?

We'll assume that Trudy can conduct a "chosen plaintext" attack; that is, she can get Alice to sign selected messages. Suppose Trudy chooses two values, Y and Z, with $Y^3 < N$ and $Z^2 < N < Z^3$ and Alice signs both.

TABLE 6.7. Efficient mod function.

$$\text{mod}(x, N)$$
```
if x >= N
    x = x % N
end if
return x
```

Let $x = Y$ and consider the $j = 1$ step in the repeated squaring algorithm of Table 6.6. We have

$$x = \text{mod}(x^2, N)$$

and since $x^3 < N$, the "%" operation does not occur. Then

$$x = \text{mod}(xY, N)$$

and, again, the "%" operation does not occur.

Now let $x = Z$ and consider the $j = 1$ step in the algorithm of Table 6.6. In this case, we have

$$x = \text{mod}(x^2, N)$$

and, since $x^2 < N < x^3$, the "%" operation does not occur. Then

$$x = \text{mod}(xZ, N)$$

and the "%" operation occurs only if $d_1 = 1$. As a result, if $d_1 = 1$ then the $j = 1$ step requires more computation and will take longer to complete for Z than for Y. If, on the other hand, $d_1 = 0$, the computations for Z and Y take about the same amount of time. Using this fact, Trudy may be able to recover the bit d_1 of the private key d. But she'll need to rely on statistics to make this reliable, particularly over a network, where random fluctuations in timings can occur.

Trudy can use the following algorithm to determine d_1. For $i = 0, 1, \dots, m - 1$, Trudy chooses Y_i with $Y_i^3 < N$. Then let y_i be the time required for Alice to sign Y_i, that is, the time required to compute $Y_i^d \mod N$. Then Trudy computes the average timing

$$y = \frac{y_0 + y_1 + \cdots + y_{m-1}}{m}.$$

Then for $i = 0, 1, \dots, m - 1$, Trudy chooses Z_i with $Z_i^2 < N < Z_i^3$. Let z_i be the time required to compute $Z_i^d \mod N$. Then Trudy computes the average timing

$$z = \frac{z_0 + z_1 + \cdots + z_{m-1}}{m}.$$

If $z > y$ then Trudy would assume that $d_1 = 1$; otherwise, she would suspect $d_1 = 0$. Once d_1 has been recovered, Trudy can use an analogous process to find d_2, though the Y and Z values will need to be chosen to satisfy different criteria. Once d_2 is known, Trudy can proceed to d_3 and so on.

The lesson of side channel attacks is an important one that goes well beyond the details of any particular attack. Side channel attacks tell us that even if crypto is secure in theory, it may not be so in practice. As a result, it's not sufficient to analyze a cipher in isolation. For a cipher to be secure in practice, it must be analyzed in the context of a specific implementation and the larger system in which it resides, even though such factors don't directly relate to the mathematical properties of the cipher itself. Schneier has an excellent article that addresses some of these issues [201].

Side channel attacks nicely illustrate that attackers don't always play by the (presumed) rules. Attackers will try to exploit the weakest link in any security system. The best way to protect against such attacks is to think like an attacker.

6.4 LATTICE REDUCTION AND THE KNAPSACK

In this section, we present the details of the successful attack on the original Merkle-Hellman knapsack cryptosystem. A more rigorous—but readable—presentation can be found in [134]. Some linear algebra is required in this section. The Appendix contains a review of the necessary material.

Let $b_1, b_2, \ldots, b_n$ be vectors in $\mathcal{R}^m$; that is, each b_i is a (column) vector consisting of exactly m real numbers. A *lattice* is the set of all multiples of the vector b_i of the form

$$\alpha_1 b_1 + \alpha_2 b_2 + \cdots + \alpha_n b_n,$$

where each α_i in an integer.

For example, consider the vectors

$$b_1 = \begin{bmatrix} -1 \\ 1 \end{bmatrix} \quad \text{and} \quad b_2 = \begin{bmatrix} 1 \\ 2 \end{bmatrix}. \tag{6.26}$$

Since b_1 and b_2 are linearly independent, any point in the plane can be written as $\alpha_1 b_1 + \alpha_2 b_2$ for some real numbers α_1 and α_2. We say that the plane $\mathcal{R}^2$ is *spanned* by the pair (b_1, b_2). If we restrict α_1 and α_2 to integers, then the resulting span, that is all points of the form $\alpha_1 b_1 + \alpha_2 b_2$, is a *lattice*. A lattice consists of a discrete set of points. For example, the lattice spanned by the the vectors in *equation 6.26* is illustrated in Figure 6.3.

Many combinatorial problems can be reduced to the problem of finding a "short" vector in a lattice. The knapsack is one such problem. Short vectors in a lattice can be found using a technique known as *lattice reduction*.

Before discussing the lattice reduction attack on the knapsack, let's first consider another combinatorial problem that can be solved using this technique. The problem that we'll consider is the *exact cover*, which can be stated as follows. Given a set S and a collection of subsets of S, find a collection of these subsets where each element of S is

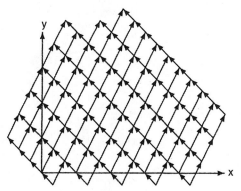

Figure 6.3. A lattice in the plane.

in exactly one subset. It's not always possible to find such a collection of subsets, but, if it is, we'll see that the solution is a short vector in a particular lattice.

Consider the following example of the exact cover problem. Let

$$S = \{0, 1, 2, 3, 4, 5, 6\}$$

and suppose we are given the following 13 subsets of S, which we label s_0 through s_{12},

$$s_0 = \{0, 1, 3\}, s_1 = \{0, 1, 5\}, s_2 = \{0, 2, 4\}, s_3 = \{0, 2, 5\},$$

$$s_4 = \{0, 3, 6\}, s_5 = \{1, 2, 4\}, s_6 = \{1, 2, 6\}, s_7 = \{1, 3, 5\},$$

$$s_8 = \{1, 4, 6\}, s_9 = \{1\}, s_{10} = \{2, 5, 6\}, s_{11} = \{3, 4, 5\}, s_{12} = \{3, 4, 6\}.$$

Denote the number of elements of S by m and the number of subsets by n. In this example, we have $m = 7$ and $n = 13$. Can we find a collection of these 13 subsets where each element of S is in exactly one subset?

There are 2^{13} different collections of the 13 subsets, so we could exhaustively search through all possible collections until we find such a collection—or until we've tried them all, in which case we would conclude that no such collection exists. But if there are too many subsets, then we need an alternative approach.

One alternative is to try a *heuristic search* technique. There are many different types of heuristic search strategies, but what they all have in common is that they search through the set of possible solutions in a nonrandom manner. The goal of such a search strategy is to search in a "smart" way, to improve the odds of finding a solution sooner than in an exhaustive search.

Lattice reduction can be viewed as a form of heuristic search. As a result, we are not assured of finding a solution using lattice reduction, but for many problems this techniques yields a solution with a high probability, yet the work required is small in comparison to an exhaustive search.

Before we can apply the lattice reduction method, we first need to rewrite the exact cover problem in matrix form. We define an $m \times n$ matrix A, where $a_{ij} = 1$ if element i

of S is in subset s_j. Otherwise, let $a_{ij} = 0$. Also, we define B to be a vector of length m consisting of all 1s. Then, if we can solve $AU = B$ for a vector U of 0s and 1s, we have solved the exact cover problem.

For the exact cover example discussed above, the matrix equation $AU = B$ has the form

$$
\begin{bmatrix}
1 & 1 & 1 & 1 & 1 & 0 & 0 & 0 & 0 & 0 & 0 & 0 & 0 \\
1 & 1 & 0 & 0 & 0 & 1 & 1 & 1 & 1 & 1 & 0 & 0 & 0 \\
0 & 0 & 1 & 1 & 0 & 1 & 1 & 0 & 0 & 0 & 1 & 0 & 0 \\
1 & 0 & 0 & 0 & 1 & 0 & 0 & 1 & 0 & 0 & 0 & 1 & 1 \\
0 & 0 & 1 & 1 & 0 & 1 & 1 & 0 & 0 & 0 & 1 & 0 & 0 \\
0 & 1 & 0 & 1 & 0 & 0 & 0 & 1 & 0 & 0 & 1 & 1 & 0 \\
0 & 0 & 0 & 0 & 1 & 0 & 1 & 0 & 1 & 0 & 1 & 0 & 1
\end{bmatrix}
\begin{bmatrix}
u_0 \\ u_1 \\ u_2 \\ u_3 \\ u_4 \\ u_5 \\ u_6 \\ u_7 \\ u_8 \\ u_9 \\ u_{10} \\ u_{11} \\ u_{12}
\end{bmatrix}
=
\begin{bmatrix}
1 \\ 1 \\ 1 \\ 1 \\ 1 \\ 1 \\ 1
\end{bmatrix}
$$

and we seek a solution U where each $u_i \in \{0, 1\}$, that is, $u_i = 1$ if the subset s_i is in the exact cover and $u_i = 0$ if subset s_i is not in the exact cover. In this particular case, it's easy to verify that a solution is given by $U = [0001000001001]$; that is, s_3, s_9 and s_{12} form an exact cover of the set S.

We have shown that the exact cover problem can be restated as finding a solution U to a matrix equation $AU = B$, where U consists entirely of 0s and 1s. This is not a standard linear algebra problem, since solutions to linear equations are not restricted to contain only 0s and 1s. But this turns out to be a problem that can be solved using lattice reduction techniques. But first, we need an elementary fact from linear algebra.

Suppose $AU = B$ where A is a matrix and U and B are column vectors. Let $a_1, a_2, \ldots, a_n$ denote the columns of A and $u_1, u_2, \ldots, u_n$ the elements of U. Then

$$B = u_1 a_1 + u_2 a_2 + \cdots + u_n a_n. \tag{6.27}$$

For example

$$
\begin{bmatrix} 3 & 4 \\ 1 & 5 \end{bmatrix} \begin{bmatrix} 2 \\ 6 \end{bmatrix} = 2 \begin{bmatrix} 3 \\ 1 \end{bmatrix} + 6 \begin{bmatrix} 4 \\ 5 \end{bmatrix} = \begin{bmatrix} 30 \\ 32 \end{bmatrix}
$$

Now given $AU = B$, consider the matrix equation

$$
\begin{bmatrix} I_{n \times n} & 0_{n \times 1} \\ A_{m \times n} & -B_{m \times 1} \end{bmatrix} \begin{bmatrix} U_{n \times 1} \\ 1_{1 \times 1} \end{bmatrix} = \begin{bmatrix} U_{n \times 1} \\ 0_{m \times 1} \end{bmatrix}
$$

which we denote as $MV = W$. Multiplying, we find the trivial equation $U = U$ and the nontrivial equation $AU - B = 0$. Therefore, finding a solution V to $MV = W$ is equivalent to finding a solution U to the original equation $AU = B$.

The benefit of rewriting the problem as $MV = W$ is that the columns of M are linearly independent. This is easily seen to be the case, since the $n \times n$ identity matrix appears in the upper left, and the final column begins with n zeros.

Let $c_0, c_1, c_2, \dots, c_n$ be the $n + 1$ columns of M and let $v_0, v_1, v_2, \dots, v_n$ be the elements of V. Then by the observation in *equation 6.27*, we have

$$W = v_0 c_0 + v_1 c_1 + \cdots + v_n c_n. \tag{6.28}$$

Let $\mathcal{L}$ be the lattice spanned by $c_0, c_1, c_2, \dots, c_n$, the columns of M. Then $\mathcal{L}$ consists of all integer multiples of the columns of M. Recall that $MV = W$, where

$$W = \begin{bmatrix} u_0 \\ u_1 \\ \vdots \\ u_{n-1} \\ 0 \\ \vdots \\ 0 \end{bmatrix}.$$

Our goal is to find U. However, instead of solving linear equations for V, we can solve for U by finding W. By *equation 6.28*, this desired solution W is in the lattice $\mathcal{L}$.

The Euclidean length of a vector $Y = (y_0, y_1, \dots, y_{n-1}) \in \mathcal{R}^n$ is given by the formula

$$\|Y\| = \sqrt{y_0^2 + y_1^2 + \cdots + y_{n-1}^2}.$$

Then the length of W is

$$\|W\| = \sqrt{u_0^2 + u_1^2 + \cdots + u_{n-1}^2} \le \sqrt{n}.$$

Since most vectors in $\mathcal{L}$ will have a length far greater than $\sqrt{n}$, we conclude that W is a short vector in the lattice $\mathcal{L}$. Furthermore, W has a very special form, with its first n entries all equal to 0 or 1 and its last m entries all equal to 0. These facts distinguish W from typical vectors in $\mathcal{L}$. Can we use this information to find W, which would give us a solution to the exact cover problem?

In fact, there is an algorithm known as the LLL algorithm [130, 145] (because it was invented by three guys whose names start with "L") to efficiently find short vectors in a lattice. Our strategy will be to use LLL to find short vectors in $\mathcal{L}$, the lattice spanned by the columns of M. Then we'll examine these short vectors to see whether any have the special form of W. If we find such a vector, then it is highly probably that we have found a solution U to the original problem.

Pseudo-code for the LLL algorithm appears in Table 6.8, where the $(n + m) \times (n + 1)$ matrix M has columns $b_0, b_1, b_2, \dots, b_n$ and the columns of matrix X are denoted $x_0, x_1, x_2, \dots, x_n$ and the elements of Y are denoted y_{ij}. Note that the y_{ij} can be negative, so care must be taken when implementing the floor function in $\lfloor y_{ij} + 1/2 \rfloor$.

TABLE 6.8. LLL algorithm.

```
                // find short vectors in the lattice spanned
                // by columns of M = (b₀, b₁ , ... , bₙ)
                loop forever
                    (X, Y) = GS(M)
                    for j = 1 to n
                        for i = j − 1 to 0
                            if |yᵢⱼ| > 1/2 then
                                bⱼ = bⱼ − ⌊yᵢⱼ + 1/2⌋bᵢ
                            end if
                        next i
                    next j
                    (X, Y) = GS(M)
                    for j = 0 to n − 1
                        if ‖xⱼ₊₁ + yⱼ,ⱼ₊₁xⱼ‖² < ¾‖xⱼ‖²
                            swap(bⱼ, bⱼ₊₁)
                            goto abc
                        end if
                    next j
                    return(M)
        abc:        continue
                end loop
```

For completeness, we've given the Gram-Schmidt orthogonalization algorithm in Table 6.9. Combined, these two algorithms are stated in about 30 lines of pseudo-code.

It's important to realize there is no guarantee that the LLL algorithm will find the desired vector W. But for certain types of problems, the probability of success is high.

By now, you may be wondering what any of this has to do with the knapsack cryptosystem. Next, we'll show that we can attack the knapsack via lattice reduction.

TABLE 6.9. Gram-Schmidt algorithm.

```
                // Gram-Schmidt M = (b₀, b₁ , ... , bₙ)
                GS(M)
                    x₀ = b₀
                    for j = 1 to n
                        xⱼ = bⱼ
                        for i = 0 to j − 1
                            yᵢⱼ = (xᵢ · bⱼ)/‖xᵢ‖²
                            xⱼ = xⱼ − yᵢⱼxᵢ
                        next i
                    next j
                    return(X,Y)
                end GS
```

Let's consider the superincreasing knapsack

$$S = [s_0, s_1, \ldots, s_7] = [2, 3, 7, 14, 30, 57, 120, 251]$$

and let's choose the multiplier $m = 41$ and the modulus $n = 491$ (this is the same knapsack that appears in Section 4.2 of Chapter 4). Then $m^{-1} = 12 \bmod 491$. To find the corresponding public knapsack, we compute $t_i = 41 s_i \bmod 491$ for $i = 0, 1, \ldots, 7$, and the result is

$$T = [t_0, t_1, \ldots, t_7] = [82, 123, 287, 83, 248, 373, 10, 471].$$

This yields the knapsack cryptosystem defined by

Public key: T

and

Private key: S and $m^{-1} \bmod n.$

For example, 10010110 is encrypted as

$$1 \cdot t_0 + 0 \cdot t_1 + 0 \cdot t_2 + 1 \cdot t_3 + 0 \cdot t_4 + 1 \cdot t_5 + 1 \cdot t_6 + 0 \cdot t_7 = 82 + 83 + 373 + 10 = 548.$$

To decrypt the ciphertext 548, the holder of the private key computes

$$548 \cdot 12 = 193 \bmod 491$$

and then uses the superincreasing knapsack S to easily solve for the plaintext 10010110.

In this particular example, the attacker Trudy knows the public key T and the ciphertext 548. Trudy can break the system if she can find $u_i \in \{0, 1\}$ so that

$$82u_0 + 123u_1 + 287u_2 + 83u_3 + 248u_4 + 373u_5 + 10u_6 + 471u_7 = 548. \quad (6.29)$$

To put this problem into the correct framework for lattice reduction, we rewrite the problem in matrix form as

$$T \cdot U = 548$$

where T is the public knapsack and $U = [u_0, u_1, \ldots, u_7]$ appears in *equation 6.29*. This has the same form as $AU = B$ discussed above, so we rewrite this to put it into the form $MV = W$, which is then suitable for the LLL algorithm. In this case we have

$$M = \begin{bmatrix} I_{8\times8} & 0_{8\times1} \\ T_{1\times8} & -C_{1\times1} \end{bmatrix} = \left[\begin{array}{cccccccc|c} 1 & 0 & 0 & 0 & 0 & 0 & 0 & 0 & 0 \\ 0 & 1 & 0 & 0 & 0 & 0 & 0 & 0 & 0 \\ 0 & 0 & 1 & 0 & 0 & 0 & 0 & 0 & 0 \\ 0 & 0 & 0 & 1 & 0 & 0 & 0 & 0 & 0 \\ 0 & 0 & 0 & 0 & 1 & 0 & 0 & 0 & 0 \\ 0 & 0 & 0 & 0 & 0 & 1 & 0 & 0 & 0 \\ 0 & 0 & 0 & 0 & 0 & 0 & 1 & 0 & 0 \\ 0 & 0 & 0 & 0 & 0 & 0 & 0 & 1 & 0 \\ 82 & 123 & 287 & 83 & 248 & 373 & 10 & 471 & -548 \end{array} \right]$$

We can now apply LLL to the matrix M to find short vectors in the lattice spanned by the columns of M. The output of LLL, which we denote by M', is a matrix of short vectors in the lattice spanned by the columns of M. In this example, LLL yields

$$
M' =
\left[
\begin{array}{rrrrrrrr|r}
-1 & -1 & 0 & 1 & 0 & 1 & 0 & 0 & 1 \\
0 & -1 & 1 & 0 & 1 & -1 & 0 & 0 & 0 \\
0 & 1 & -1 & 0 & 0 & 0 & -1 & 1 & 2 \\
1 & -1 & -1 & 1 & 0 & -1 & 0 & -1 & 0 \\
0 & 0 & 1 & 0 & -2 & -1 & 0 & 1 & 0 \\
0 & 0 & 0 & 1 & 1 & 1 & 1 & -1 & 1 \\
0 & 0 & 0 & 1 & 0 & 0 & -1 & 0 & -1 \\
0 & 0 & 0 & 0 & 0 & 0 & 1 & 1 & -1 \\
\hline
1 & -1 & 1 & 0 & 0 & 1 & -1 & 2 & 0
\end{array}
\right]
$$

The 4th column of M' has the correct form to be a solution to the knapsack problem. For this column, Trudy obtains the putative solution

$$U = [1, 0, 0, 1, 0, 1, 1, 0]$$

and using the public key and the ciphertext, she can then easily verify that 10010110 is, in fact, the correct solution. One interesting aspect of this particular attack is that Trudy can find the plaintext from the ciphertext without recovering the private key.

The lattice reduction attack on the knapsack is fast and efficient—it was originally demonstrated using an Apple II computer in 1983 [205]. Although the attack is not always successful, the probability of success against the original Merkle-Hellman knapsack is high.

Lattice reduction was a surprising method of attack on the knapsack cryptosystem. The lesson here is that clever mathematics can break cryptosystems.

6.5 HELLMAN'S TIME-MEMORY TRADE-OFF

In a time-memory trade-off, or TMTO, the objective is to balance one-time work—the result of which is stored in "memory"—with the "time" required when the algorithm is executed. A TMTO is not an algorithm per se, but instead it's a general technique that can be applied to improve the performance of many different algorithms. In some cases, the time versus memory trade-off is obvious, but in some cases it's not.

In this section, we'll first consider a simple TMTO to illustrate the concept. Then we'll present Hellman's cryptanalytic TMTO, which is somewhat more involved.

6.5.1 Popcnt

Given a nonnegative integer x, its "population count," or $\texttt{popcnt}(x)$, is the number of ones in the binary expansion of x. For example, $\texttt{popcnt}(13) = 3$, since 13 is binary 1101.

TABLE 6.10. Simple popcnt.

$t = 0$
for $i = 0$ to 31
$\quad t = t + (x \gg i)\,\&\,1$
next i

The most obvious way to compute popcnt(x) is to simply count the number of ones in the binary expansion of x. This is precisely what the pseudo-code in Table 6.10 does, where we have assumed that x is a 32-bit integer, and we use the notation "$\gg$" for the right shift and "$\&$" is the binary AND operation. Note that the algorithm in Table 6.10 requires 32 steps.

We can obtain a faster popcnt(x) by employing a precomputation and using some memory to store the precomputed results. For example, we can precompute popcnt(y) for each byte value $y \in \{0, 1, \ldots, 255\}$ and store the resulting values in an array, say, $p[y]$. Then popcnt(x), where x is again a 32-bit integer, can be computed using the algorithm in Table 6.11.

The TMTO in Table 6.11 requires only four steps—as opposed to 32 for the version in Table 6.10—but it also requires memory of size 256, along with the one-time work of computing the values stored in $p[y]$. If popcnt(x) is to be computed for many different values of x, then the TMTO in Table 6.11 is far more efficient than the naïve approach in Table 6.10.

6.5.2 Cryptanalytic TMTO

Hellman, of Diffie-Hellman fame (and Merkle-Hellman knapsack infamy), described a cryptanalytic TMTO attack in [105]. Hellman's attack was specifically designed for DES, although the same technique is applicable to any block cipher. Hellman's TMTO is a chosen plaintext attack.

Let K be a key, P a chosen plaintext block, and $C = E(P, K)$. As usual, Trudy's goal is to recover the key K. One way to beak any cipher is via an exhaustive key search. If K is of length k, then there are 2^k possible keys and Trudy can expect to find K after trying about half of the keys. That is, in the exhaustive key search case, the "time" requirement is about 2^{k-1}, while the "memory" requirement is negligible.

At the other extreme, Trudy could precompute the ciphertext C for each possible key K for a specific chosen plaintext P. This attack requires one-time work of 2^k and storage of 2^k, but then each time Trudy conducts the attack, only a single table lookup is required. Neglecting the one-time work, the "time" per attack is negligible, but the "memory" is 2^k.

TABLE 6.11. TMTO for popcnt.

$t = p[x\,\&\,\texttt{0xff}] + p[(x \gg 8)\,\&\,\texttt{0xff}] + p[(x \gg 16)\,\&\,\texttt{0xff}] + p[(x \gg 24)\,\&\,\texttt{0xff}]$

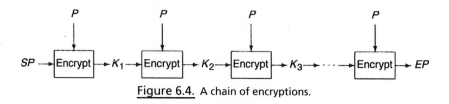

Figure 6.4. A chain of encryptions.

Hellman's TMTO attack aims for a middle ground between these two extremes. The attack requires some one-time work, producing a table (the "memory" part of the TMTO) that is then used to reduce the amount of work required (the "time" part of the TMTO) whenever the attack is executed.

To illustrate Hellman's TMTO, we'll first consider a generic block cipher with block size $n = 64$ bits and key size $k = 64$. Since the key is 64 bits, there are 2^{64} distinct keys—which is said to be equal to the number of blades of grass on earth. We'll choose a fixed plaintext P for which we obtain the corresponding ciphertext $C = E(P, K)$. The challenge is to recover the unknown key K.

Suppose we randomly select a 64-bit value SP, where SP will be the "starting point" of an encryption *chain*. We'll compute this encryption chain as

$$K_0 = SP$$
$$K_1 = E(P, SP)$$
$$K_2 = E(P, K_1)$$
$$K_3 = E(P, K_2)$$
$$\vdots$$
$$K_{t-1} = EP = E(P, K_{t-2})$$

where $EP = K_{t-1}$ is the ending point of the chain of length t. That is, we use the ciphertext generated at one step as the key at the next step. Figure 6.4 illustrates this process with a generic "black box" cipher. Another way to view the encryption chain is given in Figure 6.5, where we've illustrated the chain as a path in the space of possible keys.

Suppose we generate m chains, each of length t. Further, suppose we could choose $t = 2^{32}$ and $m = 2^{32}$ so that none of the resulting chains overlap.[1] Then each

Figure 6.5. Another view of a chain of encryptions.

------

[1]This is totally unrealistic, but it allows us to easily describe the concept behind Hellman's TMTO. We return to reality below.

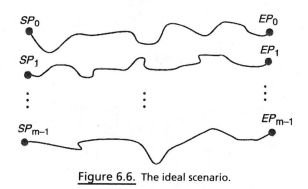

Figure 6.6. The ideal scenario.

of the 2^{64} possible key values would appear within one—and only one—chain. This idealized situation is illustrated in Figure 6.6.

The "memory" part of the TMTO is implemented by storing only the starting points and ending points of the chains; that is, we store

$$(SP_0, EP_0), (SP_1, EP_1), (SP_2, EP_2), \ldots, (SP_{m-1}, EP_{m-1}).$$

If $m = 2^{32}$, then the storage requirement, in terms of 64-bit words, is $2m = 2^{33}$. Note that this is one-time work and these tabulated results will be used each time the attack is conducted.

The actual attack—the "time" part of the TMTO—is implemented as follows. Whenever Trudy wants to conduct the attack, she will choose the specific plaintext P and somehow obtain the corresponding ciphertext C. Of course, she wants to find the key K. Trudy computes an encryption chain beginning with C as

$$X_0 = C$$
$$X_1 = E(P, X_0)$$
$$X_2 = E(P, X_1)$$
$$X_3 = E(P, X_2)$$
$$\vdots$$
$$X_{t-1} = E(P, X_{t-2})$$

where at each step $i = 1, 2, \ldots, t-1$, she compares X_i to each of the stored endpoints

$$EP_0, EP_1, \ldots, EP_{m-1}.$$

Since C is itself a possible key value, by our idealized assumption, it lies somewhere within one (and only one) chain. Suppose C lies within chain j. Then for some $i \in \{0, 1, \ldots, t-1\}$, Trudy finds $X_i = EP_j$. This situation is illustrated in Figure 6.7.

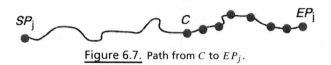

Figure 6.7. Path from C to EP_j.

Given such an i and j, Trudy can reconstruct the initial part of chain j by starting at SP_j,

$$Y_0 = SP_j$$
$$Y_1 = E(P, Y_0)$$
$$Y_2 = E(P, Y_1)$$
$$Y_3 = E(P, Y_2)$$
$$\vdots$$
$$Y_{t-i-1} = E(P, Y_{t-i-2})$$
$$Y_{t-i} = X_0 = E(P, Y_{t-i-1}).$$

Since $X_0 = C = E(P, K)$, Trudy has found the desired key, namely, $K = Y_{t-i-1}$. This is illustrated in Figure 6.8.

In this idealized example, the precomputation phase requires about $tm = 2^{64}$ work. Having paid this initial price, each time the attack is subsequently executed, only about 2^{31} encryptions will be required (on average) before an endpoint is found. Another 2^{31} encryptions (on average) are needed until C is recovered from a particular chain, giving a total work factor of about 2^{32} per attack.

If the attack is only to be executed once, a straightforward exhaustive key search will find K with an expected work of 2^{63}, in which case it would make no sense to precompute the encryption chains. However, if the attack is to be conducted many times, the precomputation work can be amortized over the number of attacks, and the work of 2^{32} per attack is negligible in comparison to an the exhaustive key search time of 2^{63}.

We could reduce the precomputation work by computing chains that only cover a part of the key space. Then the probability of successfully finding an unknown key would be equal to the proportion of the key space that is covered by chains. Out of necessity, this is the way that Hellman's cryptanalytic TMTO attack is actually implemented.

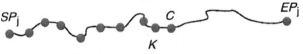

Figure 6.8. Finding K from SP_j.

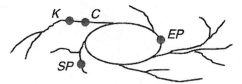

Figure 6.9. Bad chains.

6.5.3 Misbehaving Chains

In the real world, when an encryption chain is generated, bad things can happen. One bad thing occurs when a chain overlaps with itself, forming a cycle. Another bad thing occurs when two chains merge into a single chain. Both merging and cycling chains are illustrated in Figure 6.9.

Suppose we execute a TMTO attack beginning from C in Figure 6.9. Then following the algorithm described in the previous section, we eventually arrive at the endpoint EP. We then go to SP to reconstruct the chain that we expect to lead us to the key K. However, in this case, we won't find K since C is not on the (SP, EP) chain, even though we arrived at EP from C. We'll refer to this as a false alarm.

To decrease the number of false alarms, we must decrease the number of cycling and merging chains. In order to accomplish this, a "random function" F is used and a chain is computed as

$$K_0 = SP$$
$$K_1 = F(E(P, SP))$$
$$K_2 = F(E(P, K_1))$$
$$K_3 = F(E(P, K_2))$$
$$\vdots$$
$$K_{t-1} = EP = F(E(P, K_{t-2})).$$

When $n = k$, we can choose F to be a permutation. We'll need a large supply of functions F, and, fortunately, there is no shortage of permutations.

The advantage of these random functions can be seen in Figure 6.10. Without the use of these functions (or if the same function was used on both chains), once the chains collide, they will necessarily merge into a single chain. By using different functions F_0 and F_1, the chains almost certainly will not merge.

We'll choose r different functions F_i, and for each of these we'll construct m chains, each with a randomly selected starting point. As above, each chain is of length t. The set of chains that correspond to a specific function is known as a *table*. To summarize,

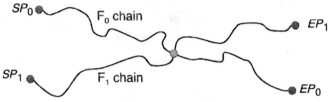

Figure 6.10. Preventing merging chains.

we have

$$r = \text{number of tables}$$
$$m = \text{number of chains in each table}$$
$$t = \text{length of each chain.}$$

The cryptanalytic TMTO precomputation will effectively cover some percentage of the key space with chains. The resulting TMTO attack will find any key that lies within some chain, but a key that doesn't appear within any chain can't be found with the TMTO attack. The attack is therefore probabilistic and the objective is to maximize the probability of success for a given amount of work.

When the key length k is equal to the cipher block length n, the algorithm for precomputing r tables of chains, each table having m chains, with each chain of length t, is given in Table 6.12.

The findChains( ) algorithm in Table 6.12 finds rm chains, each of length t and hence covers at most rmt possible keys. If the desired key K is within some chain, it will be found by the attack given in Tables 6.13 and 6.14, below.

TABLE 6.12. Algorithm to compute chains.

// Find $(SP_{i,j}, EP_{i,j})$, $i = 0, 1, \ldots, r-1$ and $j = 0, 1, \ldots, m-1$
findChains( )
    for $i = 0$ to $r - 1$
        Choose a random function F_i
        // Generate table i
        for $j = 0$ to $m - 1$
            Generate a random starting point $SP_{i,j}$
            $K_0 = SP_{i,j}$
            for $\ell = 1$ to $t - 1$
                $K_\ell = F_i(E(P, K_{\ell-1}))$
            next ℓ
            $EP_{i,j} = K_{t-1}$
        next j
    next i
end findChains

TABLE 6.13. Algorithm to find an endpoint.

```
// Search for an EP
findEP( )
        for i = 0 to r − 1
            Y = F_i(C)
            for j = 1 to t
                for ℓ = 0 to m − 1
                    if Y == EP_{i,ℓ} then
                        found = findKey(i,ℓ,j)
                        if not found
                            false alarm
                        else// found = K
                            return(found)
                        end if
                    end if
                next ℓ
                Y = F_i(E(P, Y))
            next j
        next i
        return(key not found)
end findEP
```

In an ideal world, all of the rmt chain elements would be distinct, in which case the chance of finding a randomly selected key would be $rmt/2^k$. Below, we'll see that the real world is not so kind to Trudy.

For efficient searching, the pairs $(SP_{i,j}, EP_{i,j})$, $j = 0, 1, \ldots, m − 1$, should be sorted by endpoints. The algorithm for finding a matching endpoint appears in Table 6.13. The function findKey( ) referenced in Table 6.13 is given in Table 6.14. Note that t is the length of each chain.

TABLE 6.14. Algorithm to find the key.

```
// Is key K at position t − j − 1 in chain ℓ of table i?
findKey(i,ℓ,j)
    Y = SP_{i,ℓ}
    for q = 1 to t − j − 1
        Y = F_i(E(P, Y))
    next q
    K = Y
    if C = E(P, K)
        return(K)
    else// false alarm
        return(not found)
    end if
end findKey
```

If the block length is not equal to the key length, that is, $k \neq n$, then we can't directly use ciphertext as a key for the next element in a chain. Fortunately, this situation only requires a slight modification to the algorithms above.

For concreteness, consider DES, which has a key length of $k = 56$ and a block size of $n = 64$. The only change required to the algorithms above is to modify the functions F_i. In this case, F_i cannot be a permutation, but we can take each F_i to be a truncated permutation of the form

$$F_i(x_0, x_1, \ldots, x_{63}) = (x_{i_0}, x_{i_1}, \ldots, x_{i_{55}})$$

where the indices i_j, $j = 0, 1, \ldots, 55$, are distinct elements of $\{0, 1, \ldots, 63\}$. The attack then proceeds as described above.

If $k > n$, then we require $\lceil k/n \rceil$ matching plaintext, ciphertext pairs in order to uniquely determine the key. This is easy to arrange by redefining the functions F_i to handle multiple ciphertext blocks and, if required, truncating the permutation as described in the previous paragraph.

One interesting variation on Hellman's TMTO employs "distinguished points" [31]. This variant does not use fixed-length chains; instead, a chain is constructed until a point with some distinguishing characteristic is found. For example, we could choose to construct each chain until we obtain an output of the form

$$(x_0, x_1, \ldots, x_{s-1}, \underbrace{0, 0, \ldots, 0}_{n-s}).$$

Then each chain will, on average, be of length 2^{n-s}. In practice, we would set a limit on the maximum length of a chain and reject any that exceed the limit.

Using distinguished points, the precomputation is similar to the standard case described above, except that we now retain triples

$$(SP_j, EP_j, \ell_j) \quad \text{for } j = 0, 1, 2, \ldots, rm \qquad (6.30)$$

where ℓ_j is the length of chain j. We must also keep track of the maximum length of any chain within table i, which we denote by M_i, for $i = 0, 1, \ldots, r - 1$.

The primary advantage to distinguished points is that it allows for a more efficient distributed version of the TMTO attack. Suppose r computers are available. Then each computer can search one of the r tables of chains. In this scenario, a server only needs to send computer i the function F_i along with the ciphertext C and M_i as well as the definition of a distinguished point. In particular, the triples in *equation 6.30* do not need to be transmitted to any of the r computers, which saves considerable bandwidth.

Computer i proceeds with the attack as described above; however, instead of looking for a matching EP_j at each step, it simply looks for a distinguished point. If such a point is found within M_i iterations, the distinguished point is returned to the server, which then checks to see whether it matches an actual endpoint in table i. If so, the server attempts to recover K as in the previous case.

6.5.4   Success Probability

Finally, we need to estimate the probability of success in Hellman's TMTO attack. The difficulty lies in the fact that keys can appear within more than one chain, and so we must estimate the probability of such duplication.

Perhaps the easiest way to obtain an estimate of the success probability is via the classic "occupancy problem," as described by Feller [78]. We leave the details of this derivation as a homework problem. The result is that the probability of successfully finding a key using the TMTO is approximately

$$P(\text{success}) = 1 - e^{-mtr/2^k}. \tag{6.31}$$

The approximate success probabilities for various choices of mtr are tabulated in Table 6.15. Hellman suggests choosing

$$m = t = r = 2^{k/3} \tag{6.32}$$

in which case the probability of success is, according to Table 6.15, about 0.63.

In general, the cryptanalytic TMTO precomputation requires mtr encryptions. The required "memory" is proportional to the number of chains, which is rm. Assuming the key K is in one of the computed chains and neglecting false alarms, the "time" required when the attack is executed is $t/2$ steps to find the matching EP and then another $t/2$ steps to find K within the chain, for a total expected time of t. For the parameters in *equation 6.32*, this gives a precomputation of 2^k encryptions, a memory requirement of $2^{2k/3}$, and a time requirement of $2^{2k/3}$. For DES, this implies a costly precomputation of 2^{56}, but then the resulting time and memory requirements are each less than 2^{38}, with a high probability of success. Although the attack is only probabilistic, for DES, the probability of success is extremely high for the amount of work per attack.

TABLE 6.15. Estimated TMTO success probabilities.

mtr	$P(\text{success})$
0	0
2^{k-5}	0.03
2^{k-4}	0.06
2^{k-3}	0.12
2^{k-2}	0.22
2^{k-1}	0.39
2^k	0.63
2^{k+1}	0.86
2^{k+2}	0.98
2^{k+3}	0.99
∞	1.00

Hellman's cryptanalytic TMTO does not rely on any particular properties of the DES cipher, other than the fact that DES has a small enough key length to give the TMTO a good chance of success for a feasible amount of work. This TMTO can be applied to any block cipher, provided there is sufficient computing power available for the initial precomputation and enough storage for the tabulated results. Perhaps the most interesting aspect of the attack is that it requires no knowledge of the internal workings of the cipher being attacked.

Hellman's TMTO provides a good example of the role that clever algorithms can play in breaking ciphers.

6.6 SUMMARY

In this chapter, we've presented several advanced cryptanalytic techniques. Some knowledge of differential and linear cryptanalysis is necessary to understand the trade-offs in block cipher design. We presented linear and differential attacks on TDES, a simplified version of DES, and discussed the implications of these attacks on block cipher design.

Side channel attacks have become important in recent years. It is crucial to prevent such attacks, which go beyond the traditional concept of cryptanalysis. We discussed a side channel attack on RSA to illustrate the issues involved in such attacks.

We presented a classic attack on the Merkle-Hellman knapsack public key cryptosystem. This attack illustrates that mathematical advances can have a surprising impact on cryptography.

We concluded with a discussion of Hellman's time-memory trade-off attack on DES. This attack shows the potential impact that clever algorithms can have on crypto.

Here, we've only scratched the surface of the field of cryptanalysis. Many other cryptanalytic techniques have been developed, and cryptanalysis remains an active area of research. However, the cryptanalytic attacks discussed in this chapter provide a good representative sample of the methods that are used to attacks and analyze ciphers.

6.7 PROBLEMS

1. The file `outDiff`, which is available at the textbook website, contains 100 chosen plaintext pairs P and $\tilde{P}$ that satisfy $P \oplus \tilde{P} = 0\text{x}0002$, along with the corresponding TDES-encrypted ciphertext pairs C and $\tilde{C}$. Use this information to determine the key bits $k_{13}, k_{14}, k_{15}, k_9, k_{10}, k_{11}$ using the differential cryptanalysis attack on TDES that is described in this chapter. Then use your knowledge of these key bits to exhaustively search for the remaining key bits. Give the key as $K = k_0 k_1 k_2 \cdots k_{15}$ in hexadecimal.

2. The file `outLin`, which is available at the textbook website, contains 100 known plaintext P along with the corresponding TDES-encrypted ciphertext C. Use this information to determine the value of $k_0 \oplus k_1$ and $k_2 \oplus k_7$ using the linear cryptanalysis attack on TDES that is described in this chapter. Then use your knowledge

of these key bits to exhaustively search for the remaining key bits. Give the key as $K = k_0 k_1 k_2 \cdots k_{15}$ in hexadecimal.

3. Find a 16-bit key that encrypts

$$\text{plaintext} = \texttt{0x1223} = 0001001000100011$$

to

$$\text{ciphertext} = \texttt{0x5B0C} = 0101101100001100$$

using the cipher TDES.

4. Consider a block cipher with a 32-bit block size and a 32-bit key length. In Hellman's TMTO, suppose the initial value of a chain is X and the known plaintext value is P. Give the formulas for a chain of encryptions of length four, beginning with X.

5. Implement Hellman's TMTO attack on TDES. Let $m = t = r = 2^5$. Empirically determine the probability of success.

6. Suppose that a DES-like cipher uses the S-box below.

	0000 0001 0010 0011 0100 0101 0110 0111 1000 1001 1010 1011 1100 1101 1110 1111
00	0100 0110 1000 1001 1110 0101 1010 1100 0000 0010 1111 1011 0001 0111 1101 0011
01	0110 0100 1010 1011 0011 0000 0111 1110 0010 1100 1000 1001 1101 0101 1111 0001
10	1000 0101 0000 1011 1101 0110 1110 1100 1111 0111 0100 1001 1010 0010 0001 0011
11	1010 0010 0110 1001 1111 0100 0000 1110 1101 0101 0111 1100 1000 1011 0011 0001

If the input to this S-box is 011101, what is the output? Suppose input X_1 and X_2 yield output Y_1 and Y_2, respectively. If $X_1 \oplus X_2 = 000001$ what is the most likely value for $Y_1 \oplus Y_2$ and what is its probability?

7. Consider the S-box below. For the input $x_0 x_1 x_2$ the bit x_0 indexes the row, while $x_1 x_2$ is the column index. We denote the output by $y_0 y_1$.

	00	01	10	11
0	10	01	00	11
1	11	00	01	10

Find the best linear approximation to y_1 in terms of x_0, x_1, and x_2. With what probability does this approximation hold?

8. Construct a difference table analogous to that in Table 6.1 for S-box 1 of DES (see Appendix A-3). What is the most biased difference and what is the bias?

9. Construct a difference table analogous to that in Table 6.1 for the right S-box of TDES. Verify the results in *equation 6.8*. What is the second most biased difference, and what is the bias?

10. Construct a linear approximation table analogous to that in Table 6.2 for S-box 1 of DES (see Appendix A-3). Note that the table will have 64 rows and 15 columns. What is the best linear approximation, and how well does it approximate?

11. Construct a linear approximation table analogous to that in Table 6.2 for the left S-box of TDES. Verify the results in *equation 6.20*. What is the next best linear approximation, and how well does it approximate?

12. The Enigma cipher is illustrated below. To encrypt, a plaintext letter is entered on the keyboard. This letter passes through the plugboard, or *stecker*, then through each of the three rotors, through the reflector, back through the three rotors, back through the stecker, and the resulting ciphertext letter is illuminated on the lightboard. To decrypt, the ciphertext letter is typed on the keyboard and the corresponding plaintext letter is illuminated on the lightboard. Each rotor, as well as the reflector, is hard-wired with a permutation of the 26 letters.

In the example illustrated below, the plaintext letter C is typed on the keyboard, which becomes S due to the stecker cable connecting C to S. The letter S then passes through the rotors and reflector, which, effectively, performs a permutation. In this example, S has been permuted to Z, which becomes L due to the stecker cable between L and Z. Then the ciphertext L lights up on the lightboard.

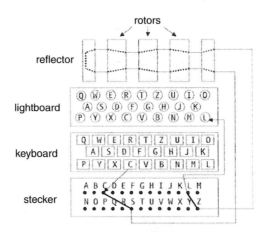

Each time a keyboard letter is typed, the rightmost rotor steps one position, and the other rotors step in an odometer-like fashion. That is, the middle rotor steps once for each 26 steps of the right rotor and the left rotor steps once for each 26 steps of the middle rotor (the reflector does not rotate). As a result, the overall permutation will be different for each letter typed. The Enigma is a substitution cipher where each letter is encrypted based on a permutation of the alphabet. But the Enigma is far from simple since each time a letter is encrypted (or decrypted), the permutation changes.

The cryptographically significant components of the Enigma cipher are the stecker, the three rotors and the reflector. The Enigma key consists of

 (i) The choice of rotors

 (ii) The position of a movable ring on both of the right two rotors that controls the rotation of the rotor to its immediate left (that is, the ring determines at which point the odometer effect occurs)

(iii) The initial position of each rotor

(iv) The number and plugging of the wires in the stecker

(v) The choice of reflector

Each rotor implements a permutation of the 26 letters of the alphabet. The movable rings can be set to any of 26 positions corresponding to the letters. Each rotor is initially set to one of the 26 letters on the rotor. The stecker is similar to an old-fashioned telephone switchboard, with 26 holes, each labeled with a letter of the alphabet. The stecker can have anywhere from 0 to 13 cables, where each cable connects a pair of letters. The reflector implements a permutation of the 26 letters.

a. How many Enigma keys are possible? Give you answer in terms of bits, that is, give your answer in the form 2^n for some n.

b. In WWII, the German's always used 10 cables on the stecker, only five different rotors were in general use, only one reflector was used, and the reflector and the five rotors were known to the Allies. Under these restrictions, how many Enigma keys are possible? Again, give your answer in bits.

c. If you ignore stecker, then what is the answer in part b?

13. The purpose of this problem is to show that the Enigma is insecure (the Enigma cipher is described in Problem 12., above). Recall that, by our definition, a cipher is insecure if any shortcut attack exists. The shortcut attack that we'll consider requires known plaintext. Suppose the following known plaintext is available:

	0 1 2 3 4 5 6 7 8 9 10 11 12 13 14 15 16 17 18 19 20 21 22 23
Plaintext	O B E R K O M M A N D O D E R W E H R M A C H T
Ciphertext	Z M G E R F E W M L K M T A W X T S W V U I N Z

Let $S(x)$ be the effect of the stecker when x passes through the stecker from the keyboard to the rotors. Then the inverse of S, denoted $S^{-1}(x)$, is the effect of the stecker when x passes through the stecker in the other direction. Let $P_i(x)$ be the permutation at step i. Note that P_i is the permutation determined by the composition of the three rotors together with the reflector. Since P_i is a permutation, its inverse, P_i^{-1} exists. Due to the rotation of the rotors, P_i changes for each i.

The weakness of Enigma that we'll highlight results from "cycles" that occur in the known plaintext and corresponding ciphertext. Consider position 8 in the table of matched plaintext and ciphertext above. The plaintext letter A passes through the stecker, then through P_8 and, finally, through S^{-1} to yield the ciphertext M, that is, $S^{-1}(P_8(S(A))) = M$ which we can rewrite as $P_8(S(A)) = S(M)$. From the known plaintext above, we find the following equations

$$P_8(S(A)) = S(M)$$
$$P_6(S(M)) = S(E)$$
$$P_{13}(S(E)) = S(A)$$

which can be combined to yield the cycle

$$S(E) = P_6(P_8(P_{13}(S(E)))) \qquad (6.33)$$

Now suppose that we guess $S(E) = G$; that is, we guess that E and G are connected by a cable in the stecker plugboard. If so, then from *equation 6.33* we have

$$G = P_6(P_8(P_{13}(G))).$$

If our guess is correct, then this equation must hold for the correct choice of key.

a. Find another cycle involving $S(E)$ in the matched plaintext and ciphertext given above. Hint: Inverse permutations can be part of a cycle.

b. Describe a shortcut attack on the Enigma using the two cycles involving $S(E)$.

14. Prove that the Enigma is its own inverse; that is, prove that for the Enigma cipher, the same key and the same circuitry encrypts the plaintext and decrypts the ciphertext (the Enigma is described in Problem 12, above). Hint: Suppose that the ith plaintext letter is X, and that the corresponding ith ciphertext letter is Y. This implies that when the ith letter typed into the keyboard is X, the letter Y is illuminated on the lightboard. Show that, for the same key settings, if the ith letter typed into the keyboard is Y, then the letter X is illuminated on the lightboard.

15. What is the advantage of a cipher (such as the Enigma) that is its own inverse?

16. An exhaustive key search attack on A5/1 has an expected work of 2^{63}. Describe and provide pseudo-code for a shortcut attack on A5/1. What is the expected work for your attack?

17. Recall the linear cryptanalysis attack on TDES discussed in Section 6.2.6. Assume that *equation 6.24* holds with probability $(3/4)^3 \approx 0.42$. Also assume that the key satisfies $k_0 \oplus k_1 = 0$. Then if we conduct the attack using 100 known plaintexts, what are the expected counts for $c_1 \oplus p_{10} = 0$ and $c_1 \oplus p_{10} = 1$? Compare your answer with the empirical results presented in the text. Why do you think the theoretical and empirical results differ?

18. Derive the formula in *equation 6.31* for the success probability in Hellman's TMTO. Hint: See the discussion of the "occupancy problem" in Feller [78].

19. Suppose that Bob's knapsack public key is

$$T = [168, 280, 560, 393, 171, 230, 684, 418].$$

Suppose that Alice encrypts a message with Bob's public key and the resulting ciphertext is $C_1 = 1135$. Implement the LLL attack and use your program to solve for the plaintext P_1. For the same public key, find the plaintext P_2 for the ciphertext $C_2 = 2055$. Can you determine the private key?

20. Suppose that Bob's knapsack public key is

$$T = [2195, 4390, 1318, 2197, 7467, 5716, 3974, 3996, 7551, 668].$$

Suppose that Alice encrypts a message with Bob's public key and the resulting ciphertext is $C_1 = 8155$. Implement the LLL attack and use your program to solve for the plaintext P_1. For the same public key, find the plaintext P_2 for the ciphertext $C_2 = 14748$. Can you determine the private key?

21. Extend the timing attack on RSA to recover the bit d_2. That is, assuming that bit d_1 has been recovered, modify the attack presented in the text to find d_2.

22. Write a program to recover the 64-bit key for STEA (Simplified TEA) given one known plaintext block and the corresponding ciphertext block. The STEA algorithm and a description of the attack on STEA can be found at [160].

23. If DES were a *group* [85], then given keys K_1 and K_2, there would exist a key K_3 such that

$$E(P, K_3) = E(E(P, K_1), K_2) \text{ for all plaintext } P \qquad (6.34)$$

and we could also find such a key K_3 if any of the encryptions were replaced by decryptions. If *equation 6.34* holds, then triple DES is no more secure than single DES. It was established in [35] that DES is not a group and, consequently, triple DES is more secure than single DES. Show that TDES is not a group. Hint: Select TDES keys K_1 and K_2. You will be finished if you can verify that there does not exist any key K_3 for which $E(P, K_3) = E(E(P, K_1), K_2)$ for all possible choices of P.

Part II

ACCESS CONTROL

7

AUTHENTICATION

*Humans are incapable of securely storing high-quality cryptographic keys,
and they have unacceptable speed and accuracy when performing
cryptographic operations. (They are also large, expensive to maintain,
difficult to manage, and they pollute the environment. It is astonishing
that these devices continue to be manufactured and deployed.)*
—in Kaufman, Perlman, and Speciner [122]

7.1 INTRODUCTION

We'll use the term *access control* to refer to issues concerning access of system resources. Under this broad definition, there are two primary parts to access control, namely, authentication and authorization.

Authentication deals with the problem of determining whether a user (or other entity) should be allowed access to a particular system or resource. In this chapter, our focus is on the methods used by humans to authenticate themselves to machines. Authentication raises many issues related to protocols, particularly when the authentication occurs over a network. This is also the environment where most machine-to-machine authentication occurs. We'll defer these protocol-related issues to Chapter 9.

By definition, authenticated users are allowed access to system resources. However, an authenticated user is generally not given *carte blanche* access to all system resources. For example, we might only allow a privileged user—such as an administrator—to install software on a system. As a result, we must somehow restrict the actions of authenticated

---

Information Security: Principles and Practice, by Mark Stamp
Copyright © 2006 John Wiley & Sons, Inc.

users. This is the field of authorization. Whereas authentication is a binary decision—access is granted or it is not—authorization deals with more find-grained restrictions and limitations on access to various system resources.

The term access control is often used as a synonym for authorization. However, in our usage, access control is more broadly defined, with authentication and authorization being under the umbrella of access control. These two aspects of access control can be summarized as

- Authentication: Who goes there?
- Authorization: Are you allowed to do that?

7.2 AUTHENTICATION METHODS

The fundamental problem that we'll consider in this chapter is that of authenticating a human to a machine. That is, we want to convince an ignorant machine that someone or something claiming to be Alice is indeed Alice and not, say, Trudy.

You, the human, can be authenticated to a machine based on any combination of the following [14].

- Something you know
- Something you have
- Something you are

A password is an example of "something you know." It's generally agreed that passwords represent a severe weak link in many modern information security systems. We'll spend some time discussing the many problems with passwords.

An example of "something you have" is an ATM card or a smartcard. The "something you are" category is synonymous with the rapidly expanding field of biometrics. For example, today you can purchase a thumbprint mouse, which scans your thumbprint and uses the result for authentication. We'll briefly discuss a few biometric methods later in this chapter.

7.3 PASSWORDS

> *Your password must be at least 18770 characters*
> *and cannot repeat any of your previous 30689 passwords.*
> —Microsoft Knowledge Base Article 276304

An ideal password is something that you know, something that a computer can verify that you know, and something nobody else can guess—even with access to unlimited computing resources. We'll see that in practice it's difficult to even come close to this ideal.

Undoubtedly you are familiar with passwords. It's virtually impossible to use a computer today without accumulating a significant number of passwords. One important fact regarding passwords is that many things act as passwords. For example, the PIN number for an ATM card is equivalent to a password. And if you forget your "real" password, a friendly website might authenticate you based on your social security number, your mother's maiden name, or your date of birth, in which case, these "things that you know" are acting as passwords. An obvious problem is that these things are not secret.

We'll see that, when users select passwords, they tend to select bad passwords, which makes password "cracking" surprisingly easy. In fact, we'll provide some basic mathematical arguments to show that it's inherently difficult to achieve security via passwords.

One solution to the password problem would be to use randomly generated cryptographic keys in place of passwords. Then the work of cracking a password would be equivalent to the work of a brute force exhaustive key search. The problem with such an approach is that humans must remember their passwords.

But we're getting ahead of ourselves. First, we need to understand why passwords are so popular. That is, why is "something you know" more popular than "something you have" and "something you are," when the latter two are, presumably, more secure? The answer is, primarily, cost,[1] and secondarily, convenience. Passwords are free, while smartcards and biometric devices cost money. Also, it's more convenient for an overworked system administrator to issue a new password than to provide and configure a new smartcard. And, of course, it's much more convenient to reset a compromised password than to issue a user a new thumb.

7.3.1 Keys Versus Passwords

We've already claimed that cryptographic keys would solve some of the problems with passwords. To see why this is so, let's compare keys to passwords. On the one hand, suppose our generic attacker, Trudy, is confronted with a 64-bit cryptographic key. Then there are 2^{64} possible keys, and, if the key was chosen at random (and assuming the crypto algorithm is secure), Trudy must on average try 2^{63} keys before she expects to find the correct one.

On the other hand, suppose Trudy is confronted with a password that is known to be eight characters long, with 256 possible choices for each character. Then there are $256^8 = 2^{64}$ possible passwords, and this appears to be equivalent to the key search problem. Unfortunately (or, from Trudy's perspective, fortunately) users don't select passwords at random. Primarily, this is because users must remember their passwords. As a result, a user is far more likely to choose an 8-character password such as

```
password
```

than, say,

```
kf&Yw!a[
```

---

[1] In security, as in many other topics relevant to the real world, cost is generally the reason why things are done as they are.

As a result, a clever attacker like Trudy can make far fewer than 2^{63} guesses and have a high probability of successfully cracking a password. For example, a carefully selected "dictionary" of $2^{20} \approx 1,000,000$ passwords would likely give Trudy a reasonable probability of cracking any given password. On the other hand, if Trudy were to try to find a randomly generated 64-bit key by trying any set of 2^{20} possible keys, her chance of success would be a mere $2^{20}/2^{64} = 1/2^{44}$, or less than 1 in 17 trillion. The nonrandomness of passwords is at the root of many of the most serious problems with passwords.

7.3.2   Choosing Passwords

Certainly some passwords are better than others. For example, everyone would probably agree that the following passwords are weak

- Frank
- Pikachu
- 10251960
- AustinStamp

especially if your name is Frank, or Austin Stamp, or your birthday is 10/25/1960.

Security often rests on passwords and, consequently, users should have passwords that are difficult to guess. However, users must also remember their passwords. With that in mind, are the following passwords better than the weak passwords above?

- jfIej(43j-EmmL+y
- 09864376537263
- POkemON
- FSa7Yago

The first password, jfIej(43j-EmmL+y, would certainly be difficult for Trudy to guess, but it would also be difficult for Alice to remember. As a result, Alice is likely to write her password down, and her password might end up on the proverbial post-it note stuck to the front of her computer. This could make Trudy's job easier than if Alice had selected a typical password.

The second password is also probably too much for most users to remember. Even the highly-trained military personal responsible for launching nuclear missiles are only expected to remember 12-digit firing codes [14].

The password POkemON might be difficult to guess, since it's not a standard dictionary word due to the digits and the upper case letters. However, if the user were known to be a fan of Pokémon, this password might be relatively easy prey.

The final password, FSa7Yago, might appear to reside in the "difficult to guess, but too difficult to remember" category. However, there is a trick to help the user remember this—it's based on a *passphrase*. That is, FSa7Yago is derived from "four score and seven years ago." Consequently, this password should be relatively easy for Alice to remember, and yet relatively difficult for Trudy to guess.

In a password experiment described in [14], users were divided into three groups, and given the following advice regarding password selection:

- **Group A:** Select passwords consisting of at least six characters, with at least one non-letter. This is typical password selection advice.
- **Group B:** Select passwords based on passphrases.
- **Group C:** Select passwords consisting of eight randomly selected characters.

The experimenters then tried to crack the passwords of users in each of the three groups. The results of this exercise were as follows:

- **Group A:** About 30% of passwords were easy to crack. Users in this group found their passwords easy to remember.
- **Group B:** About 10% of the passwords were cracked, and, as with users in Group A, users in this group found their passwords easy to remember.
- **Group C:** About 10% of the passwords were cracked. Not surprisingly, the users in this group found their passwords difficult to remember.

These results indicate that passphrases provide the best option for password selection, since the resulting passwords are more difficult to crack, yet relatively easy to remember.

This password experiment also demonstrated that user compliance is hard to achieve. In each of groups A, B, and C, about one-third of the users did not comply with the instructions. Assuming that noncompliant users tend to select passwords similar to Group A, about one-third of these passwords were easy to crack. As a result, nearly 10% of passwords are likely to be easy to crack, regardless of the advice given.

In some situations, it makes sense to assign passwords, and if this is the case, noncompliance with the password policy is not an issue—although users are likely to have a much harder time remembering assigned passwords. But if users are allowed to choose passwords, then the best advice is to choose passwords based on passphrases. In addition, the administrator should use a password-cracking tool to test for weak passwords, since attackers certainly will.

It is also suggested that periodic password changes should be required. However, users can be very clever at overcoming such requirements, invariably to the detriment of security. For example, Alice might simply "change" her password without changing it. In response to such users, the system might remember, say, five previous passwords. But a clever user like Alice will soon learn that she can cycle through five password changes before resetting her password to its original value. Or if Alice is required to choose a new password each month she might select `marlon01` for January, `marlon02` for February and so on. Forcing reluctant users to choose reasonably strong passwords is not a trivial matter.

7.3.3 Attacking Systems via Passwords

Suppose that the attacker Trudy is an "outsider," that is, she has no access to a particular system. A common attack path for Trudy would be

$$\text{outsider} \longrightarrow \text{normal user} \longrightarrow \text{administrator.}$$

In other words, Trudy will initially seek access to any account on the system and then attempt to upgrade her level of privilege. In this scenario, one weak password on a system—or in the extreme, one weak password on an entire network—could be enough for the first stage of the attack to succeed. The bottom line is that one weak password may be one too many.

Another interesting issue concerns the proper response when a password attack occurs. For example, systems often lock after three bad passwords attempts. If this is the case, how long should the system lock? Five seconds? Five minutes? Or until the administrator manually restores service? Five seconds might be insufficient to deter an automated attack. If it takes more than five seconds for Trudy to make three password guesses for every user on the system, then she could simply cycle through all accounts, making three guesses on each. By the time she returns to a particular user's account, more than five seconds will have elapsed and she will be able to make three more guesses without any delay. On the other hand, five minutes might open the door to a denial of service attack, where Trudy is able to lock accounts indefinitely by making three password guesses on each account within five minutes. The "correct" answer to this dilemma is not readily apparent.

7.3.4 Password Verification

Next, we move on to the issue of verifying that an entered password is correct. For a computer to determine the validity of an entered password, the computer must have something to compare against. That is, the computer must have access to the correct password. But it's probably a bad idea to simply store passwords in a file, since this would be a prime target for Trudy. Here, as in many other areas in information security, cryptography comes to our rescue.

Instead of storing "raw" passwords in a file, it's far more secure to store hashed passwords. That is, if the password is FSa7Yago, we'll store

$$y = h(\texttt{FSa7Yago})$$

in a file, where h is a secure hash function. The entered password x is hashed and compared to y, and if $y = h(x)$ then the entered password is assumed to be correct and the user is authenticated. The advantage of this approach is that, if Trudy obtains the password file, she does not have the actual passwords—instead she only has the hashed passwords. Of course, if Trudy knows the hash value y, she can guess likely passwords x until she finds an x for which $y = h(x)$, at which point she will have found the password. But at least Trudy has work to do after she has obtained the password file.

Suppose Trudy has a "dictionary" containing N common passwords, say

$$d_0, d_1, d_2, \ldots, d_{N-1}.$$

Then she could precompute the hash of each password in the dictionary, that is,

$$y_0 = h(d_0), \, y_1 = h(d_1), \, \ldots, \, y_{N-1} = h(d_{N-1}).$$

If Trudy then gets access to a password file containing hashed passwords, she only needs to compare the entries in the password file to the entries in her precomputed dictionary of hashes. Furthermore, the precomputed dictionary could be reused for each password file, thereby saving Trudy the work of recomputing the hashes. Provided Trudy obtains at least two password files to attack, this approach saves her work. From the good guy's point of view, this is a bad thing. Can we prevent this attack or at least make Trudy's job more difficult?

We can make life more difficult for the bad guys such as Trudy by hashing each password with a *salt* value. A salt serves a similar purpose as an initialization vector, or IV, for a block cipher in cipher block chaining (CBC) mode. Recall that an IV is a non-secret value that causes identical plaintext blocks to encrypt to different ciphertext values.

Let p be a given password. Then we generate a random salt value s and compute $y = h(p, s)$ and store the pair (s, y) in the password file. Note that the salt s is not secret. To verify an entered password z, we retrieve (s, y) from the password file, compute $h(z, s)$, and compare this result with the stored value y.

Salted password verification is just as easy as it was in the unsalted case. But Trudy's job has become much more difficult. Suppose Alice's password is hashed with salt value s_a and Bob's password is hashed with salt value s_b. Then, to crack Alice's password using her dictionary of likely passwords, Trudy must compute hashes of words in her dictionary with salt value s_a, but to crack Bob's password, Trudy must recompute the hashes using salt value s_b. For a password file with N users, Trudy's work has increased by factor of N. Trudy can't be pleased with this turn of events.

7.3.5 Math of Password Cracking

Now we'll take a closer look at the mathematics behind password cracking. In this section, we'll assume that all passwords are eight characters in length and that there are 128 choices for each character, resulting in

$$128^8 = 2^{56}$$

possible passwords. We'll also assume that passwords are stored in a password file that contains 2^{10} hashed passwords, and that Trudy has a dictionary of 2^{20} common passwords. From experience, Trudy expects that any given password will appear in her dictionary with a probability of about $1/4$. Also, "work" is measured by the number of hashes computed. In particular, comparisons are free.

Under these assumptions, we'll determine the probability of success in each of the following four cases.

I. Trudy wants to find Alice's password (perhaps Alice is the administrator) without using the dictionary of likely passwords.

II. Trudy wants to find Alice's password using the dictionary.

III. Trudy wants to find any password in the hashed password file, without using the dictionary.

IV. Trudy wants to find any password in the hashed password file, using the dictionary.

In each of these cases, we'll consider both salted and unsalted password files.

- **Case I:** Trudy decides that she wants to find Alice's password. Trudy, who is somewhat absent-minded, has forgotten that she has a password dictionary available. In this case, Trudy has no choice but to try all passwords until she happens to come across the correct password. This is precisely equivalent to an exhaustive key search and the expected work is

$$2^{56}/2 = 2^{55}.$$

The result here is the same whether the passwords are salted or not, unless—in the unsalted case—Trudy can precompute and store the hashes of all possible passwords. This is a great deal of work, and we'll assume that it is beyond Trudy's capability.

- **Case II:** Trudy again wants to recover Alice's password, but she is going to use her dictionary of common passwords. With probability $1/4$, Alice's password will appear in the dictionary, in which case Trudy would expect to find it after hashing half of the words in the dictionary, that is, after 2^{19} tries. With probability $3/4$ the password is not in the dictionary, in which case Trudy would expect to find it after about 2^{55} tries. Then the expected work is

$$\frac{1}{4}\left(2^{19}\right) + \frac{3}{4}\left(2^{55}\right) \approx 2^{54.6}.$$

The expected work is almost the same as in the previous case, where Trudy did not use her dictionary. However, in practice, Trudy could simply try all in words in her dictionary and quit if she did not find Alice's password. Then the work would be at most 2^{20} and the probability of success would be $1/4$.

If the passwords are unsalted, Trudy could precompute the hashes of all 2^{20} password in her dictionary. Then ignoring the one-time work of computing the dictionary hashes, the term involving 2^{19} would vanish from the calculation above.

- **Case III:** In this case, Trudy will be satisfied to find any one of the 1024 passwords in the hashed password file. Trudy has again forgotten about her dictionary.

Let $y_0, y_1, \ldots, y_{1023}$ be the password hashes. We'll assume that all 2^{10} passwords in the file are distinct. Let $p_0, p_1, \ldots, p_{2^{56}-1}$ be a list of all 2^{56} possible passwords. Trudy needs to make 2^{55} distinct comparisons before she expects to find a match.

If the passwords are not salted, then Trudy computes $h(p_0)$ and compares it with each y_i, for $i = 0, 1, 2, \ldots, 1023$. Next she computes $h(p_1)$ and compares it with all y_i and so on. Then each hash computation provides Trudy with 2^{10} comparisons with hashed passwords. Since work is measured only in terms of hashes, the expected work is

$$2^{55}/2^{10} = 2^{45}.$$

On the other hand, if the passwords are salted, denote the salt value for y_i as s_i. Then Trudy computes $h(p_0, s_0)$ and compares it with y_0. Next, she computes $h(p_0, s_1)$ and compares it with y_1 and she continues in this manner up to $h(p_0, s_{1023})$. Then Trudy must repeat this entire process with password p_1 and then with password p_2 and so on. In this case, each hash computation only yields one usable comparison and consequently the expected work is 2^{55}, which is the same as in Case I, above.

- **Case IV:** Finally, suppose that Trudy wants to find any one of the 1024 passwords in the hashed password file, and she will make use of her dictionary. The probability that at least one password is in dictionary is

$$1 - \left(\frac{3}{4}\right)^{1024} \approx 1$$

so we can safely ignore the case where no password in the file appears in Trudy's dictionary. If the passwords are not salted, then, since we are assuming at least one of the passwords is in the dictionary, Trudy only needs to make about 2^{19} comparisons before she expects to find a password. As in *Case III*, each hash computation yields 2^{10} comparisons, so the expected work is about

$$2^{19}/2^{10} = 2^9.$$

In the salted case, let $y_0, y_1, \ldots, y_{1023}$ be the password hashes and let $s_0, s_1, \ldots, s_{1023}$ be the corresponding salt values. Also, let $d_0, d_1, \ldots, d_{2^{20}-1}$ be the dictionary words. Suppose that Trudy first computes $h(d_0, s_0)$ and compares it to y_0, then she compute $h(d_1, s_0)$ and compares it to y_0 and so on. That is, Trudy first compares y_0 to all of her (hashed) dictionary words. Then she compares y_1 to all of her dictionary words and so on. If y_0 is in the dictionary (which has probability $1/4$), Trudy can expect to find it after about 2^{19} hashes, and if it is not in the dictionary (which has probability 3/4) Trudy will compute 2^{20} hashes. If Trudy finds y_0 in the dictionary then she's done. If not, Trudy will have computed 2^{20} hashes before she moves on to y_1. Continuing, in this manner we find that the expected work is about

$$\frac{1}{4}(2^{19}) + \frac{3}{4} \cdot \frac{1}{4}(2^{20} + 2^{19}) + \left(\frac{3}{4}\right)^2 \frac{1}{4}(2 \cdot 2^{20} + 2^{19}) + \cdots$$

$$+ \left(\frac{3}{4}\right)^{1023} \frac{1}{4}(1023 \cdot 2^{20} + 2^{19}) < 2^{22}.$$

This calculation shows the tremendous impact of a relatively small dictionary that has a reasonable chance of containing a password, together with a password file of a reasonable size. Salting doesn't help too much here as the work is (roughly) bounded by the size of the dictionary. Also note that the result is the same regardless of the number of possible passwords, provided all other assumptions remain unchanged.

The bottom line is that password cracking is too easy, particularly in situations where one weak password may be sufficient to break the security of an entire system—which is often the case. In password cracking, the numbers strongly favor the bad guys.

7.3.6 Other Password Issues

As bad as it is, password cracking is only part of the problem with passwords. Today, most users require multiple passwords, but users can't remember a large number of passwords. This results in password reuse, and any password is only as secure as the least secure place it's used. If Trudy finds one of your passwords, she would be wise to try it (and slight variations of it) other places where you use a password.

"Social engineering" is also a major concern with passwords. If someone calls you, claiming to be a system administrator who needs your password in order to correct a problem with your account, would you give out your password? According to a recent survey, 34% of users will give out their password if you ask for it, and 70% will give their password away for a candy bar [176].

Keystroke logging software and similar spyware are also serious threats to password-based security. The failure to change default passwords is a major source of attacks as well [253].

An interesting question is, who suffers from bad passwords? The answer is that it depends. If you choose your birthday as your ATM PIN number, only you stand to lose.[2] On the other hand, if you choose a weak password, every user of the system stands to lose.

There are many popular password cracking tools, including L0phtCrack [2] (for Windows) and John the Ripper [117] (for Unix). These tools come with preconfigured dictionaries, and they make it easy to produce customized dictionaries. These are good examples of the types of tools that are available to hackers. Virtually no skill is required for an attacker to leverage these powerful tools.

---

[2]Perhaps your bank will lose too, but only if you live in the United States and you have a very good lawyer.

Passwords are one of the most severe real-world security problems today. The bad guys clearly have the advantage when it comes to passwords. In the next section, we'll look at biometrics, which—together with smartcards—are often touted as the way to escape from the multitude of problems inherent with passwords.

7.4 BIOMETRICS

> *If McDonalds offered a free Big Mac in exchange for a DNA sample,*
> *there'd be lines around the block.*
> —Bruce Schneier

Biometrics are the "something you are" method of authentication or, in Schneier's immortal words, "you are your key" [200]. There are many different types of biometrics, including such traditional examples as fingerprints and handwritten signatures. More recently, biometrics based on automated facial recognition, speech recognition, gait (walking) recognition, and even a "digital doggie" (odor recognition), among many others, have been introduced. The field of biometrics is currently a very active research area [112, 135].

In the information security arena, the main impetus behind biometrics is as a replacement for passwords. But for this to be practical, a cheap and reliable biometric is needed. Today, usable biometric authentication systems exist, including the thumbprint mouse, palm print systems for secure entry into restricted spaces, the use of fingerprints to unlock car doors and so on. But given the potential of biometrics—and the corresponding weakness of passwords—it's surprising that biometrics are not more widely used for authentication.

Ideally, a biometric should be

- Universal: The ideal biometric should apply to virtually everyone. In reality, no biometric applies to everyone. For example, a small percentage of people do not have fingerprints.

- Distinguishing: The ideal biometric should distinguish with virtual certainty. In reality, we can't hope for 100% certainty, although in theory, some methods can distinguish with very low error rates.

- Permanent: Ideally, the physical characteristic being measured should never change. In practice, it's sufficient if the characteristic remains stable over a reasonably long period of time.

- Collectable: The physical characteristic should be easy to collect without any potential to cause harm to the subject. In practice, collectability depends heavily on whether the subject is cooperative or not.

- Reliable, robust, and user-friendly: To be useful in practice, the biometric system must be reliable, robust, and user-friendly under real-world conditions. Some biometrics that have shown promise in laboratory conditions have subsequently failed to deliver similar performance in practice.

Biometrics can be used for *identification* or authentication. In identification, the goal is to identify the subject from a list of many possible subjects. This occurs, for example, when a suspicious fingerprint from a crime scene is sent to the FBI fingerprint database for comparison with all records on file. In this case, the comparison is one to many.

In authentication the comparison is one to one. For example, if someone claiming to be Alice uses a thumbprint mouse biometric, the captured thumbprint image is only compared with the stored thumbprint of Alice. The identification problem is more difficult and subject to a higher error rate. In this section, we are primarily concerned with the authentication problem.

There are two phases to a biometric system. First, there is an *enrollment phase*, where subjects have their biometric information entered into a database. Typically, during this phase very carefully measurement of the pertinent physical information is required. Since this is one-time work (per subject), it's acceptable if the process is slow and multiple measurements are required. In some fielded systems, enrollment has proven to be a weak point since it may be difficult to obtain results that are as robust as those obtained under laboratory conditions.

The second phase in a biometric system is the *recognition phase*. This occurs when the biometric detection system is used in practice to determine whether (for the authentication problem) to authenticate the user or not. This phase must be quick, simple, and accurate.

We'll assume that subjects are cooperative, that is, they are willing to have the appropriate physical characteristic measured. This is a reasonable assumption in the authentication case, since authentication is generally required for access to certain information or entry into a restricted area.

For the identification problem, it is often the case that subjects are uncooperative. For example, consider a facial recognition system used for identification. One suggested use for such a system is by Las Vegas casinos, where the system would be used to detect known cheaters as they attempt to enter a casino [228]. Such systems have also been proposed as a way to detect terrorists in airports. In such cases, the enrollment conditions are probably far from ideal, and in the recognition phase, the subjects are certainly uncooperative and they will likely do everything possible to avoid detection. Cooperative subjects make the biometric problem much more tractable. For the remainder of this discussion, we'll focus on the authentication problem and we'll assume that the subjects are cooperative.

7.4.1 Types of Errors

There are two types of errors that can occur in biometric recognition. Suppose Bob poses as Alice and the system mistakenly authenticates Bob as Alice. The rate at which such misauthentication occurs is the *fraud rate*. Now suppose that Alice tries to authenticate as herself, but the system fails to authenticate her. The rate at which this type of error occurs is the *insult rate* [14].

For any biometric, we can decrease the fraud or insult rate at the expense of the other. For example, if we require a 99% voiceprint match, then we can obtain a low fraud rate, but the insult rate will be very high. On the other hand, if we set the threshold at a 10% voiceprint match, the the fraud rate will be high, but the system will have a low insult rate.

The *equal error rate* is the rate at which the fraud and insult rates are the same. This is a useful measure for compare different biometric systems.

7.4.2 Biometric Examples

In this section, we'll briefly discuss three common biometrics. First, we'll consider fingerprints, which are a well-established biometric. Fingerprints are just beginning to be widely used in computing applications. Then we'll discuss palm prints and iris scans.

7.4.2.1 Fingerprints. Fingerprints were used in ancient China as a form of signature, and they have served a similar purpose at other times in history. But the use of fingerprints as a scientific form of identification is a relatively recent phenomenon.

The first significant analysis of fingerprints occurred in 1798 when J. C. Mayer suggested that fingerprints might be unique. In 1823, Johannes Evangelist Purkinje discussed nine "fingerprint patterns," but this work was a biological treatise and did not suggest using fingerprints as a form of identification. The first modern use of fingerprints for identification occurred in 1858 in India, when Sir William Hershel used palm prints and fingerprints as a form of signature on contracts.

In 1880, Dr. Henry Faulds published an article in *Nature* that discussed the use of fingerprints for identification purposes. In Mark Twain's *Life on the Mississippi*, which was published in 1883, a murderer is identified by a fingerprint. The widespread use of fingerprinting only became possible in 1892 when Sir Francis Galton (a cousin of Darwin) developed a classification system based on "minutia" that is still in use today [144].

Examples of the different types of minutia in Galton's classification system appear in Figure 7.1. Galton's classification system allowed for efficient searching, even in the pre-computer era. Galton also verified that fingerprints do not change over time.

Today, fingerprints are routinely used for identification, particularly in criminal cases. It is interesting that the standard for determining a match varies widely. For

Loop (double)   Whorl   Arch

Figure 7.1. Examples of Galton's minutia.

Figure 7.2. Automatic extraction of minutia.

example in Britain, fingerprints must match in 16 minutia, or points, whereas in the litigious United States, no fixed number of points are required.

A fingerprint biometric works by first capturing an image of the fingerprint. The image is then enhanced using various image-processing techniques, and the minutia are identified and extracted from the enhanced image. This process is illustrated in Figure 7.2.

The minutia extracted by the biometric system are compared in a manner that is analogous to the manual analysis of fingerprints. For authentication, the extracted minutia are compared with the claimed user's minutia, which have previously been captured (during the enrollment phase) and are stored in a database. The system determines whether a statistical match occurs, with some pre-determined level of confidence. This comparison process is illustrated in Figure 7.3.

7.4.2.2 Hand Geometry. Another popular form of biometric—particularly for entry into secure facilities—is hand geometry [102, 197]. In this system, the shape of the hand is carefully measured, including the width and length of the hand and fingers. The paper [113] describes 16 such measurements, of which 14 are illustrated in Figure 7.4 (the other two measure the thickness of the hand). Human hands are not nearly as unique as fingerprints, but hand geometry is easy and quick to measure, while being sufficiently robust for many authentication uses. However, hand geometry would not be suitable for identification, since there would be many false matches.

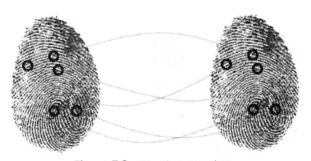

Figure 7.3. Minutia comparison.

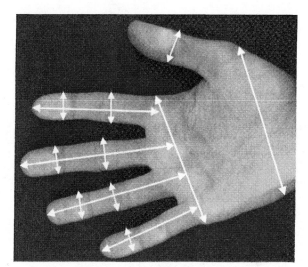

Figure 7.4. Hand geometry measurements.

One advantage of hand geometry systems is that they are fast, taking less than one minute in the enrollment phase and less than five seconds in the recognition phase. Another advantage is that human hands are symmetric, so if the enrolled hand is, say, in a cast, the other hand can be used for recognition by placing it palm side up. In this sense, the system is very robust. Some disadvantages of hand geometry include that it cannot be used on the young or the very old, and, as we'll discuss in a moment, the system has a relatively high equal error rate.

7.4.2.3 Iris Scan. The biometric that is, in theory, the best for authentication is the iris scan. The development of the iris (the colored part of the eye) is "chaotic," so that minor variations lead to large differences. There is little or no genetic influence on the iris pattern, so that the measured pattern is uncorrelated for identical twins and even for the two eyes of one individual. Another desirable property is the fact that the pattern is stable throughout a human lifetime [110].

The development of iris scan technology is relatively new. In 1936, the idea of using the human iris for identification was suggested by Frank Burch. In the 1980s, the idea resurfaced in James Bond films, but it was not until 1986 that the first patents appeared—a sure sign that people foresaw money to be made on the technology. In 1994, John Daugman, a researcher at Cambridge University, patented what is generally accepted as the current best approach to iris scanning [55].

An automated iris scanner must first locate the iris. It then takes a black and white photo of the eye. The resulting image is processed using a two-dimensional wavelet transform, the result of which is a 256-byte (that is, 2048 bit) "iris code."

Iris codes are compared based on the Hamming distance between the codes. Suppose that Alice is trying to authenticate using an iris scan. Let x be the iris code computed from

Alice's iris in the recognition phase, while y is Alice's iris scan stored in the scanner's database, from the enrollment phase. Then x and y are compared by computing the distance $d(x, y)$ between x and y as defined by

$$d(x, y) = \text{number of non-match bits/number of bits compared.}$$

For example, $d(0010, 0101) = 3/4$ and $d(101111, 101001) = 1/3$.

For an iris scan, $d(x, y)$ is computed on the 2048-bit iris code. A perfect match corresponds to $d(x, y) = 0$, but we can't expect perfection in practice. Under laboratory conditions, for the same iris the expected distance is 0.08 and for a different irises, the expect distance is 0.50. The usual thresholding scheme is to accept the comparison as a match if the distance is less than 0.32 and otherwise consider it a non-match [55]. An image of an iris appears in Figure 7.5.

Define the *match* cases to be those where, for example, Alice's data from the enrollment phase is compared to her scan data from the recognition phase. Define the *no-match* cases to be when, for example, Alice's enrollment data is compared to Bob's recognition phase data (or vice versa). Then the left histogram in Figure 7.6 represents the match data, whereas the right histogram represents the no-match data. Note that the match data provide information on the insult rate, whereas the no-match data provide information on the fraud rate.

The iris scan is often cited as the ultimate biometric for authentication. The histogram in Figure 7.6, which is based on 2.3 million comparisons, tends to support this view, since the overlapping region between the "same" (match) and "different" (no-match) cases—the region where a misidentification can occur—appears to be virtually nonexistent.

The iris scan distances for the match data in Table 7.1 provide a more detailed view of the "same" histogram in Figure 7.6. From Figure 7.6, we see that the equal error rate—that is, the crossover point between the two graphs—occurs somewhere near distance 0.34, which, from Table 7.1 implies an equal error rate of about 10^{-5}.

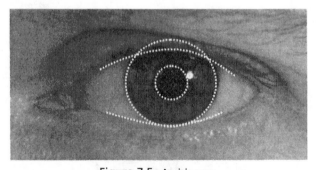

Figure 7.5. An iris scan.

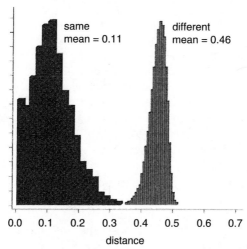

Figure 7.6. Histogram of iris scan results [110].

Is it possible to attack an iris-scanning system? Suppose Bob has a good photo of Alice's eye. Then he can claim to be Alice and try to use the photo to trick the system into authenticating him as Alice. This is not as far-fetched as it might seem. In fact, an Afghan woman whose photo appeared on a famous *National Geographic* magazine cover in 1984 was positively identified 17 years later by comparing her then-current iris scan with an iris scan taken from the 1984 photo. The magazine cover, the woman's photo, and the fascinating story can be found at [22].

To prevent such attacks, some iris-scanning systems first shine a light on the eye to verify that the pupil contracts before taking the photo. This eliminates the particular "replay" attack discussed above.

TABLE 7.1. Iris scan match scores and error rates [110].

Score	Probability
0.29	1 in 1.3×10^{10}
0.30	1 in 1.5×10^{9}
0.31	1 in 1.8×10^{8}
0.32	1 in 2.6×10^{7}
0.33	1 in 4.0×10^{6}
0.34	1 in 6.9×10^{5}
0.35	1 in 1.3×10^{5}

7.4.3   Biometric Error Rates

A comparison of biometric error rates is instructive. The equal error rate, the point at which the fraud rate equals the insult rate, is the best measure for comparing biometric systems. For fielded fingerprint biometric systems, the equal error rate is typically about 5%, while hand geometry has an equal error rate of about 10^{-3}. Although this may seem surprising, most fingerprint biometrics are relatively cheap devices, such as a thumbprint mouse. On the other hand, hand geometry biometric devices are more expensive and sophisticated devices. Consequently, the fingerprint biometrics may not be achieving anywhere near the true potential for the technology.

In theory, iris scanning has an equal error rate of about 10^{-5}. But in practice, it may be difficult to achieve such results. This is apparently because the enrollment phase must be extremely accurate in order to achieve near-optimal error rates. In practice, the people responsible for enrollment (and the equipment itself) may not be up to the laboratory standards on which the theoretical results rest.

In practice, most other biometrics are worse than fingerprints. And biometrics have a very poor record with respect to the identification problem.

7.4.4   Biometric Conclusions

Biometrics clearly have tremendous potential advantages. In particular, biometrics are difficult, although not impossible, to forge. In the case of fingerprints, Trudy could steal Alice's thumb, or, in a less gruesome attack, Trudy might be able to use a copy of Alice's fingerprint. Of course, a more sophisticated system might be able to detect such an attack, but then the system will be more costly, thereby reducing its desirability as a replacement for passwords, which will remain free.

There are also many potential software-based attacks on biometrics. For example, it may be possible to subvert the software that does the comparison or to manipulate the database that contains the enrollment data.

While a broken cryptographic key or password can be revoked and replaced, it's not clear how to revoke a "broken" biometric. This and other biometric pitfalls are discussed by Schneier [200].

Biometrics have a great deal of potential as a substitute for passwords, but biometrics are not foolproof. And given the enormous problems with passwords and the great potential of biometrics, it's surprising that biometrics are not more widespread today. This should change in the future as biometrics become more robust and inexpensive.

7.5   SOMETHING YOU HAVE

Smartcards can be used for authentication based on "something you have." A smartcard looks like a credit card but includes a small amount of memory and computing resources, so that it is able to store cryptographic keys or other secrets, and perhaps do some

Figure 7.7. A smartcard reader. (Courtesy of Athena, Inc.)

computations on the card. A special-purpose smartcard reader, as appears in Figure 7.7, is used to verify the information stored on the card.

There are several other examples of "something you have" authentication, including a laptop computer (or its MAC address), an ATM card, or a password generator. We'll briefly discuss a password generator.

A password generator is a device, about the size of a calculator, that the user must possess in order to log in to a system. Suppose Alice has a password generator, and Alice wants to authenticate herself to Bob. Bob sends a random "challenge" R to Alice, which Alice then inputs into the password generator, along with her PIN number. The password generator then produces a response, which Alice sends back to Bob. Bob can then verify whether the response is correct or not. If the response is correct, Bob is convinced that he's indeed talking to Alice, since only Alice is supposed to have the password generator. This process is illustrated in Figure 7.8. We'll see more examples of the use of challenge-response mechanisms in the protocol chapters.

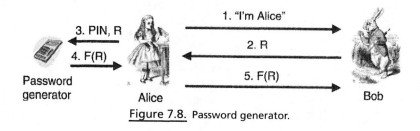

Figure 7.8. Password generator.

7.6 TWO-FACTOR AUTHENTICATION

In fact, the password generator scheme in Figure 7.8 requires both "something you have" (the password generator) and "something you know" (the PIN). Requiring two out of the three methods of authentication is known as *two-factor authentication*. Another example of a two-factor authentication system is an ATM card, which works in a similar manner to the password generator described above. Other examples of two-factor authentication include a credit card together with a signature, a biometric thumbprint mouse that also requires a password, and a smartcard with a PIN.

7.7 SINGLE SIGN-ON AND WEB COOKIES

Before leaving authentication, we'll briefly mention two additional authentication-related topics. First, we'll discuss *single sign-on*, which, in the context of the Internet, has recently become a security topic of considerable interest. We'll also mention *Web cookies*, which are often used as a weak form of authentication.

Users find it troublesome to enter their authentication information (typically, passwords) repeatedly. For example, when browsing the Web, it is not unusual for websites to require a password. While this is sensible from a security perspective, it places a burden on a typical user such as Alice, who must either remember different passwords for many different websites or compromise her security by reusing passwords.

A better solution would be to require users to authenticate only once and to have their "credentials" stay with them wherever they go on the Internet. Then subsequent authentications would be transparent to the user. This is known as single sign-on, and single sign-on for the Internet recently has become a hot security topic.

As with many computing topics, there are competing and incompatible approaches to single sign-on for the Internet. The approach favored by Microsoft goes by the name of Passport [131, 158]. The method preferred by nearly everybody else goes by the name of Liberty Alliance [74, 148], which is based on the Security Assertion Markup Language, or SAML [57]. There is clearly a need for single sign-on for the Internet, and it will be interesting to see which (if either) of these approaches becomes the preferred method.

Finally, we mention Web cookies. Suppose Alice is surfing the Web. Many websites will provide Alice with a Web cookie, which is simply a numerical value that is stored and managed by Alice's browser on her machine. The website uses the cookie value as an index into a database where it retains information about Alice.

When Alice returns to a website for which she has a cookie, the cookie is automatically passed by her browser to the website. The website can then access its database in order to "remember" important information about Alice. In this way, cookies maintain state across sessions. Since the Web uses HTTP, which is a stateless protocol, cookies are also used to maintain state within a session.

In a sense, cookies can act as a single sign-on method for a website. That is, a website can choose to authenticate Alice based simply on the possession of Alice's Web cookie. This is a very weak form of authentication, but it illustrates the (often irresistible) temptation to use whatever is available and convenient as a means of authentication. Security is, unfortunately, a secondary concern.

7.8 SUMMARY

Authentication of a human to a machine can occur based on "something you know," "something you have," or "something you are." Passwords are synonymous with the "something you know" method of authentication. In this chapter, we discussed passwords at length. The bottom line is that passwords are a very unsatisfactory method of authentication, but they are likely to remain popular for the foreseeable future.

We also discussed "something you are," or biometrics, which potentially offer much greater security than passwords. However, biometrics cost money, and they are not without problems.

We briefly mentioned "something you have" methods of authentication, as well as two-factor authentication, which combines any two of the three methods. And we mentioned single sign-on and Web cookies.

In the next section, we'll discuss authorization, which deals with restrictions placed on authenticated users. We'll return to authentication in upcoming chapters on security protocols, where we'll see that authentication over a network creates many interesting challenges.

7.9 PROBLEMS

1. Derive two passwords from the passphrase "Gentlemen do not read other gentlemen's mail."

2. List two passphrases, and, for each of these, give three passwords derived from the passphrase.

3. What passphrase might the password `PokeGCTall150` have been derived from?

4. In the context of biometrics, define the terms *fraud rate* and *insult rate*. In statistics, one of these is known as a Type I error, whereas the other is a Type II error. Which is which?

5. In some applications, a passcode consisting of some number of digits is required (for example, a PIN). Using the number-to-letter conversion on a telephone,

   a. What passcode corresponds to the password "hello"?

   b. Find as many passwords as you can that correspond to the passcode 5465. Your passwords must be English dictionary words.

6. Suppose that on a particular system, all passwords are 10 characters, there are 64 possible choices for each character, and the system has a password file containing 512 password hashes. Trudy has a dictionary of 2^{20} common passwords. Give

pseudo-code for an efficient algorithm that Trudy can use to attack the password file using her dictionary, assuming

a. The password hashes are not salted.

b. The password hashes are salted.

7. Why is it a good idea to hash passwords that are stored in a file? What is a "salt" and why should a salt be used whenever passwords are hashed?

8. On a particular system, all passwords are 8 characters and there are 128 possible choices for each character. There is a password file containing the hashes of 2^{10} passwords. Trudy has a dictionary of 2^{30} passwords, and the probability that a randomly selected password is in her dictionary is $1/4$. Work is measured in terms of the number of hashes computed.

a. Suppose that Trudy wants to recover Alice's password. Using the dictionary, what is the expected work to crack this particular password?

b. What is the probability that at least one of the passwords in the password file is in Trudy's dictionary?

9. Suppose you are a merchant and you decide to use a biometric fingerprint device to authenticate people who make credit card purchases at your store. You can choose between two different systems: System A has a fraud rate of 1% and an insult rate of 5%, whereas System B has a fraud rate of 5% and an insult rate of 1%. Which system would you choose and why?

10. Research has shown that most people cannot accurately identify an individual from a photo. For example, one study found that most people will generally accept an ID with any photo that has a picture of a person of the same gender and race as the presenter. Yet, it has also been demonstrated that, if photos are added to credit cards, then credit card fraud drops significantly. Explain this apparent contradiction.

11. Suppose all passwords on a given system are 8 characters long and that each character can have any one of 64 different values. The passwords are hashed (with a salt) and stored in a password file. Now suppose Trudy has a password cracking program that can test 64 passwords per second. Trudy also has a dictionary of 2^{30} common passwords and the probability that any given password is in her dictionary is $1/4$. The password file on this system contains 256 password hashes.

a. How many different passwords are possible?

b. How long, on average, will it take Trudy to "crack" the password for the administrator's account?

c. What is the probability that at least one of the 256 passwords in the password file is in the dictionary?

d. What is the expected work for Trudy to recover any one of the passwords in the password file?

12. Let h be a secure hash function. For this problem, a password consists of a maximum of 14 characters and there are 32 possible choices for each character. If a password is less than 14 characters, it's padded with nulls to exactly 14 characters. Let P be the resulting 14 character password. Consider the following two password hashing schemes.

(i) The password P is split into two parts, with X equal to the first 7 characters and Y equal to the last 7 characters. The password is stored as $(h(X), h(Y))$. No salt is used.

(ii) The password is stored as $h(P)$. Again, no salt is used.

Assuming a brute force attack, precisely how much easier is it to crack the password if *scheme* (i) is used compared with *scheme* (ii)? If *scheme* (i) is used, why might a 10-character password be *less* secure than a 7-character password? Note: The method in *scheme* (i) is used by Windows to store the so-called LANMAN password.

13. Many websites require that users register in order to access information or services. Suppose that you register at such a website, but when you return later you've forgotten your password. The website then asks you to enter your e-mail address and, if the address matches any e-mail address in the website's registration database, the corresponding password is e-mailed to that address.

   a. Discuss some security concerns with this approach to dealing with forgotten passwords.

   b. What can you conclude about the method used by the website to store and verify passwords?

14. Consider the password generator in Figure 7.8. If R is repeated, is the protocol secure? If R is predictable, is the protocol secure?

15. Describe a simple attack on the Web cookie authentication method discussed in the text.

16. Write a one-page description of the technical differences between Passport, Liberty Alliance, and SAML.

17. Explain how the MAC address on your computer could be used as a "something you have" form of authentication. How could you make this into a two-factor authentication scheme? How secure is this authentication scheme?

18. Suppose you have six accounts, each of which requires a password. If the probability that any one password is in Trudy's password dictionary is $1/4$, what is the probability that at least one of your passwords is in Trudy's dictionary? If the probability that any one of your passwords is in Trudy's dictionary is reduced to $1/10$, what is the probability that at least one of your passwords is in Trudy's dictionary?

19. Suppose Alice requires passwords for eight different accounts. She could choose the same password for all of these accounts. With just a single password to remember, Alice might be more likely to choose a strong password. On the other hand, Alice could choose different passwords for each account. In this case, she might be tempted to choose weaker passwords, since this will make it easier for her to remember all of her passwords. What are the trade-offs between one well-chosen password versus several weaker passwords? Is there a third approach that is more secure than either of these options?

20. Consider *Case I* from Section 7.3.5.

   a. If the passwords are unsalted, how much work is it for Trudy to precompute all possible hash values?

   b. If each password is salted with a 16-bit value, how much work is it for Trudy to precompute all possible hash values?

   c. If each password is salted with a 64-bit value, how much work is it for Trudy to precompute all possible hash values?

21. Suppose that Trudy has a dictionary of 2^n passwords and that the probability that a given password is in her dictionary is p. If Trudy obtains a file containing a

large number of salted password hashes, show that the expected work for Trudy to recover a password is less than $2^{n-1}(1 + 2(1 - p)/p)$. Hint: As in Section 7.3.5, *Case IV*, you can ignore the improbable case in which none of the passwords in the file appears in Trudy's dictionary. Then make use of the facts $\sum_{k=0}^{\infty} x^k = 1/(1 - x)$ and $\sum_{k=1}^{\infty} kx^k = x/(1 - x)^2$, provided $|x| < 1$.

22. Suppose that the chance of a false match is 1 in 10^{10} when a fingerprint is compared with one other (non-matching) fingerprint.[3] If the FBI fingerprint database contains 10^7 fingerprints, how many false matches will occur when 100,000 suspect's fingerprints are each compared with the entire database? For any individual suspect, what in the chance of a false match?

23. Suppose DNA matching could be done in real time. Describe a biometric for secure entry into a restricted facility based on this technique. Discuss one security concern and one privacy concern of such a system.

24. Gait recognition is a biometric that distinguishes based on the way that a person walks, whereas a "digital doggie" is a biometric that distinguishes based on odor.

    a. Describe an attack on gait recognition when it's used for identification.

    b. Describe an attack on a digital doggie when it's used for identification.

---

[3]This is approximately the rate when 16 points are required to determine a match, which is the British legal standard. In the U.S. legal system, matches can be found with far less than 16 points.

8

AUTHORIZATION

It is easier to exclude harmful passions than to rule them,
and to deny them admittance than to control them after they have been admitted.
—Seneca

Wherever there is authority, there is a natural inclination to disobedience.
—Thomas Haliburton

8.1 INTRODUCTION

Authorization is the part of access control concerned with restrictions on the actions of authenticated users. In our terminology, authorization is one aspect of access control and authentication is another. Many other authors use the term access control as a synonym for authorization.

In the previous chapter, we discussed authentication, where the issue is one of establishing identity. In its traditional form, authorization deals with the situation where we've already authenticated Alice and we want to enforce restrictions on what she is allowed to do. Although authentication is binary—either a user is authenticated or not—authorization is more fine grained.

In this chapter, we'll extend the traditional notion of authorization to include a few additional forms of access control. We'll discuss CAPTCHAs, which are designed to restrict access to humans (as opposed to computers), and we'll consider firewalls, which can be viewed as a form of access control for networks. We'll follow up the section on

Information Security: Principles and Practice, by Mark Stamp
Copyright © 2006 John Wiley & Sons, Inc.

firewalls with a discussion of intrusion detection systems, which come into play when firewalls fail to keep the bad guys out.

8.2 ACCESS CONTROL MATRIX

We'll define a *subject* as a user of a system (not necessarily a human user) and an *object* as a system resource. Two fundamental concepts in the field authorization are *access control lists*, or ACLs, and *capabilities*, or C-lists. Both ACLs and C-lists are derived from Lampson's *access control matrix*, which has a row for every subject and a column for every object. The access allowed by subject S to object O is stored at the intersection of the row indexed by S and the column indexed by O. An example of an access control matrix appears in Table 8.1, where we use x, r, and w for execute, read, and write privileges, respectively.

Notice that, in Table 8.1, the accounting program is treated as both an object and a subject. In this way, we can enforce the restriction that the accounting data can only be modified by the accounting program. As discussed in [14], the intent here is to make corruption of the accounting data more difficult, since any changes to the accounting data must be done by software that, presumably, includes standard accounting checks and balances. However, this does not prevent all possible attacks, since the system administrator, Sam, could replace the accounting program with a corrupt (or fraudulent) version and bypass this protection. But this trick does allow Alice and Bob to access the accounting data without allowing them to corrupt it—either intentionally or unintentionally.

8.2.1 ACLs and Capabilities

Since all subjects and all objects appear in the access control matrix, it contains all of the relevant information on which authorization decisions can be based. However, there is a practical issue in managing a large access control matrix. Realistically, a system could have hundreds of subjects and tens of thousands of objects, in which case, an access control matrix with millions of entries would need to be consulted before any operation by any subject on any object. Dealing with such a large matrix would impose an unacceptable burden on virtually any conceivable system.

TABLE 8.1. Access control matrix.

	OS	Accounting Program	Accounting Data	Insurance Data	Payroll Data
Bob	rx	rx	r	—	—
Alice	rx	rx	r	rw	rw
Sam	rwx	rwx	r	rw	rw
acct. program	rx	rx	rw	rw	r

To obtain acceptable performance for authorization operations, the access control matrix is split into more manageable pieces. There are two sensible ways to split the access control matrix. First, we could split the matrix into its columns and store each column with its corresponding object. Then, whenever an object is accessed, its column of the access control matrix could be consulted to see whether the operation is allowed. These columns are known as access control lists, or ACLs. For example, the ACL corresponding to insurance data in Table 8.1 is

$$(Bob, \text{---}), (Alice, rw), (Sam, rw), (Accounting\ program, rw)\ .$$

Alternatively, we could store the access control matrix by row, where each row is stored with its corresponding subject. Then, whenever a subject tries to perform an operation, we can consult its row of the access control matrix to see if the operation is allowed. This approach is know as capabilities, or C-lists. For example, Alice's C-list in Table 8.1 is

$$(OS, rx), (accounting\ program, rx),\ (accounting\ data, r),$$
$$(insurance\ data, rw), (payroll\ data, rw).$$

It might seem that ACLs and C-lists are equivalent, since the simply provide different ways of storing the same information. However, there are some subtle differences between the two approaches. Consider the comparison of ACLs and capabilities illustrated in Figure 8.1. Notice that the arrows in Figure 8.1 point in opposite directions; that is, for ACLs, the arrows point from the resources to the users, while, for capabilities, the arrows point from the users to the resources. This seemingly trivial difference has real significance. In particular, with capabilities, the association between users and files is built into the system, while for an ACL-based system, a separate method for associating users to files is required. This illustrates one of the inherent advantages of capabilities. In fact, capabilities have several security advantages, over ACLs, and for this reason, C-lists are much beloved within the research community [159]. In the next section, we discuss one security advantage of capabilities over ACLs.

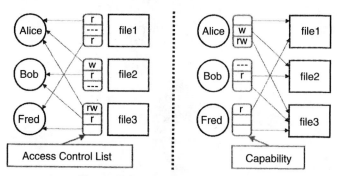

Figure 8.1. ACLs versus capabilities.

TABLE 8.2. Access control matrix for confused deputy problem.

	Compiler	BILL
Alice	x	—
Compiler	rx	rw

8.2.2 Confused Deputy

The "confused deputy" illustrates a classic security problem [103]. In this problem, there are two system resources, a compiler and a file named BILL that contains critical billing information, and there is one user, Alice. The compiler can write to any file, including BILL, while Alice can invoke the compiler and she can provide a filename where debugging information will be written. However, Alice is not allowed to write to the file BILL, since she might corrupt the billing information. The access control matrix for this scenario appears in Table 8.2.

Now suppose that Alice invokes the compiler, and she provides BILL as the debug filename. Alice does not have the privilege to access the file BILL, so this command should fail. However, the compiler, which is acting on Alice's behalf, does have the privilege to overwrite BILL. The result of Alice's command is likely to be the trashing of the BILL file, as illustrated in Figure 8.2.

Why is this problem known as the confused deputy? The compiler is acting on Alice's behalf, so it is her deputy. The compiler is confused since it is acting based on it's own privileges when it should be acting based on Alice's privileges.

With ACLs, it's difficult to avoid the confused deputy. But with capabilities, it's relatively easy to prevent this problem. The reason for this is that capabilities are easily delegated, while ACLs are not. In a capabilities-based system, when Alice invokes the compiler she can simply give her C-list to the compiler. The compiler then consults Alice's C-list when checking privileges before attempting to create the debug file. Since Alice does not have the privilege to overwrite BILL, the situation in Figure 8.2 can be avoided.

A comparison of the relative advantages of ACLs and capabilities is instructive. ACLs are preferable when users manage their own files and when protection is data oriented. With ACLs, it's also easy to change rights to a particular resource. On the other

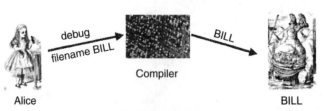

Figure 8.2. The confused deputy.

hand, with capabilities it's easy to delegate, and it's easier to add or delete users. Due to the ability to delegate, it's easy to avoid the confused deputy when using capabilities. However, capabilities are more complex to implement and they have somewhat higher overhead. For these reasons, ACLs are used in practice far more often than capabilities.

8.3 MULTILEVEL SECURITY MODELS

In this section we'll discuss security modeling in the context of multilevel security. Security models are often presented at great length in information security textbooks, but here we'll only mention two of the best-known models, and we only present an overview of these two models. For a more thorough introduction to MLS and related security models, see [213] or Gollmann's book [94].

In general, security models are descriptive, not proscriptive. That is, these models tell us what needs to be protected, but they don't attempt to answer the challenging questions concerning how to provide such protection. This is not a flaw in the models, as they are simply trying to set the framework for protection, but it is an inherent limitation on the practical utility of security modeling.

Multilevel security, or MLS, is familiar to all fans of spy novels, where "classified" information often figures prominently. In MLS, as above, the subjects are the users (generally, human) and the objects are the data to be protected (for example, documents). *Classifications* apply to objects while *clearances* apply to subjects.

The U.S. Department of Defense, or DoD, employs four levels of classifications and clearances, which can be ordered as

$$\text{TOP SECRET} > \text{SECRET} > \text{CONFIDENTIAL} > \text{UNCLASSIFIED.} \qquad (8.1)$$

A subject with, for example, a SECRET clearance is allowed access to objects classified SECRET or lower but not to objects classified TOP SECRET. For some unknown reason, security levels are generally rendered in upper case.

Let O be an object and S a subject. Then O has a classification and S has a clearance. The security *level* of O is denoted $L(O)$, and the security level of S is denoted $L(S)$. In the DoD system, the four levels shown above in *equation 8.1* are used for both clearances and classifications. Also, for a subject to obtain a SECRET clearance a more-or-less routine background check is required, while a TOP SECRET clearance requires an extensive background check and a polygraph test.

There are many practical problems related to the classification of information. For example, the proper classification is not always clear, and two experienced users might have widely differing views. Also, the level of granularity at which to apply classifications can be an issue. It's entirely possible to construct a document where each paragraph, taken individually, is UNCLASSIFIED, yet the overall document is TOP SECRET. This problem is even worse when source code must be classified, which is sometimes the case within the DoD. The flip side of granularity is aggregation. An adversary might be able to glean TOP SECRET information from a careful analysis of UNCLASSIFIED documents.

Multilevel security is needed when subjects and objects at different levels use the same system resources. The purpose of an MLS system is to enforce a form of access control by restricting subjects to objects for which they have the necessary clearance. Military and governments have long had an interest in MLS. The U.S. government, in particular, has funded a great deal of research into MLS and, as a consequence, the strengths and weaknesses of MLS are relatively well understood.

Today, there are many potential uses for MLS outside of its traditional classified government setting. For example, most businesses have information that is restricted to, say, senior management, and other information that is available to all management, while still other proprietary information is available to everyone in the company and some information is available to everyone, including the general public. If this information is stored on a single system, the company must deal with MLS issues, even if they don't realize it.

There is also interest in MLS in such applications as network firewalls. The goal in such an application is to keep an intruder such as Trudy at a low level to limit the damage that she can inflict even after she breaches the firewall. Another MLS application that we'll examine in more detail below deals with private medical information.

Again, our emphasis here is on MLS models, which explain what needs to be done but do not tell us how to implement such protection. In other words, we should view these models as high-level descriptions, not as security algorithms or protocols. There are many MLS models—we'll only discuss the most elementary. Other models tend to be more realistic, but they are also more complex, more difficult to enforce, and harder to analyze and verify.

Ideally, we would like to prove results about security models. Then any system that satisfies the assumptions of the model automatically inherits all of the results that have been proved about the model. However, we will not delve so deeply into security models in this book.

8.3.1 Bell-LaPadula

The first security model that we'll consider is Bell-LaPadula, or BLP, which, believe it or not, was named after its inventors, Elliot Bell and Len LaPadula. The purpose of BLP is to capture the minimal requirements with respect to confidentiality that any MLS system must satisfy. BLP consists of the following two statements:

Simple Security Condition: Subject S can read object O if and only if $L(O) \leq L(S)$.

*-Property (Star Property): Subject S can write object O if and only if $L(S) \leq L(O)$.

The simple security condition merely states that Alice, for example, cannot read a document for which she lacks the appropriate clearance. This condition is clearly required of any MLS system.

The star property is somewhat less obvious. This property is designed to prevent, say, TOP SECRET information from being written to, say, a SECRET document. This would break MLS security since a user with a SECRET clearance could then read TOP SECRET information. The writing could occur, for example, as the result of a computer virus. In his groundbreaking work on viruses, Cohen was able to break MLS systems using computer viruses, as discussed in [45], and such attacks remain a very real threat to MLS systems today.

The simple security condition can be summarized as "no read up," while the star property implies "no write down." Consequently, BLP can be succinctly stated as "no read up, no write down." It's difficult to imagine a security model that's any simpler.

Although simplicity in security is usually good—since it generally implies analyzability—BLP may be too simple. At least that is the conclusion of BLPs harshest critic, McLean, who states that BLP is "so trivial that it is hard to imagine a realistic security model for which it does not hold" [153]. In an attempt to poke holes in BLP, McLean defined "system Z" in which an administrator is allowed to temporarily reclassify objects, at which point they can be "written down" without violating BLP. System Z clearly violates the spirit of BLP, but, since it is not expressly forbidden, it must be allowed.

In response to McLean's criticisms, Bell and LaPadula fortified BLP with a *tranquility property*. Actually, there are two versions of this property. The strong tranquility property states that security labels can never change. This removes McLean's system Z from the BLP realm, but it's also impractical in the real world, since security labels must sometimes change. For one example, the DoD regularly declassifies documents, which would be impossible under the strong tranquility property. For another example, it is often desirable to enforce *least privilege*. If a user has, say, a TOP SECRET clearance but is only browsing UNCLASSIFIED Web pages, it is desirable to only give the user an UNCLASSIFIED clearance, so as to avoid accidentally divulging classified information. If the user later needs a higher clearance, his active clearance can be upgraded. This is known as the *high water mark principle*, and we'll see it again when we discuss Biba's model, below.

Bell and Lapadula also offered a weak tranquility property in which security label can change, provided such a change does not violate an "established security policy." Weak tranquility can defeat system Z, and it can allow for least privilege, but the property is so vague as to be nearly meaningless for analytic purposes.

The debate concerning BLP and system Z is discussed thoroughly in [27], where the author points out that BLP proponents and McLean are each making fundamentally different assumptions about modeling. This debate gives rise to some interesting issues concerning the nature—and limits—of modeling.

The bottom line regarding BLP is that it's very simple, and as a result it's one of the few models for which it's possible to prove things about systems. Unfortunately, BLP may be too simple to be of great practical benefit.

BLP has inspired many other security models, most of which strive to be more realistic. The price that these systems pay for more reality is more complexity. This makes most other models more difficult to analyze and more difficult to "apply," that is, it's more difficult to show that a real-world system satisfies the requirements of the model.

8.3.2   Biba's Model

In this section, we'll look briefly at Biba's model. Whereas BLP deals with confidentiality, Biba's model deals with integrity. In fact, Biba's model is essentially an integrity version of BLP.

If we trust the integrity of object O_1 but not that of object O_2, then if object O is composed of O_1 and O_2, we cannot trust the integrity of object O. In other words, the integrity level of O is the minimum of the integrity of any object contained in O. In confidentiality, a high water mark principle applies, while for integrity, a low water mark principle holds.

To state Biba's model formally, let $I(O)$ denote the integrity of object O and $I(S)$ the integrity of subject S. Biba's model is specified by the two statements below:

Write Access Rule: Subject S can write object O if and only if $I(O) \leq I(S)$.

Biba's Model: Subject S can read object O if and only if $I(S) \leq I(O)$.

The write access rule states that we don't trust anything that S writes any more than we trust S. Biba's model states that we can't trust S any more than the lowest integrity object that S has read. In essence, we are concerned that S will be "contaminated" by lower integrity objects, so S is forbidden from viewing such objects.

Biba's model is actually very restrictive, since it prevents S from ever viewing objects at a lower integrity level. It's possible—and often desirable—to replace Biba's model with the following:

Low Water Mark Policy: If subject S reads object O, then $I(S) = \min\left(I(S), I(O)\right)$.

Under the low water mark principle, subject S can read anything, under the condition that S's integrity is downgraded after accessing an object at a lower level.

Figure 8.3 illustrates the difference between BLP and Biba's model. The fundamental difference is that BLP is for confidentiality, which implies a high water mark principle, while Biba is for integrity, which implies a low water mark principle.

8.4   MULTILATERAL SECURITY

Multilevel security systems enforce access control (or information flow) "up and down" where the security levels are ordered in a hierarchy, such as *equation 8.1*. Usually, a simple hierarchy of security labels is not flexible enough to deal with a realistic situation. *Multilateral security* uses *compartments* to further restrict information flow "across" security levels.

We use the notation

SECURITY LEVEL {COMPARTMENT}

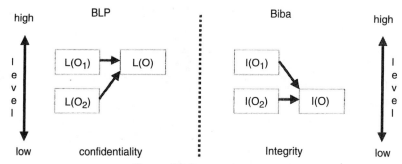

Figure 8.3. BLP versus Biba.

to denote a security level and its associated multilateral security compartment or compartments. For example, if we have compartments "CAT" and "DOG" within the TOP SECRET level, we would denote these compartments as TOP SECRET {CAT} and TOP SECRET {DOG}, and TOP SECRET {CAT,DOG}. While each of these compartments is TOP SECRET, a subject S with a TOP SECRET clearance can only access a compartment if S is specifically allowed to do so. As a result, compartments have the effect of restricting information flow across security levels.

Compartments serve to enforce the *need to know* principle; that is, subjects are only allowed access to the information that they must know. If a subject does not have a legitimate need to know everything at, say, the TOP SECRET level, then compartments can be used to limit the TOP SECRET information that the subject can access.

Why create compartments instead of simply creating a new classification level in the MLS model? It may be the case that, for example, TOP SECRET {CAT} and TOP SECRET {DOG} are not comparable, that is, neither

TOP SECRET {CAT} $\leq$ TOP SECRET {DOG}

nor

TOP SECRET {CAT} $\geq$ TOP SECRET {DOG}

holds. Using a strict MLS hierarchy, one of these two conditions must hold true.

Consider the multilateral security model in Figure 8.4, where the arrows represent "$\geq$" relationships. In this example, a subject with a TOP SECRET {CAT} clearance does not have access to information in the TOP SECRET {DOG} compartment. In addition, a subject with a TOP SECRET {CAT} clearance has access to the SECRET {CAT} compartment but not to the compartment SECRET {CAT,DOG}, even though the subject has a TOP SECRET clearance. Again, the purpose of compartments is to enforce the need to know principle.

Multilevel security can be used without multilateral security (compartments) and vice versa, but the two are usually used together. An interesting example described in [14] concerns the protection of personal medical records by the British Medical Association, or BMA. The law that required protection of medical records mandated a multilevel security system—apparently because lawmakers were familiar with MLS. Certain medical

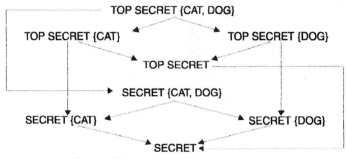

Figure 8.4. Multilateral security example.

conditions, such as AIDS, were considered to be the equivalent of TOP SECRET, while other less sensitive information, such as drug prescriptions, was considered SECRET. But if a subject had been prescribed AIDS drugs, anyone with a SECRET clearance could easily deduce TOP SECRET information. As a result, all information tended to be classified at the highest level, and consequently all users required the highest level of clearance, which defeated the purpose of the system. Eventually, the BMA system was changed to a multilateral security system, which effectively solved the problem. Then, for example, AIDS prescription information could be compartmented from general prescription information, thereby enforcing the desired need to know principle.

In the next two sections we'll discuss covert channels and inference control. These topics can arise in many different contexts, but they are particularly acute in multilevel and multilateral security environments.

8.5 COVERT CHANNEL

We'll define a *covert channel* as a communication path not intended as such by system's designers. Covert channels arise in many situations, particularly in network communications. Covert channels are virtually impossible to eliminate, and the emphasis is instead on limiting the capacity of such channels.

MLS systems are designed to restrict legitimate channels of communication. But a covert channel provides another way for information to flow. Below, we'll give an example where resources shared by subjects at different security levels can be used to pass information, thereby violating the "no read up, no write down" BLP restriction.

For example, suppose Alice has a TOP SECRET clearance while Bob only has a CONFIDENTIAL clearance. If the file space is shared by all users then Alice and Bob can agree that if Alice wants to send a 1 to Bob, she will create a file named, say, FileXYzW and if she wants to send a 0 she will not create such a file. Bob can check to see whether file FileXYzW exists, and, if it does he knows Alice has sent him a 1, and if it does not, Alice has sent him a 0. In this way, a single bit of information has been passed through a covert channel, that is, through a means that was not intended for

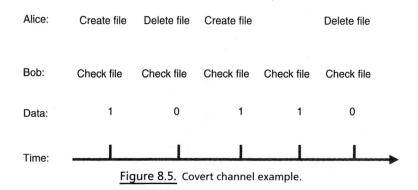

Figure 8.5. Covert channel example.

communication by the designers of the system. Note that Bob cannot look inside the file FileXYzW since he does not have the required clearance, but we are assuming that he can query the file system to see if such a file exists.

A single bit leaking from Alice to Bob is probably not a concern, but Alice could leak any amount of information by synchronizing with Bob. For example, Alice and Bob could agree that Bob will check for the file FileXYzW once each minute. As before, if the file does not exist, Alice has sent 0, and, if it does exists, Alice has sent a 1. In this way Alice can (slowly) leak TOP SECRET information to Bob. This process is illustrated in Figure 8.5.

Covert channels can be created in many ways. For example, the print queue could be used to signal information in much the same way as in the file example above. Network traffic is a rich source of potential covert channels, and, in fact, several hacking tools exist that exploit these covert channels.

Three things are required for a covert channel to exist. First, the sender and receiver must have access to a shared resource. Second, the sender must be able to vary some property of the shared resource that the receiver can observe. Finally, the sender and receiver must be able to synchronize their communication. From this description, it's apparent that covert channels are extremely common. Probably the only way to completely eliminate all covert channels is to eliminate all shared resources and all communication.

The conclusion here is that it's virtually impossible to eliminate all covert channels in any useful system. The DoD apparently agrees, since their guidelines merely call for reducing covert channel capacity to no more than one bit per second [3]. The implication is that DoD has given up trying to eliminate covert channels.

Is a limit of one bit per second sufficient covert channel protection? Consider a TOP SECRET file that is 100 MB in size. Suppose the plaintext version of this file is stored in a TOP SECRET file system, while an encrypted version of the file—encrypted with AES and a 256-bit key—is stored in an UNCLASSIFIED location. Suppose that following the DoD guidelines we are able to reduce the covert channel capacity of this system to 1 bit per second. Then it would take more than 25 years to leak the entire 100 MB document through a covert channel. However, it would take less than 5 minutes to leak the 256-bit AES key through the same covert channel. In other words, reducing covert channel capacity can be useful, but it is unlikely to be sufficient in all cases.

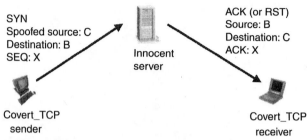

Figure 8.6. Covert channel using TCP sequence number.

For a real-world example of a covert channel, consider the transmission control protocol, or TCP. The TCP header, which appears in the Appendix in Figure A-3, includes a "reserved" field which is not used. This field can certainly be used to pass information covertly.

It's also easy to hide information in the TCP sequence number or ACK field and thereby create a covert channel between sender and receiver. Figure 8.6 illustrates the method used by the tool Covert_TCP to pass information in the sequence number. The sender hides the information in the sequence number X and the packet—with its source address forged to be the address of the intended recipient—is sent to any server. When the server acknowledges the packet, it unwittingly completes the covert channel by passing the information contained in X to the intended recipient. This stealthy covert channel is often employed in network attacks [210].

8.6 INFERENCE CONTROL

Consider a database that includes information on college faculty in California. Suppose we query the database and ask for the average salary of female computer science professors at San Jose State University and we receive the answer $100,000. We then query the database and ask for the number of female computer science professors at San Jose State University, and the answer is one. In this case, specific information has leaked from responses to general questions. The goal of inference control is to prevent this from happening.

A database that contains medical records may be of considerable interest to researchers. For example, by searching for statistical correlations, it may be possible to determine causes or risk factors for certain diseases. But patients might want to keep their medical information private. What is the best way to allow access to the statistically significant data while protecting privacy?

Can we ensure privacy by simply removing all names and addresses from the medical records? The college professor example above shows that this is far from sufficient. What more can be done to provide stronger inference control?

Several techniques used in inference control are discussed in [14]. One such technique is *query set size control,* in which no response is returned if the size of the set it too small. This approach would prevent anyone from determining the college professor's salary in the example above. However, if medical research is focused on a rare disease, query set size control could also prevent important research.

Another technique is known as the *N-respondent, k% dominance rule*, whereby data is not released if $k\%$ or more of the result is contributed by N or fewer subjects. For example, we might query a database and ask for the average salary in Bill Gates' neighborhood. Any reasonable setting for N and k would make it difficult to determine Mr. Gates salary from such a query. In fact, this technique is applied to information collected by the United States Census Bureau.

Another approach to inference control is *randomization*, where a small amount of random noise is added to the data. This is problematic in situations such as research into rare medical conditions, where the noise might swamp the legitimate data.

Many other methods of inference control have been proposed, but none are completely satisfactory. It appears that strong inference control may be impossible to achieve in practice, yet it seems equally obvious that employing some inference control, even if it's weak, is better than no inference control at all. Any reasonable inference control will make Trudy's job more difficult, and it will almost certainly reduce the amount of information that leaks, thereby limiting the damage.

As an aside, does this same logic hold for crypto? That is, is it better to use some crypto, even if it's weak, than no crypto at all? Surprisingly, for crypto, the answer is not so clear. Encryption tends to indicate important data. If there is a lot of data being sent (e.g., over the Internet), then Trudy might face an enormous challenge filtering your data from the mass of data. However, if your data is encrypted, it may be easier to filter, since encrypted data looks random, whereas unencrypted data tends to be highly patterned. And if your encryption is weak, you may have solved Trudy's filtering problem, while providing no significant protection from a cryptanalytic attack [14].

8.7 CAPTCHA

The Turing test was proposed by computing pioneer (and breaker of the Enigma) Alan Turing in 1950. The test has a human ask questions to one other human and one computer. The questioner, who can't see either respondent, must try to determine which respondent is the human and which is the computer. If the human questioner can't solve this puzzle, the computer passes the Turing test. This test is the "gold standard" in artificial intelligence, and no computer has yet come close to passing the Turing test.

A "completely automated public Turing test to tell computers and humans apart," or *CAPTCHA* is a test that a human can pass, but a computer can't pass with a probability better than guessing [243]. This could be considered as an inverse Turing test.[1] The assumptions here are that the test is generated by a computer program and graded by a computer program, yet no computer can pass the test, even if that computer has access to the source code used to generate the test. In other words, a "CAPTCHA is a program that

---

[1]Well, sort of.

can generate and grade tests that it itself cannot pass, much like some professors" [243]. It seems paradoxical that a computer can create and scores a test that it cannot pass.

Since CAPTCHAs are designed to restrict access to resources to humans, a CAPTCHA can be viewed as a form of access control. The original motivation for CAPTCHAs was an online poll that asked users to vote for the best computer science graduate program. It quickly become obvious that automated responses from MIT and Carnegie-Mellon were skewing the results [244]. So researchers developed the idea of a CAPTCHA to prevent automated "bots" from voting. Today, CAPTCHAs are used by free e-mail services, such as Yahoo, to prevent spammers from automatically signing up for large numbers of e-mail accounts.

The requirements for a CAPTCHA are that it must be easy for most humans to pass and that it must be difficult or impossible for a machines to pass, even if the machine has access to the CAPTCHA software. From the attacker's perspective, the only unknown is some randomness that is used to generate the specific CAPTCHA. It is also desirable to have different types of CAPTCHAs in case some person cannot pass one particular type. For example, blind individuals can't pass a visual CAPTCHA.

Do CAPTCHAs really exist? In fact they do—an example from [244] appears in Figure 8.7. In this case, a human might be asked to find three words that appear in the image. This is a relatively easy problem for humans but a difficult computing problem.

For the example in Figure 8.7, Trudy would know the set of possible words that could appear and she would know the general format of the image. The only unknown is a random number that is used to select the overlapping words and to distort the resulting images.

There are several types of visual CAPTCHAs of which Figure 8.7 is one example. There are also audio CAPTCHAs in which the audio is distorted in some way. The human ear is very good at removing such distortion, while automated methods are relatively easy to confuse. Currently, there are no text-based CAPTCHAs.

The computing problems that must be solved to break CAPTCHAs can be viewed as difficult problems in artificial intelligence, or AI. For example, automatic recognition of distorted text is a challenging AI problem, and the same is true of problems related

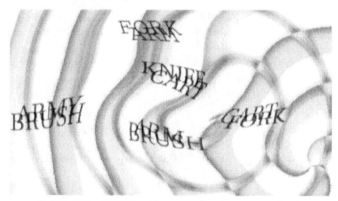

Figure 8.7. CAPTCHA (Courtesy of Luis von Ahn [244]).

to distorted audio. If attackers are able to break such CAPTCHAs, they have solved a hard AI problem. As a result, attacker's efforts are being put to good use.

8.8 FIREWALLS

Suppose you want to meet with the chairperson of a computer science department. First, you will probably need to contact the computer science department secretary. If the secretary deems that a meeting is warranted, she will schedule it; otherwise, she will not. In this way, the secretary filters out many requests that should not occupy the chair's time.

A *firewall* acts like a lot like a secretary for your network. The firewall examines requests to access the network, and it decides whether they pass a reasonableness test. If so, they are allowed through, and, if not, they are refused.

If you want to meet the chair of the computer science department, the secretary does a certain level of filtering; however, if you want to meet the President of the United States, his secretary will perform a much different level of filtering. This is analogous to firewalls, where some simple firewalls only filter out obviously bogus requests and other types of firewalls make a much greater effort to filter suspicious things.

A network firewall, as illustrated in Figure 8.8, is placed between the internal network, which might be considered relatively safe,[2] and the external network (the Internet), which is known to be unsafe. The job of the firewall is to determine what to let into and out of the internal network. In this way, a firewall acts as a form of access control for the network.

There is no standard firewall terminology. But whatever you choose to call them, there are essentially three types of firewalls—regardless of the marketing hype from firewall vendors. Each type of firewall filters packets by examining the data up to a particular layer of the network protocol stack. We'll adopt the following terminology for the classification of firewalls.

- A *packet filter* is a firewall that lives at the network layer.
- A *stateful packet filter* is a firewall that operates at the transport layer.
- An *application proxy* is, as the name suggests, a firewall that operates at the application layer where it functions as a proxy.

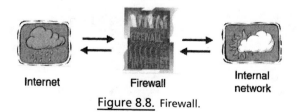

Internet   Firewall   Internal network

Figure 8.8. Firewall.

---

[2]This is probably not a valid assumption. It's estimated that about 80% of all computer attacks are due to insiders [37].

In addition, there are personal firewalls, which can be any of the types above but which are designed for one user or, at most, a small home network.

8.8.1   Packet Filter

A packet filter firewall examines packets up to the network layer, as indicated in Figure 8.9. As a result, this type of firewall can only filters packets based on the information that is available at the network layer. The information at this layer includes the source IP address, the destination IP address, the source port, the destination port and the TCP flag bits (SYN, ACK, RST, etc.). Such a firewall can filter packets based on ingress or egress; that is, it can have different filtering rules for incoming and outgoing packets.

The primary advantage of a packet filter firewall is efficiency. Since packets only need to be processed up to the network layer and only header information is examined, the entire operation should be very efficient. However, there are several disadvantages to the simple approach employed by a packet filter. First, the firewall has no concept of state, so each packet is treated independently of all others. In particular, a packet filter can't examine a TCP connection. We'll see in a moment that this is a serious limitation. In addition, a packet filter firewall is blind to application data, which is where many viruses reside today.

Packet filters are configured using access control lists, or ACLs. In this context, ACL has a different meaning than in the traditional access control terminology, as discussed above. An example of a packet filter ACL appears in Table 8.3. The purpose of the ACL in Table 8.3 is to restrict incoming packets to Web responses, which should have source port 80. The ACL is also designed to allow all outbound Web traffic, which should be destined to port 80.

How might Trudy take advantage of the inherent limitations of a packet filter firewall? She could, for example, send an initial packet that has the ACK bit set, without the prior two steps of the TCP three-way handshake. Such a packet violates the TCP protocol, since the initial packet must have the SYN bit set. Since the packet filter has no concept of state, it will assume that this packet is part of an established connection and let it

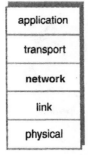

Figure 8.9. Packet filter.

TABLE 8.3. Typical ACL.

Action	Source IP	Dest IP	Source Port	Dest Port	Protocol	Flag Bits
Allow	Inside	Outside	Any	80	HTTP	Any
Allow	Outside	Inside	80	>1023	HTTP	ACK
Deny	All	All	All	All	All	All

through. When this forged packet reaches a host on the internal network, the host will realize that there is a problem (since the packet is not part of an established connection) and respond with a RST packet, which is supposed to tell the sender to terminate the connection. While this process may seem harmless, it allows Trudy to scan for open ports through the firewall. That is, Trudy can send an initial packet with the ACK flag set to a particular port p. If no response is received, then the firewall is not forwarding packets destined for port p into the internal network. However, if a RST packet is received, then the packet was allowed through port p into the internal network. This technique, which is known as a TCP "ACK scan," is illustrated in Figure 8.10.

From the ACK scan in Figure 8.10, Trudy has learned that port 1209 is open through the firewall. To prevent this attack, the firewall would need to remember existing TCP connections, so that it will know that the ACK scan packets are not part of any legitimate connection. Next, we'll discuss stateful packet filter firewalls, which keep track of connections and are therefore able to prevent this ACK scan attack.

8.8.2 Stateful Packet Filter

As the name implies, a stateful packet filter adds state to a packet filter firewall. This means that the firewall keeps track of TCP connections, and it can remember UDP "connections" as well. Conceptually, a stateful packet filter operates at the transport layer, since it is maintaining information about connections. This is illustrated in Figure 8.11.

The primary advantage of a stateful packet filter is that, in addition to all of the features of a packet filter, it also keeps track of ongoing connection. This prevents many attacks, such as the TCP ACK scan discussed in the previous section. The disadvantages of a stateful packet filter are that it cannot examine application data, and, all else being equal, it's slower than a packet filtering firewall since more processing is required.

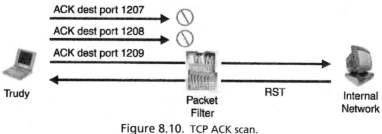

Figure 8.10. TCP ACK scan.

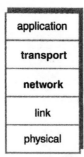

Figure 8.11. Stateful packet filter.

8.8.3 Application Proxy

A proxy is something that acts on your behalf. An application proxy firewall processes incoming packets all the way up to the application layer, as indicated in Figure 8.12. The firewall, acting on your behalf, is then able to verify that the packet appears to be legitimate (as with a stateful packet filter) and, in addition, that the data inside the packet is safe.

The primary advantage of the application proxy is that it has a complete view of connections and the application data. In other words, it has a truly comprehensive view. As a result, the application proxy is able to filter bad data at the application layer (such as viruses) while also filtering bad packets at the transport layer. The disadvantage of an application proxy is speed or, more precisely, the potential lack thereof. Since the firewall is processing packets to the application layer and examining the resulting data, it is doing a great deal more work than the simple packet filtering firewalls that we discussed above.

One interesting feature of an application proxy is that the incoming packet is destroyed and a new packet is created when the data passes through the firewall. Although this might seem like an insignificant point, it's actually a security feature. To see why this is beneficial, we'll consider the tool known as Firewalk, which is designed to

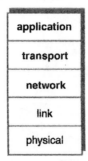

Figure 8.12. Application proxy.

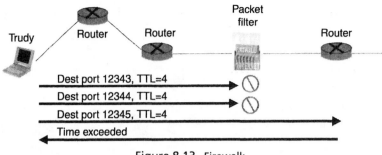

Figure 8.13. Firewalk.

scan for open ports through a firewall. While the purpose of `Firewalk` is the same as the TCP ACK scan discussed above, the implementation is completely different.

The time to live, or TTL, field in an IP packet contains the number of hops that the packet will travel before it is terminated. When a packet is terminated due to the TTL field, an ICMP "time exceeded" error message is sent back to the source.

Suppose Trudy knows the IP address of the firewall, the IP address of one system inside the firewall, and the number of hops to the firewall. Then she can send a packet to the IP address of the known host inside the firewall, with the TTL field in this packet set to one more than the number of hops to the firewall. Suppose Trudy sets the destination port of this packet to p. If the firewall does not let data through on port p, there will be no response. If, on the other hand, the firewall does let data through on port p, Trudy will receive a time exceeded error message from the first router inside the firewall that receives the packet. Trudy can then repeat this process for different ports p to determine which ports are open through the firewall. This attack is illustrated in Figure 8.13.

`Firewalk` won't work through an application proxy, since each packet that is forwarded through the firewall is a new packet. In particular, the TTL will have been reset to some default value, and the host that receives the packet will therefore not respond with a time exceeded error message.

The effect of an application proxy is that it forces Trudy to talk to the proxy and convince it to forward her messages. Since the proxy is likely to be well configured and carefully managed—compared with a typical host—this may prove difficult.

8.8.4   Personal Firewall

A personal firewall is used to protect a single host or a small network, such as a home network. Any of the three methods discussed above (packet filter, stateful packet filter, or application proxy) can be used, but generally such firewalls are relatively simple for the sake of efficiency.

8.8.5   Defense in Depth

Finally, we'll consider a network configuration that includes several layers of protection. Figure 8.14 gives a schematic for a network that includes a packet filter

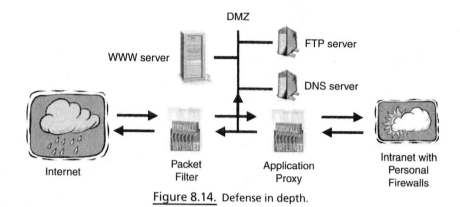

Figure 8.14. Defense in depth.

firewall, an application proxy and personal firewalls, as well as a "demilitarized zone," or DMZ.

The packet filter in Figure 8.14 is used to prevent low-level attacks on the systems in the DMZ. The systems in the DMZ are those that must be exposed to the outside world. These systems receive most of the outside traffic, so a simple packet filter is used for the sake of efficiency. The systems in the DMZ must be carefully maintained by the administrator since they are the most exposed to attack. However, if an attack succeeds on a system in the DMZ, the consequences for the company may be annoying, but they will probably not be life threatening, since the internal network will be largely unaffected.

In Figure 8.14, an application proxy firewall sits between the internal network and the DMZ. This provides the strongest possible firewall protection for the internal network. The amount of traffic into the internal network is likely to be relatively small, so an application proxy in this position will not create a bottleneck. As a final layer of protection, personal firewalls could be deployed on the individual hosts inside the corporate network.

The architecture in Figure 8.14 is an example of *defense in depth*, which is a good strategy in many security applications. If one layer of the defense is breached, there are more layers that the attacker must overcome. If Trudy is skilled enough to break through one level, then she probably has the necessary skills to penetrate other levels. But it's likely to take her some time to do so and the longer time that the administrator has to detect Trudy's attack in progress, the better chance there is of preventing it from ultimately succeeding.

Regardless of the strength of a firewall (or firewalls), some attacks will still succeed. Or an attack might be due to an insider. In any case, when an attack succeeds, we would like to detect is as soon as possible. In the next section we'll consider this intrusion detection problem.

8.9 INTRUSION DETECTION

The primary focus of computer security is *intrusion prevention*, where the goal is to keep bad guys out of your system or network. Authentication can be viewed as a way to prevent intrusions, and firewalls are certainly a form of intrusion prevention, as are most types of virus protection. Intrusion prevention can be viewed as the information security analog of locking the doors on your car.

But even if you lock the doors on your car, it might still get stolen. In information security, no matter how much effort you put into intrusion prevention, occasionally the bad guys will be successful and an intrusion will occur.

What can we do when intrusion prevention fails? *Intrusion detection systems*, or IDSs, are a relatively recent development in information security. The purpose of an IDS is to detect attacks before, during, and after they have occurred.

The basic approach employed by IDSs is to look for "unusual" activity. In the past, an administrator would scan through log files looking for signs of unusual activity. Automated intrusion detection is a natural outgrowth of such manual log file analysis.

Intrusion detection is currently a very active research topic. As a result, there are many claims in the field that have yet to be substantiated and it's far from clear how successful or useful some of these techniques will prove, particularly in the face of increasingly sophisticated attacks.

Before discussing the main threads in IDS, we mention in passing that *intrusion response* is another important topic. We'll see below that in some cases IDSs provide little specific information on the nature of an attack. In such cases, determining the proper response is not easy. In any case, we won't deal further with the topic of intrusion response here.

Who are the intruders that an IDS is trying to detect? An intruder could be a hacker who got through your network defenses and is now launching an attack on the internal network. Or, even more insidious, the "intrusion" could be due to an evil insider, such as a disgruntled employee.

What sorts of attacks might an intruder launch? An intruder with limited skills (a "script kiddie") would likely attempt a well-known attack or a slight variation on such an attack. A more skilled attacker might be capable of launching a variation on a well-known attack or a little-known attack or an entirely new attack. Or the attacker might simply use the breached system as a base from which to launch attacks on other systems.

There are essentially only two methods of intrusion detection.

- *Signature-based IDSs* attempt to detect attacks based on known "signatures" or patterns. This is analogous to signature-based virus detection, which is discussed in Chapter 11.
- *Anomaly-based IDSs* attempt to define a baseline, or normal, behavior of a system and provide a warning whenever the system strays too far from this baseline.

We'll have more to say about signature-based and anomaly-base intrusion detection below.

There are also two basic architectures for IDSs.

- *Host-based IDSs* apply their detection method or methods to activity that occurs on hosts. These systems are designed to detect attacks such as buffer overflows and escalation of privilege. Host-based systems have little or no view of network activities.

- *Network-based IDSs* apply their detection methods to network traffic. These systems are designed to detect attacks such as denial of service, network probes, and malformed packets. These systems may have some overlap with firewalls. Network-based systems have little or no direct view of host-based attacks.

Of course, various combinations of these types of IDSs are possible. For example a host-based system could use both signature-based and anomaly-based techniques, or a signature-based system might employ aspects of both host-based and network-based detection.

8.9.1   Signature-Based IDS

Failed login attempts may be indicative of a password cracking attack, so an IDS might consider "N failed login attempts in M seconds" an indication, or *signature*, of an attack. Then anytime that N or more failed login attempts occur within M seconds, the IDS would issue a warning that a password cracking attack is suspected.

Suppose that Trudy happens to know that Alice's IDS issues a warning whenever N or more failed logins occur within M seconds. Then Trudy can safely guess $N - 1$ passwords every M seconds. In this case, the signature detection slows Trudy's password guessing attack, but it might not prevent the attack. Another concern with such a scheme is that N and M must be set so that the number of false alarms is not excessive.

Many techniques are used to make signature-based detection more robust. The goal of such efforts is to detect "almost" signatures. For example, if about N login attempts occur in about M seconds, then the system could warn of a possible password cracking attempt, perhaps with a degree of confidence, based on the number of attempts and the time interval. But it's not easy to determine reasonable values for "about." Statistical analysis and heuristics are useful, but care must be taken to keep the false alarm rate to a manageable level.

The advantages of signature-based detection include simplicity, efficiency (provided the number of signatures is not excessive), and an excellent ability to detect known attacks. Another major benefit is that the warning that is issued is specific, which is generally not the case for anomaly-based systems. With a specific warning, an administrator can quickly determine whether the suspected attack is real or a false alarm and, if it is real, respond appropriately.

The disadvantages of signature detection include the fact that the signature file must be current, the number of signatures may become large thereby reducing efficiency, and the system can only detect known attacks. Even slight variations on known attack are likely to be missed by signature-based systems.

Anomaly-based IDSs attempt to overcome some of the shortcomings inherent in signature-based schemes. But no anomaly-based scheme available today could reasonably claim to be a replacement for signature-based detection. Instead, anomaly-based systems can only be used to supplement the performance of signature-based systems, not to replace them.

8.9.2 Anomaly-Based IDS

Anomaly-based IDSs look for unusual or abnormal behavior. There are several major challenges inherent in such an approach. First, we must determine what is normal for a system. Second, it is crucial that the definition of "normal" can adapt as system usage changes and evolves. Third, there are difficult statistical thresholding issues involved. For example, we must have a reasonable idea of how far abnormal lives from normal.

Statistics is obviously necessary in the development of an anomaly-based IDS. Recall that the mean defines statistically "normal" while the variance gives us a way to measure how far a result lies from normal.

How can we measure normal system behavior? Whatever characteristics we decide to measure, we must take the measurements during times of representative behavior. In particular, we must not set the baseline measurements during an attack or else an attack will seem normal. Measuring abnormal or, more precisely, determining where to separate normal variation from an attack, is an equally challenging problem. Abnormal must be measured relative to some specific value of normal. We'll view "abnormal" as a synonym for "attack."

Statistical discrimination techniques are often used to separate normal for abnormal. These techniques include Bayesian analysis, linear discriminant analysis, or LDA, quadratic discriminant analysis, or QDA, neural nets, and hidden Markov models, or HMMs, among others. In addition, some anomaly detection researchers employ advanced modeling techniques in artificial intelligence and artificial immune system principles. Such approaches are beyond the scope of this book.

Next, we'll consider two simplified examples of anomaly detection. The first example is simple, but not very realistic, whereas the second is slightly more realistic.

Suppose that we monitor the use of the three commands

```
open, read, close.
```

We find that under normal use, Alice uses the series of commands

```
open, read, close, open, open, read, close.
```

We'll consider pairs of consecutive commands and try to devise a measure of normal behavior for Alice. From Alice's series of commands above, we observe that, of the six possible ordered pairs or commands, four pairs are normal for Alice, namely,

```
(open,read), (read,close), (close,open), (open,open)
```

and the other two pairs,

```
(read,open), (close,read),
```

are abnormal. We can use this observation to identify potentially unusual behavior by Alice, or an intruder posing as Alice. We can then monitor the use of these three commands by Alice. If the ratio of abnormal to normal pairs is "too high," we would warn the administrator of a possible attack.

TABLE 8.4. Alice's initial file access rates.

H_0	H_1	H_2	H_3
.10	.40	.40	.10

This simple anomaly detection scheme could be improved. For example, we could include the expected frequency of each "normal" pair in the calculation, and if the observed pairs differ significantly from the expected distribution, we would warn of a possible attack. We might also improve the anomaly detection by using more than two consecutive commands, or by including more commands, or by including other user behavior in the model, or by using a sophisticated statistical discrimination technique.

For a slightly more plausible anomaly detection scheme, let's focus on file access. Suppose that, over time, Alice has accessed the four files F_0, F_1, F_2, and F_3 at the rates H_0, H_1, H_2, and H_3, respectively, as indicated in the Table 8.4.

Now suppose that over some recent time interval, Alice has accessed file F_i at the rate A_i for $i = 0, 1, 2, 3$ as given in Table 8.5. Do Alice's recent file access rates represent normal use? We'll employ the statistic

$$S = (H_0 - A_0)^2 + (H_1 - A_1)^2 + (H_2 - A_2)^2 + (H_3 - A_3)^2 \qquad (8.2)$$

to answer this question, where we'll define $S < 0.1$ as normal. In this case, we have

$$S = (.1 - .1)^2 + (.4 - .4)^2 + (.4 - .3)^2 + (.1 - .2)^2 = .02,$$

and we conclude that Alice's recent use is normal—at least according to this one statistic.

Alice's access rate of files can be expected to vary over time, and we need to account for this in our IDS. We do so by updating Alice's long-term history values H_i according to the formula

$$H_i = 0.2 \cdot A_i + 0.8 \cdot H_i \quad \text{for } i = 0, 1, 2, 3. \qquad (8.3)$$

From the data in Tables 8.4 and 8.5, we find that the updated values of H_0 and H_1 are the same as the previous values, whereas

$$H_2 = .2 \cdot .3 + .8 \cdot .4 = .38 \quad \text{and} \quad H_3 = .2 \cdot .2 + .8 \cdot .1 = .12.$$

The updated values appear in Table 8.6.

TABLE 8.5. Alice's recent file access rates.

A_0	A_1	A_2	A_3
.10	.40	.30	.20

TABLE 8.6. Alice's updated file access rates.

H_0	H_1	H_2	H_3
.10	.40	.38	.12

Suppose that over the next time interval Alice's measured access rates are those given in Table 8.7. Then we compute the statistic S using the values in Tables 8.6 and 8.7 and the formula in *equation 8.2* to find

$$S = (.1 - .1)^2 + (.4 - .3)^2 + (.38 - .3)^2 + (.12 - .3)^2 = .0488.$$

Since $S = .0488 < 0.1$ we again conclude that this is normal use for Alice. Again, we update Alice's long term averages using the formula in *equation 8.3* and the data in Tables 8.6 and 8.7. In this case, we obtain the results in Table 8.8.

Comparing Alice's long-term file access rates in Table 8.4 with her long-term averages after two updates as given in Table 8.8, we see that the rates have changed significantly over time. It is necessary that the IDS adapt over time to avoid a large number of false alarms (and a very annoyed system administrator) as Alice's actual behavior changes. However, this also presents an opportunity for the attacker, Trudy.

Since the H_i values slowly evolve to match Alice's behavior, Trudy can pose as Alice, provided she doesn't stray too far from Alice's usual behavior. But even more disturbing is the fact that Trudy can eventually convince the anomaly detection algorithm that her evil behavior is normal for Alice, provided Trudy has enough patience. For example, suppose that Trudy, posing as Alice, wants to always access file F_3. Then initially, she can access file F_3 at a slightly higher rate than is normal for Alice. After the next update of the H_i values, Trudy will be able to access file F_3 at an even higher rate without triggering a warning from the anomaly detection software. By going slowly, Trudy will eventually convince the anomaly detector that it's normal for "Alice" to only access file F_3.

Note that $H_3 = .1$ in Table 8.4 and, two iterations later, $H_3 = .156$ in Table 8.8, and these changes did not trigger a warning by the anomaly detector. Does this change represent a new usage pattern by Alice, or does it indicate an attempt by Trudy to trick the anomaly detector?

To make this anomaly detection scheme more robust, we should also incorporate the variance. In addition, we would certainly need to measure more than one statistic. If

TABLE 8.7. Alice's more recent file access rates.

A_0	A_1	A_2	A_3
.10	.30	.30	.30

TABLE 8.8. Alice's second updated access rates.

H_0	H_1	H_2	H_3
.10	.38	.364	.156

we measured N different statistics, $S_1, S_2, \ldots S_N$, we might combine them according to a formula such as

$$T = (S_1 + S_2 + S_3 + \cdots + S_N)/N$$

and make the determination of normal versus abnormal based on the statistic T. This would provide a more comprehensive view of normal behavior and make it more difficult for Trudy, as she would need to approximate more of Alice's normal behavior. A similar—though more sophisticated—approach is used in a popular IDS known as NIDES [9, 115]. NIDES incorporates both anomaly-based and signature-based IDSs. A good elementary introduction to NIDES, as well as several other IDSs, can be found in [233].

Robust anomaly detection is a difficult problem for a number of reasons. For one, system usage and user behavior constantly evolves and, therefore, so must the anomaly detector. Otherwise, false alarms would soon overwhelm the administrator. But an evolving anomaly detector means that it's possible for Trudy to slowly convince the anomaly detector that an attack is normal.

Another fundamental issue with anomaly detection is that a warning of abnormal behavior may not provide much specific information to the administrator. A vague warning that the system may be under attack could make it difficult to take concrete action. In contrast, a signature-based IDS will provide the administrator with precise information about the nature of the suspected attack.

The primary potential advantage of anomaly detection is that there is a chance of detecting previously unknown attacks. It's also sometimes argued that anomaly detection can be more efficient than signature detection, particularly if the signature file is large. In any case, the current generation of anomaly detectors must be used with signature-base IDS since they are not sufficiently robust to act as stand-alone systems.

The fact that anomaly detectors can't stand on their own is one of the more significant disadvantages of such systems. Other disadvantages include, as mentioned above, the nonspecific nature of the warnings provided and the potential for attackers to retrain the system to accept an attack as normal.

Anomaly-based intrusion detection is an active research topic, and many security professionals have high hopes for its ultimate success. Anomaly detection in general is often cited as key future security technology [89]. But it appears that the hackers are not convinced, at least based on the title of a talk presented at a recent Defcon[3] conference, "Why anomaly-based intrusion detection systems are a hacker's best friend" [58].

The bottom line is that anomaly detection is a difficult and tricky problem. It also appears to have parallels with the field of artificial intelligence. More than a quarter century has passed since predictions were made of "robots on your doorstep" [248]. Such predictions appear no more plausible today than at the time that they were made. If anomaly-based intrusion detection proves to be anywhere near as challenging as AI, it may never live up to its claimed potential.

8.10 SUMMARY

In this chapter, we've covered the basics of traditional authorization, including ACLs and capabilities. We highlighted the differences between ACLs and capabilities using the classic "confused deputy" problem. We then presented some of the security issues related to multilevel and multilateral security, as well as the related topics of covert channels and inference control. MLS naturally led us into the rarified air of security modeling, where we briefly discussed Bell-LaPadula and Biba's Model.

After covering the basics of security modeling, we pulled our heads out of the clouds, put our feet back on *terra firma*, and proceeded to discuss a few important non-traditional access control topics, including CAPTCHAs and firewalls. We concluded the chapter by stretching the definition of access control to cover intrusion detection systems. The issues we discussed concerning the various types of IDSs will resurface when we discuss virus detection in Chapter 11.

8.11 PROBLEMS

1. Discuss two advantaged of capabilities over ACLs. Discuss two advantages of ACLs over capabilities.

2. Briefly discuss one application not mentioned in the text where multilevel security is applicable.

3. What is the "need to know" principle and how does multilateral security enforce this principle?

4. List the three types of firewalls discussed in the book. At which layer of the Internet protocol stack does each operate? Find information on one commercial firewall product and explain (using the terminology presented in this chapter) which type of firewall it is.

---

[3]Defcon is the oldest, largest, and best-known hackers convention. It's held in Las Vegas each August, and it's inexpensive, totally chaotic, lots of fun, and hot (literally).

5. Discuss one method of inference control not mentioned in the book. What are its strengths and weaknesses?

6. Suppose that you work in a classified environment where MLS is employed and you have a TOP SECRET clearance. Describe a potential covert channel involving the User Datagram Protocol, or UDP. How could you minimize this covert channel, while still allowing network access by users with different clearance levels?

7. Define *high water mark principle* and *low water mark principle* as they relate to multilevel security. Can BLP enforce the high water mark principle, the low water mark principle, or neither? Can Biba's Model enforce the high water mark principle, the low water mark principle, or neither? Justify your answers.

8. Suppose Alice has a TOP SECRET clearance and Bob has a CONFIDENTIAL clearance. Both Alice and Bob have access to an MLS system. Describe a covert channel involving the print queue. Estimate the capacity of your covert channel.

9. Covert channels are discussed in [3]. Read and briefly summarize two of the following sections: 2.2, 3.2, 3.3, 4.1, 4.2, 5.2, 5.3, 5.4.

10. Ross Anderson claims that "Some kinds of security mechanisms may be worse than useless if they can be compromised" [14]. Does this hold true for inference control? Does this hold true for encryption? Does this hold true for methods that are used to reduce the capacity of covert channels?

11. In the text, we showed that it's easy to delegate using capabilities. Explain how it's possible to delegate using ACLs. Suppose Alice delegates to Bill who then delegates to Charlie. How would this be accomplished using capabilities? How would this be accomplished using ACLs? Which is easier and why?

12. Suppose Alice wants to temporarily delegate her C-list to Bob. Alice thinks that it would be more secure for her to digitally sign her C-list before giving it to Bob. Is this a good idea? Why or why not?

13. Combine BLP and Biba's Model into a single MLS security model that covers both confidentiality and integrity.

14. BLP can be stated as "no read up, no write down." What is the analogous statement for Biba's Model?

15. Describe the visual CAPTCHA known as Gimpy. How secure is EZ Gimpy compared with Hard Gimpy? Discuss the most successful attack on each type of Gimpy. Hint: See the article at [190].

16. Describe a visual CAPTCHA not discussed in the text. Explain how this CAPTCHA works; that is, explain how a program would generate the CAPTCHA and score the result and what a human would need to do to pass the test. Clearly specify what information is available to an attacker.

17. Describe an audio CAPTCHA not discussed in the text. Explain how this CAPTCHA works; that is, explain how a program would generate the CAPTCHA and score the result and what a human would need to do to pass the test. Clearly specify what information is available to an attacker.

18. If a packet filter firewall does not allow reset (RST) packets out, then the TCP ACK scan described in the text will not succeed. What are some drawbacks to this approach?

19. Suppose that a packet filter firewall resets the TTL field to 255 for each packet that it allows through the firewall. Then the `Firewalk` example described in the text will fail. Is there any problem with this solution? Could `Firewalk` be modified to work against such a system?

20. An application proxy firewall is able to scan all incoming application data for viruses. It would be more efficient to have each host scan the application data it receives for viruses, since this would distribute the workload among the hosts. Why might it still be preferable to have the application proxy perform this function?

21. Suppose incoming packets are encrypted with a symmetric key that is known only by the sender and the intended recipient. Which types of firewall (packet filter, stateful packet filter, application proxy) will work with such packets?

22. Suppose incoming packets are encrypted with a symmetric key known only to the sender and the receiving firewall. Which fields of the IP header can be encrypted and which cannot? Which fields of the IP header can be integrity protected and which cannot?

23. Defense in depth using firewalls is illustrated in Figure 8.14. Describe another security application where defense in depth is a sensible strategy.

24. Suppose that at the time interval following the results in Table 8.8, Alice's file use statistics are $A_0 = .05$, $A_1 = .25$, $A_2 = .25$, and $A_3 = .45$. Is this normal for Alice? Give the updated values for H_0 through H_3.

25. Beginning with the values of H_0 through H_3 in Table 8.4, what is the minimum number of iterations required until it is possible that $H_3 > .9$, without the IDS triggering a warning at any step?

26. In the time interval following the results in Table 8.6, what is the largest value that Trudy can have for A_3 without triggering a warning from the IDS? Also, give values for A_0, A_1, and A_2 that are compatible with your specified A_3 value and compute the statistic S, using the H_i values in Table 8.6.

Part III

PROTOCOLS

9

SIMPLE AUTHENTICATION PROTOCOLS

"I quite agree with you," said the Duchess; "and the moral of that is—'Be what you would seem to be'—or, if you'd like it put more simply—'Never imagine yourself not to be otherwise than what it might appear to others what you were or might have been was not otherwise than what you had been would have appeared to them to be otherwise.'"
—Lewis Carroll, *Alice in Wonderland*

Seek simplicity, and distrust it.
—Alfred North Whitehead

9.1 INTRODUCTION

Protocols are the rules that must be followed in some particular interaction. For example, there is a protocol that you follow if you want to ask a question in class. First, you raise your hand and eventually, the teacher calls on you. You can then ask your question, and the teacher will attempt to respond. There are a vast number of other human protocols, some of which can be very intricate.

In the context of networking, protocols are the rules followed in networked communication systems. Examples of formal networking protocols include HTTP, FTP, TCP, UDP, PPP, and many, many more.

Security protocols are the communication rules followed in security applications. In Chapter 10 we'll look closely at several real-world security protocols including SSL, IPSec, and Kerberos. In this chapter, we'll consider generic authentication protocols in order to better understand the fundamental issues involved in the design of such protocols.

Information Security: Principles and Practice, by Mark Stamp
Copyright © 2006 John Wiley & Sons, Inc.

In Chapter 7, we discussed methods that are used, primarily, to authenticate humans to a machines. In this chapter, we'll discuss authentication protocols. Although it might seem that these two authentication topics must be closely related, in fact, they are almost completely different. Here, we'll deal with the security issues related to the messages that must be sent—usually over a network—for authentication to occur. There are certain common classes of attacks that we'll be concerned with, most notably, replay and man-in-the-middle (MiM) attacks. These attacks depend only on the messages that are passed in the protocol and not the actual method used to authenticate (that is, something you know, something you have, or something you are).

Protocols can be very subtle. Often, a seemingly innocuous change can make a significant difference in a protocol. Security protocols are particularly subtle, since the attacker can actively intervene in the process in a variety of ways. As an indication of the challenges inherent in security protocols, many well-known security protocols—including IPSec, WEP and GSM—have serious security flaws. And even if the protocol itself is not flawed, a particular implementation can be.

Obviously, a security protocol must meet the specified security requirements. But we also want protocols to be efficient, both in computational cost and in bandwidth usage and delays. Also, an ideal security protocol should not be too fragile; that is, the protocol should continue to work even when an attacker actively tries to break it. And a security protocol should continue to work even if the environment in which it's deployed changes. Of course, it's difficult to protect against the unknown, but protocol developers can try to anticipate likely changes in the environment and build in some protections. Some of the most serious security challenges today are due to the fact that protocols are being used in environments for which they were not initially designed. For example, many Internet protocols were designed for a friendly, academic environment, which is about as far from the reality of the Internet of today as is possible. Ease of use, ease of implementation, flexibility, and so on are also desirable features in a protocol. Obviously, it's going to be difficult to satisfy all—or even most—of these requirements.

9.2 SIMPLE SECURITY PROTOCOLS

The first security protocol that we'll consider is a protocol that could be used for entry into a secure facility, such as the National Security Agency. Employees are given a badge that they must wear at all times when in the secure facility. To enter the building, the badge is inserted into a card reader and the employee must provide a PIN number. The secure entry protocol can be described as follows:

1. Insert badge into reader
2. Enter PIN
3. Is the PIN correct?
    - Yes: Enter the building
    - No: Get shot by a security guard

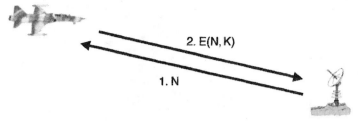

Figure 9.1. Identify friend or foe.

When you withdraw money from an ATM machine, the protocol is virtually identical to the secure entry protocol entry above, but without the violent ending:

1. Insert ATM card into reader
2. Enter PIN
3. Is the PIN correct?
   - Yes: Conduct your transactions
   - No: Machine eats your ATM card

The military has a need for many specialized security protocols. One such class of protocols is used to *identify friend or foe*, or IFF. These protocols are designed to prevent friendly fire incidents—where soldiers accidentally attack soldiers on their own side—while not seriously hampering the fight against the enemy.

A simple example of an IFF protocol appears in Figure 9.1. This protocol was reputedly used by the South African Air Force, or SAAF, when fighting in Angola [14]. The South Africans were based in Namibia, and they were fighting Cuban soldiers stationed in Angola, who were flying Soviet MiG aircraft.[1] In this IFF protocol, when the SAAF radar detected an aircraft approaching, a random number, or *challenge*, N was sent to the aircraft. All SAAF aircraft knew a key K that they used to encrypt the challenge, $E(N, K)$, which was then sent back to the radar station. Since enemy aircraft did not know K, they could not send back the required response. The radar station would then know whether to let the aircraft approach (friend) or to shoot it down (foe).

There is a clever attack on the IFF system in Figure 9.1. Anderson has dubbed this attack the "MiG-in-the-middle" [14], which is a pun on man-in-the-middle. The scenario for the attack, which is illustrated in Figure 9.2, is as follows. A Cuban-piloted MiG aircraft (the foe of the SAAF) is loitering just outside of the range of the SAAF radar in Namibia, while an SAAF Impala fighter is flying a mission over Angola. When the Impala fighter is within range of the Cuban radar station in Angola, the MiG moves within range of the SAAF radar. As specified by the protocol, the SAAF radar sends the challenge N. To avoid being shot down, the MiG needs to respond with $E(N, K)$ and quickly. Because the MiG does not know the key K, its situation appears hopeless.

---

[1]This was one of the hot wars that erupted during the Cold War.

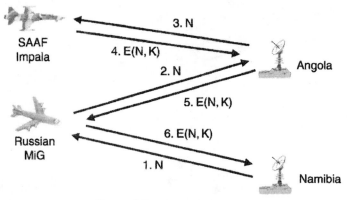

Figure 9.2. MiG-in-the-middle.

However, the MiG can forward the challenge N to it's radar station in Angola, which, in turn, can forward it to the SAAF Impala. The Impala fighter—not realizing that it has received the challenge from an enemy radar site—responds with $E(N, K)$. At this point, the Cuban radar relays the response $E(N, K)$ to the MiG, which can then provide it to the SAAF radar. Provided this all happens quickly enough, the SAAF radar will assume that the MiG is a friend, with disastrous consequences for the SAAF radar station and its operators.

Apparently, the MiG-in-the-middle attack never actually occurred [15], but it does nicely illustrate a subtle security failure. This is our first illustration of a security protocol failure, but it certainly won't be our last.

9.3 AUTHENTICATION PROTOCOLS

> *"I can't explain myself, I'm afraid, Sir,"* said Alice, *"because I'm not myself you see."*
> —Lewis Carroll, *Alice in Wonderland*

Suppose that Alice must prove to Bob that she's Alice, where, typically, Alice and Bob are communicating over a network. Keep in mind that Alice can be a human or a machine, as can Bob.

In many cases, it's sufficient for Alice to prove her identity to Bob, without Bob proving his identity to Alice. But sometimes *mutual authentication* is required; that is, Bob must also prove his identity to Alice. It seems obvious that if Alice can prove her identity to Bob, then precisely the same protocol can be used in the other direction for Bob to prove his identity to Alice. We'll see that, in security protocols, the obvious approach is often not secure.

In addition to authentication, a symmetric key is often required. The symmetric key is generally used as a session key, that is, a key for confidentiality or integrity protection (or both) for the current session.

In certain situations, there may be other requirements placed on a security protocol. For example, we might require that the protocol use public keys, or symmetric keys,

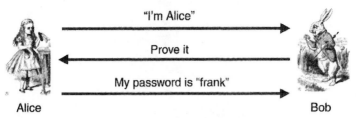

Figure 9.3. Simple authentication.

or hash functions. In addition some situations might call for anonymity or plausible deniability (discussed below).

We've previously considered the security issues associated with authentication on stand-alone computer systems. While such authentication presents its own set of challenges, from the protocol perspective, it's straightforward. In contrast, authentication over a network requires very careful attention to protocol issues. An attacker, Trudy, can passively observe messages, she can replay messages, and she can also conduct active attacks such as inserting, deleting, or changing messages. In this book, we haven't previously encountered anything comparable to these types of attacks.

Our first attempt at authentication over a network is the protocol shown in Figure 9.3. This three-message protocol requires that Alice first initiate contact with Bob and state her identity. Then Bob asks for proof of Alice's identity, and Alice responds with her password, which Bob uses to authenticate Alice.

Although the protocol in Figure 9.3 is certainly simple, it has some serious flaws. For one thing, if Trudy is able to passively observe the messages that are passed in Figure 9.3, she can later replay the messages to convince Bob that she is Alice, as illustrated in Figure 9.4.

Another issue with the simple authentication in Figure 9.3 is that Alice's password is sent in the clear. Suppose Trudy passively observes Alice's password. Then Trudy can pose as Alice on any site where Alice has reused her password "frank." Another password concern is that Bob must know Alice's password in order to authenticate her.

This simple authentication protocol is also inefficient, since the same effect could be accomplished in a single message from Alice to Bob. Finally, note that this protocol does not attempt to provide mutual authentication, which may be required in some cases.

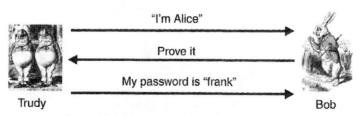

Figure 9.4. Simple authentication replay attack.

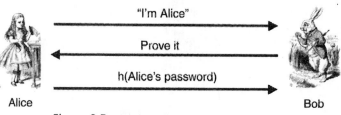

Figure 9.5. Simple authentication with a hash.

For our next attempt at an authentication protocol, consider Figure 9.5. This protocol solves some of the problems of our previous simple authentication protocol. In this version, a passive observer, Trudy, will not learn Alice's password and Bob no longer needs to know Alice's password—although he must know the hash of Alice's password.

The major flaw in the protocol of Figure 9.5 is that—as with the protocol in Figure 9.3—it's subject to a replay attack, where Trudy records Alice's messages and later replays them to Bob. In this way, Trudy would be authenticated as Alice, without knowledge of Alice's password.

To securely authenticate Alice, Bob will need to employ a "challenge-response" mechanism. That is, Bob will send a challenge to Alice, and the response from Alice will be something that only Alice can provide and that Bob can verify. To prevent a replay attack, Bob can employ a "number used once," or *nonce*, as the challenge. That is, Bob will send a unique challenge each time, and the challenge will be required in order to compute the appropriate response. Bob can thereby distinguish the current response from a replay of a previous response. In other words, the nonce is used to ensure the "freshness" of the response. This general approach to authentication with replay prevention appears in Figure 9.6.

We can design such an authentication protocol around Alice's password, since a password is something only Alice should know and Bob can verify. Our first serious attempt at an authentication protocol that is resistant to replay appears in Figure 9.7. In this protocol a nonce is sent from Bob to Alice. This nonce is the challenge. Alice must respond with the hash of her password, which proves that the response was generated by Alice, and the nonce, which proves that the response is fresh and not a replay.

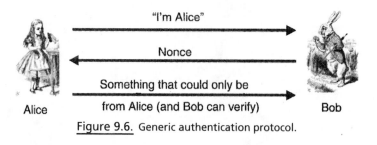

Figure 9.6. Generic authentication protocol.

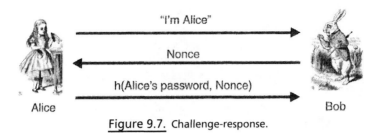

"I'm Alice"

Nonce

h(Alice's password, Nonce)

Alice   Bob

Figure 9.7. Challenge-response.

One problem with the protocol in Figure 9.7 is that Bob must know Alice's password. Our next goal will be to obtain a similar result as in Figure 9.7 without requiring Bob to know Alice's password.

9.3.1 Authentication Using Symmetric Keys

Since a hash proved useful in the previous section, perhaps some other form of cryptography will be useful as well. Let's see whether we can design a secure authentication protocol based on symmetric key cryptography. Recall that our notation for encrypting plaintext P with key K to obtain ciphertext C is $C = E(P, K)$ and the notation for decrypting ciphertext C with key K to recover the plaintext P is $P = D(C, K)$. Here, we are primarily concerned with attacks on protocols, not attacks on the cryptography used in the protocols. As a result, we'll assume that secure ciphers are used.

Suppose that Alice and Bob share symmetric key K_{AB} and that this key is known only to Alice and Bob. Authenticate can be accomplished by proving knowledge of this shared symmetric key. In the process of authenticating, the key K_{AB} must not be revealed to Trudy, and we must protect against a replay attack.

Our first symmetric key authentication protocol is analogous to the challenge-response protocol in Figure 9.7; however, instead of hashing a nonce with a password, we'll encrypt the nonce R with the key K_{AB}. This protocol is illustrated in Figure 9.8.

The symmetric key authentication protocol in Figure 9.8 allows Bob to authenticate Alice, and it prevents a replay attack. The protocol lacks mutual authentication, so our next task will be to develop a mutual authentication protocol.

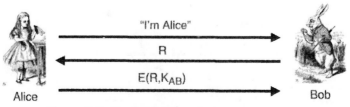

"I'm Alice"

R

$E(R, K_{AB})$

Alice   Bob

Figure 9.8. Symmetric key authentication protocol.

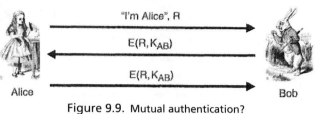

Figure 9.9. Mutual authentication?

Our first attempt at mutual authentication based on a shared symmetric key appears in Figure 9.9. This protocol is certainly efficient, and it does use symmetric key cryptography, but it has an obvious flaw. The third message in this protocol is simply a replay of the second, and consequently it proves nothing about the sender, be it Alice or Trudy.

A more plausible approach to mutual authentication would be to use the secure authentication protocol in Figure 9.8 and repeat the process twice, once for Bob to authenticate Alice and once more for Alice to authenticate Bob. We've illustrated this approach in Figure 9.10, where we've simply combined a few messages for the sake of efficiency.

However, the protocol in Figure 9.10 is subject to a man-in-the-middle, or MiM, attack, which is reminiscent of the MiG-in-the-middle attack discussed earlier. In this attack, as illustrated in Figure 9.11, Trudy initiates a conversation with Bob by claiming to be Alice and sends the challenge R_A to Bob. Bob encrypts the challenge R_A and sends it, along with a challenge R_B, to Trudy. At this point Trudy appears to be stuck, since she doesn't know the key K_{AB}, and therefore she can't respond to Bob's challenge. However, Trudy cleverly opens a new connection to Bob where she again claims to be Alice and this time sends Bob the "random" challenge R_B. Bob, following the protocol, responds with $E(R_B, K_{AB})$, which Trudy can now use to complete the first connection. Trudy can leave the second connection to time out, since she has—in the first connection—convinced Bob that she is Alice.

The conclusion is that a one-way authentication protocol may not be secure for mutual authentication. Another conclusion is that protocols—and attacks on protocols—can be subtle. Yet another conclusion is that "obvious" changes to protocols can raise serious security issues.

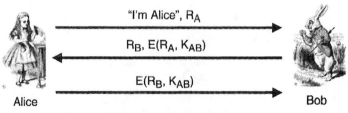

Figure 9.10. Secure mutual authentication?

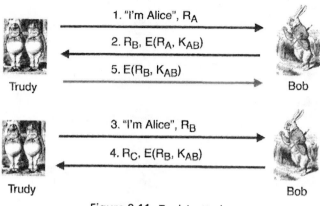

Figure 9.11. Trudy's attack.

In Figure 9.12, we've made a couple of minor changes to the insecure mutual authentication protocol of Figure 9.10. In particular, we've included the user's identity with the encryption of the nonce. This change is sufficient to prevent Trudy's previous attack since she cannot use a response from Bob for the third message.

One lesson here is that it's a bad idea to have the two sides in a protocol do exactly the same thing, since this opens the door to a replay attack. Another lesson is that small changes to a protocol can result in big changes in security.

9.3.2 Authentication Using Public Keys

Since we can devise a secure mutual authentication protocol using symmetric key technology, can we do the same using public key cryptography? First, recall that we denote the encryption of a message M with Alice's public key by $C = \{M\}_{\text{Alice}}$. To decrypt C, and thereby recover the plaintext M, we write $M = [C]_{\text{Alice}}$. Also, to sign the message M with Alice's private key we have $S = [M]_{\text{Alice}}$. Of course, encryption and decryption are inverse operation, as are encryption and signing; that is

$$[\{M\}_{\text{Alice}}]_{\text{Alice}} = M \quad \text{and} \quad \{[M]_{\text{Alice}}\}_{\text{Alice}} = M.$$

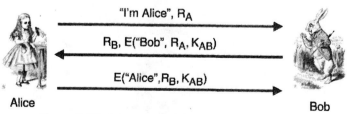

Figure 9.12. A better mutual authentication protocol.

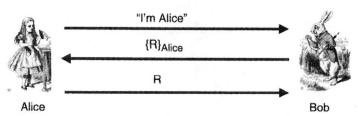

Figure 9.13. Authentication with public key encryption.

Two crucial facts regarding public key cryptography are that anybody can do public key operations, while only Alice can use her private key.

Our first attempt at authentication using public key cryptography appears in Figure 9.13. This protocol allows Bob to authenticate Alice, since only Alice can compute the private key operation that is required in order to reply with R in the third message.

If Alice uses the same key pair to encrypt as she uses for authentication, then there is a serious problem with the protocol in Figure 9.13. Suppose Trudy has previously intercepted a message encrypted with Alice's public key, say, $C = \{M\}_{\text{Alice}}$. Then Trudy can pose as Bob and send C to Alice in message two, and Alice will decrypt it and send the plaintext to Trudy. The moral of the story is that you should never use the same key pair for signing as you use for encryption.

The protocol in Figure 9.13 accomplishes authentication using public key encryption. Is it possible to accomplish the same feat using digital signatures? In fact, it is, as illustrated in Figure 9.14.

The protocol in Figure 9.14 has similar security issues as the public key encryption protocol in Figure 9.13. In Figure 9.14, if Trudy can pose as Bob, she can get Alice to sign anything. Again, the solution to this problem is to always use different key pairs for signing and encryption.

9.3.3 Session Keys

In addition to authentication, a session key is often required. Even when a symmetric key is used for authentication, it is desirable to use a separate session key to encrypt data within each connection. This limits the data encrypted with one particular key and also

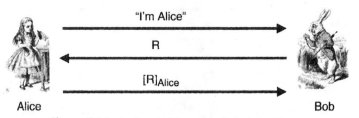

Figure 9.14. Authentication with digital signature.

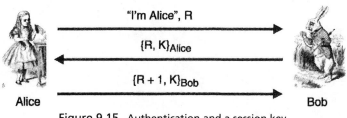

Figure 9.15. Authentication and a session key.

limits the damage if one session key is compromised. Of course, a session key may be used for confidentiality or integrity protection, or both.

Our next goal is to design a protocol for authentication that also allows us to establish a shared symmetric key. It looks to be straightforward to include a session key in our secure public key authentication protocol. Such a protocol appears in Figure 9.15.

One concern with the protocol of Figure 9.15 is that it does not provide for mutual authentication. But before we tackle that issue, can we modify the protocol in Figure 9.15 so that it uses digital signatures instead of encryption? This also seems straightforward, and the result appears in Figure 9.16.

However, there is a fatal flaw in Figure 9.16. Since the key is signed, anybody can use Bob's (or Alice's) public key and find the session key K. A session key that is public knowledge is not particularly useful! But before we dismiss this protocol entirely, note that it does provide mutual authentication, whereas the public key encryption protocol in Figure 9.15 does not. Can we improve on these protocols to achieve both mutual authentication and a secure session key?

Suppose that instead of merely signing the messages, as in Figure 9.16, we instead sign and encrypt the messages as in Figure 9.17. This appears to provide the desired mutual authentication and session key.

Since Figure 9.17 achieves our goal using "sign and encrypt," surely "encrypt and sign" must work as well. An encrypt and sign mutual authentication and key establishment protocol appears in Figure 9.18.

Note that the values $\{R, K\}_{\text{Alice}}$ and $\{R + 1, K\}_{\text{Bob}}$ in Figure 9.18 are available to anyone who has access to Alice's or Bob's public keys (which is, by assumption, anybody who wants them). Since this is not the case in Figure 9.17, it might seem that sign and encrypt somehow reveals less information than encrypt and sign. However,

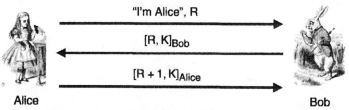

Figure 9.16. Signature-based authentication and session key.

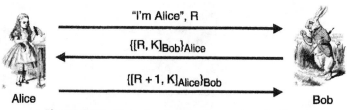

Figure 9.17. Mutual authentication and session key.

there is no security difference between the two, since an attacker must break the public key encryption to recover K in either case.

9.3.4 Perfect Forward Secrecy

Now that we have conquered mutual authentication and session key establishment (using public keys), we turn our attention to a property that is sometimes desired for session keys, namely, *perfect forward secrecy*, or PFS. The motivation behind PFS is the following. Suppose that Alice encrypts a message with a shared symmetric key K_{AB} and sends the resulting ciphertext to Bob. If Trudy records the ciphertext and later attacks Alice's computer and finds the shared key K_{AB}, then Trudy can decrypt the recorded ciphertext. The purpose of PFS is to prevent this from happening. That is, even if Trudy records all ciphertext messages and she later finds all long-term secrets (symmetric key or private key), she cannot decrypt the recorded messages. It's not obvious that this is possible.

Suppose Bob and Alice share a long-term symmetric key K_{AB}. Then if they want PFS, they can't use K_{AB} for encryption. Instead, Alice and Bob must use a session key K_S and "forget" this key after it's been used. So the PFS problem can be reduced to finding a way for Alice and Bob to agree on a session key K_S, using a long-term symmetric key K_{AB}.

A first attempt at PFS is illustrated in Figure 9.19. But this protocol fails to provide PFS, since Trudy could also record the first message $E(K_S, K_{AB})$ along with the ciphertext encrypted with K_S. Then if she later recovers K_{AB}, she can recover the session key K_S and use it to decrypt the recorded ciphertext messages. This is precisely what PFS is supposed to prevent.

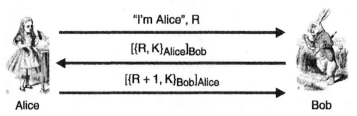

Figure 9.18. Encrypt and sign mutual authentication.

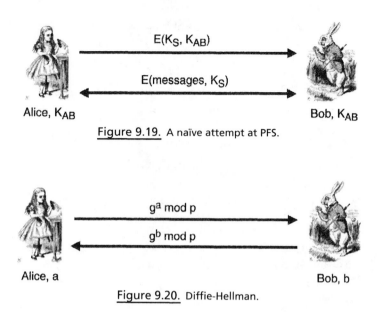

Figure 9.19. A naïve attempt at PFS.

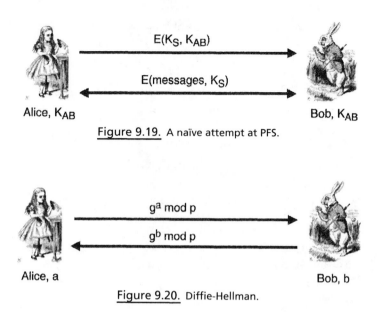

Figure 9.20. Diffie-Hellman.

There are actually several ways to achieve PFS, but perhaps the most elegant approach is with an *ephemeral Diffie-Hellman* key exchange. The usual Diffie-Hellman key exchange protocol appears in Figure 9.20. In this protocol, g and p are public, and Alice chooses a secret exponent a and Bob a secret exponent b. Then Alice sends $g^a \bmod p$ to Bob and Bob sends $g^b \bmod p$ to Alice. Alice and Bob can then each compute the shared secret $g^{ab} \bmod p$. Recall that the crucial weakness with Diffie-Hellman is that it is subject to a man-in-the-middle attack, as discussed in Section 4.4 of Chapter 4.

If we are to use Diffie-Hellman to achieve PFS, we must prevent the man-in-the-middle attack, and, of course, we must somehow assure PFS. The aforementioned ephemeral Diffie-Hellman can accomplish both. In order to prevent the MiM attack, Alice and Bob can use their shared symmetric key K_{AB} to encrypt the Diffie-Hellman exchange. Then to attain PFS, all that is required is that, once Alice has computed the shared session key $K_S = g^{ab} \bmod p$, she must forget her secret exponent a and, similarly, Bob must forget his secret exponent b. This protocol is illustrated in Figure 9.21.

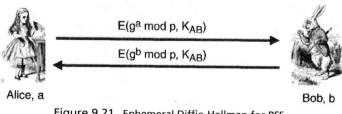

Figure 9.21. Ephemeral Diffie-Hellman for PFS.

One interesting feature of the PFS protocol in Figure 9.21 is that, once Alice and Bob have forgotten their respective secret exponents, even they can't reconstruct the session key K_S. If Alice and Bob can't recover the session key, certainly Trudy has no better chance. If Trudy records the conversation in Figure 9.21 and later is able to find K_{AB}, she will not be able to recover the session key K_S unless she can break Diffie-Hellman. This satisfies our requirements for PFS.

9.3.5   Mutual Authentication, Session Key, and PFS

Now let's put it all together and design a mutual authentication protocol that establishes a session key with PFS. The protocol in Figure 9.22, which is a slightly modified form of the encrypt and sign protocol in Figure 9.18, appears to fill the bill.

Now that we've apparently developed a secure protocol that achieves everything desired, we can turn our attention to questions of efficiency. That is, we'll try to reduce the number of messages in the protocol or increase the efficiency is some other way, such as by reducing the number of public key operations.

9.3.6   Timestamps

A *timestamp T*, contains the current time. With some care, a timestamp can be used in place of a nonce, since a current timestamp ensures freshness. The benefit of a timestamp is that we don't need to waste any messages exchanging nonces, assuming the current time is known to both Alice and Bob. Timestamps are used in many real-world security protocols, such as Kerberos—which we'll discuss in the next chapter.

Along with the potential benefit of increased efficiency, timestamps create some security concerns as well. For one thing, the use of timestamps implies that time is a security-critical parameter. For another, we can't rely on clocks to be perfectly synchronized, so we must allow for some *clock skew*; that is, we must accept any timestamp that is close to the current time. In some cases, this can open a small window to a replay attack. As a result, we would like to minimize the clock skew without causing excessive failures due to inconsistent time between Alice and Bob.

To see the potential value of a timestamp, consider the authentication protocol in Figure 9.23. This is equivalent to the sign and encrypt authentication protocol in Figure 9.17, but, by using the timestamp T, we've reduced the number of messages by a third.

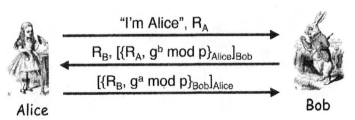

Figure 9.22. Mutual authentication, session key, and PFS.

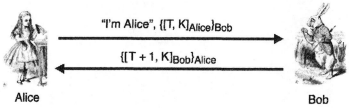

Figure 9.23. Authentication using a timestamp.

The protocol in Figure 9.23 uses a timestamp with the sign and encrypt authentication protocol, so obviously the timestamp version of encrypt and sign must also be secure. This is illustrated in Figure 9.24.

Unfortunately, with protocols, the obvious is not always true. In fact, the protocol in Figure 9.24 is subject to attack. Trudy can recover $\{T, K\}_{Bob}$ by applying Alice's public key. Then Trudy can open a connection to Bob and send $\{T, K\}_{Bob}$ in message one, as illustrated in Figure 9.25. Bob will then send the key K to Trudy in a form that Trudy can decrypt. This is not good, since K is the session key shared by Alice and Bob.

The attack in Figure 9.25 shows that our encrypt and sign is not secure when we use a timestamp. But our sign and encrypt protocol seems to be secure when a timestamp is used. In addition, the non-timestamp versions of both sign and encrypt as well as encrypt and sign are secure (see Figures 9.17 and 9.18). These examples clearly illustrate that, when it comes to security protocols, we can never take anything for granted.

Before leaving the flawed protocol in Figure 9.24, we mention that there are several ways that it can be fixed. For example, there's no reason to return the key K in the second message, since Alice already knows K and the only purpose of this message is to authenticate Bob. This secure version of the encrypt and sign protocol is illustrated in Figure 9.26.

In the next chapter, we'll discuss several well-known real-world security protocols. These protocols use many of the ideas that we've presented in this section. But before that, we briefly look at a weak form of authentication using TCP that is sometimes used in practice. Then we consider the Fiat-Shamir protocol, which is a method for zero knowledge proofs. We'll come across Fiat-Shamir again in upcoming chapters.

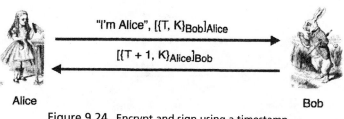

Figure 9.24. Encrypt and sign using a timestamp.

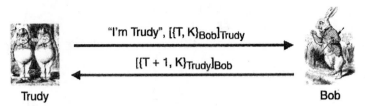

Figure 9.25. Trudy's attack on encrypt and sign.

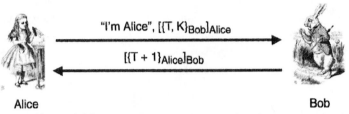

Figure 9.26. Secure encrypt and sign with a timestamp.

9.4 AUTHENTICATION AND TCP

In this section we'll take a quick look at how TCP is sometimes used for authentication. TCP was not designed to be used in this manner, and, not surprisingly, this authentication method is not particularly secure. But it does illustrate some interesting networking security issues.

Although TCP was not designed as a security protocol, it's tempting to use the IP address in a TCP connection for authentication. Even the IPSec protocol (which we discuss in the next chapter) relies on the IP address for user identity. Below, we'll show one scenario in which this can cause problems. But first we need to quickly review the TCP three-way handshake, which is illustrated in Figure 9.27. The first message is a synchronization request, or SYN, whereas the second message, which acknowledges the synchronization request, is a SYN-ACK, and the third message—which can also contain data—acknowledges the previous message, and is simply known as an ACK.

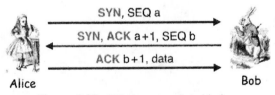

Figure 9.27. TCP three-way handshake.

Suppose that Bob relies on the completed three-way handshake to verify that he is connected to a specific IP address, which he knows belongs to Alice. In effect, he is using the TCP connection to authenticate Alice. Since Bob sends the SYN-ACK to Alice's IP address, it is tempting to assume that the corresponding ACK must have come from Alice. In particular, if Bob verifies that ACK $b + 1$ appears in message three, he has some reason to believe that Alice, at her known IP address, has received and responded to message two, since message two contains SEQ b. An underlying assumption here is that Trudy can't see the SYN-ACK packet—otherwise she would know b and she could easily forge the ACK. Clearly, this is not a strong form of authentication, but it is often used in practice.

One serious flaw with this TCP authentication scheme occurs if Trudy can predict the initial SEQ number sent by Bob. If so, the attack scenario illustrated in Figure 9.28 may be feasible. In this attack, Trudy first sends an ordinary SYN packet to Bob, who responds with a SYN-ACK. Trudy examines the SEQ value b_1 in this SYN-ACK packet. Suppose now that Trudy can use b_1 to predict Bob's next initial SEQ value b_2. Then Trudy can send a packet to Bob with the source IP address forged to be Alice's IP address. Then Bob will send the SYN-ACK to Alice's IP address which, by assumption, Trudy can't see. But since Trudy can guess b_2, she can complete the three-way handshake by sending ACK $b_2 + 1$ to Bob. As a result, Bob will believe that data from Trudy on this particular TCP connection actually came from Alice.

Note that Bob always responds to Alice's IP address and, by assumption, Trudy cannot see his responses. But Bob will accept data from Trudy, thinking it came from Alice, as long as the connection remains active. However, when the data sent by Bob to Alice's IP address reaches Alice, Alice will terminate the connection since she has not completed the three-way handshake. In order to prevent this from happening, Trudy could mount a denial of service attack on Alice by sending enough messages so that

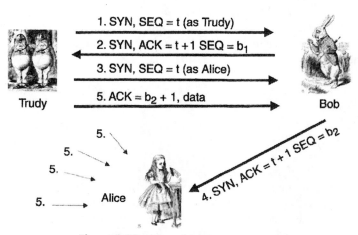

Figure 9.28. TCP authentication attack.

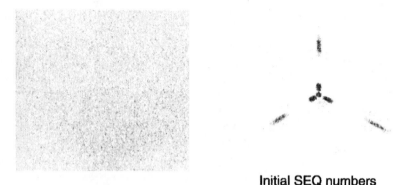

Random SEQ numbers

Initial SEQ numbers
Mac OS X

Figure 9.29. Plots of initial SEQ numbers (Courtesy of Michal Zalewski [250]).

Bob's messages can't get through—or, even if they do get through, Alice can't respond. This denial of service is illustrated by the messages labeled with 5s from Trudy to Alice. If Alice happens to be offline, Trudy could conduct the attack without this denial of service phase.

This attack is well known, and as a result it's known that initial SEQ numbers must be random. So how random are initial SEQ numbers? Surprisingly, they're often not very random at all. For example, Figure 9.29 provides a visual comparison of random initial SEQ numbers versus the highly biased initial SEQ numbers generated under Mac OS X. The Mac OS X numbers are biased enough that the attack in Figure 9.28 would have a reasonable chance of success. Many other vendors fail to generate reasonably random initial SEQ numbers, as can be seen from the fascinating pictures at [250].

Even if initial SEQ numbers are random, it's a bad idea to rely on a TCP connection for authentication. A much better approach would be to employ a secure authentication protocol after the three-way handshake has completed. Even a simple password scheme would be far superior to relying on TCP. But, as often occurs in security, the TCP authentication method is often used in practice simply because it's convenient, not because it's secure.

9.5 ZERO KNOWLEDGE PROOFS

In this section we'll discuss a fascinating authentication scheme developed by Fiege, Fiat, and Shamir [79] (yes, that Shamir), but usually known as simply Fiat-Shamir. Although this scheme might seem like little more than a clever academic exercise, we'll see this method again in Chapter 13 when we discuss Microsoft's new trusted operating system.

In a *zero knowledge proof*, or ZKP, Alice wants to prove to Bob that she knows a secret without revealing any information to anyone (including Bob) about the secret.

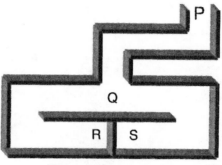

Figure 9.30. Bob's Cave.

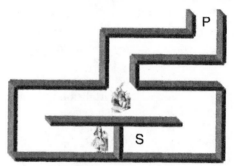

Figure 9.31. Bob's Cave protocol.

Bob must be able to verify that Alice knows the secret, even though he gains no information about the secret. On the face of it, this sounds impossible. However, there is a probabilistic process whereby Bob can verify that Alice knows a secret to an arbitrarily high probability. This is an example of an "interactive proof system."

To see how such a protocol might work, consider Bob's Cave[2] in Figure 9.30. Suppose that Alice claims to know the secret phrase "open sarsaparilla,"[3] which opens a path between R and S in Figure 9.30. Can Alice convince Bob that she knows the secret phrase without revealing any information about it?

Suppose Alice enters Bob's Cave and flips a coin to decide whether to position herself at point R or S. Bob then enters the cave and proceeds to point Q. Suppose Alice happens to be positioned at point R. This situation is illustrated in Figure 9.31.

Then Bob randomly selects one side or the other and asks Alice to appear from that side. If Bob happens to select side R, then Alice would appear at side R whether she knows the secret phrase or not. But if Bob happens to choose side S, then Alice can only

---

[2]Traditionally, Ali Baba's Cave is used here.

[3]Traditionally, the secret phrase is "open says me," which sounds a lot like "open sesame." In the cartoon world, "open sesame" somehow became "open sarsaparilla" [183].

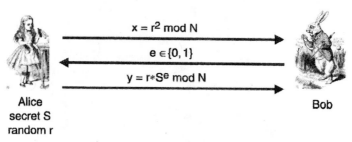

$x = r^2 \bmod N$

$e \in \{0, 1\}$

$y = r * S^e \bmod N$

Alice
secret S
random r

Bob

Figure 9.32. Fiat-Shamir protocol.

appear on side S if she knows the secret phrase that opens the door between R and S. In other words, if Alice doesn't know the secret phrase, she can trick Bob into believing that she does with a probability of $\frac{1}{2}$. But if the protocol is repeated n times, then the probability that Alice can trick Bob is only $(\frac{1}{2})^n$. Therefore, Bob can be convinced with an arbitrarily high degree of confidence that Alice indeed knows the secret phrase.

While Bob's Cave indicates that a zero knowledge proof is possible in principle, cave-based protocols are not particularly useful. Can we achieve the same effect without the cave? The answer is yes, thanks to the Fiat-Shamir protocol.

Fiat-Shamir relies on the fact that finding a square root modulo N is comparable in difficulty to factoring. Suppose $N = pq$, where p and q are prime. Alice knows a secret S which is, naturally, secret. The numbers N and $v = S^2 \bmod N$ are public. Alice must convince Bob that she knows S without revealing any information about S.

The Fiat-Shamir protocol, as illustrated in Figure 9.32, proceeds as follows. Alice selects a random r, and she sends $x = r^2 \bmod N$ to Bob. Bob then chooses a random value $e \in \{0, 1\}$, which he sends to Alice. In the third message, Alice responds with $y = rS^e \bmod N$ and Bob then verifies that

$$y^2 = xv^e \bmod N$$

which holds true since

$$y^2 = r^2 S^{2e} = r^2(S^2)^e = xv^e \bmod N. \tag{9.1}$$

Let's consider the cases $e = 0$ and $e = 1$ separately. If $e = 1$, then Alice responds with $y = r \cdot S \bmod N$ in the third message, and *equation 9.1* becomes

$$y^2 = r^2 \cdot S^2 = r^2 \cdot (S^2) = x \cdot v \bmod N.$$

In particular, when $e = 1$, Alice must know the secret S.

If $e = 0$ in Fiat-Shamir, then Alice responds in the third message with $y = r \bmod N$ and *equation 9.1* becomes

$$y^2 = r^2 = x \bmod N.$$

Alice does not need to know the secret S in this case. This may seem strange, but it's equivalent to the situation in Bob's Cave where Alice did not need to open the secret passage in order to come out on the correct side. While it might seem tempting for Bob to always send $e = 1$, we'll see in a moment that that this would not be wise.

The first message in the Fiat-Shamir protocol is known as the *commitment* phase since Alice commits to her choice of r by sending $x = r^2 \bmod N$ to Bob. The second message is the *challenge* phase since Bob is challenging Alice to provide the correct response. The third message is the *response* phase, since Alice must respond with the correct value, which Bob can verify using *equation 9.1*. These phases correspond to the three steps in Bob's Cave protocol in Figure 9.31.

The mathematics behind the Fiat-Shamir protocol works; that is, Bob can verify $y^2 = xv^e \bmod N$ from the information he receives. But this does not establish the security of the protocol. To do so, we must determine whether an attacker, Trudy, can convince Bob that she knows S and thereby convince Bob that she is Alice.

Suppose Trudy expects Bob to send the challenge $e = 0$ in message two. Then Trudy can send $x = r^2 \bmod N$ in message one and $y = r \bmod N$ in message three. In other words, Trudy simply follows the protocol in this case, since she does not need to know the secret S.

On the other hand, if Trudy expects Bob to send $e = 1$, then she can send $x = r^2v^{-1} \bmod N$ in message one and $y = r \bmod N$ in message three. Then Bob will compute $y^2 = r^2$ and $xv^e = r^2v^{-1}v = r^2$ and he will find that *equation 9.1* holds, and he will accept the result as valid. But if Bob chooses $e \in \{0, 1\}$ at random (as required by the protocol), then Trudy can only fool Bob with probability $\frac{1}{2}$. And, as with Bob's Cave, after n iterations, the probability that Trudy can fool Bob is only $(\frac{1}{2})^n$.

Fiat-Shamir requires that Bob's challenge $e \in \{0, 1\}$ be unpredictable. In addition, Alice must generate a random r at each iteration of the protocol (see Problem 28 at the end of this chapter).

Is the Fiat-Shamir protocol really "zero knowledge"? Can Bob—or anyone else—learn anything about Alice's secret S? Recall that $v = S^2 \bmod N$ and the modulus N are public. In addition, Bob sees $r^2 \bmod N$ in message one, and, assuming $e = 1$, Bob sees $rS \bmod N$ in message three. If Bob can find r from $r^2 \bmod N$, then he can find S. But we're assuming that finding a modular square root is computationally infeasible. And if Bob were somehow able to find such square roots, he could obtain S directly from the public value v without bothering with the protocol at all. While this is not a rigorous proof that Fiat-Shamir is zero knowledge, it does indicate that the protocol itself does not help Bob to find the secret S.

What is the security benefit of Fiat-Shamir? If public keys are used for authentication, then the public keys must be in the possession of both sides. For example, if Alice does not know Bob's public key, then Bob would typically send his certificate to Alice. But the certificate identifies Bob, and consequently this exchange would enable Trudy to determine that Bob is a party to a particular transaction. In other words, it is difficult in practice to maintain anonymity when public keys are used.

A significant advantage of zero knowledge proofs is that they allow for authentication with anonymity. In Fiat-Shamir, both sides must know the public value v, but there is nothing in v that identifies Alice, and there is nothing in the messages that are passed that must identify Alice. This is a significant advantage that has led Microsoft to include support for zero knowledge proofs in its "next generation secure computing base," or

NGSCB, which we'll discuss in Chapter 13. The bottom line is that Fiat-Shamir is not just fun and games for mathematicians.

9.6 THE BEST AUTHENTICATION PROTOCOL?

In general there is no best authentication protocol. What is best for a particular situation will depend on many factors. At a minimum, we need to consider the following questions.

- What is the sensitivity of the application?
- What delay is tolerable?
- What type of crypto is supported—public key, symmetric key, or hash functions?
- Is mutual authentication required?
- Is a session key required?
- Is perfect forward secrecy desired?
- Is anonymity a concern?

In the next chapter, we'll see that there are other issues that can influence our choice of protocol.

9.7 SUMMARY

In this chapter we discussed several different ways to authenticate and establish a session key over a network. We can accomplish these feats using symmetric keys, public keys, or hash functions. We also learned how to achieve perfect forward secrecy, and we considered the benefits (and potential drawbacks) of using timestamps.

Along the way, we came across many security pitfalls. You should now have some appreciation for the subtle issues that can arise with security protocols. This will be useful in the next chapter where we look closely at several real-world security protocols. We'll see that, despite extensive development efforts, such protocols are not immune to some of the security flaws highlighted in this chapter.

9.8 PROBLEMS

1. Modify the secure authentication protocol in Figure 9.12 to use a hash function instead of symmetric key encryption. The resulting protocol must still be secure.
2. Design a secure mutual authentication and key establishment protocol using symmetric key cryptography.
3. Provide a way to achieve perfect forward secrecy that does not use Diffie-Hellman.
4. The insecure protocol in Figure 9.24 was modified to be secure in Figure 9.26. Find two other ways to slightly modify the protocol in Figure 9.24 so that the resulting protocol is secure. Your protocols must use a timestamp and "encrypt and sign."

5. We want to design a secure mutual authentication protocol based on a shared symmetric key. We also want to establish a session key, and we want to achieve perfect forward secrecy. Design such a protocol that uses three messages. Can you reduce the protocol to two messages?

6. Consider the following mutual authentication protocol, where K_{AB} is a shared symmetric key:

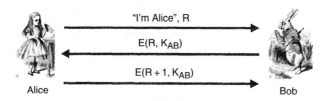

"I'm Alice", R

$E(R, K_{AB})$

$E(R + 1, K_{AB})$

Alice   Bob

Give two different attacks that Trudy can use to convince Bob that she is Alice. Hint: A man-in-the-middle attack doesn't work.

7. Consider the attack on TCP authentication illustrated in Figure 9.28. Suppose that Trudy cannot guess the initial sequence number b_2 exactly. Instead, Trudy can only narrow b_2 down to one of, say, 1,000 possible values. How can Trudy conduct the attack so that she is almost certain to succeed?

8. What is the primary advantage of using timestamps in an authentication protocol. What is the primary disadvantage of using timestamps?

9. Consider the following protocol, where $K = h(S, R_A, R_B)$ and CLNT and SRVR are constants:

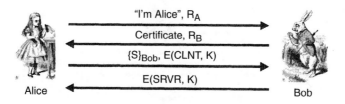

"I'm Alice", R_A

Certificate, R_B

$\{S\}_{Bob}, E(CLNT, K)$

$E(SRVR, K)$

Alice   Bob

a. Does Alice authenticate Bob? Why or why not?

b. Does Bob authenticate Alice? Why or why not?

10. Consider the following protocol, where $K = h(S, R_A, R_B)$ and CLNT and SRVR are constants and K_{AB} is a shared symmetric key.

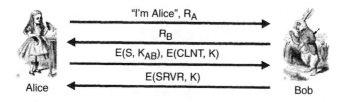

"I'm Alice", R_A

R_B

$E(S, K_{AB}), E(CLNT, K)$

$E(SRVR, K)$

Alice   Bob

    a. Does Alice authenticate Bob? Why or why not?

    b. Does Bob authenticate Alice? Why or why not?

11. The following two-message protocol is designed for mutual authentication and to establish a shared symmetric key K. Here, T is a timestamp.

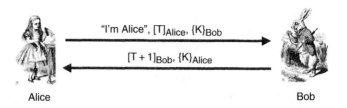

Alice   Bob

    This protocol is insecure. Illustrate a successful attack by Trudy.

12. Suppose R is a random challenge sent in the clear from Alice to Bob and K is a symmetric key known to both Alice and Bob. Which of the following are secure session keys and which are not: $R \oplus K$, $E(R, K)$, $E(K, R)$, $h(K, R)$, $h(R, K)$?

13. Design a secure two-message authentication protocol that achieves mutual authentication and establishes a session key K. Assume that Alice and Bob know each other's public keys beforehand. Does your protocol protect the anonymity of Alice and Bob from a passive attacker? If not, can you modify your protocol so that it does?

14. If Trudy can construct messages that appear to any observer (including Alice or Bob) to be valid messages between Alice and Bob, then the protocol is said to provide *plausible deniability*. Consider the following protocol

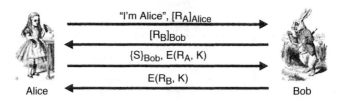

Alice   Bob

    where $K = h(R_A, R_B, S)$. Does this protocol provide plausible deniability? If so, why? If not, slightly modify the protocol so that it does, while still providing mutual authentication and a session key.

15. Consider the following protocol

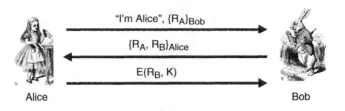

Alice   Bob

where $K = h(R_A, R_B)$. Does this protocol provide for plausible deniability (see Problem 14, above)? If so, why? If not, slightly modify the protocol so that it does, while still providing mutual authentication and a secure session key.

16. Design a mutual authentication protocol that only employs digital signatures and provides plausible deniability (see Problem 14, above).

17. Is plausible deniability (see Problem 14, above) a feature or a security flaw?

18. The following mutual authentication protocol is based on a shared symmetric key K_{AB}.

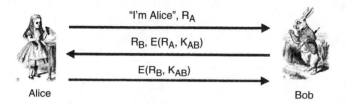

"I'm Alice", R_A

R_B, $E(R_A, K_{AB})$

$E(R_B, K_{AB})$

Alice   Bob

Show that Trudy can attack the protocol to convince Bob that she is Alice, where we assume that the cryptography is secure. Modify the protocol to prevent such an attack by Trudy.

19. Consider the following mutual authentication and key establishment protocol. This protocol uses a timestamp T and public key cryptography.

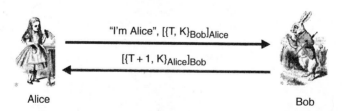

"I'm Alice", $[\{T, K\}_{Bob}]_{Alice}$

$[\{T + 1, K\}_{Alice}]_{Bob}$

Alice   Bob

Show that Trudy can attack the protocol to discover the key K. We assume that the cryptography is secure. Modify the protocol to prevent such an attack by Trudy.

20. Suppose we remove R_B from the protocol in Figure 9.22. Show that Trudy can convince Bob that she is Alice.

21. In the text, we claimed that the protocol in Figure 9.18 is secure, while the similar protocol in Figure 9.24 is insecure. Why does the attack on the latter protocol not succeed against the former protocol?

22. The protocol in Figure 9.23 is subject to a replay attack, provided Trudy can act within the allowed clock skew. How can Bob prevent such an attack?

23. Modify the identify friend or foe (IFF) protocol discussed at the beginning of the chapter so that it's no longer susceptible to the MiG-in-the-middle attack.

24. Can you achieve perfect forward secrecy using only symmetric key cryptography? If so, give such a protocol. If not, why not?

25. Design a zero knowledge protocol that uses Bob's Cave and only requires one iteration to determine with certainty whether Alice knows the secret phrase.

26. Suppose that in the Fiat-Shamir protocol in Figure 9.32 we have $N = 55$ and Alice's secret is $S = 9$. What is v? Suppose Alice chooses $r = 10$. What does Alice send in the first message? What does Alice send in the third message, assuming Bob chooses $e = 0$? What does Alice send in the third message, assuming Bob chooses $e = 1$?

27. Suppose that in the Fiat-Shamir protocol in Figure 9.32, we have $N = 55$ and $v = 5$. Suppose Alice sends $x = 4$ in the first message, Bob sends $e = 1$ in the second message, and Alice sends $y = 30$ in message three. Show that Bob will verify Alice's response in this case. Can you find Alice's secret S?

28. In the Fiat-Shamir protocol in Figure 9.32, suppose that Alice gets lazy and she decides to use the same "random" r each iteration. Show that Bob can determine Alice's secret S. Is this a security concern?

29. Suppose that in the Fiat-Shamir protocol illustrated in Figure 9.32, we have $N = 27,331$ and $v = 7,339$. Suppose that Alice sends $x = 21,684$ in message one, Bob sends $e = 0$ in message two, and Alice sends $y = 657$ in the third message. Show that Bob verifies Alice's response in this case. At the next iteration, Alice again sends $x = 21,684$ in message one, but Bob sends $e = 1$ in message two, and Alice responds with $y = 26,938$ in message three. Show that Bob again verifies Alice's response. Determine Alice's secret S. Hint: $657^{-1} = 208 \bmod 27,331$.

10

REAL-WORLD SECURITY PROTOCOLS

The wire protocol guys don't worry about security because
that's really a network protocol problem. The network protocol
guys don't worry about it because, really, it's an application problem.
The application guys don't worry about it because,
after all, they can just use the IP address and trust the network.
—Marcus J. Ranum

In the real world, nothing happens at the right place at the right time.
It is the job of journalists and historians to correct that.
—Mark Twain

10.1 INTRODUCTION

In this chapter, we'll discuss four security protocols that are used extensively in the real world. First on the agenda is the Secure Socket Layer, or SSL, which is used to secure most Internet transactions today. The second protocol that we'll consider in detail is IPSec, which is a complex and over-engineered protocol with several security flaws. Then we will discuss Kerberos, a popular authentication protocol built on symmetric key cryptography. The final real-world protocol we'll consider is GSM, which is used to secure mobile telephone conversations. The GSM protocol is relatively simple, but it's an interesting case study due to the large number of successful attacks that are known.

Information Security: Principles and Practice, by Mark Stamp
Copyright © 2006 John Wiley & Sons, Inc.

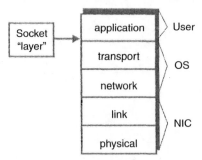

Figure 10.1. Socket layer.

10.2 SECURE SOCKET LAYER

The "socket layer" lives between the application layer and the transport layer in the Internet protocol stack. In practice, SSL most often deals with Web browsing, in which case the application layer protocol is HTTP and the transport layer protocol is TCP. The socket layer is illustrated in Figure 10.1.

SSL is the protocol that is used for the vast majority of secure transactions over the Internet. For example, suppose that you want to buy a book at amazon.com. Before you provide your credit card information, you want to be sure you are dealing with Amazon; that is, you must authenticate Amazon. Generally, Amazon doesn't care who you are, as long as you have money. As a result, the authentication need not be mutual.

After you are satisfied that you are dealing with Amazon, you will provide Amazon with private information, such as your credit card number, your address, and so on. You probably want this information protected in transit. In most cases, you want both confidentiality (to protect your privacy) and integrity protection (to assure the transaction is received correctly).

The general idea behind SSL is illustrated in Figure 10.2. In this protocol, Alice (the client) informs Bob (the server) that she wants to conduct a secure transaction. Bob responds with his certificate. Alice needs to verify the signature on the certificate, at which point she will be confident that she has Bob's certificate—although she cannot yet be certain that she's talking to Bob. Then Alice will encrypt a symmetric key K_{AB}

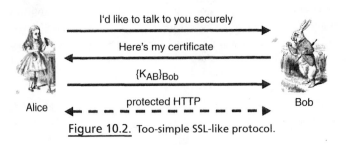

Figure 10.2. Too-simple SSL-like protocol.

with Bob's public key and send the encrypted key to Bob. This symmetric key can then be used to encrypt and integrity protect subsequent communications.

The protocol in Figure 10.2 is not useful as it stands. For one thing, Bob is not explicitly authenticated and the only way Alice will know she is talking to Bob is when the encrypted data decrypts correctly. Also, Alice is not authenticated to Bob at all, which is probably reasonable given the discussion above.

In Figure 10.3, we've given a reasonably complete view of the basic SSL protocol. In this protocol,

$$S = \text{the "pre-master secret"}$$

$$K = h(S, R_A, R_B)$$

$$\text{msgs} = \text{shorthand for "all previous messages"}$$

$$\text{CLNT} = \text{literal string}$$

$$\text{SRVR} = \text{literal string}$$

where h is a secure hash function. The actual SSL protocol is more complex than what is given in Figure 10.3, but this simplified version is sufficient for our purposes. The complete SSL specification can be found at [195].

Next, let's briefly discuss each of the messages sent in the simplified SSL protocol in Figure 10.3. In the first message, Alice informs Bob that she would like to establish an SSL connection, and she passes a list of ciphers that she supports, along with a nonce R_A. In the second message, Bob responds with his certificate, he selects one of the ciphers from the ciphers list that Alice sent in message one, and he sends a nonce R_B.

In the third message, Alice sends the "pre-master secret" S that she generated, along with a hash that is encrypted with the key K. In this hash, "msgs" includes all previous messages and CLNT is a literal string. The hash is used to verify that the previous messages have been received correctly.

In the fourth message, Bob responds with a similar hash. Alice can thereby verify that Bob received the messages correctly, and, more importantly, she can authenticate Bob, since only Bob could have decrypted S, which is required to generate the key K. At this point, Alice has authenticated Bob, and Alice and Bob have a shared symmetric key K, which they can use to encrypt and integrity protect subsequent messages.

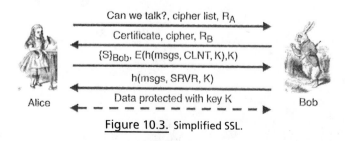

Figure 10.3. Simplified SSL.

The following six quantities are derived from $K = h(S, R_A, R_B)$.

- Two encryption keys, one for sending and one for receiving data.
- Two integrity keys, one for sending and one for receiving.
- Two initialization vectors (IVs), one for sending and one for receiving.

Different keys in each direction may help to prevent certain types of replay attacks.

You may be wondering why $h(\text{msgs}, \text{CLNT}, K)$ is encrypted and integrity protected in messages three and four. In fact, this adds no security, though it does add extra work, so this could be considered a minor flaw in the protocol.

In the SSL protocol of Figure 10.3, Alice, the client, authenticates Bob, the server, but not vice versa. With SSL, it is possible for the server to authenticate the client. If this is desired, Bob sends a "certificate request" in message two. However, this is seldom used, since it requires users to have valid certificates. If the server wants to authenticate the client, the server could simply require an encrypted or hashed password from the client. Such authentication would be separate from the SSL protocol.

10.2.1   SSL and the Man-in-the-Middle

SSL is designed to protect against the man-in-the-middle, or MiM, attack illustrated in Figure 10.4. What mechanism in SSL prevents this MiM attack? Bob's certificate must be signed by a certificate authority (such as VeriSign). The attacker Trudy could send Bob's certificate to Alice, but then Trudy could not authenticate herself as Bob. If Trudy sends her own certificate instead of Bob's, the attack should fail when Alice attempts to verify the signature on the certificate.

Suppose SSL is being used in a Web browsing session (as is the usual case for SSL). If the the signature on a certificate is not valid, what does Alice's Web browser do? It provides Alice with a warning. And what does Alice then do? Most users would probably ignore such a warning and allow the connection to proceed. If Alice ignores this warning, then Trudy's MiM attack in Figure 10.4 will succeed.

10.2.2   SSL Connections

An SSL *session* is established as shown in Figure 10.3. This session establishment protocol is relatively expensive, since public key operations are required.

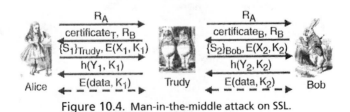

Figure 10.4. Man-in-the-middle attack on SSL.

SSL was originally developed by Netscape, specifically for use in Web browsing. The application layer protocol for the Web is HTTP, and two versions of it are in common usage, HTTP 1.0 and HTTP 1.1. With HTTP 1.0, it is common practice for the Web browser to open multiple parallel connections in order to improve performance. If we had to establish a new SSL session for each of these HTTP connections, then there could be a significant performance problem, due to the large number of the public key operations. The designers of SSL were aware of this potential problem, so they included an efficient protocol for opening new SSL *connections* provided that an SSL session already exists. If an SSL session exists, then Alice and Bob share a symmetric key K which can be used to establish new connections, thereby avoiding expensive public key operations.

The SSL connection protocol is given in Figure 10.5. The protocol is similar to the SSL session establishment protocol, except that the symmetric key K is used in order to avoid public key operation. Given one (expensive) session, SSL can create any number of (cheap) connections.

10.2.3 SSL Versus IPSec

In the next section, we'll discuss IPSec. In many ways, IPSec is similar to SSL, but in some important ways it's very different. IPSec is complex, so before we discuss it in detail, we'll first give a quick comparison of SSL versus IPSec. SSL (and the IEEE standard known as TLS) lives at the socket layer. As a result, SSL resides in user space. IPSec, on the other hand, lives at the network layer and is therefore part of the operating system. Logically, this is the fundamental distinction between SSL and IPSec.

Both SSL and IPSec provide encryption, integrity protection, and authentication. SSL is relatively simple and well-designed, whereas IPSec is overly complex and includes some significant flaws.

Since IPSec is part of the OS, changes to the OS are required in order to implement IPSec. In contrast, SSL is part of user space, so it requires no changes to the OS. IPSec also requires no changes to applications, since all of the work occurs in the OS. But to use SSL, existing applications must be modified.

SSL was built into Web application early on, and its primary use remains secure Web transactions. IPSec is often used to secure a "virtual private network," or VPN,

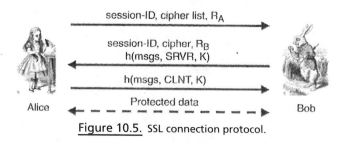

Figure 10.5. SSL connection protocol.

an application that creates a secure tunnel between the endpoints. Also, IPSec is required in IP version 6 (IPv6).

There is, understandably, a reluctance to retrofit applications for SSL. There is, also understandably, a reluctance to use IPSec due to its complexity and interoperability issues. The net result is that the Internet is less secure than it should be.

10.3 IPSec

Figure 10.6 illustrates the primary logical difference between SSL, which lives at the socket layer, and IPSec, which lives at the network layer. The major advantage of IPSec is that it's transparent to applications.

The major drawback to IPSec is that it's a complex protocol, which can best be described as "over-engineered." IPSec has many dubious features, which makes implementation difficult. Also, IPSec is flawed, probably as a direct result of its complexity. In fact, IPSec includes some serious security flaws as we'll discuss below. There are also interoperability issues with IPSec, again due to the complexity of it specification, which seems to run contrary to the point of having a standard. Another complicating factor is that the IPSec specification is split into three pieces, to be found in RFC 2407 [181], RFC 2408 [152], and RFC 2409 [104], and these RFCs were written by disjoint sets of authors.

The two main parts to IPSec are

- The Internet Key Exchange, or *IKE*, which provides for mutual authentication and establishment of a shared symmetric key. There are two phases of IKE, which are analogous to SSL sessions and connections.
- The Encapsulating Security Payload and Authentication Header, or *ESP/AH*, which together make up the second part of IPSec. ESP provides for encryption or integrity of IP packets, whereas AH provides for integrity only.

First, we'll consider IKE and then ESP/AH. IKE is by far the more complex of the two parts.

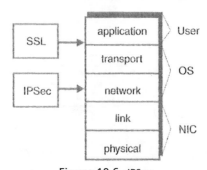

Figure 10.6. IPSec.

IKE consists of two phases, which are cleverly labeled Phase 1 and Phase 2. Phase 1 is the more complex of the two. In Phase 1, an IKE security association, or SA, is established, while in Phase 2, an IPSec security association is established. Phase 1 is roughly equivalent to an SSL session establishment, whereas Phase 2 is comparable to an SSL connection establishment. But unlike SSL, there is no obvious need for two phases in IKE. And if multiple Phase 2s do not occur, then it's more expensive to require two phases. This is the first hint of the over-engineering aspects of IPSec.

In IKE Phase 1, there are four different "key options."

- Public key encryption (original version)
- Public key encryption (improved version)
- Digital signature
- Symmetric key

For each of the key options there is a "main mode" and an "aggressive mode." As a result, there are a staggering eight versions of IKE Phase 1. Here is yet more evidence that IPSec is over-engineered.

You may be wondering why there is a public key encryption and a digital signature option in IKE Phase 1. The answer is that Alice always knows her own private key, but she may not initially know Bob's public key. With the signature version of IKE Phase 1, Alice does not need to know Bob's public key beforehand—or waste a message retrieving Bob's public key.

We'll discuss six of the eight Phase 1 variants, namely, digital signatures (main and aggressive modes), symmetric key (main and aggressive modes), and public key encryption (main and aggressive). We'll consider the original version of public key encryption, since it's slightly simpler, although less efficient than the improved version.

Each of the Phase 1 variants use an ephemeral Diffie-Hellman key exchange to establish a session key. The benefit of this approach is that it achieves perfect forward secrecy, or PFS. In each of the variants we discuss, we'll use the following notation. Let a be Alice's (ephemeral) Diffie-Hellman exponent and let b be Bob's (ephemeral) Diffie-Hellman exponent. Let g be the generator and p the prime for use in Diffie-Hellman. Recall that p and g are public.

10.3.1 IKE Phase 1: Digital Signature

The first Phase 1 variant that we'll discuss is digital signature, main mode. This six message protocol is illustrated in Figure 10.7, where

$$CP = \text{crypto proposed}$$

$$CS = \text{crypto selected}$$

$$IC = \text{initiator "cookie"}$$

$$RC = \text{responder "cookie"}$$

$$K = h(IC, RC, g^{ab} \bmod p, R_A, R_B)$$

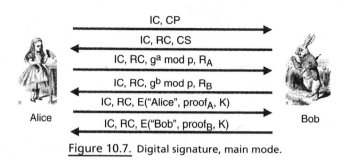

Figure 10.7. Digital signature, main mode.

$$\text{SKEYID} = h(R_A, R_B, g^{ab} \bmod p)$$

$$\text{proof}_A = [h(\text{SKEYID}, g^a \bmod p, g^b \bmod p, \text{IC}, \text{RC}, \text{CP}, \text{``Alice''})]_{\text{Alice}}$$

Here, h is a hash function and proof_B is similar to proof_A.

Let's briefly consider each of the six messages in Figure 10.7. In the first message Alice provides information on the ciphers that she supports along with a "cookie" (discussed below). In message two, Bob selects from Alice's crypto proposal and sends the cookies. The third message includes a nonce and Alice's Diffie-Hellman value. Bob responds similarly in message four, providing a nonce and his Diffie-Hellman value. In the final two messages, Alice and Bob authenticate each other using digital signatures.

In the protocol of Figure 10.7, a passive attacker cannot discern Alice or Bob's identity, so this protocol provides anonymity. In the aggressive mode version of digital signatures, which appears in Figure 10.8, there is no attempt to hide the identities of Alice or Bob, which simplifies the protocol considerably. The notation in Figure 10.8 is the same as that used in Figure 10.7.

One subtle difference between digital signature main and aggressive modes is that in main mode it is possible to negotiate the values of g and p as part of the "crypto proposed" and "crypt accepted" messages. However, this is not the case in aggressive mode, since the Diffie-Hellman value $g^a \bmod p$ is part of the first message.

For each of the key options main mode must be implemented, while aggressive mode "should" be implemented. In [122], the authors interpret this to mean that if aggressive mode is not implemented, "you should feel guilty about it".

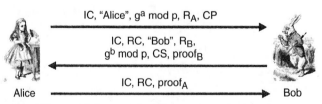

Figure 10.8. Digital signature, aggressive mode.

For the digital signature version of Phase 1, a passive attacker knows the identities of Alice and Bob in aggressive mode but not in main mode. However, an active attacker can also determine Alice's identity in main mode.

10.3.2 IKE Phase 1: Symmetric Key

The next version of Phase 1 that we'll consider is the symmetric key option—both main mode and aggressive mode. As above, the main mode is a six message protocol, where the format is the same as in Figure 10.7, above, except that

$$K_{AB} = \text{symmetric key shared in advance}$$

$$K = h(\text{IC}, \text{RC}, g^{ab} \bmod p, R_A, R_B, K_{AB})$$

$$\text{SKEYID} = h(K, g^{ab} \bmod p)$$

$$\text{proof}_A = h(\text{SKEYID}, g^a \bmod p, g^b \bmod p, \text{IC}, \text{RC}, \text{CP}, \text{Alice})$$

The primary advantage of the complex main mode over the aggressive mode is that main mode is supposed to hide identities from a passive attacker. But there is a Catch–22 in symmetric key main mode. That is, Alice sends her identity, encrypted with key K, in message five. To determine the key K, Bob must know K_{AB}, but how can Bob know to use key K_{AB} until he knows that he's talking to Alice?

The consequence of this snafu is that Alice's IP address acts as her identity since Bob must have a way to identify Alice that is independent of the protocol. There are a couple of unpleasant implications of this. First, symmetric key main mode is useless if Alice's IP address can change. A more fundamental issue is that the protocol is complex and uses six messages, presumably to hide identities, but it fails to hide identities, unless you consider an IP address to be secret. So it would seem pointless to use symmetric key main mode instead of the simpler and more efficient aggressive mode, which we describe next.

IPSec symmetric key aggressive mode follows the same format as the digital signature aggressive mode in Figure 10.8, with the key and signature computed as in symmetric key main mode. As with the digital signature variant, the main difference from main mode is that aggressive mode does not attempt to hide identities. Since symmetric key main mode also fails to hide Alice's identity, this is not a serious limitation of aggressive mode in this case.

10.3.3 IKE Phase 1: Public Key Encryption

Next, we'll consider the public key encryption versions of IKE Phase 1, both main and aggressive modes. We've already seen the digital signature versions. In the main mode of the encryption version, Alice must know Bob's public key in advance and vice versa. Though it would be possible to exchange certificates, that would reveal the identities of Alice and Bob, defeating the primary advantage of main mode.

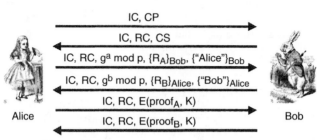

Figure 10.9. Public key encryption, main mode.

The public key encryption main mode protocol is given in Figure 10.9, where the notation is as above, except

$$K = h(\text{IC}, \text{RC}, g^{ab} \bmod p, R_A, R_B)$$

$$\text{SKEYID} = h(R_A, R_B, g^{ab} \bmod p)$$

$$\text{proof}_A = h(\text{SKEYID}, g^a \bmod p, g^b \bmod p, \text{IC}, \text{RC}, \text{CP}, \text{"Alice"}).$$

Public key encryption, aggressive mode, is given in Figure 10.10, where the notation is similar to the main mode. Note that, unlike the other aggressive modes, public key encryption aggressive mode allows Alice and Bob to remain anonymous. It is left as an exercise for the reader to determine any possible advantage of main mode over aggressive mode—see Problem 20 at the end of the chapter.

There is an interesting security issue that arises in the public key encryption versions—both main and aggressive modes. To make it concrete, let's consider aggressive mode. Suppose Trudy generates Diffie-Hellman exponents a and b and random nonces R_A and R_B. Then Trudy can compute all of the remaining quantities that appear in the protocol in Figure 10.10, namely $g^{ab} \bmod p$, K, SKEYID, proof_A and proof_B. The reason that Trudy can do this is that the public keys of Alice and Bob are public.

Why would Trudy go to the trouble of generating all of the values that Alice and Bob generate when they want to communicate? Once Trudy has all of these quantities,

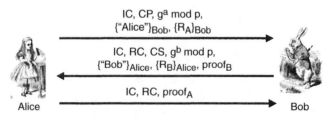

Figure 10.10. Public key encryption, aggressive mode.

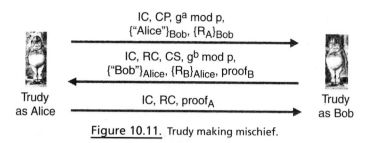

$$\text{IC, CP, } g^a \text{ mod p,}$$
$$\{\text{"Alice"}\}_{Bob}, \{R_A\}_{Bob}$$

$$\text{IC, RC, CS, } g^b \text{ mod p,}$$
$$\{\text{"Bob"}\}_{Alice}, \{R_B\}_{Alice}, \text{proof}_B$$

Trudy
as Alice $$\text{IC, RC, proof}_A$$ Trudy
as Bob

Figure 10.11. Trudy making mischief.

she can create an entire conversation that appears to be a valid IPSec transaction between Alice and Bob, as indicated in Figure 10.11. Amazingly, this conversation appears to be valid to any observer, including Alice or Bob!

Surely, the fact that Trudy can create an entire fake conversation that appears to be between Alice and Bob is a security flaw. Surprisingly, in IPSec this is actually considered a security feature, which goes by the name of *plausible deniability*. A protocol that includes plausible deniability allows Alice and Bob to deny that a conversation took place, since Trudy could have faked the whole thing. In some situations, this is a highly desirable feature. But in some situations it might be a security problem. For example, if Alice makes a purchase from Bob, she could later repudiate it—unless Bob had required a digital signature from Alice.

10.3.4 IPSec Cookies

The "cookies" IC and RC that appear in the IPSec protocols above are referred to as "anti-clogging tokens" in the relevant RFCs. These IPSec cookies have no relation to Web cookies, which are used to maintain state. Instead, the stated purpose of IPSec cookies is to make denial of service, or DoS, attacks more difficult.

Consider TCP SYN flooding, which is a prototypical DoS attack. Each TCP SYN request causes the server to do a little bit of work (create a SEQ number, for example) and to keep some amount of "state," since the server must remember the half-open connection when the corresponding ACK arrives in the third step of the three-way handshake. It is this keeping of state that an attacker can exploit to create a DoS. If the attacker bombards a server with a large number of SYN packets and never completes the resulting half-open connections, the server will eventually deplete its resources. When this occurs, the server cannot handle legitimate SYN requests and a DoS results.

To reduce the threat of DoS in IPSec, the server Bob would like to remain stateless for as long as possible. The IPSec cookies are supposed to accomplish this. However, they fail to achieve their design goal. In each of the main mode protocols, Bob must remember the crypto proposal, CP, from message one, since it is required in message six in order for Bob to compute proof$_B$. Consequently, Bob must keep state beginning with the first message. The IPSec cookies therefore offer little DoS protection.

10.3.5 IKE Phase 1 Summary

Regardless of which of the eight versions is used, the final results of IKE Phase 1 are

- Mutual authentication
- A shared symmetric key
- An IKE security association (SA)

IKE Phase 1 is computationally expensive in any of the public key modes, and the main modes require six messages, which may be costly in some situations. Developers of IKE assumed that it would be used for lots of things, not just IPSec (which partly explains the over-engineering). So they included an inexpensive Phase 2, that can only be used after an IKE SA has been established in Phase 1.

IKE Phase 2 establishes a so-called IPSec security association, or IPSec SA. The comparison to SSL is that IKE Phase 1 is more or less equivalent to establishing an SSL session, whereas IKE Phase 2 is more or less equivalent to establishing an SSL connection, using an existing session. Again, the designers of IPSec wanted to make it as flexible as possible, since they assumed it would be used for lots of things other than IPSec. In fact, IKE could be used for lots of things other than IPSec; however, in practice, it's not.

10.3.6 IKE Phase 2

IKE Phase 2 is mercifully simple—at least in comparison to IKE Phase 1. Before IKE Phase 2 can be attempted, IKE Phase 1 must be completed, in which case a shared symmetric key K, the IPSec cookies, IC, RC, and the IKE security association have all been established and are known. Given that this is the case, the IKE Phase 2 protocol appears in Figure 10.12, where

- The crypto proposal includes ESP or AH (or both)
- SA identifies the IKE security association
- Hashes 1, 2, and 3 depend on SKEYID, R_A, R_B, and the IKE SA from Phase 1
- The keys are derived from KEYMAT $= h($SKEYID, R_A, R_B, junk$)$, where the "junk" is known to all (including an attacker)
- The value of SKEYID depends on the Phase 1 key method
- Optional PFS can be used, which is achieved via an ephemeral Diffie-Hellman exchange

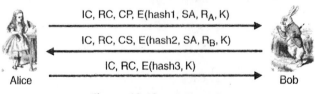

Figure 10.12. IKE Phase 2.

Note that R_A and R_B in Figure 10.12 are not the same as those from IKE Phase 1. As a result, the keys generated in each Phase 2 "connection" are different.

After completing IKE Phase 1, we have established an IKE security association, and after completing IKE Phase 2, we have established an IPSec security association. At this point, both Alice and Bob have been authenticated and both sides have a shared symmetric key for use in the current connection.

The goals of IPSec are mutual authentication and protection of IP packets, which are also know as IP datagrams. Mutual authentication is accomplished in IKE Phase 1. We'll next discuss the protection of IP datagrams, but first, let's consider what an IP datagram looks like from the perspective of IPSec.

10.3.7   IPSec and IP Datagrams

An IP datagram consists of a header and data. The IP header appears in the Appendix in Figure A-5. If the `options` field is empty (as it usually is), then the IP header consists of 20 bytes. For the purposes of IPSec, one important point is that routers must see the IP header in order to route the packet, and, as a result, IPSec can't encrypt the IP header. A second important point is that some of the fields in the IP header change as the packet is forwarded. For example, the TTL field, which contains the number of hops remaining before the packet is discarded, is decremented by each router that the packet passes through. Any header fields that change (in IPSec-speak, such fields are "mutable") cannot be integrity protected.

Consider, for example, a Web browsing session. The application layer protocol for such traffic is HTTP, and the transport layer protocol is TCP. In this situation, IP encapsulates a TCP packet, which encapsulates an HTTP packet. This is illustrated in Figure 10.13. The point here is that, from the perspective of IP, the "data" includes the TCP header and the HTTP header.

IPSec uses either ESP or AH (to be described shortly) to protect an IP datagram. Depending on which is selected, an ESP header or an AH header will be included in the new IPSec-protected datagram.

10.3.8   Transport and Tunnel Modes

Independent of whether ESP or AH is used, IPSec can use either *transport mode* or *tunnel mode*. In transport mode, as illustrated in Figure 10.14, the new ESP/AH header is sandwiched between the IP header and the data. Transport mode is efficient since it adds a minimal amount of additional header information. Also note that the original IP

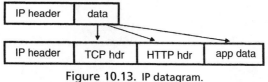

Figure 10.13. IP datagram.

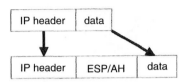

Figure 10.14. IPSec transport mode.

header remains intact. The downside of transport mode is that a passive attacker can see the headers. Transport mode is designed for host-to-host communication.

In tunnel mode, as illustrated in Figure 10.15, the entire IP packet is encapsulated in a new IP packet. One advantage of this approach is that the original IP header is no longer visible to an attacker—assuming the packet is encrypted. This is particularly valuable if tunnel mode is used from firewall to firewall, which is the case for which tunnel mode was designed. When tunnel mode is used from firewall to firewall, an attacker does not know which hosts are communicating. The disadvantage of tunnel mode is the overhead of an additional IP header.

Transport mode is not necessary, since we could always encapsulate the original IP packet in a new secure IPSec packet. For firewall-to-firewall-protected traffic, tunnel mode is necessary, as we must preserve the original IP header to correctly route the packet from the destination firewall to the destination host. But transport mode is more efficient, which makes it preferable when traffic is protected from host-to-host. Note that tunnel mode would not protect the source and destination addresses in the host-to-host case, since these addresses would be repeated in the new IP header.

10.3.9 ESP and AH

Once we've decided whether to use transport mode or tunnel mode, then we must consider the type of protection we want to apply to the IP datagrams. The choices are confidentiality, integrity, or both. But we also must consider the protection—if any—that we would like to apply to the header. In IPSec, the only choices are AH and ESP, so what protection options do each of these provide?

AH, the authentication header, provides integrity only; that is, with AH there is no encryption. The AH integrity protection applies to everything beyond the IP header and some fields of the header. As previously mentioned, not all fields of the IP header can

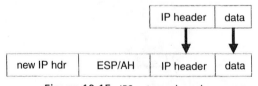

Figure 10.15. IPSec tunnel mode.

be integrity protected (TTL, for example). AH classifies IP header fields as mutable or immutable, and it applies its integrity protection to all of the immutable fields.

ESP, the encapsulating security payload, provides integrity and confidentiality. Both the confidentiality and integrity protection are applied to everything beyond the IP header, that is, the data (from the perspective of IP).

There is a clever trick whereby ESP can be used for integrity only. In ESP, Alice and Bob negotiate the cipher that they will use. One of the ciphers that must be supported is the "NULL" cipher, which is described in RFC 2410 [92]:

- NULL encryption "is a block cipher the origins of which appear to be lost in antiquity"
- "Despite rumors," there is no evidence that NSA "suppressed publication of this algorithm"
- Evidence suggests it was developed in Roman times as exportable version of Caesar's cipher
- NULL encryption can make use of keys of varying length
- No IV is required
- NULL encryption is defined by $\text{Null}(P, K) = P$ for any plaintext P and any key K

This RFC proves that security people are strange.

If the NULL cipher is selected in ESP, then no encryption is applied but the data is still integrity protected. Since this looks like the same service provided by AH, why does AH exist?

There are three reasons given for the existence of AH. As previously noted, the IP header can't be encrypted since routers must see the header in order to route packets. But AH does provide integrity protection to the immutable fields in the IP header, whereas ESP provides no protection to the header.

A second reason for the existence of AH is that ESP encrypts everything beyond the IP header, provided a non-NULL cipher is selected. If ESP is used and the packet is encrypted, a firewall can't look inside the packet to examine the TCP header. Surprisingly, ESP with NULL encryption doesn't solve this problem. When the firewall sees the ESP header, it will know that ESP is being used. However, the header does not say that the NULL cipher is used (that was negotiated between Alice and Bob), so the firewall can't know whether it can read the TCP header or not.

Both of these reasons for the existence of AH are fairly weak. The designers of AH/ESP could have made minor modifications to the protocol so that ESP alone could overcome these drawbacks. But a third reason has been given for the existence of AH. At one meeting where the IPSec standard was being developed, "someone from Microsoft gave an impassioned speech about how AH was useless ..." and "... everyone in the room looked around and said, Hmm. He's right, and we hate AH also, but if it annoys Microsoft let's leave it in since we hate Microsoft more than we hate AH" [122]. So now you know the real reason why AH exists.

10.4 KERBEROS

In Greek mythology, Kerberos is a three-headed dog that guards the entrance to Hades. In security, Kerberos is an authentication system that uses symmetric key cryptography. Kerberos originated at MIT and is based on work by Needham and Schroeder [166]. Whereas SSL and IPSec are designed for the Internet, Kerberos is designed for smaller scale use, such as on a local area network.

In authentication systems based on public key cryptography, if there are N users, each user requires a public-private key pair, and, consequently, N key pairs are needed. In authentication systems based on symmetric keys, if there are N users, then each pair of users must share a symmetric key, in which case $N(N-1)/2 \approx N^2$ keys are required. As a result, authentication based on symmetric keys doesn't scale. However, Kerberos is based on symmetric keys but only requires N symmetric keys for N users. The way that Kerberos is able to achieve this is by relying on a trusted third party, or TTP.

The Kerberos TTP is a security critical component of the system that must be protected from attack. This is certainly a security concern, but the advantage of Kerberos over a system that uses public keys is that no public key infrastructure, or PKI, is required. As we discussed in Chapter 4, PKI presents a substantial challenge in practice.

Kerberos employs a *key distribution center*, or KDC, that acts as the TTP. Since the KDC acts as a TTP, if it's compromised, the security of the entire system is lost. The KDC shares a symmetric key K_A with user Alice, and it shares a symmetric key K_B with Bob, and it shares a symmetric key K_C with Carol, and so on. The KDC has a master key K_{KDC}, which is known only to the KDC. Although it might seem senseless to have a key that only the KDC knows, we'll see that the key K_{KDC} plays a critical role. In particular, the key K_{KDC} allows the KDC to remain stateless, which eliminates the possibility of most denial of service attacks. A stateless KDC is one of the primary design goals in Kerberos—a goal that was successfully achieved in Kerberos, unlike the failed attempt at statelessness in IPSec.

Kerberos is used for authentication and to establish a session key that can be used for confidentiality and integrity. In principle, any symmetric cipher can be used with Kerberos; however, in practice, the crypto algorithm that is used today is the Data Encryption Standard (DES).

The KDC issues various types of *tickets*. Understanding these tickets is crucial to understanding Kerberos. A ticket contains the keys and other information required in order to access a network resource. One special ticket that the KDC issues is the all-important *ticket-granting ticket*, or TGT. These TGTs are used by the recipient to obtain (ordinary) tickets that are then used to allow access to network resources. The use of TGTs is a crucial part of the stateless design of Kerberos.

Each TGT contains a session key, the user ID of the user to whom the TGT is issued, and an expiration time. Below, we'll ignore the expiration time, but it's important to remember that every TGT has an expiration time built into it. Every TGT is encrypted with K_{KDC} before it is sent to the intended recipient. As a result, a TGT can only be read by the KDC. It might seem strange to encrypt a TGT with a key that only the KDC knows and then send that TGT to a user. However, we'll see that this is one of the more clever design features in Kerberos.

10.4.1 Kerberized Login

To understand Kerberos, let's first consider how a "Kerberized" login works; that is, we'll examine the steps that occur when Alice logs in to a system where Kerberos is used for authentication. As on most systems, Alice first enters her password. Alice's computer then derives the key K_A from Alice's password, where K_A is the key that Alice and the KDC share. Alice's computer uses K_A to obtain a TGT for Alice from the KDC. Alice can then use this TGT (referred to as her "credentials") to securely access network resources.

A Kerberized login is illustrated in Figure 10.16, where

- The key K_A is derived from Alice's password as $K_A = h$(Alice's password).
- The KDC creates the session key S_A.
- Alice's computer decrypts using K_A to obtain S_A and the TGT, and then the computer forgets K_A.
- TGT $= E$("Alice", S_A; K_{KDC}).

One major advantage to the Kerberized login is that the entire security process (beyond the password entry) is entirely transparent to Alice. The major disadvantage is that the reliance on the security of the KDC is total.

10.4.2 Kerberos Ticket

Once Alice's computer receives the TGT, it can then use the TGT to request access to network resources. For example, let's suppose that Alice wants to talk to Bob. Then Alice's computer presents Alice's TGT to the KDC, along with an "authenticator" that is designed to avoid a replay. After the KDC verifies Alice's authenticator, it responds with a "ticket to Bob." Alice's computer can then use the ticket to Bob to communicate with Bob via his computer. Alice's acquisition of the ticket to Bob is illustrated in Figure 10.17, where

$$\text{REQUEST} = (\text{TGT, authenticator})$$

$$\text{authenticator} = E(\text{timestamp}, S_A)$$

$$\text{REPLY} = E(\text{"Bob"}, K_{AB}, \text{ticket to Bob}; S_A)$$

$$\text{ticket to Bob} = E(\text{"Alice"}, K_{AB}; K_B)$$

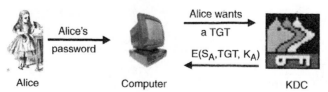

Figure 10.16. Kerberized login.

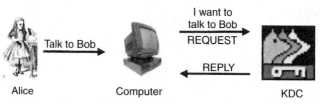

Figure 10.17. Alice gets ticket to Bob.

Note that Kerberos uses timestamps. In Figure 10.17, the KDC obtains the key S_A from the TGT and uses this key to verify the timestamp. Also, the key K_{AB} is the session key that Alice and Bob will use for their session.

Once Alice has obtained the "ticket to Bob," she can then securely communicate with Bob. This process is illustrated in Figure 10.18, where ticket to Bob is as above and

$$\text{authenticator} = E(\text{timestamp}, K_{AB}).$$

Note that Bob decrypts "ticket to Bob" with his key K_B in order to obtain K_{AB}, which he then uses to verify the timestamp. The key K_{AB} is also used for confidentiality and integrity of the subsequent conversation between Alice and Bob.

Since timestamps are used for mutual authentication, Kerberos minimizes the number of messages that must be sent. As we mentioned in the previous chapter, the primary drawback of using timestamps is that time becomes a security-critical parameter. Another issue with timestamps is that we can't expect all clocks to be perfectly synchronized and therefore some clock skew must be tolerated. In Kerberos, this clock skew is typically set at five minutes—which is an eternity in a networked world.

10.4.3 Kerberos Security

Next, we'll discuss some of the design features of Kerberos. Recall that, when Alice logs in, the KDC sends $E(S_A, \text{TGT}; K_A)$ to Alice, where $\text{TGT} = E(\text{"Alice"}, S_A; K_{KDC})$. Since the TGT is encrypted with K_{KDC}, why is the TGT encrypted again with the key K_A? The answer is that this is a minor flaw in Kerberos, since it's extra work that provides no additional security. If the key K_{KDC} is compromised, the entire security of the system

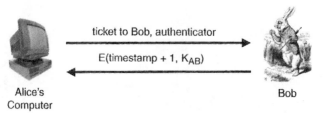

Figure 10.18. Alice contacts Bob.

is broken, so there can be no added benefit to encrypting the TGT again after it's already encrypted with K_{KDC}.

Notice that, in Figure 10.17, Alice remains anonymous in the REQUEST. This is a nice security feature that is a side benefit of the fact that the TGT is encrypted with the key K_{KDC}. That is, the KDC does not need to know who is making the REQUEST in order to decrypt it, since all TGTs are encrypted with K_{KDC}.

In the Kerberos example above, why is "ticket to Bob" sent to Alice, when Alice simply forwards it on to Bob? Apparently, it would be more efficient to have the KDC send the ticket to Bob directly to Bob. However, if the ticket to Bob arrives at Bob before Alice initiates contact with Bob, then Bob would have to remember the key K_{AB} and the fact that this key is to be used in a transaction with Alice. That is, Bob would need to maintain state. Kerberos is very good at avoiding state as much as possible.

Finally, how does Kerberos prevent replay attacks? Replay prevention relies on the timestamps used in the authenticators. But there is still an issue of replay within the clock skew. To prevent such replay attacks, the KDC would need to remember all timestamps received within the most recent clock skew interval of time (typically, five minutes). However, most Kerberos implementations apparently don't bother to do this [122].

Before leaving Kerberos, we consider two design alternatives. First, Kerberos could have chosen to have Alice's computer remember her password and use that for authentication. This would eliminate the need for the KDC, but the scaling issue becomes a problem, and it's difficult to protect passwords on a computer. In effect, every computer on the network would become a TTP. This is certainly not a desirable situation.

A more sensible alternative would be to have the KDC remember session keys instead of putting these in the TGT. This design would completely eliminate the need for TGTs. But it would also require the KDC to maintain state, and a stateless KDC is one of the most impressive design features in Kerberos.

10.5 GSM

Some unique security concerns arise in wireless environments. To date, wireless protocols, such as WEP, have a poor track record for security [16, 30, 68]. In this section we'll discuss the security of GSM cell phones. GSM illustrates some of the unique security problems that arise in a wireless situation. It's also an excellent example of how mistakes at the design phase are extremely difficult to correct later. But before we get to GSM security, we need some background on the development of cell phone technology.

Back in the computing dark ages (prior to the early 1980s, that is) cell phones were expensive, completely insecure, and as large as a brick. These *first-generation* cell phones were analog, not digital, and there were few standards and little or no thought was given to security.

The biggest security issue with early cell phones was their susceptibility to *cloning*. These cell phones would broadcast their identity in the clear when a phone call was placed, and this identity was used to determine who to bill for the phone call. Since this ID was broadcast over a wireless media, it could easily be captured and later used to make a "clone," or copy, of the phone. This allowed the bad guys to make free phone calls, which did not please the legitimate consumers or the cellular phone companies. Cell phone cloning became a big business, with fake base stations created simply to gather IDs [14].

Into this environment came GSM, which began in 1982 as Groupe Spéciale Mobile, but in 1986—as a tribute to the universality of three-letter acronyms—it was formally rechristened as Global System for Mobile Communications. The founding of GSM marks the official beginning of *second-generation* cell phone technology [106]. We'll have much more to say about GSM security below.

Yes Virginia, there is a *third generation* as well, which is promoted by the 3rd Generation Partnership Project, or 3GPP [1]. We'll briefly mention the security improvements offered by 3GPP after we complete our survey of GSM security.

10.5.1 GSM Architecture

The general architecture of the GSM system appears in Figure 10.19, where

- The *mobile* is the cell phone.
- The *air interface* is the wireless transmission from the cell phone to a base station.
- The *visited network* includes multiple base stations and a *base station controller*, which acts as a hub for connecting the base stations under its control to the rest of the GSM network. The base station controller includes a *visitor location registry*, or VLR, that is used to keep tabs on all mobiles currently accessing the GSM network via any of the base station controller's network of base stations.
- The *public switched telephone network*, or PSTN, is the ordinary (non-cellular) telephone system. The PSTN is also referred to as "land lines" to distinguish it from the wireless network.

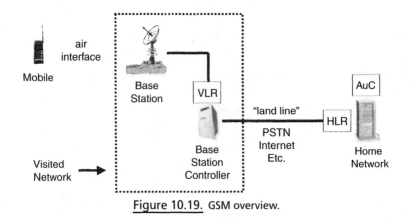

Figure 10.19. GSM overview.

- The *home network* is the network where the mobile is registered. Each mobile is associated with a unique home network. The home network includes a *home location registry*, or HLR, which keeps track of the most recent location of all mobiles that belong to the particular home network. The *authentication center*, or AuC, maintains the crucial billing information for all mobiles for which this particular home network is home.

We'll discuss each of these pieces of the GSM architecture in more detail below.

Each GSM mobile phone contains a Subscriber Identity Module, or *SIM*, which is a smartcard. On the SIM smartcard, there is an International Mobile Subscriber ID, or *IMSI*, which, not surprisingly, is used to identify the mobile. The SIM also contains a 128-bit key that is only known to the mobile and its home network. This key is universally know as Ki, so we'll follow the standard notation. The purpose of the SIM smartcard is to provide an inexpensive form of tamper-resistant hardware. The SIM card also implements two-factor authentication, relying on "something you have" (the SIM itself) and "something you know" in the form of a four-digit PIN. However, the PIN is usually treated as an annoyance by most users, and it's generally not used.

Again, the visited network is the network where the mobile is currently located. A base station is one "cell" in the cellular system, whereas the base station controller manages a collection of cells. The VLR has information on all mobiles currently visiting the base station controller's territory.

The home network stores a given mobile's crucial information, that is, its IMSI and Ki. The HLR keeps track of the most recent location of mobiles that have this home network as their home, while the AuC contains the IMSI-to-Ki mapping.

10.5.2   GSM Security Architecture

Now we're ready to begin our discussion of GSM security issues. The primary security goals set forth by the designers of GSM were

- Make GSM as secure as ordinary telephones (the PSTN).
- Prevent cell phone cloning.

In particular, GSM was not designed to resist an active attack. At the time, active attacks were considered infeasible, since the necessary equipment was extremely costly. However, today the cost of such equipment is little more than that of a good laptop computer. The designers of GSM considered the biggest threats to be insecure billing, corruption, and similar low-tech attacks.

GSM attempts to deal with three security issues: anonymity, authentication and confidentiality. The anonymity goal for GSM is to prevent intercepted traffic from being used to identify the caller. This particular feature is not especially important to the phone companies, but might be important to customers. Authentication, on the other hand is of paramount importance to the phone companies, since correct authentication is necessary for proper billing. The cloning problems with first generation phones can be viewed as an authentication failure. Confidentiality of calls over the air interface may be important to customers, and, if so, it's important to the phone companies, at least from a marketing perspective.

Next, we'll look at GSM's approach to anonymity, authentication, and confidentiality in more detail. Then we'll discuss some of the many security shortcomings of GSM.

10.5.2.1 Anonymity.
GSM provides a very limited form of anonymity. The IMSI is used to initially identify the caller. Then a Temporary Mobile Subscriber ID, or *TMSI*, is assigned to the caller, and the TMSI is subsequently used to identify the caller. In addition, the TMSI changes frequently. The net effect is that if an attacker captures the initial part of the call, where the IMSI is passed, the anonymity is not assured. But if the attacker misses the initial part of the call, then the anonymity is reasonably strong. Although this is not a particularly strong form of anonymity, it may be sufficient for many practical situations where an attacker could have difficulty filtering the IMSIs out of a large volume of traffic. Perhaps the GSM designers were more concerned with having a simple and "marketable" form of anonymity than providing a strong form of anonymity.

10.5.2.2 Authentication.
Authentication is, from the phone company's perspective, the most crucial aspect of GSM security. More precisely, authenticating the user to the base station is critical to the phone company; otherwise, they might not get paid for the service they provide. In GSM, the caller is authenticated to the base station, but the authentication is not mutual. The GSM designers apparently decided that it was not critical that the caller know he is talking to a legitimate base station. We'll see that this was a critical security oversight.

GSM authentication employs a challenge-response mechanism. The home network—which knows the Ki that corresponds to the caller's IMSI—is informed of the IMSI of the caller. The home network then generates a random challenge RAND and computes the "expected response," $XRES = A3(RAND, Ki)$, where A3 is a hash function, and RAND and XRES are sent to the base station. The base station sends RAND, the challenge, to the mobile. The mobile's response is denoted SRES, where SRES is computed by the mobile as $SRES = A3(RAND, Ki)$. To complete the authentication, the base station verifies that $SRES = XRES$. One nice feature of this authentication method is that the caller's key Ki never leaves its home network.

10.5.2.3 Confidentiality.
GSM uses a stream cipher to encrypt the data. The reason for this choice is due to the high error rate, which is typically about 1 in 1,000 bits, in the cell phone environment. With a block cipher, each transmission error causes one or two entire plaintext blocks to be garbled (depending on the mode), while a stream cipher garbles only those plaintext bits corresponding to the specific ciphertext bits that are in error.

The GSM encryption key is universally denoted as Kc, so we'll follow that convention. When the home network receives the IMSI from the base station controller, the home network computes $Kc = A8(RAND, Ki)$, where A8 is a hash function. Then Kc is sent to the base station as part of the triple (RAND, XRES, Kc).

The base station receives the GSM triple (RAND, XRES, Kc) and completes the authentication as described above. If this succeeds, the mobile computes $Kc = $ A8(RAND, Ki). The base station already knows Kc, so the mobile and base station have established a shared symmetric key with which to encrypt the conversation. As mentioned above, the data is encrypted with a stream cipher. The keystream is generated as A5(Kc), where A5 is a stream cipher. As with authentication, the caller's master key Ki never leaves its home network.

10.5.3 GSM Authentication Protocol

The GSM protocol between the mobile and the base station is illustrated in Figure 10.20. A few security concerns with this protocol are as follows [172].

- The RAND is hashed together with Ki to produce the encryption key Kc. Also, the value of RAND is hashed with Ki to generate SRES, which a passive attacker can see. As a result, it's necessary that SRES and Kc be uncorrelated. This is easy to achieve if the hash functions A3 and A8 are reasonably secure.

- It must not be possible to deduce Ki from known RAND and SRES pairs, since such pairs are available to a passive attacker. This is equivalent to a known plaintext attack on the hash function.

- It must not be possible to deduce Ki from chosen RAND and SRES pairs, which is equivalent to a chosen plaintext attack on the hash function. Although this attack might seem implausible, with possession of the SIM card, an attacker can choose the RAND values and observe the corresponding SRES values.

10.5.4 GSM Security Flaws

Next, we'll discuss several security flaws in GSM. There are cryptographic flaws in GSM and there are protocol flaws as well. But we'll see that the most devastating attacks on GSM are due to invalid security assumptions made by the original designers of GSM.

10.5.4.1 *Crypto Flaws.* There are several cryptographic flaws in GSM. The hashes A3 and A8 both rely on a hash function known as COMP128. The hash COMP128 was developed as a secret design, in violation of Kerckhoffs Principle. Not surprisingly,

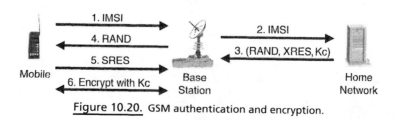

Figure 10.20. GSM authentication and encryption.

COMP128 was later found to be weak—it can be broken by 150,000 chosen plaintexts [86]. What this means in practice is that an attacker who has access to a SIM card can determine the key Ki in 2 to 10 hours, depending in the speed of the card. In particular, an unscrupulous seller of cell phones could determine Ki before selling a phone, then create clones that would have their calls billed to the purchaser of the phone. Below, we'll mention another attack on COMP128.

There are actually two different forms of the encryption algorithm A5, which are known as A5/1 and A5/2. We discussed A5/1 in the symmetric key cryptography chapter. As with COMP128, both of these were developed in violation of Kerckhoffs Principle and both are weak. The A5/2 algorithm is weak [21, 178] and a feasible attack on A5/1 is known [26].

10.5.4.2 Invalid Assumptions. There is a serious design flaw in the GSM protocol itself. A GSM phone call is encrypted between the mobile and the base station but not from the base station to the base station controller. Recall that a design goal of GSM was to develop a system as secure as the public switched telephone network (PSTN). As a result, if a GSM phone call is routed over the PSTN, then from that point on, no further special protection is required. In other words, the emphasis of GSM security is on protecting the phone call over the air interface, between the mobile and the base station.

The designers of GSM assumed that once the call reached the base station, it would be routed over the PSTN to the base station controller. This is implied by the solid line between the base station and base station controller in Figure 10.19. As a result of this assumption, the GSM security protocol does not protect the conversation when it is sent from the base station to the base station controller. However, many GSM systems today transmit calls between a base station and its base station controller over a microwave link [172]. Since microwave is a wireless media, it is possible for an attacker to eavesdrop on unprotected calls over this link, rendering the encryption over the air interface useless.

10.5.4.3 SIM Attacks. Several attacks were developed on various types of SIM cards. In one attack, known as *optical fault induction*, an attacker could force a SIM card to divulge its Ki by using an ordinary flashbulb [209]. In another class of attacks, known as *partitioning attacks*, timing and power consumption analysis could be used to recover Ki using as few as eight adaptively chosen plaintexts [184]. As a result, an attacker who has possession of the SIM could recover Ki in seconds and, consequently, a misplaced cell phone could be cloned in seconds. We'll see below that a fake base station could also be used to clone GSM phones.

10.5.4.4 Fake Base Station. Another serious flaw with the GSM protocol is the threat posed by a fake base station. This attack, which is illustrated in Figure 10.21, exploits two flaws in the protocol. First, the authentication is not mutual. While the caller is authenticated to the base station (which is necessary for proper billing), the designers of GSM felt it was not worth the extra effort to authenticate the base station to

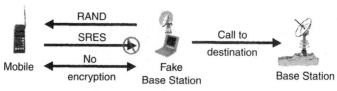

Figure 10.21. GSM fake base station.

the caller. Although they were aware of the possibility of a fake base station, apparently the protocol designers believed that the probability of such an attack was too remote to justify the (small) additional cost of mutual authentication. The second flaw that this attack exploits is that encryption over the air interface is not automatic. Instead, the base station determines whether the call is encrypted or not.

In the attack illustrated in Figure 10.21, the fake base station sends a random value to the mobile, which the mobile assumes is RAND. The mobile replies with the corresponding SRES, which the fake base station discards, since it does not need to authenticate the caller (and it cannot authenticate the caller). The fake base station then tells the mobile not to encrypt the call. Unbeknownst to either the caller or the recipient, the fake base station then places a call to the the intended recipient and forwards the conversation from the caller to the recipient and vice versa. The fake base station can then eavesdrop on the entire conversation.

An interesting fact concerning this fake base station attack is that if the call from the fake base station to the legitimate base station is an ordinary GSM phone call, then it is encrypted. Another interesting fact is that the fake base station will be billed for the call, although to avoid detection the fake base station might use a cloned GSM phone for its "call forwarding" service.

Since the fake base station sends any RAND it chooses and receives the corresponding SRES, it can conduct a chosen plaintext attack on the SIM without possessing the SIM card. The SIM attack mentioned above that requires only eight adaptively chosen plaintexts would be entirely feasible with a fake base station.

Another major flaw with the GSM protocol is that it provides no replay protection. A base station (or a fake base station) can replay a compromised triple (RAND, XRES, Kc) forever. As a result, one compromised triple gives an attacker a key Kc that is valid forever. A clever fake base station operator could use a compromised triple to "protect" the conversation between the mobile and the fake base station so that nobody else could eavesdrop on the conversation.

Denial of service is relatively easy in a wireless environment, since the signal can be jammed. GSM offers no special protection from such an attack.

10.5.5 GSM Conclusions

From our discussion of GSM security flaws, it seems that GSM is a security failure—though it is certainly a commercial success, which raises some questions about the commercial significance of good security. However, it is perhaps more relevant to consider whether GSM achieved its security design goals. Recall that the two security goals set forth by the designers of GSM were to eliminate the cloning that had plagued first-generation systems and to make the air interface as secure as the PSTN. Although it is possible to clone GSM phones, it has never become a significant problem in practice. So GSM does appear to have achieved its first goal.

Does GSM make the air interface as secure as the PSTN? There certainly are attacks on the GSM air interface (most notably the fake base station), but there are also attacks on the PSTN (tapping a line) that are at least as severe. So it could be argued that GSM also achieved its second design goal.

The real problem with GSM security is that the initial design goals were too limited. The major insecurities in GSM include weak crypto, SIM issues, the fake base station attack, and a total lack of replay protection. In the PSTN, the primary insecurity is tapping, though there are others threats, such as attacks on cordless phones. In this light, GSM should probably be considered a modest security success.

10.5.6   3GPP

The security designers of the next generation of cell phones, 3GPP, have set their sights higher than the designers of GSM. The security of 3GPP is built on the GSM security model, but the 3GPP developers have carefully patched all of the known GSM vulnerabilities. For example, 3GPP includes mutual authentication and integrity protection of all signaling, including the "start encryption" command from the base station to the mobile. These improvements eliminate the GSM-style fake base station attack. Also, in 3GPP, the keys can't be reused and triples can't be replayed. The weak proprietary crypto algorithms of GSM (COMP128, A5/1 and A5/2) have been replaced by a strong encryption algorithm known as KASUMI, which has undergone rigorous peer review. In addition, the encryption has been extended from the mobile all the way to the base station controller.

The history of mobile phones, from the first-generation phones to GSM and now 3GPP, nicely illustrates the usual evolution that occurs in security. As the attackers develop new attacks, the defenders respond with new protections, which the attackers again probe for weaknesses. Ideally, this "arms race" approach to security could be avoided by a careful analysis of the threat prior to the initial development. However, it's unrealistic to believe that the designers of first-generation cell phones could have imagined the world of today. Attacks such as the fake base station, which would have seemed unlikely at one time, are now easily implemented. With this in mind, we should realize that, although 3GPP clearly promises more security than GSM could deliver, it's almost certain that attacks will eventually surface. In short, the security arms race continues!

10.6   SUMMARY

In this chapter, we discussed four real-world security protocols in detail. We saw that SSL is a well-designed protocol that is used to authenticate the client to the server and establish a shared symmetric key.

We saw that IPSec is a complex protocol with some serious security flaws. The designers of IPSec over-engineered the protocol, which makes it complex. IPSec provides an excellent illustration of the generally accepted principle that "complexity is the enemy of security."

Kerberos is a widely deployed authentication protocol that relies on symmetric key cryptography. The ability of the Kerberos KDC to remain stateless is one of the many clever features of the protocol.

We finished the chapter with a discussion of GSM. The actual GSM security protocol is simple, but it provides an interesting case study due to the large number of attacks that have surfaced. While complexity might be the enemy of security, GSM nicely illustrates that simplicity isn't necessarily security's best friend. The major flaw with GSM is that its designers were not ambitious enough, since they didn't design GSM to withstand attacks that are feasible today. This is perhaps excusable given that some of these attacks seemed far fetched in 1982 when GSM was developed. GSM also shows that it's difficult to overcome security flaws that are introduced at the design phase.

The security of 3GPP cell phones—the next generation of cell phones—is built on the GSM model, with all of the known security flaws in GSM having been patched. It will be interesting to see how 3GPP security holds up in practice.

10.7 PROBLEMS

1. In the Kerberos interaction discussed in Section 10.4.2, the "ticket to Bob" is sent to Alice who must forward it to Bob, instead of being sent directly to Bob. Why is Kerbero's implemented in this way?

2. The SSL protocol discussed in Section 10.2 relies on public key cryptography. Design a variant that is based on symmetric key cryptography. Is your protocol resistant to a man-in-the-middle attack?

3. What is the primary advantage of SSL over IPSec? What is the primary advantage of IPSec over SSL?

4. Consider the Kerberos interaction discussed in Section 10.4.2. In the REPLY message, why is "ticket to Bob" encrypted with the key S_A?

5. Consider the GSM security protocol in Figure 10.20. Modify this protocol so that it achieves mutual authentication.

6. Consider the Kerberized login discussed in the book.
   a. What is the TGT and what is its purpose?
   b. Why is the TGT sent to Alice instead of being stored on the KDC?
   c. Why is the TGT encrypted with K_A when it is sent from the KDC to Alice's computer?

7. Briefly describe one security flaw in GSM that is not discussed in the text.

8. Consider a man-in-the-middle attack on an SSL connection between Alice and Bob.
   a. At what point should this attack fail?
   b. What mistake might Alice reasonably make that would allow this attack to succeed?

9. In Kerberos, Alice's key K_A, which is shared by Alice and the KDC, is computed (on Alice's computer) as $K_A = h$(Alice's password). Instead, this could have been implemented as follows. Initially, the key K_A is randomly generated on Alice's computer. The key is then stored on the computer as $E(K_A, K)$ where the key K is computed as $K = h$(Alice's password). The key K_A is also stored on the KDC. What are the advantages and disadvantages to this alternative approach to generating and storing K_A?

10. Suppose we use symmetric keys for authentication and each of N users must be able to communicate with any of the other $N - 1$ users. Evidently, such a system will require one symmetric key for each pair of users, or about N^2 keys. On the other hand, if we use public keys, only N key pairs are required, but we must then deal with PKI issues. Kerberos provides authentication using symmetric keys, yet Kerberos only requires N symmetric keys for N users. The Kerberos KDC makes this possible. Is it possible to achieve a similar result without the KDC?

11. Consider the SSL protocol in Figure 10.3. Modify the protocol to use digital signatures instead of public key encryption. Your protocol must provide authentication and a session key.

12. Consider the SSL protocol in Figure 10.3. This protocol does not allow Bob to remain anonymous, since his certificate identifies him. Modify the protocol so that Bob can remain anonymous. Hint: The IPSec main mode public key protocols allow the users to remain anonymous.

13. Dog race tracks often employ Automatic Betting Machines (ABMs), which are somewhat analogous to ATM machines. An ABM is a terminal where Alice can place her own bets and scan her winning tickets. An ABM does not accept or dispense cash. Instead, an ABM only accepts and dispenses *vouchers*. A voucher can also be purchased from a special voucher machine for cash, but a voucher can only be converted into cash by a human teller.

   A voucher includes 15 hexadecimal digits, which can be read by a human or scanned by a machine that reads a bar code on the voucher. When a voucher is redeemed, the information is recorded in the voucher database and a paper receipt is printed. For security reasons, the teller must submit the paper receipt which serves as the physical record that the voucher was cashed.

   A voucher is valid for one year from its date of issue. However, the older that a voucher is, the more likely that it has been lost and will never be redeemed. Since vouchers are printed on cheap paper, they are often damaged to the point where they fail to scan, and they can even be difficult for human tellers to process manually.

   A list of all outstanding vouchers is kept in a database. Any human teller can read the first 10 hex digits from this database for any outstanding voucher. But, for security reasons, the last five hex digits are not available to a teller.

   If Ted the teller is given a valid voucher that doesn't scan, he must manually enter the hex digits in order to cash the voucher. Using the database, it's easy for Ted to match the first 10 hex digits. However, the last five hex digits must be determined from the voucher itself. Determining these last five hex digits can be difficult, particularly if the voucher is in poor condition.

In order to help overworked tellers, Carl, a clever programmer, added a wildcard feature to the manual voucher entry routine. Using this feature, Ted (or any other teller) can enter any of the last five hex digits that are readable and "*" for any unreadable digits. Carl's program will then inform Ted whether an outstanding voucher exists that matches in the digits that were entered, ignoring any position with a "*." Note that this routine does not give Ted the missing digits, but instead, it simply returns a yes or no answer.

Suppose that Ted is given a voucher for which none of the last five hex digits can be read.

   a. Without the wildcard feature, how many guesses must Ted make, on average, in order to recover the last five hex digits of this voucher?

   b. Using the wildcard feature, how many guesses, on average, must Ted make to recover the last five hex digits of this voucher?

   c. How could Dave, a dishonest teller, exploit the wildcard feature in order to cheat the system? Hint: Dave would want to concentrate on vouchers that are nearly one year old since such vouchers are likely to have been lost. Dave would need to use the wildcard feature in order to cash such a voucher, since the voucher is not in his possession.

   d. What is the risk for Dave? That is, how might Dave get caught under the current system?

   e. Modify the system so that it allows tellers to securely and efficiently deal with vouchers that fail to scan automatically, but also makes it impossible (or at least very difficult) for Dave to cheat the system.

14. The Wired Equivalency Protocol, or WEP, is used to protect data sent over a wireless link. WEP has many security flaws, one of which involves its use of initialization vectors, or IVs. WEP IVs are 24 bits long. WEP uses a fixed long-term key K. For each packet, WEP sends an IV in the clear along with the encrypted packet. The packet is encrypted with a stream cipher using the key $K_S = (\text{IV}, K)$, that is, the IV is pre-pended to the key K. Suppose that a particular WEP connection sends packets containing 1500 bytes over a 11 Mbps WEP link.

   a. If the IVs are chosen at random, what is the expected amount of time until the first IV repeats? What is the expected amount of time until some IV is repeated?

   b. If the IVs are not selected at random but are instead selected in sequence, say, $\text{IV}_i = i$ for $i = 0, 1, 2, \ldots, 2^{24} - 1$, what is the expected amount of time until the first IV repeats? What is the expected amount of time until some IV is repeated?

   c. Why is a repeated IV a security concern?

   d. Why is WEP "unsafe at any key length" [245]? That is, why is WEP no more secure if K is 256 bits than if K is 40 bits? Hint: See [80] for the definitive answer.

15. In GSM, each home network has an AuC database containing user keys Ki. Instead, a process known as *key diversification* could be used, which would eliminate the need for such a database. Key diversification works as follows. Let h be a secure hash function and let K_M be a master key known only to the AuCs. In GSM, each user has a unique ID known as an IMSI. A user's key Ki would be $Ki = h(K_M, \text{IMSI})$, and this key would be stored on the mobile. Given any IMSI, the AuC would compute the key Ki as $Ki = h(K_M, \text{IMSI})$. The primary advantage of this approach is that no database is required. What is the primary disadvantage? Why do you think the designers of GSM chose not to employ key diversification?

16. IKE has two phases, Phase 1 and Phase 2. In IKE Phase 1, there are four key options and, for each of these, there is a main mode and an aggressive mode.

    a. What is the primary difference between main mode and aggressive mode?

    b. What is the primary advantage of the Phase 1 digital signature key option over Phase 1 public key encryption?

17. IKE has two phases, Phase 1 and Phase 2. In IKE Phase 1, there are four key options and, for each of these, there is a main mode and an aggressive mode.

    a. Explain the difference between Phase 1 and Phase 2.

    b. What is the primary advantage of Phase 1 public key encryption main mode over Phase 1 symmetric key encryption main mode?

18. IPSec cookies are also known as "anti-clogging tokens."

    a. What is the intended security purpose of IPSec cookies?

    b. Why do IPSec cookies fail to fulfill their intended purpose?

    c. Redesign the IPSEC Phase 1 symmetric key signing main mode so that the IPSec cookies do serve their intended purpose.

19. In IKE Phase 1 digital signature main mode, proof$_A$ and proof$_B$ are signed by Alice and Bob, respectively. However, in IKE Phase 1, public key encryption main mode, proof$_A$ and proof$_B$ are neither signed nor encrypted with public keys. Why is it necessary to sign these values in digital signature mode, yet it is not necessary to public key encrypt (or sign) them in public key encryption mode?

20. As noted in the text, IKE Phase 1 public key encryption aggressive mode allows Alice and Bob to remain anonymous. Since anonymity is usually given as the primary advantage of main mode over aggressive mode, is there any reason to ever use public key encryption main mode?

21. IKE Phase 1 uses ephemeral Diffie–Hellman for perfect forward secrecy, or PFS. Recall that, in our example of PFS in Section 9.3.4 of Chapter 9, we encrypted the Diffie–Hellman values with a symmetric key in order to prevent the man-in-the-middle attack. However, the Diffie–Hellman values are not encrypted in IKE. Is this a security flaw? Explain.

22. How can an active attacker determine Alice's identity in IKE Phase 1 digital signature main mode?

23. Why does IPSec tunnel mode fail to hide the header information when used from host to host? Is this also the case when tunnel mode is used from firewall to firewall? Why or why not?

24. ESP requires both encryption and integrity, yet it is possible to use ESP for integrity only. Explain this apparent contradiction.

25. In Kerberos, why can Alice remain anonymous when requesting a "ticket to Bob"?

26. Give a one-message protocol that prevents cell phone cloning and establishes a shared encryption key.

27. Give a two-message protocol that prevents cell phone cloning, prevents a fake base station attack, and establishes a shared session key.

Part IV

SOFTWARE

11

SOFTWARE FLAWS AND MALWARE

*If automobiles had followed the same development cycle as the computer,
a Rolls-Royce would today cost $100, get a million miles per gallon,
and explode once a year, killing everyone inside.*
—Robert X. Cringely

I think that's the last bug.
—Deluded programmer

11.1 INTRODUCTION

In security, why should software be on the same level as crypto, access control, and protocols? For one thing, virtually all of information security is implemented in software. In effect, software is the foundation on which all of these other security mechanisms rest. We'll see that software provides a very weak foundation on which to build reliable security.

In this chapter, we'll discuss several security issues related to software. First, we'll consider unintentional software flaws [142] that can lead to security problems. A classic example of such a flaw is the buffer overflow, which we'll discuss in some detail. Then we consider malicious software, or malware, which is intentionally designed to do bad things. Computer viruses and worms are examples of malware. We'll also consider the intriguing prospects for the future of malware, and we'll present a few miscellaneous software-based attacks. Software is a big topic, so we continue with this general theme in the next chapter.

Information Security: Principles and Practice, by Mark Stamp
Copyright © 2006 John Wiley & Sons, Inc.

11.2 SOFTWARE FLAWS

Bad software is everywhere [107]. For example, the NASA Mars Lander, which cost $165 million, crashed into Mars due to a software error in converting between English and metric units of measure [111]. Another infamous example of bad software was the Denver airport baggage handling system. Bugs in this software delayed the airport opening by 11 months at a cost of about $1 million per day [91]. Software failures have also occurred in the MV-22 Osprey, an advanced military aircraft. Lives have been lost due to this faulty software [137]. There are many more examples of such failures.

In this section, we're interested in the security implications of software flaws. With faulty software everywhere, it shouldn't be surprising that bad guys have found ways to take advantage of this situation.

Normal users of software find bugs and flaws more or less by accident. Such users hate buggy software, but, out of necessity, they've learned to live with it. Users have, in fact, become very skilled at making bad software work.

Attackers, on the other hand, look at buggy software as an opportunity, not a problem. They actively search for bugs and flaws in software, and they like bad software. Attackers try to make software misbehave, and flaws often prove very useful in this regard. We'll see that buggy software is at the core of many attacks.

It's generally accepted among computer security professionals that "complexity is the enemy of security" [53], and modern software is extremely complex. In fact, the complexity of software has far outstripped the abilities of humans to manage the complexity. The numbers in Table 11.1 hint at the complexity of large-scale software projects.

A conservative estimate places the number of bugs in software at 5 per 1,000 lines of code, or LOC [241]. A typical computer might have 3,000 executable files, each of which contains, perhaps, 100,000 LOC, on average. Then, on average, each executable has 50 bugs, which implies about 150,000 bugs for a single computer.

If we extend this calculation to a a medium-sized corporate network with 30,000 nodes, we'd expect to find about 4.5 billion bugs in the network. Of course, many of these bugs would be duplicates, but it's still a staggering number. Now suppose that only 10% of these bugs are security critical and that only 10% of these security-critical bugs are remotely exploitable. Then there are "only" 4.5 million serious security flaws due to bad software in this network!

TABLE 11.1. Software complexity.

System	Lines of Code
Netscape	17 million
Space shuttle	10 million
Linux	1.5 million
Windows XP	40 million
Boeing 777	7 million

The simple arithmetic of bug counting is good news for the bad guys and very bad news for the good guys. We'll return to this later, but the crucial point is that we are not going to eliminate software security flaws any time soon—if ever. We'll discuss ways to reduce the number of flaws, but we must be realistic and realize that many flaws will remain. The best we can realistically hope for is to effectively manage the security risk created by buggy and complex software. Absolute security is often unobtainable, and software is definitely no exception in this regard.

In this section, we'll focus on program flaws. These are unintentional software bugs that can have security implications. The specific classes of flaws that we'll consider are the following.

- Buffer overflow
- Race conditions
- Incomplete mediation

In the next section, we'll consider malicious software, or malware, which is intended by it's developer to do bad things.

A programming mistake, or bug, is an *error*. When a program with an error is executed, the error may cause the program to reach an incorrect internal state, which is known as a *fault*. A fault may cause the system to depart from its expected behavior, which is a *failure* [179]. In other words, an error is a human-created bug, while a fault is internal to the software, and a failure is externally observable.

For example, the C program in Table 11.2 has an error, since buffer[20] has not been allocated. This error might cause a fault, where the program reaches an incorrect internal state. If a fault occurs, it might lead to a failure, where the program behaves incorrectly. Whether a fault occurs, and whether this leads to a failure, depends on what resides in the memory location where buffer[20] is written.

Below, we use the term *flaw* as a synonym for error, fault, or failure. The severity of the flaw should be apparent from the context.

One of the goals of software engineering is to ensure that a program does what it's supposed to do. However, for software to be secure, a much higher standard is required—secure software software must do what it's supposed to do and nothing more [241].

Next, we'll consider three specific types of program flaws that can create serious security vulnerabilities. The first of these is the infamous buffer overflow, also known as smashing the stack. Buffer overflow has been called the "attack of the decade" [14] for the 1990s, and it's likely to be the attack of the decade for the current decade as well.

The second class of software flaws we'll consider are race conditions. These are common, but generally more difficult to exploit than buffer overflows. The third major

TABLE 11.2. A flawed program.

```
int main(){
    int buffer[10];
    buffer[20] = 37;}
```

software vulnerability that we consider is incomplete mediation. This flaw often makes buffer overflow conditions exploitable. There are other types of software flaws, but these three are the most common and cause most of the problems.

11.2.1 Buffer Overflow

Trudy says, "My cup runneth over, what a blessing."
Alice says, "My cup runneth over, what a mess."
—Anonymous

Before we discuss the specifics of buffer overflow attacks, let's consider a typical scenario where such an attack might occur. Suppose that a Web form asks the user to enter data, such as name, age, date of birth, and so on. This data is then sent to a server that writes the data to buffer that can hold N characters. If the server software does not verify that the length of the data is at most N characters, then a buffer overflow can occur.

It might seem that a buffer overflow is relatively harmless, but we'll see that this is far from the case. At the least, it's reasonably likely that overflowing data will cause a computer to crash. Trudy could take advantage of this to launch a denial of service (DoS) attack. And under certain conditions, Trudy can do much more—she can have code of her choosing execute on the affected machine. It's remarkable that a common programming bug can lead to such an outcome.

Consider again the C source code in Table 11.2. When this code is executed, a buffer overflow occurs. The effect of this buffer overflow depends on what resides in memory at location `buffer[20]`. The buffer overflow might overwrite user data or code, or it could overwrite system data or code.

Consider, for example, software that is used for authentication. Ultimately, the authentication decision resides in a single bit. If a buffer overflow overwrites this authentication bit, then Trudy can authenticate herself as, say, Alice.

This situation is illustrated in Figure 11.1, where the "F" in the position of the boolean flag indicates failed authentication.

If a buffer overflow overwrites the memory position where the boolean flag is stored, Trudy can overwrite "F" with "T," and the software will then believe that Trudy has been authenticated. This is illustrated in Figure 11.2.

Before we can discuss the more sophisticated forms of buffer overflow attacks, we need an overview of the memory organization of a typical processor. A simplified view of memory organization—which is sufficient for our purposes—appears in Figure 11.3.

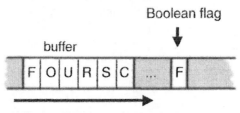

Figure 11.1. Buffer and a boolean flag.

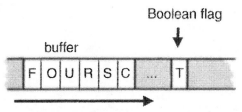

Figure 11.2. Simple buffer overflow.

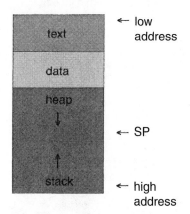

Figure 11.3. Memory organization.

The *text* section is for code, while the *data* section holds static variables. The *heap* is for dynamic data, while the *stack* can be viewed as "scratch paper" for the processor. For example, dynamic local variables, parameters to functions, and the return address of a function call are all stored on the stack. The *stack pointer*, or SP, indicates the top of the stack. Notice that the stack grows up from the bottom in Figure 11.3, while the heap grows down.

We are interested in the use of the stack during a function call. To see how the stack is used in this case, consider the example in Table 11.3. When the function func in Table 11.3 is called, the values that are pushed onto the stack are those given in Figure 11.4. In particular, note that the stack is being used (like scratch paper) to hold the array buffer while the function executes. The stack also holds the return address where control will be passed after the function finishes executing. Also note that buffer

TABLE 11.3. Example of code.

```
void func(int a, int b){
    char buffer[10];
}
void main(){
    func(1,2);
}
```

is positioned above the return address on the stack; that is, buffer is pushed onto the stack after the return address.

The buffer in Table 11.3 holds 10 characters. What happens if we put more than 10 characters into buffer? The buffer will "overflow," analogous to the way that a 5-gallon gas tank will overflow if we try to add 10 gallons of gas. In both cases, the overflow will likely cause a mess. In the case of our buffer overflow, Figure 11.4 indicates that the buffer will overflow into the space where the return address is located. If Trudy overflows the return address with random bits, as illustrated in Figure 11.5, then the most likely outcome is that the program will crash, since the program will jump to a random memory location when the function has finished executing.

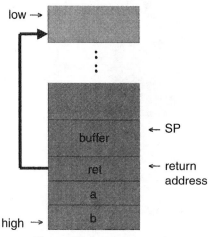

Figure 11.4. Stack example.

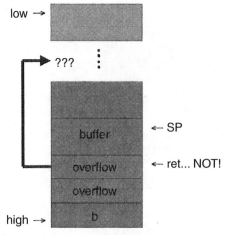

Figure 11.5. Buffer overflow causes a problem.

Trudy might be satisfied with simply crashing a program. But then again, Trudy might realize that there's much more potential to cause trouble in this "stack smashing" attack than simply crashing a computer. Since Trudy can overwrite the return address with a random address, can she also overwrite it with a specific address of her choosing? Often, the answer is yes. But what specific address should Trudy choose?

With some trial and error, Trudy can probably overwrite the return address with the address of the start of the buffer. Trudy can choose the data that goes into the buffer, so if Trudy can insert executable code into the buffer and overwrite the return address with the starting address of this code, Trudy can execute code of her choosing on the victim's machine! This amazing phenomenon is illustrated in Figure 11.6.

It's worth reflecting on the buffer overflow attack illustrated in Figure 11.6. Simply because of an unintentional programming error, Trudy may be able to execute code of her choosing on a remote machine. The security implications of such an attack are truly mind-boggling.

From Trudy's point of view, there are a couple of difficulties with the stack smashing attack described above. First, she may not know the precise address of the evil code she has inserted, and, second, she may not know the precise location of the return address on the stack. Neither of these presents an insurmountable obstacle.

Two simple tricks make a buffer overflow attack much easier to mount. For one thing, Trudy can precede the injected evil code with a NOP "landing pad" and, for another, she can insert the desired return address repeatedly. Then, if any of the multiple return addresses overwrite the true return address, execution will jump to the specified address. And if this specified address lands on any of the inserted NOPs, the evil code will be executed immediately after the last NOP in the landing pad. This improved stack smashing attack is illustrated in Figure 11.7.

For a buffer overflow attack to succeed, the program must contain a buffer overflow flaw. Not all buffer overflows are exploitable, but those that are enable Trudy to inject

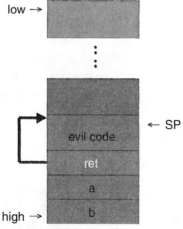

Figure 11.6. Evil buffer overflow.

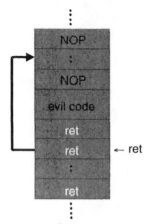

Figure 11.7. Improved evil buffer overflow.

code into the system. That is, if Trudy finds an exploitable buffer overflow, she can execute code of her choosing on the affected system. Trudy will probably have to work for some time in order to develop a useful attack. The standard reference on buffer overflow attacks is [7].

11.2.1.1 Buffer Overflow Example.
In this section, we'll examine code that contains an exploitable buffer overflow and we'll demonstrate an attack on this code. We'll be working from Trudy's perspective.

The program that Trudy is confronted with asks for a serial number that Trudy doesn't know. Trudy doesn't have the source code, but she does possess the executable.

When Trudy runs the program and enters an incorrect serial number, the program halts without further comment, as indicated in Figure 11.8. Trudy proceeds to try a few different serial numbers, but, as expected, she is unable to guess the correct serial number.

Trudy then tries entering unusual input values to see how the program reacts. She is hoping that the program will misbehave in some way and that she might have a chance of exploiting the incorrect behavior. Trudy realizes she's in luck when she observes the result in Figure 11.9, which indicates that the program contains a buffer overflow. Note that $0x41$ is the ASCII code for the character A. By carefully examining the error

Figure 11.8. Serial number program.

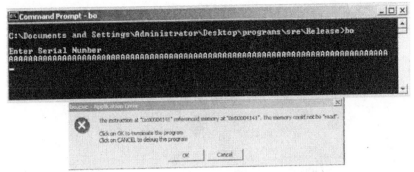

Figure 11.9. Buffer overflow in serial number program.

```
.text:00401000          sub     esp, 1Ch
.text:00401000          push    offset aEnterSerialNum ; "\nEnter Serial Number\n"
.text:00401003          call    sub_40109F
.text:00401008          lea     eax, [esp+20h+var_1C]
.text:00401000          push    eax
.text:00401011          push    offset aS        ; "%s"
.text:00401012          call    sub_401088
.text:00401017          push    8
.text:0040101C          lea     ecx, [esp+2Ch+var_1C]
.text:0040101E          push    offset aS123n456 ; "S123N456"
.text:00401022          push    ecx
.text:00401027          call    sub_401050
.text:00401028          add     esp, 18h
.text:0040102D          test    eax, eax
.text:00401030          jnz     short loc_401041
.text:00401032          push    offset aSerialNumberIs ; "Serial number is correct.\n"
.text:00401034          call    sub_40109F
.text:00401039          add     esp, 4
.text:0040103E
```

Figure 11.10. Disassembled serial number program.

message, Trudy realizes that she has overwritten two bytes of the return address with the character A.

Trudy then disassembles[1] the executable file and obtains the assembly code in Figure 11.10. The significant information in this code is the "Serial number is correct" message, which appears at address $0\text{x}401034$. If Trudy can overwrite the return address with the address $0\text{x}401034$, then the program will jump to the "Serial number is correct" branch and she will have obtained access to the code, without knowing the correct serial number.

But Trudy can't directly enter a hex address as input for the serial number, since the input is interpreted as ASCII text. Trudy finds that $0\text{x}401034$ is "@^P4" in ASCII, where "^P" is control-P. Confident of success, Trudy overwrites the return address with "@^P4." To her surprise, Trudy obtains the results in Figure 11.11.

A careful examination of the error message shows that the address where the error arose was $0\text{x}341040$. Apparently, Trudy caused the program to jump to this address instead of $0\text{x}401034$ as she had intended. Trudy notices that the intended address

---

[1]We'll have more to say about disassemblers in the next chapter.

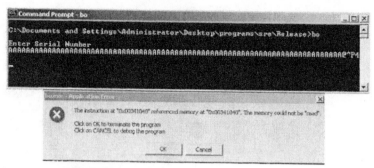

Figure 11.11. Failed buffer overflow attempt.

of $0x401034$ and the address $0x341040$ are byte reversed. The problem here is that the machine Trudy is dealing with uses the "little endian" convention, so that the low-order byte is first and the high-order byte comes last. That is, the address that Trudy wants, namely, $0x401034$, is stored internally as $0x341040$. So Trudy changes her attack slightly and overwrites the return address with $0x341040$, which in ASCII is "4^P@." With this change, Trudy is successful, as shown in Figure 11.12.

The important point of this buffer overflow example is that, even without access to the source code, Trudy was able to break the security of the software. The only tool she used was a disassembler to determine the address that she needed to use to overwrite the return address. In principle, this address could be found by trial and error, though that would certainly be tedious, and if Trudy has the executable it would be foolish of her not to employ a disassembler.

For the sake of completeness, we provide the C source code, bo.c, corresponding to the executable, bo.exe. This source code appears in Table 11.4.

Again, Trudy was able to complete her buffer overflow attack without access to the source code in Table 11.3. We provide the source code here simply for reference.

11.2.1.2 Stack Smashing Prevention.

There are several possible ways to prevent stack smashing attacks. One obvious approach is to eliminate all buffer overflows from software. Another option is to detect buffer overflows as they occur and respond accordingly. Yet another option for preventing the worst effects of such attacks is to not

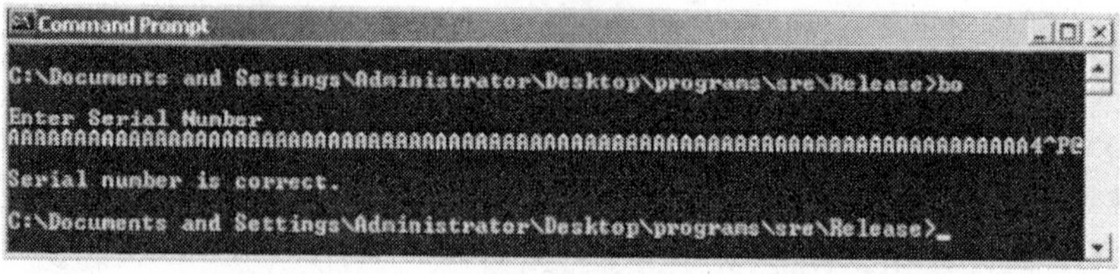

Figure 11.12. Successful buffer overflow attack.

TABLE 11.4. Source code for serial number example.

```
main()
{
    char in[75];
    printf("\nEnter Serial Number\n");
    scanf("%s", in);
    if(!strncmp(in, "S123N456", 8))
    {
        printf("Serial number is correct.\n");
    }
}
```

allow code to execute on the stack. In this section, we'll briefly discuss each of these options.

A good way to minimize the damage caused by the stack-based buffer overflows is to make the stack non-executable. Some hardware (and many operating systems) support the "no execute" or NX bit [97]. Using the NX bit, memory can be flagged so that code can't execute in a specified location. In this way the stack (as well as the heap and data sections) can be protected from the worst effects of a buffer overflow. Microsoft Windows has recently added support for the NX bit [238], although the NX bit is not present in most hardware on the market today. As the NX approach becomes more widely deployed, we should see a decline in the number and overall severity of buffer overflow attacks. However, as discussed in the problems at the end of this chapter, NX will not prevent all buffer overflow attacks; see [132] for further information.

Using "safe" programming languages such as JAVA or C# will eliminate most buffer overflows at the source. These languages are safe because at runtime they automatically check that all memory accesses are within the declared array bounds. There is a performance penalty for such checking, and for that reason much code will continue to be written in C. In contrast to these safe languages, there are several C functions that are known to be unsafe and these functions are the source of the vast majority of buffer overflow attacks. There are safer alternatives to all of the unsafe C functions and so the unsafe functions should never be used.

Runtime stack checking can be used to preventing stack smashing attacks. In this approach, when the return address is popped off of the stack, it's checked to verify that it hasn't changed. This can be accomplished by pushing a special value onto the stack immediately after the return address. Then, in order to overwrite the return address, this special value must first be overwritten. This special value is usually referred to as a "canary," in reference to the coal miner's canary.[2]

An anti-stack-smashing canary can be a specific value, or a value that depends on the return address. A specific value that is used is the constant $0x000aff0d$. This constant includes $0x00$ as the first byte since this is the string terminating byte. Any string that

---

[2]Coal miners would take a canary with them underground into the mine. If the canary died, the coal miners knew there was a problem with the air and they needed to get out of the mine as soon as possible.

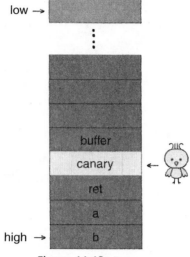

Figure 11.13. A canary.

overflows a buffer can't include 0×00 or it will be terminated at that point, and no more data will be overwritten. Consequently, an attacker can't use a string input to overwrite the constant $0\times000\text{aff}0\text{d}$ with itself, and any other value that overwrites the canary will be detected. The use of a canary is illustrated in Figure 11.13.

Microsoft recently added a canary feature to its C++ compiler based on an approach discussed in [186]. Any program that was compiled with the /GS compiler flag would use a canary—or, in Microsoft-speak, a "security cookie"—in order to detect a buffer overflow. But the Microsoft implementation was apparently flawed. When the canary died, the program passed control to a user-supplied handler function. It was claimed that an attacker could specify this handler function, thereby executing arbitrary code on the victim machine [185], though this was denied by Microsoft [143]. If the claimed flaw really was a flaw, then all buffer overflows were exploitable if compiled under the /GS option, even those that would not have been exploitable without the /GS option.

11.2.1.3 Buffer Overflow: The Last Word. Buffer overflow was unquestionably the attack of the decade for the 1990s, and it's almost certain to be the attack of the current decade as well. This is in spite of the fact that buffer overflow attacks have been known since the 1970s and it's possible to prevent such attacks by using the NX bit approach or to drastically reduce such attacks by using safe programming languages. Even with an unsafe language such as C, buffer overflow attacks can be greatly reduced by using the safer versions of the unsafe functions.

Developers must be educated, and tools for preventing and detecting buffer overflow conditions must be used. If it's available on a given platform, the NX bit should certainly be employed. In any case, buffer overflows will exist for a long time to come due to the large amount of legacy code and older machines that will continue to be in service for the foreseeable future.

11.2.2   Incomplete Mediation

The C function `strcpy(buffer, input)` copies the contents of the input string `input` to the array `buffer`. As we discovered above, a buffer overflow will occur if the length of `input` is greater than the length of `buffer`. To prevent such a buffer overflow, the program must *validate* the input by checking the length of `input` before attempting to write it to `buffer`. Failure to do so is an example of the problem of *incomplete mediation*.

As a somewhat more subtle example of incomplete mediation, consider data that is input to a Web form. Such data is often transferred to the server by including it in a URL, and that's the method we'll use in this example.

Suppose the input is validated on the client. For example, suppose the following order has been checked by the client:

```
http://www.things.com/orders/final&custID=112&
num=55A&qty=20&price=10&shipping=5&total=205
```

This URL is interpreted to mean that the customer with ID number 112 has ordered 20 of item number 55, at a cost of $10 each, which, with $5 shipping, gives a total cost of $205. Since the input was checked on the client, the developer of the server software believes it would be wasted effort to check it again on the server.

But instead of using the client software, Trudy can directly send a URL to the server. Suppose Trudy sends the following URL to the server:

```
http://www.things.com/orders/final&custID=112&
num=55A&qty=20&price=10&shipping=5&total=25
```

Since the server doesn't bother to validate the input, Trudy can obtain the same order as above, but for the bargain price of $25 instead of the legitimate price of $205.

Recent research [58] has revealed numerous buffer overflows in the Linux kernel, and most of these are due to incomplete mediation. This is somewhat surprising since the Linux kernel is usually considered to be very good software. After all, it is open source, so anyone can look for flaws in the code (we'll have much more to say about this topic in the next chapter) and it is the kernel, so it must have been written by experienced programmers. If such problems are common in the Linux kernel, they are undoubtedly more common in most other code.

There are tools available to help find likely cases of incomplete mediation. These tools should be more widely used, but they are not a cure-all since this problem can be subtle, and therefore difficult to detect automatically. And, as with most security tools, these tools can be as useful to the bad guys as they are to the good guys.

11.2.3   Race Conditions

Security processes should be *atomic*, that is, they should occur "all at once." Race conditions can arise when a security-critical process occurs in stages. In such cases,

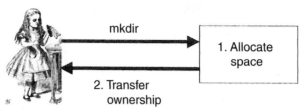

Figure 11.14. How mkdir is supposed to work.

an attacker may be able to make a change between the stages and thereby break the security. The term race condition refers to a "race" between the attacker and the next stage of the process—though it's not so much a race as a matter of careful timing for the attacker.

The race condition that we'll consider occurs in an outdated version of the Unix command mkdir, which creates a new directory. With this version of mkdir, there is a stage that determines authorization followed by a stage that transfers ownership. If Trudy can make a change after the authorization stage but before the transfer of ownership, then she can become the owner of any directory on the system.

The way that this version of mkdir is supposed to work is illustrated in Figure 11.14. Note that mkdir is not atomic and that is what makes it susceptible to a race condition.

Trudy can exploit the mkdir race condition if she can somehow implement the attack in Figure 11.15. In this attack, after the space for the new directory is allocated to Trudy, a link is established from the the password file (which Trudy is not authorized to access) to this space before ownership of the new directory is transferred to Trudy. The attack requires careful (or lucky) timing by Trudy.

Race conditions are probably fairly common. But attacks based on race conditions require careful timing, which makes them much more difficult to exploit than buffer overflow conditions. The way to prevent race conditions is to be sure that security-critical processes are atomic. However, this is easier said than done.

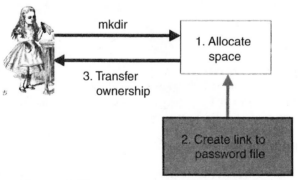

Figure 11.15. Attack on the mkdir race condition.

11.3 MALWARE

In this section, we'll discuss software that is designed to break security. Since such software is malicious in its intent, it goes by the name of *malware.*

Malware can be subdivided into many different categories. We'll use the following classification system, though there is considerable overlap between the various types.

- A *virus* is malware that relies on someone or something else to propagate from one system to another. For example, an e-mail virus attaches itself to an e-mail that is sent from one user to another. Until recently, viruses were the most popular form of malware.

- A *worm* is like a virus except that it propagates by itself without the need for outside assistance. Recently, worms have become hacker's preferred form of malware.

- A *trojan horse*, or trojan, is software that appears to be one thing but has some unexpected functionality. For example, an innocent-looking game could do something malicious while the victim is playing.

- A *trapdoor* or *backdoor* allows unauthorized access to a system.

- A *rabbit* is a malicious program that exhausts system resources. A rabbit could be implemented through a virus, a worm, or other means.

Generally, we won't be overly concerned with placing a particular piece of malware into its precise category. We'll use "virus" as shorthand for a virus, worm, or other such malware, since the term virus seems to be in common usage. But you should be aware that most recent "viruses" are actually worms, and this trend appears set to continue.

Where do viruses live on a system? It should come as no surprise that *boot sector* viruses live in the boot sector, where they are able to take control early in the boot process. Such a virus can then take steps to mask its presence before it can be detected. From a virus writer's perspective, the boot sector is a good place to be.

Another class of viruses are *memory resident*, meaning that they stay in memory. Rebooting the system may be sufficient to flush these viruses out. Viruses also can live in applications, macros, data, library routines, compilers, debuggers, and even in virus checking software.

By computing standards, malware is ancient. The first substantive work on viruses was done by Fred Cohen in the 1980s [47], who demonstrated that malware could be used to break multilevel security systems of the day. In fact, multilevel security (MLS) systems remain highly vulnerable to such attacks today.

The first virus of any significance to appear in the wild was the *Brain virus* of 1986. Brain did nothing malicious, and it was considered little more than a curiosity. As a result, it did not fully awaken people to the security implications of malware. That complacency was shaken in 1988 when the *Morris worm* appeared. This worm remains one of the more interesting pieces of malware to date, and we'll have more to say about it below. The other examples of malware that we'll discuss in some detail are *Code Red*, which appeared in 2001, and *SQL Slammer*, which appeared in the summer of 2004. We'll also present a simple example of a trojan and we'll discuss the future of malware.

11.3.1 Brain

The Brain virus of 1986 was more annoying than harmful [211]. Its importance lies in the fact that it was first, and as such it became a prototype for many later viruses. But because it was not malicious, there was little reaction by users. Despite the clear warning presented by Brain, computing systems remained extremely vulnerable to malware.

Brain placed itself in the boot sector and other places on the system. It then screened all disk access in order to avoid detection and to maintain its infection. Each disk read, Brain would check the boot sector to see if it was infected. If not, it would reinstall itself in the boot sector, which made it difficult to eliminate.

11.3.2 Morris Worm

The security outlook of the computing world changed forever when the Morris worm attacked the Internet in 1988 [29, 173]. It's important to remember that the Internet of 1988 was nothing like the Internet of today. Back then, the Internet was primarily populated by academics who exchanged e-mail and used `telnet` for remote access to supercomputers. Nevertheless, the Internet had reached a certain critical mass that made it vulnerable to self-sustaining worm attacks.

The Morris worm was a cleverly designed and sophisticated piece of software that was written by a graduate student at Cornell University.[3] Morris claimed that his worm was a test gone bad. In fact, the most serious consequence of the worm was due to a flaw (according to Morris). The worm was apparently supposed to check whether a system was already infected before trying to infect it. But this check was not always done, and so the worm tried to re-infect already-infected systems, which led to resource exhaustion. The malicious effect of the Morris worm was essentially that of a so-called rabbit.

Morris' worm was designed to do three things:

- Determine where it could spread its infection
- Spread its infection when possible
- Remain undiscovered

To spread its infection, the Morris worm had to obtain remote access to machines on the network. In order to do so, the worm attempted to guess user account passwords. If that failed, it tried to exploit a buffer overflow in `fingerd` (part of the Unix `finger` utility), and it also tried to exploit a trapdoor in `sendmail`. The flaws in `fingerd` and `sendmail` were well-known at the time but not widely patched.

---

[3]As if to add a conspiratorial overtone to the the entire affair, Morris' father was working at the National Security Agency at the time of the release of the Morris worm [189].

Once access had been obtained to a machine, the worm sent a "bootstrap loader" to the victim. This loader consisted of 99 lines of C code, which the victim machine compiled and executed. The bootstrap loader then fetched the rest of the worm. In this process, the victim machine even authenticated the sender!

The Morris worm also went to great lengths to remain undetected. If the transmission of the worm was interrupted, all of the code that had been transmitted was deleted. The code was also encrypted when it was downloaded, and the downloaded source code was deleted after it was decrypted and compiled. When the worm was running on a system, it periodically changed its name and process identifier (PID), so that a system administrator would be less likely to notice anything unusual.

It's no exaggeration to say that the Morris worm shocked the Internet community of 1988. The Internet was supposed to be able to survive a nuclear attack, yet it was brought to a grinding halt by a graduate student and a few hundred lines of C code. Few, if any, had dreamed that the Internet was so vulnerable to such an attack.

The results would have been much worse if Morris had chosen to have his worm do something truly malicious. In fact, it could be argued that the greatest damage was caused by the widespread panic the worm created. Many users simple pulled the plug, believing it to be the only way to protect their system. It turned out that users who didn't panic were the quickest to recover.

As a direct result of the Morris worm attack, the Computer Emergency Response Team (CERT) [39] was established, which continues to be a primary clearinghouse for timely computer security information. While the Morris worm greatly increased awareness of the security vulnerability of the Internet, only limited actions were taken to improve security.

After the Morris worm, viruses became the mainstay of malware writers. Only recently have worms reemerged in a big way. We'll next consider two recent worms that indicate the current trend in malware.

11.3.3   Code Red

When Code Red appeared in July of 2001, it was able to infect more than 250,000 systems in 10 to 15 hours. Before Code Red had run its course, it infected more than 750,000 out of 6,000,000 susceptible systems worldwide.

To gain access to a system, the Code Red worm exploited a buffer overflow in Microsoft IIS server software. It then monitored traffic on port 80, looking for other susceptible servers.

The malicious actions of Code Red depended on the day of the month. From day 1 to 19, it tried to spread its infection, and from day 20 to 27 it attempted a distributed denial of service, or DDoS, attack on www.whitehouse.gov.

There were many copycat versions of Code Red, one of which included a trapdoor for remote access to infected systems. This variant rebooted the system to flush all traces of the worm, leaving only the trapdoor.

It has been claimed that Code Red may have been a "beta test for information warfare" [179]. However, there seems to be little or no evidence to support such a claim.

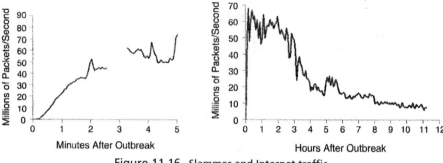

Figure 11.16. Slammer and Internet traffic.

11.3.4 SQL Slammer

The SQL Slammer worm burst onto the scene in the summer of 2004, when it infected 250,000 systems in 10 minutes. In this brief 10-minute period, Slammer reached an infection level that took Code Red 15 hours to achieve. At its peak, the number of Slammer infections doubled every 8.5 seconds [161].

Recent research has shown that Slammer spread too fast and effectively "burned out" the available bandwidth on the Internet [69]. In other words, if Slammer had been able to throttle itself slightly, it could have ultimately infected more systems. The graphs in Figure 11.16 show the increase in Internet traffic as a result of Slammer. The graph on the right shows the increase over a period of hours (note the initial spike), and the graph on the left shows the increase over the first 5 minutes.

The reason that Slammer created such a spike in Internet traffic is that each infected site searched for new susceptible sites by randomly generating IP addresses. A more efficient search strategy would have made more effective use of the available bandwidth. We'll return to this idea below when we discuss the future of malware.

Why was Slammer so successful? For one thing, the entire worm fit into a single 376-byte UDP packet. Firewalls are often configured to let a small packet through, assuming that a single packet could do no harm by itself. The firewall then monitors the connection to see whether anything unusual occurs. Since it was generally expected that much more than 376 bytes would be required for an attack, Slammer succeeded in large part by defying the assumptions of the "security experts."

11.3.5 Trojan Example

In this section, we'll present a trojan, that is, a program that appears to be something that it's not. This trojan comes from the Macintosh world, and it's totally harmless; however, its creator could just as easily have had this program do something malicious [149].

The particular trojan appears to be audio data, in the form of an mp3 audio file that we'll name `freeMusic.mp3`. The icon for this file appears in Figure 11.17. A user would almost certainly expect that double clicking on this file would automatically launch iTunes, and play the music contained in the mp3 file.

Figure 11.17. Icon for `freeMusic.mp3`.

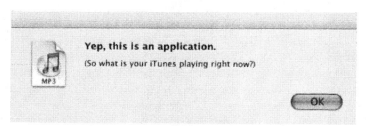

Yep, this is an application.

(So what is your iTunes playing right now?)

OK

Figure 11.18. Unexpected effect of `freeMusic.mp3` trojan.

However, after double-clicking on the icon in Figure 11.17, iTunes launches (as expected) and an mp3 file titled "Wild Laugh" plays (probably not expected). Simultaneously, and unexpectedly, the message window in Figure 11.18 appears.

What happened? This "mp3" file is a wolf in sheep's clothing—the file `freeMusic.mp3` is not an mp3 file at all. Instead, it's an application (that is, an executable file) that has had its icon changed so that it appears to be an mp3 file. A careful look at `freeMusic.mp3` reveals this fact, as shown in Figure 11.19.

Most users are unlikely to give a second thought to opening a file that appears to be an mp3. This trojan only issues a harmless warning, but that's because the author had no malicious intent and instead simply wanted to illustrate a point. The trojan could just as easily have done anything that the user who launched it is allowed to do [120].

11.3.6 Malware Detection

There are three commonly used methods for detecting malware. The first, and most common, is *signature detection*. This relies on finding a pattern or signature that is

Name	Date Modified	Size	Kind
read me	Apr 9, 2004, 7:36 PM	8 KB	Text document
freeMusic.mp3	Mar 21, 2004, 1:49 AM	88 KB	Application
query	Apr 9, 2004, 7:26 PM	12 KB	Text document
response	Apr 9, 2004, 7:25 PM	8 KB	Text document

4 items, 62.14 GB available

Figure 11.19. Trojan `freeMusic.mp3` revealed.

present in a particular piece of malware. A second approach is *change detection*, which finds files that have changed. A file that has unexpectedly changed may indicate an infection. The third approach is *anomaly detection*, where the goal is to detect unusual or "virus-like" files or behavior. We'll briefly discuss each of these and consider their relative advantages and disadvantages.

In Chapter 8, we discussed signature-based and anomaly-based intrusion detection systems (IDSs). There are parallels between such IDS systems and the corresponding virus detection methods.

11.3.6.1 Signature Detection.
A signature is generally a string of bits found in a file, although a hash value could also be used as a signature. Suppose that a virus contains the string of bits $0x23956a58bd910345$. Then we can consider this string to be a signature of the virus, and we can search for this signature in all files on a system. If we find the signature, we can't be certain that we've found the virus, since other innocent files could contain the same string of bits. If the bits in files were random, the chance of such a false match would, at $1/2^{64}$, be negligible. However, computer software and data is far from random, so there is, perhaps, a reasonable chance of a false match. This means that if a matching signature is found, further secondary testing is required to be certain that it actually represents a virus.

Signature detection is effective on malware that is known and for which each copy of the malware contains an identifiable signature. Another advantage of signature detection is that it places a minimal burden on users and administrators, since all that is required is to keep their signature files up to date and periodically scan for viruses.

A disadvantage of signature detection is that signature files can become large (tens of thousands of signatures is not uncommon), which can make scanning slow. Also, the signature files must be kept up to date. A more fundamental problem with signature detection is that it can only be used to detect known viruses—even a slight variant of a known virus might be missed.

Today, signature detection is by far the most popular malware detection method. As a result, virus writers have evolved some sophisticated means for avoiding signature detection. We'll have more to say about this below.

11.3.6.2 Change Detection.
Since malware must reside somewhere on system, if we detect a change somewhere on a system, then it may indicate an infection. That is, if we detect that a file has changed, it may be infected with a virus. We'll refer to this approach as change detection.

How can we detect changes? Hash functions are useful in this regard. Suppose we compute hashes of all files on a system and securely store these hash values. Then at regular intervals we can recompute the hashes and compare the new values with the stored values. If a file has changed in one or more bit position—as it will in the case of a virus infection—we'll find that the computed hash does not match the previously computed hash value.

One advantage of change detection is that there are virtually no false negatives; that is, if a file has been infected, we'll detect a change. Another major advantage is that we can detect previously unknown malware. But the disadvantages to change detection are many. Files on a system often change. As a result, there will be many false positives, which places a heavy burden on users and administrators. If a virus is inserted into a file that changes often, it will likely slip through a change detection regimen. And what should be done when a suspicious change is detected? A careful analysis of log files might prove useful. But it might be necessary to fall back to a signature scan, in which case the value of the change detection system is questionable.

11.3.6.3 Anomaly Detection. Anomaly detection is aimed at finding any "unusual" or "virus-like" or other potentially malicious activity or behavior. We discussed this idea in detail in an earlier section on intrusion detection systems (IDSs). The fundamental challenge with anomaly detection lies in determining what is normal and what is unusual and being able to distinguish between the two. Another serious difficulty is that the definition of "normal" can change, and the system must adapt to such changes—or risk overwhelming users with false alarms.

The major advantage of anomaly detection is that there is some chance of detecting previously unknown malware. However, the disadvantages are many. For one, anomaly detection is unproven in practice. Also, as discussed in more detail in the IDS section of Chapter 8, a patient attacker may be able to make an anomaly appear to be normal. In addition, anomaly detection is not robust enough to be used as a stand-alone detection system, so it is usually combined with a signature detection system. Although many people have high hopes for anomaly detection, it's currently a challenging research problem instead of a practical solution.

Next, we'll discuss the future of malware. This discussion will make it clear that better detection tools will be needed—and soon.

11.3.7 The Future of Malware

What does the future hold in store for malware? We'll briefly consider a few intriguing possibilities. Given the resourcefulness of malware developers, we can expect to see attacks based on these or similar ideas in the near future [19, 223].

One of the first responses of virus writers to the success of signature detection systems was *polymorphic* malware. A polymorphic worm, for example, may be encrypted with a different key each time it propagates. Often the encryption is extremely weak, such as a repeated XOR with a fixed bit pattern. The purpose of the encryption is not confidentiality, but to simply mask any possible signature. However, such a worm must include code to decrypt the worm, and this code is still subject to signature detection. As a result, polymorphic malware is more difficult—but not impossible—to detect with signature detection methods.

Metamorphic malware takes polymorphism one significant step further. A metamorphic worm "mutates" before infecting a new system. If the mutation is substantial, such a worm can likely avoid any signature-based detection system. The mutated worm will do the same thing as the original worm, but yet its internal structure must be different enough to avoid detection. Detection of metamorphic software is currently a difficult research problem.

Let's consider how a metamorphic worm might replicate [58]. First, the worm could be disassembled and the resulting code stripped to a base form. Then randomly selected variations could be inserted into the assembly code. These variations could include rearranging jumps and inserting dead code. The resulting code would then be assembled to obtain a worm with exactly the same functionality as the original but without a common signature.

According to the late pop artist Andy Warhol, "In the future everybody will be world-famous for 15 minutes" [230]. A *Warhol worm* is designed to infect the entire Internet in 15 minutes. Recall that Slammer infected 250,000 systems in 10 minutes. Slammer burned out the available bandwidth due to the way that it searched for susceptible hosts, and, as a result, Slammer was too bandwidth-intensive to have infected the entire Internet in 15 minutes. A true Warhol worm must do "better" than Slammer. Is this possible?

One approach to a Warhol worm is the following. The malware developer would do preliminary work to develop an initial "hit list" of sites that are susceptible to a particular exploit. Then the worm would be seeded with this hit list of vulnerable IP addresses. Of course, the list of IP addresses depends on the particular exploit used by the worm. Many sophisticated tools exist for identifying systems that are susceptible to a given exploit.

When this Warhol worm is launched, each of the sites on the initial hit list will be infected since they are all known to be vulnerable. Then each of these infected sites can scan a predetermined part of IP address space. This approach would avoid duplication and the resulting wasted bandwidth that caused Slammer to bog down.

Depending on the size of the initial hit list, the approach described above could conceivably infect the entire Internet in 15 minutes or less. No worm this sophisticated has yet been seen in the wild (as of mid-2005). Even Slammer relied on randomly generated IP addresses to spread its infection.

Is it possible to do better than Warhol worm? That is, can the entire Internet be infected in significantly less than 15 minutes? A *flash worm* is designed to infect the entire Internet almost instantly.

Searching for vulnerable IP addresses is the slow part of any worm attack. The Warhol worm described above uses a smart search strategy, where it relies on an initial list of susceptible systems. A flash worm could take this approach to the limit by embedding all susceptible IP addresses into the worm.

A great deal of work would be required to predetermine all vulnerable IP addresses, but there are hacker tools available that would significantly reduce this burden. Once all vulnerable IP addresses are known, they could be embedded in a single worm. This would result is an enormous worm of, perhaps, 400 KB in size [58]. But then each time the worm replicates, it would split the list of addresses embedded within it, as illustrated in Figure 11.20. In just a few generations the worm would be reduced to a reasonable size. The strength of this approach is that it results in virtually no wasted time or bandwidth.

It has been estimated that a well-designed flash worm could infect the entire Internet in as little as 15 seconds! Since this is much faster than humans could possibly respond, any defense against such an attack must be automated. A conjectured defense against

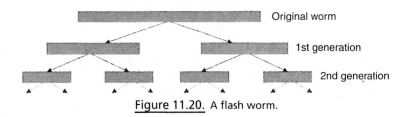

Figure 11.20. A flash worm.

flash worms [58] would be to deploy many "personal" intrusion detection systems and to have a "master" IDS monitor these personal IDSs. When the master IDS detects unusual activity, it can let it proceed on a few nodes, while temporarily blocking it elsewhere. If the sacrificial nodes are adversely affected, then an attack is in progress, and it can be prevented elsewhere. On the other hand, if it's a false alarm, the other nodes are only delayed slightly. This defensive strategy shares many of the challenges associated with anomaly-based intrusion detection systems, as discussed in Chapter 8.

11.3.8 Cyber Diseases Versus Biological Diseases

It's currently very popular to make biological analogies with computing. There are many such analogies that are applied to the field of security. In the field of malware and, in particular, computer "viruses," the analogy is fairly obvious.

There clearly are some similarities between biological and computer diseases. For example, in nature, if there are too few susceptible individuals, a disease will tend to die out. A somewhat similar situation exists on the Internet, where too few susceptible systems may not allow a worm to become self-sustaining—particularly if the worm is randomly searching for vulnerable IP addresses.

There are, however, some significant difference between cyber diseases and biological diseases. For example, there is virtually no sense of distance on the Internet, so many of the models developed for biological diseases don't apply to cyber diseases. Also, in nature, diseases attack more or less at random, while hackers specifically select the most desirable targets. As a result, computer attacks are probably more focused and damaging than biological attacks. The important point here is that, although the biological analogy is useful, it cannot be taken too literally.

11.4 MISCELLANEOUS SOFTWARE-BASED ATTACKS

In this section, we'll consider attacks that rely on software. While there are numerous such attacks, we'll restrict our attention to a few representative types of attacks. The topics we'll discuss are *salami attacks*, *linearization attacks*, *time bombs*, and the general issue of trusting software.

11.4.1 Salami Attacks

In a salami attack, a programmer "slices off" an amount of money from individual transactions. These slices must be difficult for the victim to detect. For example, it's a matter of computing folklore that a programmer for a bank used a salami attack to slice off fractional cents leftover from interest calculations. These fractional cents— which were not noticed by the customers or the bank—were supposedly deposited in the programmers account. According to the legend, the programmer made a lot of money.

Although it is not known whether this ever actually occurred, it certainly is possible. And there are many confirmed cases of similar insider attacks. The following examples of salami attacks all appear in [118]. In one documented case, a programmer added a few cents to every employee payroll tax withholding, but credited the money to his own tax. As a result, this programmer got a hefty tax refund. In another example, a rent-a-car franchise in Florida inflated gas tank capacity in order to overcharge customers. An employee at a Taco Bell location reprogrammed the cash register for the drive-through line so that $2.99 items registered as $0.01 and the employee pocketed the $2.98 difference—a rather large slice of salami!

In another salami attack, four men who owned a gas station in Los Angeles installed a computer chip that overstated the amount of gas pumped. Not surprisingly, customers complained when they had to pay for more gas than their tanks could hold. But this scam was hard to detect, since the gas station owners were clever. They had programmed the chip to give the correct amount of gas whenever exactly 5 or 10 gallons was purchased, because they knew from experience that inspectors usually asked for 5 or 10 gallons.

11.4.2 Linearization Attacks

Linearization attacks have been used to break security in a wide variety of situations. To illustrate the attack, consider the program in Table 11.5, which checks an entered number to see whether it matches the correct serial number, which in this case happens to be S123N456. For efficiency, the programmer decided to check one character at a time and to exit as soon as an incorrect character is found. Can Trudy take advantage of this?

Using the code in Table 11.5, the correct serial number will take longer to process than an incorrect serial number. Even better (for Trudy), a serial number that has the first character correct will take longer than any that has an incorrect first character. So, Trudy can select an eight-character string and vary the first character over all possibilities. If she can time the program precisely enough, she will find that the string beginning with S takes the most time. Trudy can then fix the first character as S and vary the second character, in which case she will find that 1 takes the longest. Continuing, Trudy can recover the serial number one character at a time.

What is the advantage for Trudy in this linearization attack? Suppose the serial number is eight characters long and each character has 128 possible values. Then there are $128^8 = 2^{56}$ possible serial numbers. If Trudy must randomly guess complete serial numbers, she would guess the serial number in about 2^{55} tries, which is an enormous amount of work. On the other hand, by using the linearization attack above, an average of only $128/2 = 64$ guesses are required for each letter, for a total expected work of about $8 \cdot 64 = 2^9$ guesses, which is a trivial amount of work.

A real-world example of a linearization attack occurred in TENEX [179], a time-share system used in ancient times. In TENEX, passwords were verified one character

TABLE 11.5. Serial number program.

```
int main(int argc, const char *argv[])
{
    int i;
    char serial[9]="S123N456\n";
    if(strlen(argv[1]) < 8)
    {
        printf("\nError---try again.\n\n");
        exit(0);
    }
    for(i = 0; i < 8; ++i)
    {
        if(argv[1][i] != serial[i]) break;
    }
    if(i == 8)
    {
        printf("\nSerial number is correct!\n\n");
    }
}
```

at a time, but careful timing was not even necessary. Instead, it was possible to arrange for a page fault to occur when the next unknown character was guessed correctly. Then a user-accessible page fault register would tell the attacker that a page fault had occurred and, therefore, that the next character had been guessed correctly. This attack could be used to crack any password in seconds.

11.4.3 Time Bombs

Time bombs are another interesting class of software-based attacks. We'll illustrate the concept with an infamous example. In 1986, Donald Gene Burleson told his employer to stop withholding taxes from his paycheck. Since this isn't legal, the company refused. Burleson, a tax protester, made it known that he planned to sue his company. In the process of preparing his legal documents, he used his company's computing resources. When his company discovered this behavior, they, not surprisingly, fired him [182].

It later came to light that Burleson had been developing malicious software. After Burleson was fired, he triggered this "time bomb" software, which proceeded to delete thousands of records from the company computer.

The Burleson story doesn't end here. Out of fear of embarrassment, the company was reluctant to pursue a legal case against Burleson, despite his malicious actions. Then in a bizarre twist, Burleson sued his former employer for back pay, at which point the company finally sued Burleson. The company eventually won, and in 1988 Burleson was fined $11,800. The case took two years to prosecute at a cost of thousands of dollars and resulted in little more than a slap on the wrist for Burleson. This was one of the first computer crime cases in the United States, and many cases since have followed a similar pattern. In particular, companies are often reluctant to pursue such cases out of fear of embarrassment.

11.4.4 Trusting Software

Finally, we consider a philosophical question with practical significance: Can you trust software? In a fascinating article [232], the following thought experiment is discussed. Suppose that a C compiler has a virus. When compiling the `login` program, this virus creates a backdoor in the form of an account with a known password. Also, when the C compiler is recompiled, the virus incorporates itself into the newly compiled C compiler.

Now suppose that you suspect that your system is infected with a virus. To be absolutely certain that you fix the problem, you decide to start over from scratch. First, you recompile the C compiler, and then you recompile the operating system—which includes the `login` program. In this case, you still haven't gotten rid of the problem.

In the real-world, imagine that an attacker is able to hide a virus in your virus scanner. Or consider the damage that could be done by a successful attack on online virus signature updates—or other automated software updates.

11.5 SUMMARY

In this chapter, we discussed security threats that arise from software. The threats considered in this chapter come in two basic flavors. The plain vanilla flavor consists of unintentional software flaws that attackers can sometimes exploit. The classic example of such a flaw is the buffer overflow, which we discussed in detail. Another common flaw with security implications is a race condition.

The more exotic flavor of software security threats arise from intentionally malicious software, or malware. Such malware includes the viruses and worms that plague users today, as well as trojans and backdoors. Malware writers have developed highly sophisticated techniques for avoiding detection, and they appear set to push the envelope further in the near future. Whether detection tools are up to the challenge posed by the next generation of malware is an open question.

11.6 PROBLEMS

1. It's been said that, with respect to security, complexity, extensibility, and connectivity are the "trinity of trouble" [107]. Define each of these terms and explain how each creates security problems.
2. What is a validation error, and how can such an error lead to a security flaw?
3. Discuss one example of a virus or worm that was not discussed in the text.
4. What is a race condition? Discuss an example of a race condition, other than the `mkdir` example presented in the text.

5. What is the distinction between a polymorphic and a metamorphic worm? How might metamorphic software be used for good instead of evil?

6. What is a "canary," and how is it used to prevent stack smashing attacks? How was Microsoft's implementation of this technique (the /GS compiler option) flawed?

7. Discuss one real-world example of a buffer overflow that resulted in a successful attack.

8. Explain how a heap-based buffer overflow works in contrast to the stack-based buffer overflow discussed in this chapter.

9. Read the article [238] and explain why the author (correctly) views the NX bit as only one small part of the solution to the security problems that plague computers today.

10. Recall that a trojan horse has "unexpected functionality." Write your own trojan, where the unexpected functionality is completely harmless. Explain how your trojan could be modified to do something malicious.

11. As discussed in the text, the C function `strcpy` is unsafe. The C function `strncpy` is a safer version of `strcpy`. Why is `strncpy` safer but not completely safe?

12. Suppose Alice's system employs the NX bit method of protecting against buffer overflow attacks. If Alice's system uses software that is known to harbor multiple buffer overflows, would it be possible for Trudy to conduct a denial of service attack on Alice by exploiting one of these buffer overflows? Explain.

13. Suppose that the NX bit method of protecting against buffer overflow attacks is implemented. Will the buffer overflow illustrated in Figure 11.5 succeed? Will the attack in Figure 11.6 succeed? Why will the specific buffer overflow example discussed in Section 11.2.1.1 still succeed?

14. Consider the following protocol for adding money to a debit card.

   (i) User inserts debit card into debit card machine.

   (ii) Debit card machine determines current value of card is x dollars.

   (iii) User inserts y dollars into debit card machine.

   (iv) User presses `enter` button on debit card machine.

   (v) Debit card machine writes value of $x + y$ dollars to debit card and ejects card.

   Describe an attack on this protocol that exploits a race condition. How could you change the protocol above to eliminate the race condition, or at least make it more difficult to exploit?

15. List all unsafe C functions and explain why each is unsafe. List the safer alternative to each and explain whether each is safe or only safer.

16. In contrast to a flash worm, a slow worm is designed to slowly spread its infection but remain undetected. Then, at a preset time, all of the hidden worms could emerge and do something malicious. The resulting effect is similar to that of a flash worm. Discuss one weakness (from Trudy's perspective) of a slow worm compared with a flash worm. Discuss one weakness (also from Trudy's perspective) of a flash worm compared with a slow worm.

17. Exploit the buffer overflow in the Windows executable contained in `overflow.zip` (available from the textbook website) so that you bypass its serial number check. Turn in a screen capture to verify your success. Can you determine the correct serial number?

18. Devise a linearization attack on the code in Table 11.5. Write pseudo-code to implement such an attack.

19. Obtain the Windows executable contained in `linear.zip` (available at the textbook website). Use a linearization attack to determine the correct eight-digit serial number. How many guesses were required to find the serial number? What is the expected number of guesses that would have been required if the code was not vulnerable to a linearization attack?

20. Suppose that a bank does 1,000 currency exchange transactions each day. Describe a salami attack on such transactions. How much money would Trudy expect to make using this salami attack in a day? In a week? In a year?

21. Read the article [232] and write a one-page summary.

12

INSECURITY IN SOFTWARE

*Every time I write about the impossibility of effectively protecting digital files
on a general-purpose computer, I get responses from people decrying the
death of copyright. "How will authors and artists get paid for their work?"
they ask me. Truth be told, I don't know. I feel rather like the physicist
who just explained relativity to a group of would-be interstellar travelers,
only to be asked: "How do you expect us to get to the stars, then?"
I'm sorry, but I don't know that, either.*
—Bruce Schneier

The reverse side also has a reverse side.
—Japanese proverb

12.1 INTRODUCTION

In this chapter, we'll begin with software reverse engineering, or SRE. To fully appreciate
the security difficulties inherent in software, we must look at software the way that an
attacker looks at software. Serious attackers use SRE techniques to find and exploit
flaws—or create new flaws—in software.

After our brief look at SRE, we'll be prepared to discuss digital rights management,
or DRM, which provides an excellent example of the limitations of doing security in
software. DRM also nicely illustrates the potential impact of SRE on software.

The last major topic of this chapter is software development. It was tempting to
label this section "secure software development," but truly secure software is virtually

Information Security: Principles and Practice, by Mark Stamp
Copyright © 2006 John Wiley & Sons, Inc.

impossible to achieve in practice. We'll discuss methods to improve the security of software, but we'll also see why most of the advantages lie with the bad guys. We'll illustrate this point with a timely example—a comparison of the security vulnerabilities of open source and closed source software.

12.2 SOFTWARE REVERSE ENGINEERING

SRE or software reverse engineering—which is also known as reverse code engineering, or, simply, reversing—can be used for good or not so good purposes. The good uses include understanding malware [251, 252] or legacy code. We're interested in the not-so-good uses, which include removing usage restrictions from software, finding and exploiting software flaws, cheating at games, breaking DRM systems, and many other attacks on software.

We'll assume that the reverse engineer is our old friend Trudy. Trudy only has an executable, or exe, file, and, in particular, she does not have access to the source code. Trudy might want to simply understand the software better in order to devise an attack, but more likely she wants to modify the software in some way. SRE is usually aimed at code for Microsoft Window, so we'll assume that Trudy is focused on Windows software.

The essential tools of the trade for SRE include a *disassembler*, a *debugger*, and a *hex editor*. A disassembler converts an executable into assembly code, as best it can. A disassembler can't always disassemble code correctly, since, for example, it's not always possible to distinguish code from data. This implies that in general, it's not possible to disassemble an exe file and reassemble the result into a functioning executable. This will make Trudy's task slightly more challenging but by no means insurmountable.

IDA Pro is the hacker's disassembler of choice, and it is a powerful and flexible tool [109]. IDA Pro costs a few hundred dollars, and, as with any disassembler, it converts the binary to assembly, as best it can—though IDA Pro's best is much better than the best of any other disassembler. Hackman [227] is an inexpensive shareware disassembler, although it's inferior to IDA Pro.

A debugger is used to set break points, which allows Trudy to step through the code as it executes. This is necessary to completely understand the code. Some claim that SoftICE is the "alpha and omega" of debuggers [121]. It costs several thousand dollars and is a sophisticated and complex tool with a large two-volume users manual. SoftICE is a kernel mode debugger, meaning that it can debug code even if it's not "instrumented" for debugging, that is, even if the code is not supposed to be debugged [49]. SoftICE can even be used to debug the operating system. OllyDbg [170] is a freeware debugger that is said to be a worthy competitor to SoftICE [132]. The maker of OllyDbg also provides a quality disassembler and hex editor.

A hex editor is also a necessary SRE tool. The hex editor is the tool Trudy will use to directly modify, or *patch*, the exe file. UltraEdit is a popular hex editor, and it's shareware, HIEW is another shareware hex editor that hackers like.

Other tools that might sometimes prove useful include Regmon, which monitors all accesses of the Windows registry, and Filemon, which, as you might have guessed, monitors all accesses of files. Both of these tools are freeware. VMWare [242]—which allows a user to set up virtual machines—is another potentially useful tool.

Why do we need a disassembler and a debugger? The disassembler gives a static view that provides a good overview of the program logic. But to jump to a specific place in the disassembled code would require that the attacker mentally execute the code in order to know the state of all register values. This is an insurmountable obstacle for all but the simplest code.

A debugger on the other hand is dynamic and allows Trudy to set break points. In this way, Trudy can treat complex code as a black box. Also, as we mentioned above, not all code disassembles correctly, and for such cases a debugger is required to make sense of the code. The bottom line is that both disassembler and debugger are required for any serious SRE task.

For SRE work, boundless patience and optimism are also needed, since SRE is extremely tedious and labor intensive. There are few automated tools and SRE is essentially a manual process that requires many long hours spent slogging through assembly code. For an attacker, however, the payoff can be well worth the effort.

The necessary technical skills for SRE include a working knowledge of the target assembly language and experience with the necessary tools—primarily a disassembler and a debugger. For Windows, some knowledge of the Windows portable executable, or PE, file format is also important [180]. These skills are beyond the scope of this book—see [121] for more information. Below we'll restrict our attention to a relatively simple SRE example.

The SRE example that we'll consider only requires the use of a disassembler and a hex editor. We'll disassemble the executable to understand the code. Then we'll use the hex editor to patch the code to change its behavior. It's important to realize that for most real-world code a debugger would also be required.

For our SRE example, we'll consider code that requires a serial number. The attacker Trudy doesn't know the serial number, and when she guesses (incorrectly) she obtains the results in Figure 12.1.

Trudy, being a dedicate reverser, decides the first thing she'll do is to disassemble serial.exe. Part of the resulting IDA Pro disassembly appears in Figure 12.2.

The line at address 0x401022 in Figure 12.2 indicates that the correct serial number is S123N456. Trudy tries this serial number and finds that it is indeed correct, as indicated in Figure 12.3.

Figure 12.1. Serial number program.

```
.text:00401003          push    offset aEnterSerialNum ; "\nEnter Serial Number\n"
.text:00401008          call    sub_4010AF
.text:0040100D          lea     eax, [esp+18h+var_14]
.text:00401011          push    eax
.text:00401012          push    offset aS        ; "%s"
.text:00401017          call    sub_401090
.text:0040101C          push    8
.text:0040101E          lea     ecx, [esp+24h+var_14]
.text:00401022          push    offset aS123n456 ; "S123N456"
.text:00401027          push    ecx
.text:00401028          call    sub_401060
.text:0040102D          add     esp, 18h
.text:00401030          test    eax, eax
.text:00401032          jz      short loc_401045
.text:00401034          push    offset aErrorIncorrect ; "Error! Incorrect serial number."
.text:00401039          call    sub_4010AF
```

Figure 12.2. Serial number program disassembly.

But Trudy suffers from short-term memory loss, and she has particular trouble remembering serial numbers. Trudy would like to patch the executable serial.exe so that she doesn't need to remember the serial number. Trudy looks again at the disassembly in Figure 12.2, and she notices that the test instruction at address 0x401030 is significant. If the jump instruction, jz, at 0x401032 is not true, then the error message "Error! Incorrect serial number" is printed. If Trudy can make the jz instruction always return true, then it wouldn't matter what serial number she entered.

At this point, Trudy must rely on her knowledge of assembly code. The instruction test eax,eax computes a binary AND of register eax with itself. This causes the flag bit—which is tested in the jump instruction at address 0x401032—to be zero only if the eax register contains 0. Trudy doesn't particularly care why this set of instructions is being executed, since she just wants to change things so that the jump jz is always true.

Trudy realizes that if she can replace the the instruction test eax,eax address 0x401030 with xor eax,eax, then the flag bit that is tested in line 0x401032 will always be zero (since anything XORed with itself gives zero), and the subsequent jump will therefore always be true. Trudy needs to determine whether she can patch the code to make this change without causing any unwanted side effect.

Trudy next examines the bits (in hex) at address 0x401030, and she sees the results displayed in Figure 12.4, which tells her that test eax,eax is, in hex, 0x85C0 .... Trudy, again relying on her knowledge of assembly code, knows that her desired result of xor eax,eax is, in hex, 0x33C0 .... That is, Trudy only needs to change one byte in the executable to make her desired change. It's also crucial that Trudy does not need to insert or delete any bytes, as that would almost certainly cause the resulting code to fail.

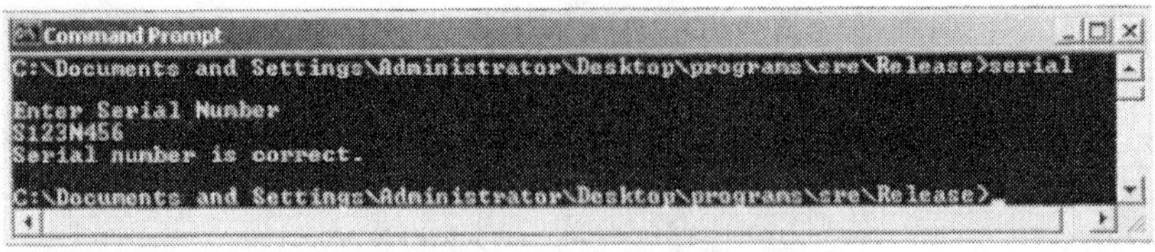

Figure 12.3. Correct serial number.

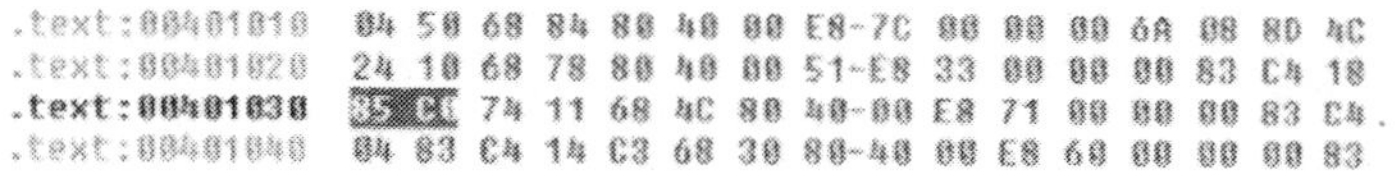

```
.text:00401010   04 50 68 84 80 40 00 E8-7C 00 00 00 6A 08 8D 4C
.text:00401020   24 10 68 78 80 40 00 51-E8 33 00 00 00 83 C4 18
.text:00401030   85 C0 74 11 68 4C 80 40-00 E8 71 00 00 00 83 C4
.text:00401040   04 83 C4 14 C3 68 30 80-40 00 E8 60 00 00 00 83
```

Figure 12.4. Hex view of `serial.exe`.

Trudy then uses her favorite hex editor to patch `serial.exe`. Since the addresses in the hex editor won't match those in the disassembler, she uses the hex editor to search through `serial.exe` to find—as can be seen in Figure 12.4—the bits 0x85C07411684C. She then changes the byte 0x85 to 0x33, and she names the resulting file `serialPatch.exe`. A comparison of the original and the patched executables appears in Figure 12.5.

Trudy then executes the patched code `serialPatch.exe` and tries an incorrect serial number. The results in Figure 12.6 indicate that the patched program accepts any serial number, which is precisely what Trudy had hoped to achieve.

Finally, we've disassembled both `serial.exe` and `serialPatch.exe` with the comparison given in Figure 12.7. These results show that the patching achieved its desired results.

Kaspersky's book [121] is an excellent source for more information on SRE techniques. The book [177] has a readable introduction to some aspects of SRE.

Before leaving the important topic of SRE, we'll briefly consider ways to make such attacks more difficult. Although it's impossible to prevent SRE on an open system such as a PC, where the attacker has full administrator privileges, we can make SRE

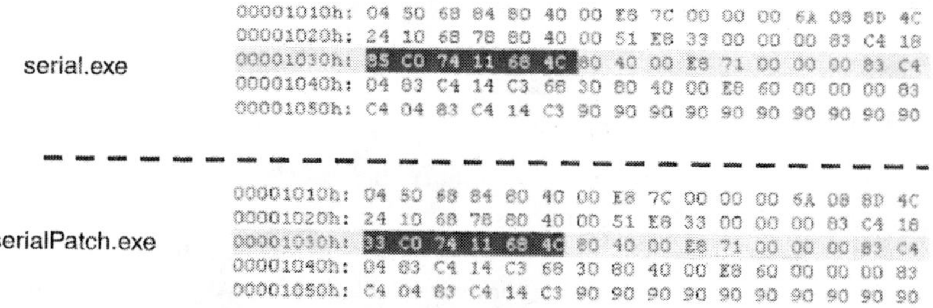

Figure 12.5. Hex view of original and patched.

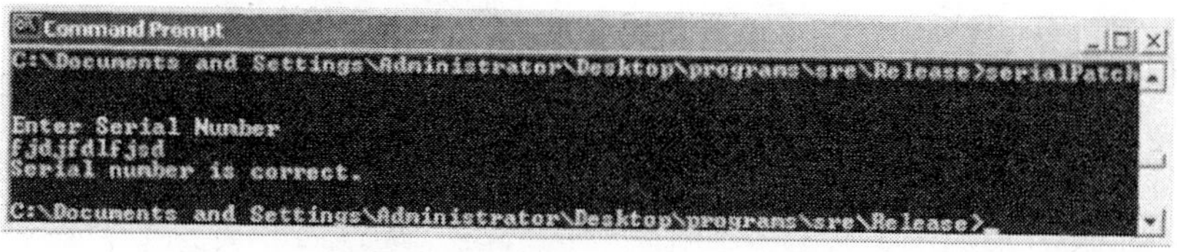

Figure 12.6. Patched executable.

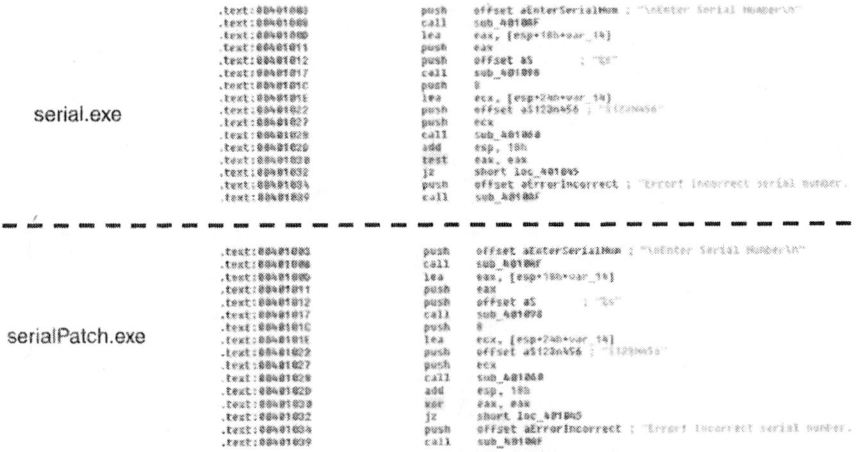

```
                    .text:00401003    push    offset aEnterSerialNum ; "\nEnter Serial Number\n"
                    .text:00401008    call    sub_40100F
                    .text:0040100D    lea     eax, [esp+18h+var_14]
                    .text:00401011    push    eax
                    .text:00401012    push    offset aS       ; "%s"
                    .text:00401017    call    sub_401098
                    .text:0040101C    push    0
  serial.exe        .text:0040101E    lea     ecx, [esp+24h+var_14]
                    .text:00401022    push    offset aS1234n456 ; "1234n456"
                    .text:00401027    push    ecx
                    .text:00401028    call    sub_401060
                    .text:0040102D    add     esp, 18h
                    .text:00401030    test    eax, eax
                    .text:00401032    jz      short loc_401045
                    .text:00401034    push    offset aErrorIncorrect ; "Error! Incorrect serial number."
                    .text:00401039    call    sub_40100F
```

```
                    .text:00401003    push    offset aEnterSerialNum ; "\nEnter Serial Number\n"
                    .text:00401008    call    sub_40100F
                    .text:0040100D    lea     eax, [esp+18h+var_14]
                    .text:00401011    push    eax
                    .text:00401012    push    offset aS       ; "%s"
                    .text:00401017    call    sub_401098
                    .text:0040101C    push    0
serialPatch.exe     .text:0040101E    lea     ecx, [esp+24h+var_14]
                    .text:00401022    push    offset aS1234n456 ; "1234n456"
                    .text:00401027    push    ecx
                    .text:00401028    call    sub_401060
                    .text:0040102D    add     esp, 18h
                    .text:00401030    xor     eax, eax
                    .text:00401032    jz      short loc_401045
                    .text:00401034    push    offset aErrorIncorrect ; "Error! Incorrect serial number."
                    .text:00401039    call    sub_40100F
```

Figure 12.7. Disassembly of original and patched.

more difficult. A good source of information on anti-SRE techniques is [40], though the material is somewhat dated.

We'd like to find some anti-disassembly techniques that can be used to confuse a disassembler. Our goal here is to give the attacker an incorrect static view of the code— or, better yet, no static view at all. We'll also consider anti-debugging techniques that can be used to obscure the attacker's dynamic view of the code. In Section 12.3, below, we'll discuss some tamper-resistance techniques that can be applied to software in order to make the code more difficult for an attacker to understand and therefore more difficult to patch.

12.2.1 Anti-Disassembly Techniques

There are several well-known anti-disassembly methods.[1] For example, it's possible to encrypt the executable file, and, when the exe file is in encrypted form, it can't be disassembled correctly. But there is a "chicken and egg" problem here that is similar to the situation that occurs with polymorphic viruses. That is, the code must be decrypted before it can be executed. A clever attacker can examine the decryption code and thereby gain access to the decrypted executable.

Another simple but reasonably effective anti-disassembly trick is "false disassembly" [241], which is illustrated in Figure 12.8. In this example, the top part of the figure indicates the actual assembly code, while the bottom part indicates the false disassembly. In the top part of the figure, the second instruction is a jump that jumps over the section labeled "junk," which is filled with invalid instructions.

---

[1]I was tempted to title this section "Anti-Disassemblymentarianism." Fortunately, I resisted the temptation.

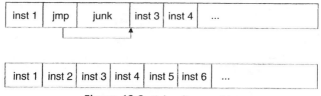

Figure 12.8. False disassembly.

In the false disassembly in the bottom part of Figure 12.8, every "instruction" from inst 3 on is incorrect. Note that the jump instruction actually jumps into the middle of the disassembled (and incorrect) inst 4, causing all subsequent instructions to be disassembled incorrectly. If Trudy carefully studies the false disassembly in Figure 12.8, she will eventually realize that inst 2 jumps into the middle of inst 4, and she can then undo the effects of the false disassembly.

Another sophisticated anti-disassembly trick that has been used is self-modifying code. As the name implies, self-modifying code modifies its own executable in real time [46]. This is an effective way to confuse a disassembler, but it may also confuse the developers, since it's difficult to implement and is error prone. Another sophisticated attempt to make code tamper resistant is discussed in [17].

12.2.2 Anti-Debugging Techniques

There are also several methods that can be used to make debugging more difficult. Since a debugger uses certain debug registers, a program can monitor the use of these registers and stop (or crash) if these registers are in use. A program can also monitor for inserted breakpoints, which is another telltale sign of a debugger.

Debuggers sometimes don't handle threads well, so interacting threads may confuse the debugger. There are many other debugger-unfriendly tricks, one of which we'll discuss below. But it is worth noting that it's possible to implement a hardware-based debugger (known as a HardICE) that can't be detected or confused by the tricks discussed here.

A simple anti-debugging technique is illustrated in Figure 12.9, where the top part of the figure illustrates the series of instructions that are to be executed. Suppose that, for efficiency, when the processor fetches inst 1, it also prefetches inst 2, inst 3,

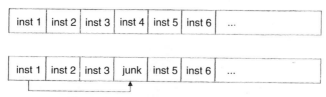

Figure 12.9. Anti-debugging example.

and inst 4. However, when the debugger executes inst 1, it does not prefetch instructions. Then we can take advantage of this difference to confuse the debugger, as illustrated in the bottom half of Figure 12.9, where inst 1 overwrites the memory location of inst 4. When the program is not being debugged, this causes no problem since inst 1 through inst 4 are all fetched at the same time. But a debugger does not prefetch inst 4, so it will be confused when it tries to execute the "junk" that has overwritten inst 4 [241].

There are some potential problems with the anti-debugging method in Figure 12.9. First, if the program tries to execute this segment of code more than once, the "junk" code will be executed. Also, this code is extremely platform dependent. And, as with the anti-disassembling example above, if Trudy has enough patience and skill, she will eventually unravel this trick and eliminate its effect.

12.3   SOFTWARE TAMPER RESISTANCE

In this section, we discuss several methods that can be employed to make software more tamper resistant. The goal of tamper resistance is to make patching more difficult, either by making the code more difficult to understand or by making the code likely to fail if it's patched. The techniques we'll discuss have been used in practice, but there's little (if any) empirical evidence to support the effectiveness of such methods.

12.3.1   Guards

It's possible to have the code hash sections of itself as it executes and compare the computed hash values with the known hash values of the original code. If tampering occurs, a hash check will fail and the program can take evasive action. These hash checks are sometimes know as guards. Guards can be viewed as a way to make the code "fragile", that is, the code breaks when tampering occurs.

Research has shown that by using guards it's possible to obtain good coverage of software with a minimal performance penalty [42, 108]. But there are some subtle issues. For example, if all guards are similar, then it would be relatively easy for an attacker to automatically detect and remove them. For more information on this and other issues related to guards, see [208].

12.3.2   Obfuscation

Another popular form of tamper resistance is code obfuscation. Here, the goal is to make the code difficult to understand. The rationale is that Trudy can't patch the code if she can't understand it. In a sense, this is the opposite of good software engineering practices.

As a simple example, "spaghetti code" can be viewed as a form of obfuscation. There has been much research into more robust methods of obfuscation, and one of the strongest appears to be the *opaque predicate* [48]. For example, consider the following pseudo-code:

$$\text{int } x, y;$$

$$\vdots$$

$$\text{if}((x - y)(x - y) > (x^2 - 2xy + y^2))\{\ldots\}$$

Notice that the if conditional is always false, since

$$(x - y)(x - y) = x^2 - 2xy + y^2$$

for any values of x and y. But an attacker might waste a significant amount of time analyzing the "dead" code that follows this if conditional. While this particular opaque predicate is not particularly opaque, many non-obvious opaque predicates have been developed. Again, this technique will not necessarily prevent an attack, but it should substantially increase the time required for a successful attack.

Code obfuscation has sometimes been promoted as a powerful security technique. In fact, Diffie and Hellman's original conception of public key cryptography suggested obfuscation as a likely way to develop a such a cryptosystem [67]. But recently it has been argued that obfuscation cannot possibly provide strong security in, say, the same sense as cryptography [20]. Nevertheless, obfuscation might still have a significant practical benefit in the challenging area of software protection.

For example, consider a piece of software that is used to determine authentication. Ultimately, authentication is a one-bit decision, regardless of the precise details of the method used. Therefore, somewhere in the authentication software there is, effectively, a single bit that determines whether authentication succeeds or fails. If Trudy can find this bit, she can force authentication to always succeed and thereby break the security. Obfuscation can make Trudy's job of finding this crucial bit into a challenging game of "hide and seek" in software. Obfuscation can effectively "smear" this one bit of information over a large body of code, thereby forcing Trudy to analyze a considerable amount of code. If the time and difficulty required to sufficiently understand the obfuscated code is sufficiently high, Trudy might simply give up. If so, the obfuscation has served its purpose.

Obfuscation can also be combined with other methods, including anti-disassembly, anti-debugging, and anti-patching techniques. All of these will tend to increase Trudy's work. However, unlike, say, a secure block cipher, we can probably never hope to drive the cost so high that an army of persistent attackers cannot eventually defeat the obfuscation.

12.3.3 Metamorphism Revisited

The usual practice in software development is to distribute identical copies, or clones, of a particular piece of software to each customer. This has obvious benefits with regard to development, maintainability, and so on. But software cloning has some negative security implications. In particular, if an attack is found on any one copy, the exact same attack will work on all of the copies. That is, the software has no resistance to *break once, break everywhere*, or BOBE (this is sometimes rendered as "break once run anywhere," or BORA).

In the previous chapter, we saw that metamorphic software is used by virus writers in an effort to avoid detection. Might a similar technique be used for good instead of evil? For example, suppose we develop a piece of software, but instead of distributing clones of this software, we distribute metamorphic copies. That is, each copy of our software differs internally, but all copies are functionally identical [216]. This is analogous to the metamorphic malware that we discussed in Chapter 11.

Suppose we distribute N cloned copies of a particular piece of software. Then one successful attack breaks all N clones. In other words, this software has no BOBE resistance. On the other hand, if we distribute N metamorphic copies of the software, where each of these N is functionally identical, but they differ in their internal structure, then an attack on one instance will not necessarily work against other instances. The strength of such an approach depends heavily on how different the non-clones are, but, in the best case, N times as much work is required to break all N instances. This is the best possible situation with respect to BOBE resistance.

Thanks to open platforms and SRE, we cannot prevent attacks on software. Arguably, the best we can hope for is increased BOBE resistance. Metamorphism is one possible way to achieve a reasonable level of BOBE resistance.

An analogy is often made between software diversity (or metamorphism) and genetic diversity in biological systems [44, 46, 82, 83, 168, 174, 175, 222]. For example, if all plants in a field are genetically identical, then one disease can kill all of the plants. But if the plants in a field are genetically diverse, then one disease can only kill some of the plants. This is essentially the same reasoning that lies behind metamorphic software.

To illustrate the potential benefits of metamorphism, suppose that our software has a common program flaw, say, an exploitable buffer overflow. If we clone this software, then the same buffer overflow attack will work against all cloned copies of the software. Suppose instead that the software is metamorphic. Now even if the buffer overflow exists in all instances, the same attack code will almost certainly not work against all instances, since buffer overflow attacks are, as we saw in Chapter 11, fairly delicate.

Metamorphic software is an intriguing concept that has been used in some applications [36, 217]. The use of metamorphism raises concerns regarding software development, software upgrades, and so on. Also, metamorphism does not prevent SRE, although it does appear to provide significant BOBE resistance. Metamorphism is used in malware, but perhaps it's not just for evil anymore!

12.4 DIGITAL RIGHTS MANAGEMENT

Digital rights management, or DRM, provides an excellent example of the limitations of doing security in software. The topics discussed in the previous section are particularly relevant to the DRM problem.

In this section, we'll discuss what DRM is and is not, and we'll describe an actual DRM system designed to protect PDF documents. We'll then briefly outline a DRM system designed to protect streaming media, and we'll discuss a particular peer-to-peer application that employs DRM. We'll also consider the use of DRM to protect documents distributed within an enterprise.

12.4.1 What is DRM?

At its most fundamental level, DRM is an attempt to provide "remote control" over digital content. We would like to distribute digital content, but we want to retain some control—remote control—over its use after it has been delivered [90].

Suppose Trudy wants to sell her new book, *For the Hack of It*, in digital form online. Since there is a huge potential market on the Internet and Trudy can keep all of the profits and she won't need to pay any shipping, this seems like an ideal solution. However, after a few moments of reflection Trudy realizes that there is a serious problem. What happens if, say, Alice buys Trudy's digital book and then redistributes it for free online? In the worst case, Trudy might only sell one copy [219, 221].

The fundamental problem is that it's trivial to make a perfect copy of digital content and almost as easy to redistribute it to virtually anyone. This is a dramatic change from the pre-digital era, when copying a book was costly, and redistributing it was relatively difficult. For an excellent discussion of the challenges faced in the digital age compared with those of the pre-digital era, see the paper [25].

In this section, we'll focus on the digital book example. However, similar comments hold for other digital media, including audio and video.

Persistent protection is the buzzword for the required level of DRM protection. That is, we must protect the digital content so that the protection stays with the content after it's delivered. Examples of the kinds of persistent protection restrictions that we might want to enforce on a digital book include the following:

- No copying
- Read once
- Do not open until Christmas
- No forwarding

among many other possibilities.

What can be done to enforce persistent protection? One option is to rely on the honor system, whereby we do not actually force users to obey the rules but instead simply expect that they will, since most people are good, honest, decent, and trustworthy. Surprisingly, this has actually been tried. Stephen King, the horror novel writer, published a book *The Plant* online in installments [191, 198]. King said that he would only continue to publish installments if a high enough rate of users paid.

Of the planned seven installments of *The Plant*, only the first six appeared online. Stephen King's spokesman claimed that the rate of payers had dropped so low that Mr. King would not publish the remaining installments online, leaving some angry customers who had paid $7 for 6/7ths of a book [191]. Before dismissing the honor system entirely, it's worth noting that shareware essentially follows the honor system model.

Another DRM option is to simply give up on enforcing DRM on an open platform such as a PC. In the previous section, we saw that SRE attacks render software on a PC highly vulnerable. This implies that, if we try to enforce persistent protection through software in a PC, we are likely doomed to failure.

However, the lure of Internet sales has created a strong interest in DRM, even if it can't be made perfectly robust. We'll also see that companies have an interest in DRM as a way to comply with certain government regulations.

If we decide that it's worthwhile to attempt DRM on a PC, one option is to build a weak software-based DRM. Several of these type of systems have been deployed, and most are extremely weak. For example, such a DRM system for protecting digital documents might be defeated by a user who is knowledgeable enough to operate a screen capture program.

Another option would be to develop the strongest possible DRM system in software. In the next section we'll describe a system that strives for just such a level of DRM protection. The design we'll describe is based on a real DRM system developed by the author for MediaSnap, Inc., as discussed in [220].

A reasonably high level of DRM protection can be achieved. Closed systems, such as game systems, are very good at enforcing restrictions similar to the persistent protection requirements mentioned above. Currently, there is work underway to include closed system features in future PCs. In large part, this work is motivated by the desire to make DRM robust on such systems. We'll return to this topic in Chapter 13 when we discuss Microsoft's Next Generation Secure Computing Base, or NGSCB. In this chapter, we'll only consider software-based DRM.

In much of the hype surrounding DRM today, it is claimed—or at least strongly implied—that cryptography is the solution to the DRM problem. That this is not the case can easily be seen by considering the generic black box crypto diagram in Figure 12.10, which illustrates a symmetric key system.

In the standard crypto scenario, the attacker Trudy has access to the ciphertext and perhaps some plaintext and some side-channel information. In the DRM scenario, we are trying to enforce persistent protection on a remote computer. What's more, the legitimate recipient is a potential attacker.

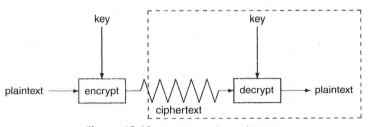

Figure 12.10. Cryptography and DRM.

Suppose Trudy is the legitimate recipient of a DRM-protected document. Then Trudy has access to everything within the dashed box in Figure 12.10. In particular, Trudy has access to the key. We certainly can't expect crypto to solve the persistent protection problem if we give the attacker the key!

With DRM it's necessary to use encryption so that the data can be securely delivered, and so that Trudy can't trivially remove the persistent protection. But if Trudy is clever, she won't try to attack the crypto directly. Instead, she will try to find the key, which is hidden somewhere in the software. One of the fundamental problems in DRM can be reduced to the problem of playing "hide and seek" with a key in software [204].

Software-based DRM systems are forced to rely on *security by obscurity*; that is, the security resides in the fact that Trudy doesn't completely understand, for example, how and where the key is hidden. Security by obscurity is generally considered a derogatory term in the security field, since once the obscurity is gone, so is the security. However, in software-based DRM, there does not appear to be any other viable option.

Software obfuscation and the other techniques discussed in the previous section are also examples of security by obscurity. It's always preferable not to rely on security by obscurity, but, when there is no other option, then we need to consider whether we can derive any useful measure of security from some clever application of obscurity.

Current DRM systems also rely heavily on secret designs, in clear violation of the spirit of Kerckhoffs Principle. Of course, this is partly due to the reliance on obscurity, but even a general overview of the security architecture is unavailable for most DRM systems. As mentioned above, current DRM systems also place excessive faith in crypto.

There is a fundamental limit on the effectiveness of any DRM system, since the so-called *analog hole* is present in any DRM system. That is, when the content is rendered, it can be captured in analog form. For example, when digital music is played, it can be recorded using a microphone, regardless of the strength of the DRM protection. Similarly, a digital book can be captured in unprotected form using a digital camera to photograph the pages displayed on a computer screen. No DRM system can prevent such attacks.

Another interesting feature of DRM is the degree to which human nature matters. For software-based systems, it's clear that absolute DRM security is impossible. So the challenge is to develop something that works in practice. Whether this is possible or not depends heavily on the context, as we'll see in the examples discussed below. The bottom line is that DRM is not strictly a technical problem. While this is also true of most security topics (recall passwords, for example), it's far more apparent in DRM than in many other security fields.

We've mentioned several times that strong software-based DRM is impossible. Let's be explicit as to why this is the case. From the previous SRE sections, it should be clear that we can't really hide a secret in software, since we can't prevent SRE. A user with full administrator privilege can eventually break any anti-SRE protection and thereby attack DRM software that is trying to enforce persistent protection. As a result, SRE is the "killer app" for attacking software-based DRM.

12.4.2   A Real-World DRM System

The information in this section is based on a DRM system designed and developed by MediaSnap, Inc., a small Silicon Valley startup company. The system is intended for use with digital documents that will be distributed via e-mail.

There are two major components to the MediaSnap DRM systems, a server component that we'll call the Secure Document Server, or SDS, and the client software, which is a software plugin to the Adobe PDF reader.

Suppose Alice wants to send a DRM-protected document to Bob. Alice first creates the document, and then attaches it to an e-mail. She selects the recipient, Bob, in the usual way, and she uses a special pull-down menu on her e-mail client to select the desired level of persistent protection. She then sends the e-mail.

The entire e-mail, including any attachements, is converted to PDF, and it is then encrypted (using standard crypto techniques) and sent to the SDS. It is the SDS that applies the desired persistent protection to the document. The SDS then packages the document so that only Bob can access it using his client DRM software. The client software will attempt to enforce the persistent protection. The resulting document is then e-mailed to Bob. This process is illustrated in Figure 12.11.

A key is required to access the DRM-protected document, and this key is stored on the SDS. Whenever Bob wants to access the protected document, he must first authenticate to the SDS and only then will the key be sent from the SDS to Bob. Bob can then access the document, but only through the DRM software. This process is illustrated in Figure 12.12.

There are security issues both on the server side and on the client side. The SDS must protect keys and authenticate users, and it must apply the required persistent protection to

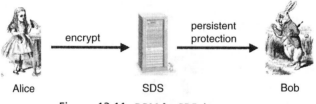

Figure 12.11. DRM for PDF documents.

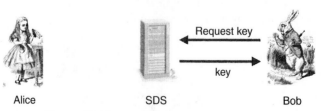

Figure 12.12. Accessing protected documents.

the document. The client must protect keys, authenticate users, and enforce the persistent protection, all while operating in a potentially hostile environment. The SDS resides at corporate headquarters and is relatively secure. The DRM client software, on the other hand, is readily available to any attacker. The discussion below concerns the client software.

The high-level design of the client software is illustrated in Figure 12.13. The software has an outer "shell" that attempts to create a tamper-resistant barrier. This includes anti-disassembly and anti-debugging techniques as discussed above. To prevent disassembly, the executable code is encrypted, and false disassembly is used to protect the part of the code that performs the decryption. In addition, the executable code is only decrypted in small slices so that it's more difficult for an attacker to obtain the entire code in decrypted form.

The anti-debugging technique is fairly sophisticated. The basic approach is to monitor for the use of the debug registers. One obvious attack on such a scheme is a man-in-the-middle, where the attacker debugs the code but responds to the anti-debugging software in such a way that it appears no debugger is running. The anti-debugging technique includes defenses against such an attack on its monitoring mechanism.

We know from the previous section that tamper-resistance techniques can delay an attacker, but they can't prevent a persistent attacker from eventual success. The software inside the tamper-resistant shell is obfuscated to further delay an attacker who has penetrated the tamper-resistant outer layer.

The obfuscation is applied to the security critical operations, including key management, authentication, and cryptography. The authentication information is cached, since we don't want to ask the user to repeatedly enter a password (or other means of authentication). Each time the authentication data is cached, it is cached in a different location in memory and in a different form.

The digital content is encrypted using the Advanced Encryption Standard (AES) block cipher. Unfortunately, standard crypto is difficult to obfuscate since the algorithms are well-known and the implementations are standardized for efficiency and to prevent implementation errors. As a result, the MediaSnap system also employs a "scrambling" algorithm, which is essentially a proprietary cipher. This scrambling is used in addition to—and not in place of—a strong cipher, so there is no violation of Kerckhoffs Principle.

The scrambling algorithm, which can itself be obfuscated, presents a much more substantial SRE challenge than a standard cipher, such as AES. The keys are also obfuscated by splitting them into multiple parts and hiding some parts in data and other parts

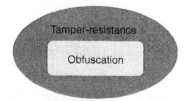

Figure 12.13. DRM software design.

in code. In short, the MediaSnap system employs multiple layers of obfuscation. But even this sophisticated obfuscation can only slow an attacker—a persistent attacker will eventually succeed.

Another security feature implemented by the system is an anti-screen capture technique, which is somewhat analogous to the anti-debugging technique mentioned above. Digital watermarking is also employed. As we learned in Chapter 5, watermarking is designed to provide the ability to trace stolen content. However, in practice, watermarking is of limited value, particularly if the attacker knows the watermarking scheme.

The MediaSnap DRM software also includes metamorphism for BOBE resistance. The metamorphism is implemented in several places, most notably in the scrambling algorithms. We'll have more to say about this below when we discuss a DRM application designed to protect streaming media.

This MediaSnap DRM system employs nearly all known software protection techniques in one form or another. It is almost certainly one of the most advanced software-based DRM systems yet devised. The only significant protection mechanism not employed is the guards or "fragilization" technique discussed above, and the only reason guards are not used is that they're incompatible with encrypted executable code.

One major security concern that we did not yet mention is the role of the operating system. In particular, if we can't trust the operating system to behave correctly, then our DRM client software can easily be undercut by attacks on the operating system. We'll return to this topic in the next chapter.

12.4.3   DRM for Streaming Media

Suppose we want to stream digital audio or video over the Internet, and this digital media is to be viewed in real time. If we want to charge money for the content, how can we protect the content from capture and redistribution? This sounds like a job for DRM. The DRM system we describe here follows the design given in [214].

Possible attacks on streaming media include spoofing the stream between the endpoints, man-in-the-middle, replay, or redistribution of the data, and the capture of the plaintext at the client. We are concerned with the latter attack. The threat here arises from unauthorized software that is used to capture the plaintext stream on the client.

The most innovative feature of our proposed design is the use of scrambling algorithms, which are encryption-like algorithms, as described in the previous section. We'll assume that we have a large number of distinct scrambling algorithms at our disposal and we'll use these to achieve a significant degree of metamorphism.

Each instance of the client software comes equipped with a large number of distinct scrambling algorithms included. Each client has a distinct subset of scrambling algorithms chosen from a master set of all scrambling algorithms, and the server knows this master set of algorithms. The client and server must negotiate a specific scrambling algorithm to be used for a particular piece of digital content. We'll describe this negotiation process in detail below.

We'll also encrypt the content so that we don't need to rely on the scrambling algorithm for cryptographic strength. The purpose of the scrambling is metamorphism—and the resulting BOBE resistance—not cryptographic security.

The data is scrambled and then encrypted on the server. On the client, the data must be decrypted and then descrambled. The descrambling occurs in a proprietary device driver, just prior to the rendering of the content. The purpose of this approach is to keep the plaintext away from an attacker, such as Trudy, until the last possible moment prior to rendering. Trudy is faced with a proprietary device driver that has a unique set of scrambling algorithms "baked in." This should provide Trudy with a significant SRE challenge and the system should have good BOBE resistance.

Suppose the server knows the N different scrambling algorithms, $s_0, s_1, \ldots, s_{N-1}$. Each client is equipped with a subset of these algorithms. For example, suppose that a particular client has the scrambling algorithms

$$\text{LIST} = \{s_{12}, s_{45}, s_2, s_{37}, s_{23}, s_{31}\}.$$

This LIST is stored on the client as $E(\text{LIST}, K_{\text{server}})$, where K_{server} is a key that only the server knows. The primary benefit of this approach is that the database that maps clients to their scrambling algorithms is distributed among the clients, eliminating a potential burden on the server. Notice that this approach is reminiscent of the way Kerberos uses TGTs to manage security-critical information.

To negotiate a scrambling algorithm, the client sends its LIST to the server. The server then decrypts the LIST and chooses one of the algorithms that is built into the client. The server must then securely communicate its scrambling algorithm choice to the client. This process is illustrated in Figure 12.14, where the server has selected the mth scrambling algorithm on the client's LIST, and the key K is a session key that has been established between the client and server.

The metamorphism provided by the scrambling algorithms is deeply embedded in the system and tied into all of the data. Furthermore, if the server knows that a particular scrambling algorithm is broken, the server won't select it. And if a particular client has too many broken algorithms, the server can force a software upgrade before agreeing to distribute the content.

The server could also distribute the client software (or some crucial component of it) immediately prior to distributing the content. This would make it more difficult for Trudy to capture the streamed media in real time. Of course, Trudy could record the stream and then attack the software at her leisure. However, in many situations, an attack that is not close to real time would be of less concern.

Since the scrambling algorithms are unknown to the attacker, they require a significant effort to reverse engineer, whereas a standard crypto algorithm does not need

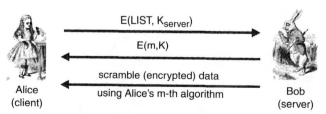

Figure 12.14. Scrambling algorithm selection.

to be reverse engineered at all—the attacker only needs to find the key. As we mentioned above, it could be argued that the use of scrambling algorithms is just security by obscurity. But in this particular application, it appears to have significant value since it improves BOBE resistance.

12.4.4   DRM for a P2P Application

Today, much digital content is delivered via peer-to-peer, or P2P, networks. Such networks contain large amounts of illegal, or pirated, music. The following scheme is designed to coerce users into paying a small fee for legal content that is distributed over a P2P network. This scheme is based on the pioneering work of Exploit Systems [77]. But before we discuss this application in detail, let's review how a P2P network works.

Suppose Alice has joined a P2P network, and she requests the song "Hey Jude." Then a query for "Hey Jude" floods through the network, and any peer who has the song—and is willing to share it—responds to Alice. This is illustrated in Figure 12.15. In this example, Alice can choose to download the song from either Carol or Pat.

Figure 12.16 illustrates the same scenario in a P2P network that includes a special peer that we'll call a *peer offering service*, or POS. The POS acts much like any other peer, except that it has only legal—and DRM-protected—music.

When Alice makes her request on a P2P network with a POS, it appears to her that she has received responses from Bill, Ben, Carol, Joe, and Pat. If Alice selects to download the music from Bill, Ben, or Joe, she will receive DRM-protected content for which she will be required to pay a small fee before she can listen to the music. On the other hand, if Alice selects either Carol or Pat, she receives the music for free, just as in the P2P network without the POS.

For the POS concept to work, it must not be apparent to Alice whether a peer is an ordinary peer or a POS peer. In addition, the POS must have a significant percentage of its "peers" appear in the top 10 responses. Let's assume that these technical challenges can be resolved in favor of the POS.

Now suppose Alice first selects Bill, Ben, or Joe. Then after downloading the music and discovering that she must pay, she is free to select another peer and, perhaps, another, until she finds one that has pirated (and free) music. But is it worth Alice's time to download the song repeatedly in order to avoid paying? If the music is priced low enough, perhaps not. In addition, the legal (DRM-protected) version can offer extras that might further entice Alice to pay a small fee.

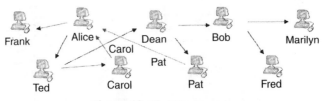

Figure 12.15. P2P network.

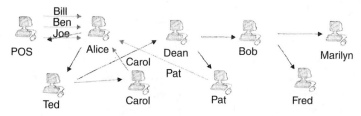

Figure 12.16. P2P network with POS.

The POS idea is clever, since it piggybacks on existing P2P networks. And in the POS scenario, weak DRM is sufficient. As long as it's more trouble for Alice to break the DRM than to click and wait for another download, the DRM has served its purpose.

To date, there has been very little interest in the POS idea from the music industry, perhaps due to the fact that the music industry does not want to be seen as legitimizing such networks. However, there has been some interest from the "adult" video industry.

12.4.5 DRM in the Enterprise

There are government regulations that require companies to protect certain types of private information, and there are similar regulations regarding certain types of business records. For example, the Health Insurance Portability and Accountability Act, or HIPAA, requires that companies protect personal medical records. HIPAA stipulates fines of up to $10,000 "per incident" for failing to provide sufficient protection. Companies that deal with medical records often need to make such records accessible to certain employees, but, due to HIPAA, they also must be certain that medical records do not leak to unauthorized recipients. DRM can be used to solve this problem.

The Sarbanes-Oxley Act, or SOA, requires that companies must preserve certain documents, such as information that might be relevant to "insider trading" stock violations. Again, DRM could be used here to be sure that such information is protected as required by law. The bottom line is that DRM-like protections are needed by corporations for regulatory compliance. We refer to this as *enterprise DRM* to distinguish it from the e-commerce DRM discussed above.

From a technical point of view, the enterprise DRM security requirements are similar to those for e-commerce. But the motivation for enterprise DRM is entirely different, since the purpose of enterprise DRM is to prevent a company from losing money (due to fines) instead of being an avenue for making money (as in e-commerce). More significantly, the human dimension is completely different. In an enterprise setting the threat of reprisals (getting fired or sued) are far more plausible than in the e-commerce setting. Also, the required level of protection is different. In enterprise DRM, a corporation has shown "due diligence" and thereby complied with the regulations, provided that an active attack on the DRM system is required in order to break its security. A moderate level of

DRM security is sufficient in this case. From a technical perspective, enterprise DRM is very much a solvable problem.

In e-commerce, the strength of the DRM system is the predominate concern. But in the enterprise setting, other more mundane issues are far more important [215]. For example, policy management is an important concern. That is, it must be easy for an administrator to set policies for individual users, groups, etc. Authentication issues are also significant, since the DRM system must interface with an existing corporate authentication system, and the system must prevent authentication spoofing. From a technical perspective, these are not major obstacles.

DRM for e-commerce and enterprise DRM face similar technical hurdles. But because the human dimension is so different, one is virtually unsolvable (at least for software-based systems), while the other is relatively easy to solve.

12.4.6   DRM Failures

There are far too many examples of failed e-commerce DRM systems to list them all here, but we'll mention a few. One infamous system could be defeated by a felt-tip pen [72], while another was defeated by holding down the "shift" key while downloading the content [6].

The Secure Digital Music Initiative, or SDMI, is an interesting case. Prior to implementing SDMI on real systems, the SDMI Consortium posted a series of challenge problems online, presumably to show how secure their system would be in practice. A group of researchers was able to completely break the security of the SDMI, and, for their hard work, they were rewarded with the threat of multiple lawsuits. Eventually the attackers' results were published, and they make fascinating reading—particularly with respect to the limitations of watermarking schemes [51].

Major technology corporations have put forth DRM systems that were easily broken. For example, Adobe eBooks security was easily defeated [18, 98], and, as in the case of SDMI, the attacker's reward consisted of legal threats that were ultimately unenforceable [237].

Another poor DRM system was Microsoft's MS-DRM (version 2). Microsoft violated Kerckhoffs Principle, which resulted in a fatally flawed block cipher algorithm. The attacker in this case was the anonymous "Beale Screamer" [23], who avoided legal reprisals, presumably due to his anonymity.

12.4.7   DRM Conclusions

DRM clearly illustrates the limitations of doing security in software, particularly when that software must function in a hostile environment. Such software is extremely vulnerable to attack, and the protection options are extremely limited. In other words, the attacker has nearly all of the advantages.

Tamper-resistant hardware and a "trusted" operating system can make a significant difference. We'll discuss these topics more in the next chapter.

In the next section, we shift gears to discuss security issues related to software development. Much of our discussion will be focused through the lens of the open source versus closed source software debate.

12.5 SOFTWARE DEVELOPMENT

The standard approach to software development is to develop a product as quickly as possible and release it without adequate testing. The code is then "patched" as flaws in the code are discovered by users. In security, this is known as *penetrate and patch*. Although penetrate and patch may be a bad way to develop software in general, it's a horrible way to develop secure software. Note that "patch" has a different meaning here than in the SRE context. Here, it is used to mean "fix the bug," whereas in SRE it refers to a change made directly to the executable code to add, remove, or modify certain features of the software.

Since it's a security liability, why is penetrate and patch the standard software development paradigm? There is more to it than simply a moral or ethical failing by software developers. In software, whoever is first to market is likely to become the market leader, even if their product ultimately is inferior to the competition. And in the computing world, the market leader tends to dominate the market more so than in most fields. This first to market advantage can't be ignored because it creates an overwhelming incentive to sell software before it's been thoroughly tested.

There also seems to be an implicit assumption that if you patch bad software long enough it will eventually become good software. This is sometimes referred to as the *penetrate and patch fallacy* [241]. Why is this a fallacy? For one thing, there is huge body of empirical evidence to the contrary. Regardless of the number of "service packs" applied, software continues to exhibit serious flaws. In fact, patches often add new flaws. And software is a moving target due to new versions, new features, a changing environment, new uses, new attacks, and so on.

Another contributing factor toward the current sorry state of software security is that users generally find it easier and safer to "follow the leader." For example, a system administrator probably won't get fired if his system has a serious flaw, provided everybody else has the same flaw. On the other hand, that same administrator probably won't receive a comparable amount of credit if his system works normally while other systems are having problems.

Yet another major impetus for doing things like everybody else is that administrators and users have more people they can ask for support. Together, these perverse economic incentives are sometimes collectively referred to as *network economics* [14].

Secure software development is difficult and costly. Development must be done carefully, with security in mind from the beginning. And, as we'll make precise below, a extraordinarily large amount of testing is required to achieve reasonably low bug (and security-flaw) rates. It's certainly cheaper and easier to let customers do the testing, particularly when there is no serious economic disincentive to do so, and, due to network economics, there is actually an incentive to rush to market.

Why is there no economic disincentive for flawed software? Even if a software flaw causes major losses to a corporation, the software vendor has no legal liability. Is any other product sold this way? It's often suggested that holding software vendors legally liable for the adverse effects of their products would be a market-friendly way to improve the quality of software. But software vendors have so far successfully argued that such liability would stifle innovation. And it's far from certain that such an approach would have a serious impact on the virtual monopoly that exists in many areas of software, which is often blamed for the lack of software quality.

12.5.1   Open Versus Closed Source Software

We'll look at some of the security problems inherent in software through the prism of the open source versus closed source debate. Some of the conclusions will probably surprise you.

With open source software, the source code is available to users. For example, the Linux operating system is open source. With closed source software, on the other hand, the source code is not available to users. Windows is an example of closed source software. In this section, we want to examine the relative security strengths and weaknesses of open source and closed source software.

The primary claimed security advantages of open source software can be summarized as "more eyeballs"; that is, the more people who look at the code, the fewer flaws that will remain undiscovered. This is really just a variant on Kerckhoffs Principle, and who could possibly argue with such a fundamental tenet of security?

However, upon closer inspection, the benefit of more eyeballs becomes more questionable, at least in this case. First, how many of these "eyeballs" are looking for security flaws? And how many eyeballs are focused on the boring parts of the code, which often harbor security flaws? Also, how many of these eyeballs belong to security experts, who would have a realistic chance of discovering subtle security flaws?

Another issue with open source is that attackers can also look for flaws in the source code. Conceivably, an ingenious evil coder might even be able to insert a security flaw into an open source project.

An interesting case study is wu-ftp. This open source software is of modest size, at about 8,000 lines of code, and it implements a security-critical application (file transfer). Yet this software was widely deployed and in use for 10 years before serious security flaws were discovered [241]. More generally, the open source movement appears to have done little to reduce security flaws. Perhaps the fundamental problem is that open source software also follows the penetrate and patch model of development.

If open source software has its security issues, certainly closed source software is worse. Or is it? The security flaws in closed source are not as visible to attackers, which could be viewed as providing a form of security by obscurity. But does this provide any real security? Given the record of attacks on closed source software, it is clear that many exploits do not require source code—our simple SRE example in Section 12.2 illustrates why this is the case. Although it is possible to analyze closed source code, it's a lot more work than for open source software.

Advocates of open source often cite the *Microsoft fallacy* as a reason why open source software is inherently superior to closed source [241]. This fallacy can be stated as

- Microsoft makes bad software
- Microsoft software is closed source
- Therefore all closed source software is bad

Why is this a fallacy? For one thing, it's not logically correct. Perhaps more relevant than Microsoft software being closed source is the fact that Microsoft follows the penetrate and patch model.

Next, we'll look at the differences between open and closed source at a slightly more theoretical level. But before we get to that, it's reasonable to wonder why—if there is no security difference between open and closed source software—is Microsoft software successfully attacked so often?

Microsoft is a big target for any attacker. An attacker who wants the most "bang for the buck" is naturally attracted to Microsoft. While there are few exploits against, say, Mac OS X, this certainly has more to do with the fact that it receives less attention from hackers (and, not coincidentally, the hacker tools are less developed) than any inherent security advantage to OS X. An attack on OS X would do far less damage overall and therefore bring less "glory" to the attacker.

Now let's consider the security implications of open and closed source software from a slightly more theoretical angle. It can be shown that the probability of a security failure after t units of testing is about K/t, where K is a constant, and this approximation holds over a large range of values for t [12]. Then the *mean time between failure*, or MTBF, is

$$MTBF = t/K. \qquad (12.1)$$

The good news here is that security improves with testing. The bad news is that security only improves linearly with testing. But is it true that software only improves linearly with testing? Empirical results have repeatedly shown that security improves linearly with testing, and it is the conventional wisdom that this is the case for any large and complex software system [14].

The implications of *equation 12.1* are profound. One implication is that to achieve a level of, say, 1,000,000 hours between security failures, software must be tested for (on the order of) 1,000,000 hours.

What does *equation 12.1* imply about the security of open source versus closed source software? Suppose an open source project has

$$MTBF = t/K. \qquad (12.2)$$

Now suppose this same project is instead closed source and that flaws are twice as hard to find in the closed source case. It seems that we then have

$$MTBF = 2t/K \qquad (12.3)$$

for the closed source case. If so, closed source software is more secure than open source. However, *equation 12.3* is not correct, since the closed source testing is only half as effective as in the open source case, so the values of t in *equations 12.2* and *12.3* are not comparable. That is, to put the closed source case on par with the open source case, we have MTBF $= 2(t/2)/K = t/K$. This shows that, in theory, the effectiveness of testing is the same for open and closed source software. This argument is due to Anderson [12].

Closed source advocates might argue that closed source software has "open source" alpha testing, where flaws are found at the higher open source rate, followed by closed source beta testing and use, which gives the attackers the lower closed source rate. But, in the larger scheme of things, alpha testing is a minor part of the total testing, particularly with the pressures to rush to market. Although this argument could, in principle, give an edge to closed source, in practice it's probably not a significant advantage. It seems that the inescapable—and surprising—conclusion is that open and closed source software are virtually indistinguishable from a security perspective.

12.5.2 Finding Flaws

A fundamental security problem with testing is that the good guys must find almost all security flaws, whereas Trudy only needs to find one flaw that the good guys haven't found. This implies that software reliability is far more challenging in security than elsewhere in software engineering.

An example from [14] nicely illustrates this asymmetry between attacker and defender. Recall that MTBF $= t/K$. Now suppose there are 10^6 security flaws in a large and complex piece of software and assume that each flaw has an MTBF $= 10^9$ hours. Then we would expect to find one flaw for every $10^9/10^6 = 10^3$ hours of testing.

Suppose that the good guys hire 10,000 testers who spend a total of 10^7 hours testing, and they find, as expected, 10^4 flaws. Trudy, by herself, spends 10^3 hours testing and finds one flaw. Since the good guys found only 1% of the flaws, the chance that these 10,000 good guys found Trudy's bug is only 1%. As we've seen in other areas of security, the mathematics overwhelmingly favors the bad guys.

12.5.3 Other Software Development Issues

Good software development practices include the following steps [179]: specify, design, implement, test, review, document, manage, and maintain. Most of these topics are beyond the scope of this book. In this section, we'll mention a few software development issues that have a significant impact on security.

We've already discussed some aspects of testing in the previous section. From this discussion, it should be clear that if we ever hope to engineer secure software, we cannot adopt the penetrate and patch model. Although penetrate and patch will always exist to some extent—since flaws that are discovered must be patched—if more care is taken in development then perhaps fewer and less severe flaws will need to be patched.

Secure software development is not easy, as our discussion of testing indicates. And testing is only part of the development process. To improve security, much more time and effort are required throughout the entire development process. Unfortunately, there is little or no economic incentive for this today.

Next, we'll briefly discuss the following security-critical software development topics:

- Design
- Hazard analysis
- Peer review
- Testing
- Configuration management
- Postmortem for mistakes

We've already discussed testing, but we'll have more to say about certain other testing-related issues below.

The design phase is critical for security since a careful initial design can avoid high-level errors that are difficult—if not impossible—to correct later. Perhaps the most important point is to design security features in from the start, since retrofitting security is difficult, if not impossible. Internet protocols offer an excellent illustration of this point. IPv4, for example, has no built-in security, while the new and improved version, IPv6, makes IPSec mandatory. However, the transition to IPv6 is proving slow (at best), and, consequently, the Internet remains much less secure than it could be.

Usually an informal approach is used at the design phase, but so-called *formal methods* can sometimes be used [32]. Using formal methods, it's possible to rigorously prove that a design is correct. Unfortunately, formal methods are generally too complex to be useful in most real-world situations.

In order to build reasonably secure software, the likely threats must be known in advance. This is where the field of *hazard analysis* comes into play. There are several informal ways to approach this problem, such as developing a hazard list containing potential security problems, or simply making a list of "what ifs." A slightly more systematic approach is Schneier's *attack tree* concept, where possible attacks are organized into a tree-like structure [199]. A nice feature of this approach is that you can prune entire branches of attacks if you can prevent the attacks closer to the root of the tree.

There are several other approaches to hazard analysis, including hazard and operability studies, or HAZOP, failure modes and effective analysis, or FMEA, and fault tree analysis, or FTA [179]. We'll not discuss these in this book.

Peer review is also a useful tool for improving security. There are three levels of peer review, which, from most informal to most formal, are sometimes called *review*, *walk-through*, and *inspection*. Each level of review is useful, and there is considerable evidence that peer review is effective [179].

Next, we'll discuss testing, but from a different perspective than in the previous section. Testing occurs at different levels of the development process, and we can categorize testing as

- *Module testing*, where small sections of the code are tested individually.
- *Component testing*, where a few modules are combined and tested together.

- *Unit testing*, where several components are combined for testing.
- *Integration testing*, where everything is put everything together and tested as a whole.

At each of these levels, security flaws can be uncovered. For example, features that interact in a new or unexpected way may evade detection at the component level but be exposed during integration testing.

Another way to view testing is based on its purpose. We can define the categories

- *Function testing*, where it's verified that the system functions as required.
- *Performance testing*, where requirements such as speed and resource use are verified.
- *Acceptance testing*, where the customer is involved.
- *Installation testing*, which, not surprisingly, is testing done at install time.
- *Regression testing*, which is testing that is done after any significant change to the system.

Again, security vulnerabilities can appear during any of these types of testing.

Another testing-related technique that should be used is *active fault detection*, where, instead of simply waiting for a system to fail, the tester actively tries to make it fail. This is the approach that an attacker will follow, and this might uncover security flaws that a more passive approach would miss.

Another useful concept is *fault injection*, where faults are inserted into the process, even if there is no obvious way for such a fault to occur. This can reveal weaknesses that would otherwise go unnoticed if the testing is restricted to expected inputs.

Bug injection is an interesting concept that can, in principle, be used to estimate the number of bugs remaining in code. Suppose we insert 100 bugs into some code, and our testers are able to find 30 of these. Then if 300 bugs were found during testing it might be reasonable to assume that roughly 700 bugs remain undiscovered. This assumes that the injected bugs are similar to the remaining bugs, which is probably not an entirely valid assumption. But bug injection may be a useful approach in order to obtain a ballpark estimate of the number of bugs and, indirectly, the number of security flaws.

A testing case history is given in [179]. In this example, the system had 184,000 lines of code. Of the flaws found,

- 17.3% were found when inspecting the system design
- 19.1% were found inspecting component design
- 15.1% were found during code inspection
- 29.4% were found during integration testing
- 16.6% were found during system and regression testing

The conclusion is that many kinds of testing must be conducted and that overlapping testing is useful because it provides a sort of defense in depth.

As we observed earlier in this chapter, security testing is far more demanding than non-security testing. In non-security testing, we need to verify that the system does what it's supposed to, while in security testing we must verify that the system does what it is supposed to and nothing more.

In any realistic scenario, it's almost certainly impossible to do exhaustive testing. And in the previous section, we noted that the MTBF formula indicates that an extraordinarily large amount of testing is required to achieve a high MTBF. But there may be a loophole. That is, if we can eliminate an entire class of flaws, then the statistical model that the MTBF is based on will break down [14]. For example, if we have a test (or a few tests) to find all buffer overflows, then we can eliminate this entire class of flaws with a relatively small amount of work. Unfortunately, it does not seem that we are close to achieving such results today.

Configuration management, that is, how we deal with changes to a system, is also a security-critical issue. Several types of changes can occur, which can be categorized as *minor changes* that are needed in order to maintain daily functioning, *adaptive changes* or modifications, *perfective changes* or improvements, and *preventive changes*, which are intended to prevent any loss of performance [179]. Any such change to a system can introduce new security flaws or can expose existing flaws.

After identifying and fixing any security flaw, it is important to carefully analyze the flaw. This sort of *postmortem analysis* is the best way to learn from the problem and thereby increase the odds that a similar problem will be avoided in the future. In security, we always learn more when things go wrong than when they go right. If we fail to analyze those cases where things go wrong then we've missed a significant opportunity. Postmortem analysis may be the most underutilized method in all of security engineering.

The bottom line on secure software development is that network economics and penetrate and patch are the enemies of secure software. Unfortunately, there is little economic incentive for secure software; until that changes, we probably can't expect significant changes in the status quo. But in those cases where security is a priority, it is possible to develop reasonably secure software. Proper development can minimize security flaws, but secure development is a costly and time-consuming proposition. For all of these reasons, we can't expect dramatic improvements in software security anytime soon.

Even with the best software development practices, security flaws will still exist. Since absolute security is almost never possible, it's not surprising that absolute security in software is impossible. But there is no excuse for the miserable state of software security today. The goal of secure software development—as in most areas of security—must be to minimize and manage the risks.

12.6 SUMMARY

In this chapter, we provided some indication as to why security in software is so difficult to achieve. We focused on three topics, namely, SRE, DRM, and software development.

Software reverse engineering, or SRE, illustrates what a skilled attacker can do to software. Even with a very limited use of the hacking tools, we were able to easily defeat the security of a program.

We then discussed DRM, which shows the challenges of attempting to enforce security through software that executes in a hostile environment. After the SRE section, this should not have come as a surprise.

Finally, we discussed the difficulties involved in secure software development. Although we looked at the problem from the perspective of open source versus closed source software, from any perspective secure software development is extremely challenging. Some elementary mathematics confirms the level of difficulty. Nevertheless, it's possible to develop reasonably secure software, even though such software is the exception rather than the rule today.

12.7 PROBLEMS

1. Can the anti-debugging technique illustrated in Figure 12.9 be implemented so that it also provides anti-disassembly protection?

2. Why are "guards" incompatible with encrypted object code?

3. Suppose that a system has 1,000,000 bugs, each with MTBF of 10,000,000 hours. The good guys work for 10,000 hours and find 1,000 bugs.

   a. If Trudy works for 10 hours and finds 1 bug, what is the probability that Trudy's bug was not found by the good guys?

   b. If Trudy works for 30 hours and finds 3 bugs, what is the probability that at least one of her bugs was not found by the good guys?

4. Suppose that a large and complex piece of software has 10,000 bugs, each with an MTBF of 1,000,000 hours. Then you expect to find a particular bug after 1,000,000 hours of testing, and—since there are 10,000 bugs—you expect to find one bug for every 100 hours of testing. Suppose the good guys do 200,000 hours of testing while the bad guy, Trudy, does 400 hours of testing.

   a. How many bugs should Trudy find? How many bugs should the good guys find?

   b. What is the probability that Trudy finds at least one bug that the good guys did not?

5. Patch the Windows executable found in the file SRE.zip on the textbook website so that any serial number results in the message "Serial number is correct!!!". Turn in a screen capture showing your results. Can you determine the correct serial number?

6. Consider a DRM system implemented in software on a PC. Why is encryption necessary but not sufficient to provide "persistent protection?"

7. What is the primary advantage to implementing DRM on a closed system? What is the primary advantage to implementing DRM on an open platform?

8. Suppose that a particular open source project has MTBF $= t/K$. Without access to the source code, it's believed that bugs in the software would be three times as hard to find as in the open source case. If this is true, what would the MTBF be if this project were closed source?

9. Suppose that MTBF $= t^2/K$ instead of t/K. Then is there an advantage to closed source software over open source, or vice versa, assuming bugs are twice as hard to find in the closed source case?

10. Suppose that there are 100 security flaws in a particular piece of software, and security flaw i requires i hours of testing to find. What is the MTBF?

11. As a deterrent to Microsoft's new Death Star [162], the planet Earth plans to build its own Death Star. Should the plans for Earth's Death Star be made public or should they be kept secret? Give several reasons to support your point of view.

12. Suppose it's impossible to patch some particular software that implements DRM protection. Is the DRM system then secure?

13. Suppose debugging is impossible. Is SRE still possible?

14. Suppose disassembly is impossible. Is SRE still possible?

15. Devise a method for caching authentication information where the information is stored in a different form each time it's cached.

16. Devise a method for storing a key K in data and in software. That is, both the code and the data are required in order to reconstruct K.

17. In [204], it's shown that keys are easy to find when hidden in data, since keys are random and most data is not random. With this in mind, devise a method for hiding a key in data.

18. Describe in detail one anti-disassembly method not discussed in the text.

19. Describe in detail one anti-debugging method not discussed in the text.

20. What is BOBE resistance? In the text, it is argued that metamorphism can increase BOBE resistance. Discuss one other method that can be used to increase BOBE resistance.

21. In the text, it is argued that metamorphism can increase the resistance of software to a buffer overflow attack. Discuss one other type of attack that metamorphism might help to prevent.

22. Suppose that you insert 100 typos into a textbook manuscript. Your editor finds 25 of these typos and, in the process, she also finds 800 other typos. After you remove all of the 100 inserted typos, estimate the number of typos remaining in the manuscript. What does this have to do with software security?

13

OPERATING SYSTEMS AND SECURITY

UNIX is basically a simple operating system,
but you have to be a genius to understand the simplicity.
—Dennis Ritchie

The purpose of OS X's giant icons, the purpose of its whole new flashy look,
is to keep the customer happy during that critical period
between the time of sale and the time the check clears.
—Bruce Tognazzini

13.1 INTRODUCTION

In this chapter, we'll look at security issues related to operating systems (OSs). OSs are large and complex pieces of software and in Chapter 11 we saw that there are certain to be many security flaws in any such program. But here we are concerned with the security protection provided by the OS, not with the threat of bad OS software. That is, we are concerned with the OS as the security enforcer. This is a large topic and we'll only highlight some of the important issues.

First, we'll describe the primary security-related functions of any modern operating system. Then we'll discuss the notion of a trusted OS, and we'll conclude with a look at Microsoft's recent effort to develop a trusted operating system, which goes by the catchy name of NGSCB.

13.2 OPERATING SYSTEM SECURITY FUNCTIONS

Ideally, the OS must be able to deal effectively with security-critical issues whether they occur accidentally or as part of a malicious attack. Modern OSs are designed for multi-user environments and multi-tasking operations, and, as a result, a modern OS must, at a minimum, deal with *separation*, *memory protection*, and *access control*. We briefly discuss each of these three topics below.

13.2.1 Separation

Arguably the most fundamental security issue for a modern OS is that of separation. The OS must keep users separate from each other as well as separating individual processes.

There are several ways that separation can be enforced [179], including

- *Physical separation*, where users are restricted to separate devices. This provides a strong form of separation, but it is often impractical.
- *Temporal separation*, where processes execute one at a time. This eliminates many problems that arise due to concurrency and simplifies the job of the OS. Generally speaking, simplicity is the friend of security.
- *Logical separation* can be implemented via sandboxing, where each process has its own sandbox. A process is free to do almost anything within its sandbox, but it's highly restricted as to what it can do outside of its sandbox.
- *Cryptographic separation* can be used to make information unintelligible to an outsider.

Of course, various combinations of these separation methods can be used as well.

13.2.2 Memory Protection

The second fundamental issue an OS must deal with is memory protection. This includes protection for the memory that the OS itself uses as well as the memory of user processes. A *fence address* can be used for memory protection. A fence is a particular address that users and their processes cannot cross—only the OS can operate on one side of the fence, and users are restricted to the other side.

A fence could be static in which case there is a fixed fence address. A major drawback to this approach (or benefit, depending on your perspective) is that it places a strict limit on the size of the OS. An alternative is a dynamic fence which can be implemented using a fence register to specify the current fence address.

In addition to the fence, base and bounds registers can be used. These registers contain the lower and upper address limits of a particular user (or process) space. The base and bounds register approach implicitly assumes that the user (or process) space is contiguous in memory.

How does the OS determine what protection to apply to a specific memory location? In some cases it might be sufficient to apply the same protection to all of a user's (or process's) memory. At the other extreme, *tagging* requires that the protection of each individual address be specified. While this is extremely fine-grained, it also introduces significant overhead. The overhead can be reduced by tagging sections of the address space instead of individual addresses. In any case, another drawback to tagging is compatibility, since tagging schemes are not in common use.

The most common methods of memory protection are *segmentation* and *paging*. While these are not as flexible as tagging, they're much more efficient. We'll discuss each of these next.

Segmentation, as illustrated in Figure 13.1, divides the memory into logical units, such as individual procedures or the data in one array. Then different access control can be enforced on different segments. Another benefit of segmentation is that any segment can be placed in any memory location—provided the location is large enough to hold the segment. The OS must keep track of the locations of all segments, which is accomplished using a <segment,offset> pair, where the cleverly named segment specifies the segment, and the offset is the starting address of the specified segment.

Other benefits of segmentation include the fact that segments can be moved to different locations in memory and they can also be moved in and out of memory. With segmentation, all address references must go through the OS, so the OS can, in this respect, achieve complete mediation. Depending on the access control applied to particular segments, users can share access to segments and specific users can be restricted to specific segments.

One serious drawback to segmentation is that the segments are of variable sizes. As a result, when the OS references <segment,offset> it must also know the size of the segment in order to be sure that the requested address is within the segment. But some segments—such as those that include dynamic memory allocation—can grow during execution. Consequently, the OS must keep track of segment sizes that can vary. And due the variability of segment sizes, memory fragmentation is a potential problem. Finally, if memory is compacted in order to make better use of the available space, the

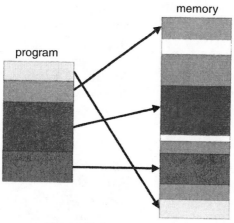

Figure 13.1. Segmentation.

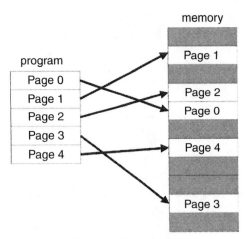

Figure 13.2. Paging.

segmentation tables change. In short, segmentation is complex and places a significant burden on the OS.

Paging is like segmentation, except that all segments are of a fixed size, as illustrated in Figure 13.2. With paging, access to a particular page uses a pair of the form `<page,offset>`. The advantages of paging over segmentation include no fragmentation, improved efficiency, and the fact that there are no variable segment sizes to worry about. The disadvantages are that there is no logical unity to pages, which makes it more difficult to determine the proper access control to apply to a given page.

13.2.3 Access Control

OSs are the ultimate enforcers of access control. This is one reason why the OS is such an attractive target for attack—a successful attack on the OS will effectively nullify any protection built in at a higher level. We discussed access control in Chapter 8 and we'll briefly return to the subject of access control in the next section when we discuss the requirements of a trusted OS.

13.3 TRUSTED OPERATING SYSTEM

> *There's none deceived but he that trusts.*
> —Benjamin Franklin

A system is *trusted* if we rely on it for security. If a trusted system fails to provide the expected security, then the security of the system fails.

There is a distinction between trust and security. Trust implies reliance, that is, trust is binary choice—either we trust or we don't. Security, on the other hand, is a judgment of the effectiveness of the security mechanisms. Security is judged relative to a specified policy or statement. However, security depends on trust, since a trusted component that fails to provide the expected security will break the security of the system. Ideally, we only trust secure systems, and, ideally, all trust relationships are explicit.

Since a trusted system is one that we rely on for security, an untrusted system must be one that we don't rely on for security. As a consequence, if all untrusted systems are compromised, the security of the system is unaffected. A curious implication of this simple observation is that only a trusted system can break security. This is an important result, and we'll have more to say about it in the next section.

The OS mediates interactions between subjects (users) and objects (resources). A trusted OS must securely enforce separation, memory protection, and access control. That is, the trusted OS must determine which objects to protect and how and which subjects are allowed to do what.

Any list of good security principles would likely include least privilege (such as the "low watermark" principle), simplicity, open design (Kerckhoffs Principle), complete mediation, white listing (in preference to black listing), separation, and ease of use. A trusted OS should securely provide all of these. However, most commercial OSs are feature-rich, which tends to lead to complexity and poor security.

13.3.1   MAC, DAC, and More

As illustrated in Figure 13.3, any OS must provide some degree of separation, memory protection, and access control. On the other hand, a trusted OS, as illustrated in Figure 13.4, must securely provide additional security, including mandatory access control, discretionary access control, object reuse protection, complete mediation, trusted path, and logs. We'll briefly discuss some of these topics below.

Mandatory access control, or MAC, is access that is not controlled by the owner of an object. For example, Alice does not decide who holds a TOP SECRET clearance, so she can't completely control the access to a document classified at this level. Discretionary access control, or DAC, is the type of access control where access is determined by the

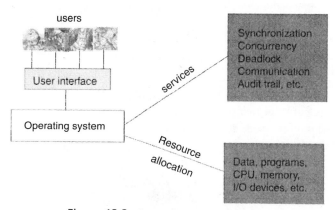

Figure 13.3. Operating system overview.

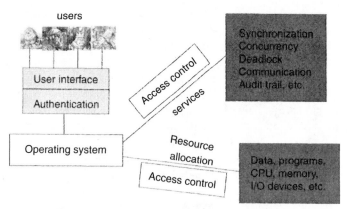

Figure 13.4. Trusted operating system overview.

owner of an object. For example, in UNIX file protection, the owner of a file controls read, write, and execute privileges.

If both DAC and MAC apply to an object, MAC wins. Suppose Alice owns a document marked TOP SECRET. Alice can set the DAC since she owns the document, but, regardless of these settings, Bob, who only has a SECRET clearance, can't access the document since he doesn't meet the MAC requirements.

A trusted OS must also prevent information from leaking from one user to another. Any OS will use some form of memory protection and access control to prevent such leaking of information. But we expect more from a trusted OS. For example, when the OS allocates space for a file, that same space may have previously been used by a different user's process. If the OS takes no additional precautions, the bits that remain from the previous process could be accessible and thereby leak information. A trusted OS should take steps to prevent this from occurring.

A related problem is *magnetic remanence*, where faint images of previously stored data can sometimes be read, even after the space has been overwritten by new data. To minimize the chance of this occurring, the DoD sets guidelines that require memory to be overwritten repeatedly with different bit patterns before it is considered safe to allow another process access to that space [4].

13.3.2 Trusted Path

When you enter your password at the login prompt, what happens to that password depends on the software that is running on your system. How can you be sure that software is not doing something evil, such as writing your password to a file that will later be e-mailed to Trudy? This is the *trusted path* problem, and as Ross Anderson [14] puts it,

> I don't know how to to be confident even of a digital signature I make on my own PC, and I've worked in security for over fifteen years. Checking all of the software in the critical path between the display and the signature software is way beyond my patience.

Ideally, a trusted OS should provide strong assurances of a trusted path.

The OS is also responsible for logging security-related events. This sort of information is necessary in order to detect attacks and for postmortem analysis. Logging is not as simple as it might seem. In particular, it is not always obvious precisely what to log. If we log too much, then we might overwhelm any human who must examine the data, and we could even overwhelm automated systems that must find the relevant needle in this haystack of data. For example, should we log incorrect passwords? If so, then "almost" passwords would appear in the log file, and log files would themselves then be security critical. If not, it may be harder to detect when a password-guessing attack is in progress.

13.3.3 Trusted Computing Base

The kernel, which is the lowest-level part of the OS, is responsible for synchronization, inter-process communication, message passing, interrupt handling, and so on. A *security kernel* is the part of the kernel that deals with security. That is, the security kernel is contained within the kernel.

Why have a security kernel? Since all accesses must go through the kernel, it is the ideal place for access control. It's probably also good practice to have security-critical functions in one location. By locating all such functions in one place, security functions are easier to test and modify.

One of the primary motivations for an attack on the OS is that the attacker can get below higher-level security functions and thereby bypass the security. By putting as many security functions as possible at the OSs lowest layer, it will be more difficult for an attacker to get below these functions.

The *reference monitor* is the part of the security kernel that deals with access control. The reference monitor mediates all access between subjects and objects, as illustrated in Figure 13.5. This crucial part of the security kernel should be tamper resistant, and, ideally, it should be analyzable, small and simple, since an error at this level would be devastating to the security of the entire system.

The *trusted computing base*, or TCB, is everything in the OS that we rely on to enforce security. Our definition of trust implies that, if everything outside TCB were subverted, the trusted OS would still be secure.

Security-critical operations will likely occur in many places within the OS. Ideally, we would design the security kernel first and then build the OS around it. Unfortunately, reality is usually just the opposite, as security tends to be an afterthought instead of a primary design goal. However, there are examples of trusted OSs that have been designed from scratch, with security as the primary objective. One such example is SCOMP, a trusted OS developed by Honeywell. SCOMP has less than 10,000 lines of code in its security kernel, and it strives for simplicity and analyzability [84]. Contrast this to

Figure 13.5. Reference monitor.

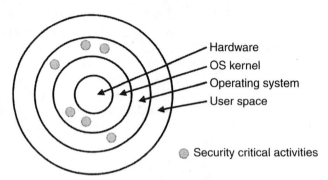

Figure 13.6. A poor TCB design.

Windows XP, which has more than 40,000,000 lines of code and numerous dubious features.

Ideally the TCB should gather all security functions into an identifiable layer. For example, the TCB illustrated in Figure 13.6 is a poor design, since security-critical features are spread throughout the OS. Any change in a security feature may have unintended consequences in other OS functionality, and the individual security operations are difficult to analyze, particularly with respect to their interactions with other security-critical components.

The TCB illustrated in Figure 13.7 is preferable, since all security functions are collected in a well-defined security kernel [179]. In this design, the security impact of any change in one security function can be analyzed by studying its effect on the security kernel. Also, an attacker who subverts OS operations at a higher level will not have defeated the TCB operations.

In summary, trust implies reliance and the TCB is everything in the OS that we rely on for security. If everything outside the TCB is subverted, we still have a trusted system, but if anything in the TCB is subverted, then the security of the system is, by definition, broken.

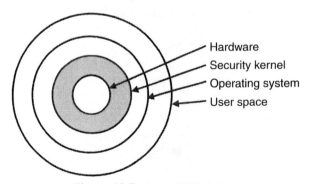

Figure 13.7. A good TCB design.

In the next section we'll examine NGSCB, which is an effort by Microsoft to develop a trusted OS for the PC platform. DRM was the original motivation for NGSCB, but it has wider security implications [76].

13.4 NEXT GENERATION SECURE COMPUTING BASE

Microsoft's Next Generation Secure Computing Base, or NGSCB (pronounced "n-scub"), was originally slated to be part of the "Longhorn" OS. But it appears that at least some of the features of NGSCB won't appear until a later release. In any case, NGSCB—in some form or another—is likely to appear relatively soon.

NGSCB is designed to work with special hardware to be developed by the Trusted Computing Group, or TCG, led by Intel [235]. NGSCB is the part of Windows that will interface with the TCG hardware. TCG was formerly known as the Trusted Computing Platform Alliance, or TCPA, and NGSCB was formerly known as Palladium. It's been theorized that the name changes are due to bad publicity surrounding the initial discussion of TCPA/Palladium [146].

The original motivation for TCPA/Palladium was digital rights management. Due to the extremely negative reaction this received in many quarters, TCG/NGSCB now downplays the DRM connection, though it clearly remains a major motivating factor. Today, TCG/NGSCB is promoted as a general security-enhancing technology, with DRM being just one of many potential applications. But, as we'll see below, not everyone is convinced that this is a good idea. Depending on who you ask, TCG/NGSCB is designed to provide trusted computing [167] or treacherous computing [13].

The underlying motivation for TCG/NGSCB is to provide some of the strengths of a closed system on the open PC platform [75, 163]. Closed systems, such as game consoles and smartcards, are very good at protecting secrets, primarily due to their tamper-resistant features. As a result, closed systems are good at forcing people to pay money for the use of copyrighted information, such as the software used to play games. The drawback to closed systems is their limited flexibility. In contrast, open systems such as PCs offer incredible flexibility, but, as we have seen, they do a poor job of protecting secrets. This is primarily because open systems have no real means to defend their own software. Ron Rivest has aptly described NGSCB as "a virtual set-top box inside your PC" [53].

TCG will provide tamper-resistant hardware that will be standard PC hardware. Conceptually, this can be viewed as a smartcard embedded within the PC hardware. This tamper-resistant hardware will provide a secure place to store cryptographic keys or other secrets. These secrets can thereby be secured, even from a user of the PC who has full administrator privileges. Prior to the TCG, nothing comparable to this existed for PCs.

The TCG tamper-resistant hardware is in addition to all of the usual PC hardware, not in place of it. To take advantage of this special hardware, the PC will need to have two OSs—its usual OS and a special trusted OS to deal with the TCG hardware. NGSCB is Microsoft's version of this trusted OS.

According to Microsoft, the design goals of NGSCB are twofold. First, it is to provide high assurance; that is, users can have a high degree of confidence that NGSCB will behave correctly, even when it's under attack. The second goal is to provide authenticated operation. In order to protect the secrets stored in the tamper-resistant hardware, it's critical that only trusted software can access this hardware. By carefully authenticating all software, NGSCB can provide this high degree of trust. Protection against hardware tampering is not a design goal of NGSCB, since that is the domain of the TCG.

Specific details concerning NGSCB are sketchy, and, based on the available information, Microsoft has not yet resolved all of the fine points. As a result, the following information is somewhat speculative. The details should become much clearer in the near future.

The high-level architecture of NGSCB is illustrated in Figure 13.8. The "left-hand side," or LHS, is where the usual, untrusted, Windows OS lives, while the "right-hand side," or RHS, is where the trusted OS resides. The *Nexus* is the trusted computing base, or TCB, of the NGSCB. *Nexus Computing Agents* or NCAs are the only software components that are allowed to talk to the (trusted) Nexus and (untrusted) LHS [50]. The NCAs are as critical to NGSCB as the Nexus.

13.4.1 NGSCB Feature Groups

NGSCB implements the following four major "feature groups":

- *Strong process isolation*, which prevents processes from interfering with each other.
- *Sealed storage*, which is the tamper-resistant hardware where secrets (that is, keys) can be stored securely.
- *Secure path*, which provides protected paths to and from the mouse, keyboard, and monitor.
- *Attestation*, which allows for "things" to be securely authenticated.

Attestation is an innovative feature that allows the TCB to be extended via NCAs. The other three feature groups are all aimed directly at protecting against malicious code. Next, we'll describe each of these feature groups in more detail.

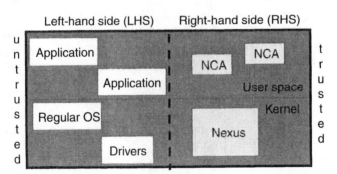

Figure 13.8. NGSCB overview.

13.4.1.1 *Process Isolation.* Process isolation is enforced by "curtained memory," which appears to be little more than a buzzword. In any case, the trusted OS (the Nexus) must be protected from the untrusted OS as well as from the BIOS, device drivers, and other low-level operations that could be used to attack it. Curtained memory is the name for the memory protection scheme that provides such protection.

Process isolation also applies to the NCAs. The NCAs must be isolated from any software that they don't trust. These trust relationships are determined by users—to an extent. That is, a user can disable a trusted NCAs (in essence, treating it as untrusted), but a user cannot make an untrusted NCA trusted. If the latter were possible, then the security of the trusted OS could be trivially broken.

13.4.1.2 *Sealed Storage.* Sealed storage contains a secret, which is most likely a key (or keys). If software X wants to access the secret, a hash of X is computed as an integrity check. The confidentiality of the secret is protected since it can only be accessed by trusted software while the integrity of the secret is assured since it resides in the sealed storage.

13.4.1.3 *Secure Path.* The details of the secure path feature are vague. It's claimed that, for input, the path from the keyboard to the Nexus and the path from the mouse to the Nexus are both "secure"—but exactly how this is implemented is not entirely clear. Apparently, digital signatures are used so that the Nexus can verify the integrity of the data [231]. For output, there is a similar secure path from the Nexus to the screen, although here the signature verification would seem to be more exposed to attack.

13.4.1.4 *Attestation.* The most innovative feature of NGSCB is attestation, which provides for the secure authentication of "things," such as devices, services, and, most importantly, software. This is separate from user authentication. Attestation is accomplished using public key cryptography, and it relies on a certified key pair, where the private key—which is not user accessible—lives in the sealed storage.

The TCB can be extended via attestation of NCAs. That is, a new NCA is trusted provided that it passes the attestation check. This is a major feature, as we'll see below.

One issue with attestation is that, since it uses public key cryptography, certificates must be exchanged. Since public keys reveal users' identities, anonymity is lost in this approach. To protect anonymity, NGSCB has support for a trusted third party, or TTP. The TTP verifies the signature and vouches for it to the recipient. Anonymity can be preserved in this way—although the TTP will know the signer's identity. It is also claimed that NGSCB provides support for zero knowledge proofs. As we discussed in Chapter 9, zero knowledge proofs allow us to verify that a user knows a secret without revealing any information about the secret. According to Microsoft, when using zero knowledge proofs in NGSCB, "anonymity is preserved unconditionally" [50].

13.4.2   NGSCB Compelling Applications

What good is TCG/NGSCB? There are several compelling applications, but, here, we'll mention only two. First, suppose that Alice types a document on her computer. She can then "move" the document to the RHS (the trusted space), read the document carefully, and then digitally sign the document before moving it back to the (untrusted) LHS. Alice can then be very confident of what she actually signed, which, as suggested by Ross Anderson's quote above, is almost impossible on a non-NGSCB computer today.

A second application where NGSCB is useful is DRM. One fundamental DRM problem that is solved by NGSCB is that of protecting a secret. We've seen that it's virtually impossible to protect a secret in software. By using tamper-resistant hardware (sealed storage) and other NGSCB features, protecting a secret is much more plausible.

The NGSCB secure path also prevents certain DRM attacks. For example, with DRM-protected digital documents, an attacker could try to "scrape data" from the screen. This should be much more difficult with the NGSCB secure path in place. NBSCB also allows for the positive identification of users. Although this can be done without NGSCB, there is a much higher degree of assurance with NGSCB, since the user's ID is (in the form of a private key) embedded in the secure storage.

13.4.3   Criticisms of NGSCB

> *Microsoft isn't evil, they just make really crappy operating systems.*
> —Linus Torvalds

According to Microsoft, everything in Windows will still work in the LHS of an NGSCB system. Microsoft also insists that the user is in charge, since the user determines

- Which Nexus (or Nexii) will run on the system
- Which NCAs are allowed to run on the system
- Which NCAs are allowed to identify the system

There is also no way for an external process to enable a Nexus or NCA—to allay the fear that Microsoft would be in charge of an NGSCB computer. In addition, Nexus source code is publicly available and the Nexus does not block, delete, or censor any data—although NCAs do. For example, if a particular NCA is part of a DRM system, then it must "censor" any data for which user Alice has not paid. But each NCA on Alice's system must be authorized by Alice, so she could choose not to authorize the particular NCA that deals with DRM. Of course, she won't have access to DRM-protected content if she chooses not to authorize the required NCA.

Microsoft goes to great lengths to argue that NGSCB is harmless. The most likely reason for this is that many people seem to be convinced that NGSCB is harmful. There are many NGSCB critics, but here we'll only consider two. The first is Ross Anderson, whose criticisms can be found at [13]. Anderson is one of the harshest TCG/NGSCB critics and perhaps the most influential. We'll then discuss the criticisms of Clark Thomborson, whose criticisms are less well known, but raise some interesting fundamental issues [231].

Anderson's primary concern is that when NGSCB is used, a digital object can be controlled by its creator, not by the user of the machine where it currently resides. For example, suppose Alice creates some digital content. With NGSCB, she can specify the NCA that must be used to access this content. Of course, Bob can refuse to accept the NCA, but in that case his access is denied. And if Bob allows the NCA, he may have restrictions placed on his actions. It's worth noting that such restrictions are exactly what is needed in certain applications such as multilevel security. But the argument is that such restrictions are inappropriate as part of a general-purpose tool, such as a PC. Anderson gives the following example. Suppose Microsoft Word encrypts all documents with key that is only made available to Microsoft products. Then it would be even more difficult to stop using Microsoft products than it is today.

Anderson also claims that files from a compromised machine could be blacklisted (for example, to prevent music piracy). As an extreme example of the effect this might have, Anderson gives an example similar to the following. Suppose that every student at San Jose State University (SJSU) uses a single pirated copy of Microsoft Word. If Microsoft stops this copy from working on all NGSCB machines, then SJSU students will simply avoid NGSCB. But if Microsoft instead makes all NGSCB machines refuse to open documents created with this copy of Word, then SJSU users can't share documents with any NGSCB user. This could be used to coerce SJSU students into using legitimate copies of Word.

Anderson makes some rather provocative statements in [13], including

The Soviet Union tried to register and control all typewriters. NGSCB attempts to register and control all computers.

and even more frightening

In 2010 President Clinton may have two red buttons on her desk—one that sends missiles to China and another that turns off all of the PCs in China....

It's not clear exactly how NGSCB would enable either of these scenarios, but these are the kinds of concerns that have been widely discussed.

Clark Thomborson has expressed some concerns that strike at the heart of the NGSCB concept [231]. In his view, NGSCB should be viewed as a security guard. By passive observation, a real-world security guard can learn a great deal about the workings of the facility he's guarding. The NGSCB "security guard" is similar, since it can passively observe a user's most sensitive information.

How can a user such as Alice be sure that NGSCB is not spying on her? Microsoft would probably argue that this can't happen since the Nexus software is public, the NCAs can be debugged (this is required for application development), and NGSCB is strictly an "opt in" technology. But there may be a loophole here. The release versions of NCAs can't be debugged and the debug and release versions will necessarily have different hash values. As a result, the release version of an NCA could conceivably do something that the debug version does not do—such as spy on Alice.

The bottom line with regard to TCG/NGCSB is that it's an attempt to embed a trusted OS within an open platform. Without something similar, there is a legitimate concern that the PC may lose popularity, particularly in entertainment-related areas, where copyright holders might insist on the security of closed-system solutions.

NGSCB critics worry that users will lose control over their PCs—or be spied on by their PC. But it could reasonably be argued that users must choose to opt in, and, if a user does not opt in, what has been lost?

More fundamentally, NGSCB is a trusted system, and, as we noted above, only a trusted system can break your security. When put in this light, the concerns surrounding NGSCB are understandable. The debate regarding TCG/NGSCB is bound to continue for some time to come.

13.5 SUMMARY

In this chapter, we considered operating system security and, more specifically, the role of a trusted OS. We then discussed Microsoft's NGSCB, which is an attempt to build a trusted OS for the PC platform. NGSCB has clear implications for DRM, a controversial topic that we presented in detail in Chapter 12. For this and other reasons, NGSCB has its critics. We discussed some of these criticisms, as well as considered possible counterarguments to the criticisms.

13.6 PROBLEMS

1. What is a trusted computing base, or TCB? What part or parts of NBSCB comprise its TCB? Why does TCG/NGSCB need to implement a TCB?

2. In this chapter, two compelling applications of NGSCB are presented. Discuss one other compelling application of a trusted OS such as NGSCB.

3. In NGSCB, what is attestation and what is its purpose? What are NCAs and what two purposes do they serve?

4. What does it mean to say that a system is "trusted"? Do you agree that "only a trusted system can break your security"? Why or why not?

5. Explain the difference between segmentation and paging. Give one significant security advantage of segmentation over paging. What is the primary advantage of paging over segmentation?

6. Explain how paging and segmentation can be combined.

7. In the text, we discussed two critics of NGSCB. Which of their criticisms do you find more compelling and why?

8. In Chapter 12, we showed that it's possible to reverse engineer software. It's also possible to reverse engineer most hardware. Since this is the case, why is DRM on an NGSCB system any more secure than on a non-NGSCB system?

9. Give two examples of closed systems. How well does each protect secrets?

10. Find an influential critic of NGSCB, other than the two critics mentioned in the text, and summarize his or her arguments against NGSCB.

11. Find a supporter of NGSCB (other than Microsoft of a TCG company) and summarize his or her arguments in favor of NGSCB.

12. Read the discussion of "treacherous computing" at [13] and summarize the author's main points.

13. Public key crypto is used in NGSCB for attestation. One problem with this approach is that anonymity is difficult to achieve. Recall that, in Kerberos, which is based on symmetric key cryptography, Alice's anonymity is protected (when Alice sends her TGT to the KDC, she doesn't need to identify herself). Since anonymity is a concern, why doesn't NGSCB use an approach similar to Kerberos?

14. Why is the NGSCB sealed storage integrity check implemented using hashing instead of public key signing?

15. Why is NGSCB attestation implemented using public key signatures instead of hashing?

16. In NGSCB, how do each of process isolation, sealed storage, secure path, and attestation help to protect against malicious software?

17. Give two reasons why NGSCB attestation is necessary.

18. Why would Trudy probably prefer to successfully subvert the OS rather than successfully attack one particular application?

19. What is black listing? What is white listing? As a general security principle, why is white listing preferable to black listing?

20. Explain Rivest's comment that TCG/NGSCB is like "a virtual set-top box inside your PC."

21. Suppose that students take in-class tests on their own laptop computers. When they finish answering the questions, they e-mail their results to the instructor using a wireless Internet connection. Assume that the network connection is open during the test.

    a. Discuss ways that students might attempt to cheat.

    b. Could NGSCB be used to make cheating more difficult?

APPENDIX

A-1 NETWORK SECURITY BASICS

There are three kinds of death in this world.
There's heart death, there's brain death, and there's being off the network.
—Guy Almes

A-1.1 Introduction

This appendix contains an abbreviated introduction to networking with the emphasis on security issues. Networking is a large and complex topic. Here, we'll cover the minimal amount of information that is required in this textbook, and we'll also add a few comments on network-specific security issues that are not directly addressed elsewhere in this book.

A network is composed of *hosts* and *routers*. The term hosts can include many kinds of devices, such as computers of all sorts, servers, and even wireless devices such as cell phones and PDAs. The purpose of the network is to transfer data between the hosts. We're primarily concerned with the Internet, the king of all networks.

A network has an *edge* and a *core*. The hosts live at the edge, while the core consists of an interconnected mesh of routers. The purpose of the core is to route data through the network from host to host. An example of a network appears in Figure A-1.

The Internet is a *packet switched* network, meaning that the data is sent in discrete chunks known as packets. In contrast, the traditional telephone system is a

Information Security: Principles and Practice, by Mark Stamp
Copyright © 2006 John Wiley & Sons, Inc.

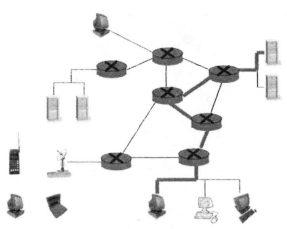

Figure A-1. A small network.

circuit switched network. For each telephone call, a dedicated circuit—with dedicated bandwidth—is established between the end points. Packet switched networks can make more efficient use of the available bandwidth, though there is some additional complexity involved, and things get particularly involved if "circuit-like" behavior is required.

The study of modern networking is largely the study of networking protocols. Networking protocols precisely specify communication rules employed by the network. For the Internet, the details are spelled out in RFCs, which are essentially Internet standards.

Protocols can be classified in many different ways, but one classification that is particularly relevant in security is *stateless* versus *stateful*. Stateless protocols don't "remember" anything, while stateful protocols do have some memory. Many security problems are related to state. For example, denial of service, or DoS, attacks often take advantage of stateful protocols, while stateless protocols can also have serious security issues, as we'll see below.

A-1.2   The Protocol Stack

It is standard practice to view networking protocols as residing within layers. When these layers are all stacked up, it is known as a *protocol stack*. It's important to realize that a protocol stack is more of a concept than an actual physical construct. Nevertheless, the idea of a protocol stack does simplify the study of networks (though newcomers to networking are excused for not believing it). The infamous OSI reference model includes seven layers, but we'll strip it down to the layers that matter so that we only need to consider the following five layers.

- The *application layer* is responsible for handling the application data that is sent from host to host. Examples of application layer protocols include HTTP, SMTP, FTP, and Gnutella.

- The *transport layer* deals with logical end-to-end transport of the data. The transport layer protocols of interest are TCP and UDP.
- The *network layer* routes the data through the network. IP is the network layer protocol that matters to us.
- The *link layer* handles the transferring of data over each individual link of the network. There are many link layer protocols, but we'll only mention two, ethernet and ARP.
- The *physical layer* sends the bits over the physical media. If you want to know about the physical layer, study electrical engineering.

Conceptually, a packet of data passes down the protocol stack at the source and then back up the protocol stack at the destination. Routers in the core of the network must process data up to the network layer in order to know where to route a packet. This is illustrated in Figure A-2.

Suppose that X is a packet of application data at the source. As X goes down protocol stack, each protocol adds a *header*, which includes the information required by that particular protocol. Let H_A be the header added at the application layer. Then the application layer passes (H_A, X) down the stack to the transport layer. If H_T is the transport layer header, then $(H_T, (H_A, X))$ is passed to the network layer where another header, say, H_N is added to give $(H_N, (H_T, (H_A, X)))$. Finally, the link layer adds a header, H_L, and the packet

$$(H_L, (H_N, (H_T, (H_A, X))))$$

is passed to the physical layer. In particular, note that the application layer header is the innermost header, which sometime seems backward to networking newbies. When the packet is processed up the protocol stack at the destination (or at a router), the headers are stripped off layer by layer—like peeling an onion—and the information in each header is used to determine the proper course of action by the corresponding protocol.

Next, we'll take a brief look at each of the layers. We'll follow [136] and go down the protocol stack from the application layer to the link layer.

A-1.3   Application Layer

Typical network applications include Web browsing, e-mail, file transfer, P2P, and so on. These are distributed applications that run on hosts. The hosts would prefer the network to be completely transparent.

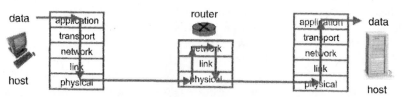

Figure A-2. Layering in action.

As mentioned above, application layer protocols include HTTP, SMTP, IMAP, FTP, Gnutella, and so on. These protocols only make up a small part of an application. For example, the e-mail application includes an e-mail client (such as Outlook or Eudora), a sending host, a receiving host, e-mail servers, and a few networking protocols such as SMTP and POP3.

Most applications are designed for the client-server paradigm, where the *client* is the host that requests a service and the *server* is the host that responds to the request. In other words, the client is the one who "speaks first" and the server is the one trying to fulfill the request. For example, if you request a Web page, you are the client and the Web server is the server, which only seems right. However, in some cases the distinction between client and server is not so obvious. For example, in a file-sharing application, your computer is a client when you request a file, and it is a server when someone downloads a file from you. Both of these events could even occur simultaneously, in which case you would be acting as both a client and a server.

Peer-to-peer, or P2P, file sharing applications offer something of an alternative to the traditional client-server model. In the P2P model, hosts act as both clients and servers, as mentioned in the previous paragraph. But the real challenge in P2P lies in locating a "server" with the content that a client desires. There are several interesting approaches to this problem. For example, some P2P systems distribute the database that maps available content to hosts among certain special peers, whereas others simply flood each request through the network. In this latter case, hosts with the desired content respond directly to the requester. KaZaA uses the distributed database approach, while Gnutella employs query flooding.

Next, we'll briefly discuss a few specific application layer protocols. First, let's consider HTTP, the HyperText Transfer Protocol, which is the application layer protocol used when you browse the Web. As mentioned above, the client requests a Web page and the server responds to the request. Since HTTP is a stateless protocol, *Web cookies* were developed as a tasty way to maintain state. When you initially contact a Web site, it can provide your browser with a cookie, which is simply an identifier that is used to index a database maintained by the Web server. When your browser subsequently sends HTTP messages to the Web server, your browser will pass the cookie to the server. The server can then consult its database and thereby remember information about you. Web cookies can keep state within a single session as well as between sessions.

Web cookies can also be used as a very weak form of authentication and enable such modern conveniences as shopping carts and recommendation lists. However, cookies do raise some privacy concerns, since a Web site with memory can learn a great deal about you. And if multiple sites pool their information, they might gain a fairly complete picture of your Web persona.

Another interesting application layer protocol is SMTP, the Simple Mail Transfer Protocol, which is used to transfer e-mail from the sender to the recipient's e-mail server. Then POP3, IMAP, or HTTP (for Web mail) is used to get the messages from the e-mail server to the recipient. An SMTP e-mail "server" can act as a server or a client (in our terminology) when e-mail is transferred.

As with many application protocols, SMTP commands are human readable. For example, the commands in Table A-1 are legitimate SMTP commands that were typed

TABLE A-1. Spoofed e-mail using SMTP.

```
C: telnet eniac.cs.sjsu.edu 25
S: 220 eniac.sjsu.edu
C: HELO ca.gov
S: 250 Hello ca.gov, pleased to meet you
C: MAIL FROM: <arnold@ca.gov>
S: 250 arnold@ca.gov... Sender ok
C: RCPT TO: <stamp@cs.sjsu.edu>
S: 250 stamp@cs.sjsu.edu ... Recipient ok
C: DATA
S: 354 Enter mail, end with "." on a line by itself
C: It is my pleasure to inform you that you
C: are terminated
C:   .
S: 250 Message accepted for delivery
C: QUIT
S: 221 eniac.sjsu.edu closing connection
```

as part of a telnet session. The user types in the lines beginning with C while the server responds with the lines marked as S. This particular session resulted in a spoofed e-mail being sent to the author, stamp@cs.sjsu.edu, from arnold@ca.gov.

Another application layer protocol with security implications is DNS, the Domain Name Service. The primary purpose of DNS is to convert a nice human readable name such as www.google.com into its equivalent 32-bit IP address (discussed below), which computers and routers prefer. DNS is implemented as a distributed heirarchical database. There are only 13 "root" DNS servers worldwide and a successful attack on these would cripple the Internet. This is perhaps as close to a single point of failure as exits in the Internet today. Attacks on root servers have succeeded; however, because of the distributed nature of the DNS, it would be necessary for such an attack to continue for several days before it would seriously affect the Internet. No attack on DNS has had such staying power—at least not yet.

A-1.4   Transport Layer

The network layer (discussed below) offers unreliable, "best effort" delivery of packets. This means that the network attempts to get packets to their destination, but if a packet fails to arrive (or its data is corrupted or a packet arrives out of order), the network takes no responsibility, much like the U.S. Postal Service. Any improved service beyond this limited best effort—such as the reliable delivery of packets—must be implemented somewhere above the network layer. Also, such additional service must be implemented on the hosts, since the core of the network only offers a best-effort delivery service. Reliable delivery of packets is the primary purpose of the transport layer.

Before we dive into the transport layer it's worth pondering why the network is unreliable. Since we are dealing with packet switched networks, it's very possible that hosts will put more packets into the network than it can handle. Routers include buffers to store extra packets until they can be forwarded, but these are finite—when a router's buffer is full, the router has no choice but to drop packets. The data in packets can also get corrupted in transit. And since routing is a dynamic process, it's possible that the packets in one particular connection can follow different paths. When this occurs, it's possible for packets to arrive at the destination in a different order than they were sent by the source. It is the job of the transport layer to deal with these types of problems.

There are two transport layer protocols of importance. The Transmission Control Protocol, or TCP, provides for reliable delivery. TCP will make sure that your packets arrive, that they are sequenced in the correct order, and that the data has not been corrupted. To greatly oversimplify things, the way that TCP provides these services is by including sequence numbers in packets and telling the sender to retransmit packets when problems are detected. Note that TCP runs on hosts, and all communication is over the unreliable network. The format of the TCP header appears in Figure A-3.

TCP assures that packets arrive at their destination and that the packets are processed in order. TCP also makes sure that packets are not sent too fast for the receiver (this is known as flow control), and TCP provides network-wide congestion control. This congestion control feature is complex, but one interesting aspect is that it attempts to give every host a fair share. That is, if congestion is detected, every TCP connection will get (over the long run) about the same amount of the available bandwidth. Of course, a host can try to cheat by opening more TCP connections.

TCP is "connection-oriented," which means that TCP will contact the server before sending data in order to be sure that the server is alive and that it is listening on the appropriate port. It's important to realize that these connections are only logical, and no true dedicated connection takes place.

The TCP connection establishment is of particular importance. A so-called *three-way handshake* is used, where the three messages are

- SYN: the client requests synchronization with the server.
- SYN-ACK: the server acknowledges receipt of the SYN request.

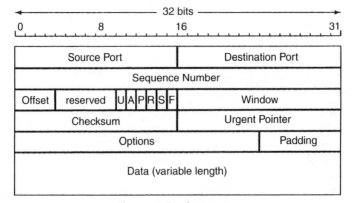

Figure A-3. TCP header.

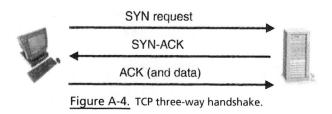

<u>Figure A-4.</u> TCP three-way handshake.

- ACK: the client acknowledges the SYN-ACK. This third message can also include data. For example, if the client is Web browsing, the client would include the request for a specific web page along with the ACK message.

The three-way handshake is illustrated in Figure A-4. TCP also provides for orderly tearing down of "connections." Connections are terminated by FIN (finish) or RST (reset) packet.

The TCP three-way handshake makes denial of service, or DoS, attacks possible. Whenever a SYN packet is received, the server must remember the "half-open" connection. This remembering consumes a small amount of server resources. As a result, too many half-open connections will cause server resources to be exhausted, at which point the server can no longer respond to any new connections.

The transport layer includes another protocol of note, the User Datagram Protocol, or UDP. Whereas TCP provides everything and the kitchen sink, UDP is a truly minimal "no frills" service. The benefit of this is that it requires minimal overhead, but the down side to UDP is that it provides no assurance that packets arrive, no assurance packets are in the proper order, and so on. In other words, UDP adds little to the unreliable network over which it operates.

Why does UDP exist? UDP is more efficient since it has a smaller header, and by not providing flow control or congestion control, it consumes less bandwdth. But the main benefit to UDP is that there are no restrictions to slow down the sender. However, if packets are sent too fast, they will be dropped—either at an intermediate router or at the destination. In some applications, delay is not tolerable, but it is acceptable to lose some fraction of the packets. Streaming audio and video fit this description, and for these applications UDP is preferable to TCP. Finally, it's worth noting that reliable data transfer is possible using UDP, but the reliability must be built in by the developer at the application layer.

A-1.5   Network Layer

The network layer is the crucial layer for the core of network. Recall that the core is an interconnected mesh of routers, and the purpose of the network layer is to provide the information needed to route packets through this mesh. The network layer protocol of interest here is the Internet Protocol, or IP. As we indicated above, IP follows a "best effort" approach. Note that IP must run in every host and router in the network. The format of the IP header appears in Figure A-5.

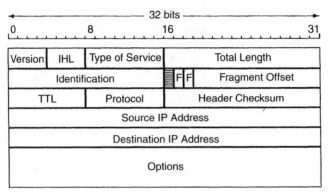

Figure A-5. IP header.

In addition to network layer protocols, routers also run routing protocols, which are used to determine the best path to use when sending packets. There are many routing protocols, but the most popular are RIP, OSPF, and BGP.

In order to route packets, every host on the Internet has a 32-bit IP address. Unfortunately, there are not enough IP addresses available, and as a result many tricks are employed to effectively extend the IP address space. IP addresses are listed in so-called dotted decimal notation of the form $W.X.Y.Z$, where each value is between 0 and 255. For example, 195.72.180.27 is a valid IP address. Note that a host's IP address can change.

Although each host has a 32-bit IP address, there can be many processes running on a single host. For example, you could browse the Web, send e-mail, and do a file transfer all at the same time. In order to effectively communicate across the network, it's necessary to distinguish these processes. The way this is accomplished is by assigning each process a 16-bit port number. The port numbers below 1024 are said to be "well-known," and they are reserved for specific applications. For example, port 80 is used for HTTP and port 110 for POP3. The port numbers from 1024 to 65535 are dynamic and assigned as needed. An IP address together with a port number defines a socket, and a socket uniquely identifies a process.

The IP header is used by routers to determine the proper route for a packet through the network. The header includes fields for the source and destination IP addresses. There is also a time to live, or TTL, field that limits the number of "hops" that a packet can travel before it is terminated. This prevents wayward packets from bouncing around the Internet for all of eternity. There are also fields that deal with our next topic, fragmentation.

Each link on the Internet limits the maximum size of packets. If a packet is too big, it is the router's job to split it into smaller packets. This process in known as *fragmentation*. To prevent multiple fragmentation and reassembly steps, the fragments are only reassembled at the their destination.

Fragmentation creates many security issues. The fundamental problem is that the actual purpose of a packet is easily disguised by breaking it into fragments. The fragments can even overlap when reassembled, which further exacerbates this problem.

The result is that the receiving host can only determine the purpose of a packet after it has received all of the fragments and reassembled the pieces. A firewall has a great deal more work to do when dealing with fragmented packets. The bottom line is that fragmentation opens the door to DoS and many other types of attacks.

The current version of IP is version 4, or IPv4. It has many shortcomings, including too small 32-bit addresses and poor security (fragmentation being just one example). As a result, a new and improved version, IP version 6, or IPv6, has been developed. IPv6 includes 128-bit addresses and strong security in the form of IPSec. Unfortunately, IPv6 is a classic example of how not to develop a replacement protocol, and it has yet to take hold on a large scale [24].

A-1.6 Link Layer

The link layer is responsible for getting the packet over each individual link in the network. That is, the link layer deals with getting a packet from a host to a router, from a router to a router, from a router to a host, or, locally, from one host to another host. As a packet traverses the network, different links can be completely different. For example, a single packet might travel over ethernet, a wired point-to-point line, and a wireless microwave link when traveling from its source to its destination.

The link layer and physical layer are implemented in a "semi-autonomous" adapter known as Network Interface Card, or NIC. Examples include ethernet cards and wireless 802.11 cards. The NIC is (mostly) out of the host's control, and that's why it's said to be semi-autonomous.

One link layer protocol of particular importance is ethernet. Ethernet is a multiple access protocol, meaning that it's used when many hosts are competing for a shared resource. Ethernet is used on a local area network, or LAN. In Ethernet, if two packets are transmitted by different hosts at the same time, they can collide, in which case both packets are corrupted. The packets must then be resent. The challenge is to efficiently handle collisions in a distributed environment. There are many possible approaches, but ethernet is by far the most popular method. We won't go into the precise details here.

While IP addresses are used at the network layer, the link layer has it's own addressing scheme. These link layer addresses go by many different names—we'll refer to them as MAC addresses, but they are also known as LAN addresses and physical addresses. MAC addresses are 48 bits, and they're globally unique. The MAC address is embedded in the NIC, and, unlike an IP address, it cannot change (unless a new NIC is installed). MAC addresses are used to forward packets at the link layer.

Why do we need both IP addresses and MAC addresses? An analogy is often made to a home addresses, which, like IP addresses, can change, and social security numbers, which, like MAC addresses, are immutable. However, this doesn't really answer the question. In fact, it would be conceivable to do away with MAC addresses, but it is somewhat more efficient to use these two forms of addressing. Fundamentally, the dual addressing is necessary due to layering, which requires that the link layer should work with any network layer addressing scheme. Other network layer protocols (such as IPX) that do not have IP addresses are used in some situations.

There are many link layer protocols. We've mentioned ethernet, and we'll mention just one more, the Address Resolution Protocol, or ARP. The primary purpose of ARP is to find the MAC address that corresponds to a given IP address for hosts on the same LAN. Each node has its own ARP table, which contains the mapping between IP addresses and MAC addresses. This ARP table—which is also known as an ARP cache—is generated automatically. The entries expire after a period of time (typically, 20 minutes) so they must be refreshed periodically. Appropriately, ARP is the protocol used to find the ARP table entries.

When a node doesn't know a particular IP-to-MAC mapping, it broadcasts an ARP request message to the LAN. The appropriate node on the LAN responds with an ARP reply and the requesting node can then fill in an entry in its ARP cache.

ARP is a stateless protocol, and, as a result, a node does not have a record of ARP requests that it has sent. As a consequence, a node will accept any ARP reply that it receives, even if it made no corresponding ARP request. This opens the door to an attack by a malicious host on the LAN. This attack—which is known as *ARP cache poisoning*—is illustrated in Figure A-6. In this example, host CC-CC-CC-CC-CC-CC has sent a bogus ARP reply to each of the other hosts, and they have updated their ARP caches accordingly. As a result, whenever AA-AA-AA-AA-AA-AA and BB-BB-BB-BB-BB-BB send packets to each other, the packets will first pass through the evil host CC-CC-CC-CC-CC-CC, who can alter the messages before passing them along (or simply delete them). This type of attack is known as a "man-in-the-middle," regardless of the gender of the attacker. Whereas TCP provided us with an example of a stateful protocol that is subject to attack, ARP is an example of a vulnerable stateless protocol.

A-1.7 Conclusions

In this section, we've barely scratched the surface of the vast topic that is networking. Tanenbaum [226] presents an excellent introduction to a wide range of networking topics, and his book is extremely well-suited to independent study. Another good introductory

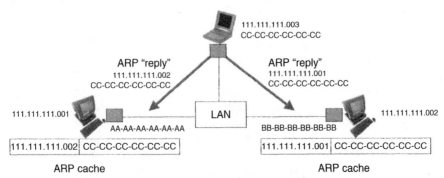

Figure A-6. ARP cache poisoning.

textbook on networking is Kurose and Ross [136]. A more detailed discussion of networking protocols can be found in [81]. If more details are needed than what is available in [81], consult the appropriate RFCs.

A-2 MATH ESSENTIALS

Medicine makes people ill, mathematics make them sad and theology makes them sinful.
                                                                —Martin Luther

A-2.1 Modular Arithmetic

For integers x and n, the value of "x modulo n," which we abbreviate as $x \bmod n$, is given by the remainder when x is divided by n. Notice that the possible remainder values when a number is divided by n are restricted to $0, 1, 2 \ldots, n - 1$.

In non-modular arithmetic, the number line is used to represent the relative positions of the numbers. For modular arithmetic, a "clock" with the integers $0, 1, 2 \ldots, n - 1$ serves a similar purpose, and for this reason modular arithmetic is sometimes known as "clock arithmetic." For example, the "clock" for mod 6 appears in Figure A-7.

We write, for example, $7 \bmod 6 = 1$ or $7 = 1 \bmod 6$. A basic property of modular addition is

$$((a \bmod n) + (b \bmod n)) \bmod n = (a + b) \bmod n$$

so that, for example,

$$(7 + 12) \bmod 6 = 19 \bmod 6 = 1 \bmod 6$$

and

$$(7 + 12) \bmod 6 = (1 + 0) \bmod 6 = 1 \bmod 6.$$

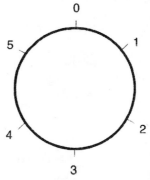

Figure A-7. The number "line" mod 6.

The point here is that we can apply the "mod" operations at any time—either before or after the addition.

The same holds true for modular multiplication, that is,

$$((a \bmod n)(b \bmod n)) \bmod n = ab \bmod n.$$

For example,

$$(7 \cdot 4) \bmod 6 = 28 \bmod 6 = 4 \bmod 6$$

and

$$(7 \cdot 4) \bmod 6 = (1 \cdot 4) \bmod 6 = 4 \bmod 6.$$

Modular inverses play an important role in public key cryptography. In ordinary addition, the inverse of x is the number that must be added to x in order to get 0, that is, the additive inverse of x is $-x$. The additive inverse of $x \bmod n$ is also denoted $-x$ and is similarly defined as the number that must be added to x to obtain $0 \bmod n$. For example, $-2 \bmod 6 = 4$, since $2 + 4 = 0 \bmod 6$.

In "ordinary" arithmetic, the multiplicative inverse of x, denoted by x^{-1}, is the number that must be multiplied by x in order to obtain the number 1. In the non-modular case, for $x \neq 0$, we have $x^{-1} = 1/x$. The multiplicative inverse of $x \bmod n$ is the number that must be multiplied by x in order to get $1 \bmod n$. For example, $3^{-1} \bmod 7 = 5$, since $3 \cdot 5 = 1 \bmod 7$.

What is $2^{-1} \bmod 6$? It's easy to verify that none of the numbers $\{0, 1, 2, 3, 4, 5\}$ work, and so 2 does not have a multiplicative inverse, modulo 6. This shows that in modular arithmetic, the multiplicative inverse does not always exist.

When does the multiplicative inverse exist? To answer that, we require an additional concept. Recall that number p is *prime* if it has no factors other than 1 and p. We say that x and y are *relatively prime* if they have no common factor other than 1. For example, 8 and 9 are relatively prime, even though neither is prime. It can be shown that $x^{-1} \bmod y$ exists if and only if x and y are relatively prime. When the modular inverse exists, it's easy to find using the Euclidean algorithm [34]. It's also easy to tell when a modular inverse doesn't exist, that is, it's easy to test whether x and y are relatively prime.

Another important elementary concept is the *totient function*, which is denoted $\phi(n)$. The value of $\phi(n)$ is the number of positive integers less than n that are relatively prime to n. For example $\phi(4) = 2$ since 4 is relatively prime to 3 and 1. Also, $\phi(5) = 4$ since 5 is relatively prime to 1, 2, 3 and 4.

For any prime number p, we have $\phi(p) = p - 1$. Furthermore, it is fairly easy to show [34] that if p and q are prime, then $\phi(pq) = (p-1)(q-1)$. These elementary properties of $\phi(n)$ are required to understand the RSA public key cryptosystem.

A-2.2 Permutations

Let S be a given set. Then a *permutation* of S is an ordered list of the elements of S in which each element appears exactly once. For example, $(3, 1, 4, 0, 5, 2)$ is a permutation of $\{0, 1, 2, 3, 4, 5\}$.

It is easy to count the number of permutations of $\{0, 1, 2, \ldots, n-1\}$. There are n ways to choose the first element of the permutation, $n-1$ selections remain for the next element of the permutation, and so on. In this way, we see that there are $n!$ permutations of $\{0, 1, 2, \ldots, n-1\}$. For example, there are 24 permutations of the set $\{0, 1, 2, 3\}$.

Permutations are surprisingly important in the study of symmetric key cryptography, as well as in several other areas of cryptography.

A-2.3 Probability

In this book, we only require a few elementary facts from the field of probability. Let $S = \{0, 1, 2, \ldots, N-1\}$ represent the set of all possible outcomes to some experiment. If each outcome is *equally likely*, then the probability of the event $X \subset S$ is

$$P(X) = \frac{\text{number of elements of } X}{\text{number of elements of } S}.$$

For example, if we roll two dice, then S consists of the 36 equally likely outcomes

$$S = \{(1, 1), (1, 2), \ldots, (1, 6), (2, 1), (2, 2), \ldots, (6, 6)\}.$$

When we roll two dice, we find, for example,

$$P(\text{sum equal } 7) = \frac{6}{36} = \frac{1}{6}$$

since 6 of the elements in S sum to 7.

Often, it's easier to compute the probability of X using the fact

$$P(X) = 1 - P(\text{complement of } X)$$

where the complement of X is the set of elements in S that are not in X. For example, when rolling two dice,

$$P(\text{sum} > 3) = 1 - P(\text{number} \leq 3) = 1 - \frac{3}{36} = \frac{11}{12}.$$

Although there are many good sources for information on discrete probability, perhaps the best reference for the types of problems that arise in security is the ancient—but excellent—book by Feller [78]. This book covers all of the basics and many advanced topics, all in a very readable style.

A-2.4 Linear Algebra

In Chapter 6, the discussion of the the attack on the knapsack cryptosystem requires a small amount of linear algebra. Here, we'll discuss only the minimum amount of linear algebra required to understand the material in that particular section.

We write $v \in \mathcal{R}^n$ to denote a vector containing n components, where each element is a real number. For example,

$$v = [v_1, v_2, v_3, v_4] = [4, 7/3, 13, -3/2] \in \mathcal{R}^4.$$

The *dot product* of two vectors $u, v \in \mathcal{R}^n$, is

$$u \cdot v = u_1 v_1 + u_2 v_2 + \cdots + u_n v_n$$

A *matrix* consists of a $n \times m$ array of numbers. For example

$$A = \begin{bmatrix} 3 & 4 & 2 \\ 1 & 7 & 9 \end{bmatrix}$$

is a 2×3 matrix, and we may write $A_{2\times3}$ to emphasize this fact. We denote the element in the ith row and jth column of A as a_{ij}. For example, in the matrix A, above, $a_{1,2} = 4$.

To multiply a matrix by a number, we simply multiply each element of the matrix by the number. For example,

$$3A = \begin{bmatrix} 3 \cdot 3 & 3 \cdot 4 & 3 \cdot 2 \\ 3 \cdot 1 & 3 \cdot 7 & 3 \cdot 9 \end{bmatrix} = \begin{bmatrix} 9 & 12 & 6 \\ 3 & 21 & 27 \end{bmatrix}$$

Addition of matrices A and B is only defined if the matrices have the same dimensions. If so, the corresponding elements are simply added. For example,

$$\begin{bmatrix} 3 & 2 \\ 1 & 5 \end{bmatrix} + \begin{bmatrix} -1 & 4 \\ 6 & 2 \end{bmatrix} = \begin{bmatrix} 2 & 6 \\ 7 & 7 \end{bmatrix}.$$

Matrix multiplication, on the other hand, is less intuitive than addition or multiplication by a number. If $A_{m\times n}$ and $B_{k\times\ell}$, then the product $C = AB$ is only defined if $n = k$, in which case the product matrix C is $m \times \ell$. When the product is defined, the element in row i and column j of C, that is c_{ij}, is given by the dot product of the ith row of A with the jth column of B. For example, with the matrix A above and

$$B = \begin{bmatrix} -1 & 2 \\ 2 & -3 \end{bmatrix}$$

the product

$$BA = C_{2\times3} = \begin{bmatrix} [-1, 2] \cdot \begin{bmatrix} 3 \\ 1 \end{bmatrix} & [-1, 2] \cdot \begin{bmatrix} 4 \\ 7 \end{bmatrix} & [-1, 2] \cdot \begin{bmatrix} 2 \\ 9 \end{bmatrix} \\ [2, -3] \cdot \begin{bmatrix} 3 \\ 1 \end{bmatrix} & [2, -3] \cdot \begin{bmatrix} 4 \\ 7 \end{bmatrix} & [2, -3] \cdot \begin{bmatrix} 2 \\ 9 \end{bmatrix} \end{bmatrix}$$

$$= \begin{bmatrix} -1 & 10 & 16 \\ 3 & -13 & -23 \end{bmatrix}$$

while AB is undefined.

For square matrices, that is, matrices with equal numbers of rows and columns, the *identity matrix* $I_{n \times n}$ has 1s on the main diagonal, and 0s elsewhere. For example, the 3×3 identity matrix is

$$I = \begin{bmatrix} 1 & 0 & 0 \\ 0 & 1 & 0 \\ 0 & 0 & 1 \end{bmatrix}$$

For square matrices, the identity matrix is the multiplicative identity, that is, $AI = IA = A$.

We can also define block matrices, where the "elements" are themselves matrices. We can multiply the blocks of such matrices, provided that the dimensions match as required for matrix multiplications. For example, if

$$M = \begin{bmatrix} I_{n \times n} & C_{n \times 1} \\ A_{m \times n} & B_{m \times 1} \end{bmatrix} \text{ and } V = \begin{bmatrix} U_{n \times \ell} \\ T_{1 \times \ell} \end{bmatrix}$$

then

$$MV = \begin{bmatrix} X_{n \times \ell} \\ Y_{m \times \ell} \end{bmatrix}$$

where $X = U + CT$ and $Y = AU + BT$. You should verify that all of the dimensions are appropriate so that all of these operations are defined.

We'll require only one more result from linear algebra. Suppose x and y are vectors in $\mathcal{R}^n$. Then we say that x and y are *linearly independent* provided that the only α and β for which $\alpha x + \beta y = 0$ is $\alpha = \beta = 0$. For example,

$$\begin{bmatrix} 1 \\ -1 \end{bmatrix} \text{ and } \begin{bmatrix} 1 \\ 2 \end{bmatrix}.$$

are linearly independent. Linear independence extends to more than two vectors. If a set of vectors are linearly independent, then none of the vectors can be written as a *linear combination* of the other vectors, that is, none of the vectors can be written as a sum of multiples of the other vectors in the set.

A-3 DES S-BOXES

Each DES S-box is constructed so that each of its four rows is a permutation of the hexadecimal digits $\{0, 1, 2, \ldots, E, F\}$. For each of the eight S-boxes below, the input to the S-box is denoted $b_0 b_1 b_2 b_3 b_4 b_5$. Note that the first and last input bits are used to index the row, while the middle four bits index the column.

$b_0 b_5$	0	1	2	3	4	5	6	$b_1 b_2 b_3 b_4$ 7	8	9	A	B	C	D	E	F
0	E	4	D	1	2	F	B	8	3	A	6	C	5	9	0	7
1	0	F	7	4	E	2	D	1	A	6	C	B	9	5	3	8
2	4	1	E	8	D	6	2	B	F	C	9	7	3	A	5	0
3	F	C	8	2	4	9	1	7	5	B	3	E	A	0	6	D

DES S-box 1

								$b_1b_2b_3b_4$								
b_0b_5	0	1	2	3	4	5	6	7	8	9	A	B	C	D	E	F
0	F	1	8	E	6	B	3	4	9	7	2	D	C	0	5	A
1	3	D	4	7	F	2	8	E	C	0	1	A	6	9	B	5
2	0	E	7	B	A	4	D	1	5	8	C	6	9	3	2	F
3	D	8	A	1	3	F	4	2	B	6	7	C	0	5	E	9

DES S-box 2

								$b_1b_2b_3b_4$								
b_0b_5	0	1	2	3	4	5	6	7	8	9	A	B	C	D	E	F
0	A	0	9	E	6	3	F	5	1	D	C	7	B	4	2	8
1	D	7	0	9	3	4	6	A	2	8	5	E	C	B	F	1
2	D	6	4	9	8	F	3	0	B	1	2	C	5	A	E	7
3	1	A	D	0	6	9	8	7	4	F	E	3	B	5	2	C

DES S-box 3

								$b_1b_2b_3b_4$								
b_0b_5	0	1	2	3	4	5	6	7	8	9	A	B	C	D	E	F
0	7	D	E	3	0	6	9	A	1	2	8	5	B	C	4	F
1	D	8	B	5	6	F	0	3	4	7	2	C	1	A	E	9
2	A	6	9	0	C	B	7	D	F	1	3	E	5	2	8	4
3	3	F	0	6	A	1	D	8	9	4	5	B	C	7	2	E

DES S-box 4

								$b_1b_2b_3b_4$								
b_0b_5	0	1	2	3	4	5	6	7	8	9	A	B	C	D	E	F
0	2	C	4	1	7	A	B	6	8	5	3	F	D	0	E	9
1	E	B	2	C	4	7	D	1	5	0	F	A	3	9	8	6
2	4	2	1	B	A	D	7	8	F	9	C	5	6	3	0	E
3	B	8	C	7	1	E	2	D	6	F	0	9	A	4	5	3

DES S-box 5

								$b_1b_2b_3b_4$								
b_0b_5	0	1	2	3	4	5	6	7	8	9	A	B	C	D	E	F
0	C	1	A	F	9	2	6	8	0	D	3	4	E	7	5	B
1	A	F	4	2	7	C	9	5	6	1	D	E	0	B	3	8
2	9	E	F	5	2	8	C	3	7	0	4	A	1	D	B	6
3	4	3	2	C	9	5	F	A	B	E	1	7	6	0	8	D

DES S-box 6

							$b_1b_2b_3b_4$									
b_0b_5	0	1	2	3	4	5	6	7	8	9	A	B	C	D	E	F
0	4	B	2	E	F	0	8	D	3	C	9	7	5	A	6	1
1	D	0	B	7	4	9	1	A	E	3	5	C	2	F	8	6
2	1	4	B	D	C	3	7	E	A	F	6	8	0	5	9	2
3	6	B	D	8	1	4	A	7	9	5	0	F	E	2	3	C

DES S-box 7

							$b_1b_2b_3b_4$									
b_0b_5	0	1	2	3	4	5	6	7	8	9	A	B	C	D	E	F
0	D	2	8	4	6	F	B	1	A	9	3	E	5	0	C	7
1	1	F	D	8	A	3	7	4	C	5	6	B	0	E	9	2
2	7	B	4	1	9	C	E	2	0	6	A	D	F	3	5	8
3	2	1	E	7	4	A	8	D	F	C	9	0	3	5	6	B

DES S-box 8

ANNOTATED BIBLIOGRAPHY

[1] 3GPP home page, at http://www.3gpp.org/

[2] @stake LC 5, at http://www.atstake.com/products/lc/
- Despite the firing of Dan Geer for his implicit criticism of Microsoft (see for example, http://dc.internet.com/news/article.php/3083901), @stake remains one of the top security companies.

[3] A guide to understanding covert channel capacity analysis of a trusted system, National computer security center, November 1993, at http://www.Fas.org/irp/nsa/rainbow/tg030.html

[4] A guide to understanding data remanence in automated information systems, NCSC-TG-025, http://www.cerberussystems.com/INFOSEC/stds/ncsctg25.htm

[5] AES algorithm (Rijndael) information, at http://csrc.nist.gov/CryptoToolkit/aes/rijndael/
- A good place to tap into the wealth of information available of Rijndael and the AES.

[6] E. Ackerman, Student skirts CD's piracy guard, SiliconValley.com, at http://www.siliconvalley.com/mld/siliconvalley/news/local/6960633.htm
- The classic "hold down the shift key" attack on a DRM system.

[7] Aleph One, Smashing the stack for fun and profit, *Phrack* 49, at http://www.phrack.org/show.php?p=49&a=14

Information Security: Principles and Practice, by Mark Stamp
Copyright © 2006 John Wiley & Sons, Inc.

- The first widely available and hacker-friendly source of information on buffer overflow attacks.

[8] Anarchriz, CRC and how to reverse it, at `http://http://its.mine.nu/html/re/essays/CRC.html`

- Typical semi-literate hacker prose, but the information appears to be sound.

[9] D. Anderson, T. Frivold, and A. Valdes, Next-generation intrusion detection expert system (NIDES): a summary, at `http://www.sdl.sri.com/papers/4/s/4sri/4sri.pdf`

- This is one in a series of papers about NIDES available at the SRI website.

[10] R. Anderson and E. Biham, Tiger: a fast new hash function, at `http://www.cs.technion.ac.il/~biham/Reports/Tiger/tiger.ps`

- Two crypto experts present the details of their hash.

[11] R. J. Anderson and M. G. Kuhn, Improved differential fault analysis, at `http://www.ftp.cl.cam.ac.uk/ftp/users/rja14/dfa`

- Along with most other security topics under the sun, Ross Anderson is an expert on side channel attacks.

[12] R. Anderson, Security in open versus closed source systems—the dance of Boltzmann, Coarse and Moore, at `http://www.ftp.cl.cam.ac.uk/ftp/users/rja14/toulouse.pdf`

- This fascinating paper gives an impressive (and elementary) argument that—from a security perspective—there's no significant difference between open and closed source software. This is Ross Anderson at his best.

[13] R. Anderson, TCPA/Palladium frequently asked questions, at `http://www.cl.cam.ac.uk/%7Erja14/tcpa-faq.html`

- A great read with—in typical Anderson fashion—several provocative statements.

[14] R. Anderson, *Security Engineering*, Wiley, 2001.

- Ross Anderson is the reigning God of information security and this book is his Bible. For the nitty-gritty details, you'll have to go elsewhere, but for the "big picture," this is a must read.

[15] R. Anderson, *Security Engineering* Errata, at `http://www.cl.cam.ac.uk/~rja14/errata.html`

- This is worth reading just for Anderson's description of the publishing process. Here you'll also learn (among other things) that the MiG-in-the-middle attack never actually occurred.

[16] W. A. Arbaugh, N. Shankar, and Y. C. J. Wan, Your 802.11 wireless network has no clothes, at `http://www.cs.umd.edu/~waa/wireless.pdf`

- Well-written description of the many security flaws in 802.11.

[17] D. Aucsmith, Tamper resistant software: an implementation, *Proceedings of the First International Information Hiding Workshop, Lecture Notes in*

Computer Science 1174, Springer-Verlag, Cambridge, UK, pp. 317–334, 1996

- Difficult to read and well-nigh impossible to comprehend. I challenge anyone to make sense of this, even with Aucsmith's patent as backup.

[18] D. V. Bailey, Inside eBook security, *Dr. Dobb's Journal*, November 2001, at `http://www.ddj.com/documents/s=1487/ddj0111d/0111d.htm`

- The weakness of eBook security is exposed.

[19] I. Balepin, Superworms and cyrptovirology: a deadly combination, at `http://www.csif.cs.ucdavis.edu/~balepin/new_pubs/worms-cryptovirology.pdf`

- The future of malware is considered.

[20] B. Barak, O. Goldreich, R. Impagliazzo, S. Rudich, A. Sahai, S. Vadhan, and K. Yang, On the (im)possibility of obfuscating programs (extended abstract), in J. Kilian, editor, *Advances in Cryptology—CRYPTO 2001, Lecture Notes in Computer Science 2139*, at `http://www.eecs.harvard.edu/~salil/papers/obfuscate-abs.html`

- This paper created quite a stir when published. The upshot is that, in some sense, obfuscation can probably never "really" be secure. There is some debate as to whether the model used is realistic and what "really" really means.

[21] E. Barkan, E. Biham, and N. Keller, Instant ciphertext-only cryptanalysis of GSM encrypted communication, at `http://cryptome.org/gsm-crack-bbk.pdf`

- Attacks on the GSM protocol as well as attacks on A5/2 and A5/1.

[22] BBC News, Afghan girl found after 17 years, at `http://news.bbc.co.uk/1/hi/world/south_asia/1870382.stm`

[23] Beale Screamer, Microsoft's digital rights management scheme—technical details, at `http://web.elastic.org/~fche/mirrors/cryptome.org/beale-sci-crypt.htm`

- Interesting and well-written, at least by hacker standards.

[24] D. J. Bernstein, The IPv6 mess, at `http://cr.yp.to/djbdns/ipv6mess.html`

[25] P. Biddle et al., The darknet and the future of content distribution, at `http://crypto.stanford.edu/DRM2002/darknet5.doc`

- A true classic. Anyone interested in DRM must read this.

[26] A. Biryukov, A. Shamir, and D. Wagner, Real time cryptanalysis of A5/1 on a PC, at `http://home.in.tum.de/~gerold/KryptDokumente/a5_Angriff/a51-bsw.htm`

- An efficient attack on A5/1 that requires huge amounts of storage.

[27] M. Bishop, *Computer Security: Art and Science*, Addison Wesley, 2003.

- In my humble opinion, this book often crosses the line into the realm of theory for the sake of theory. The book is definitely not an easy read. The best sections are those on topics that are theoretical by their very nature. For example, the discussion of security modeling is excellent.

[28] I. Blake, G. Seroussi, and N. Smart, *Elliptic Curves in Cryptography*, Cambridge University Press, 2000.

• The mathematical results are all there but without the proofs.

[29] L. Boettger, The Morris worm: how it affected computer security and lessons learned by it, at `http://www.hackersnews.org/hackerhistory/morrisworm.html`

[30] N. Borisov, I. Goldberg, and D. Wagner, Intercepting mobile communications: the insecurity of 802.11, at `http://www.isaac.cs.berkeley.edu/isaac/wep-draft.pdf`

• A good source for information concerning the many flaws of WEP.

[31] J. Borst, B. Preneel, and J. Vandewalle, On the time-memory trade-off between exhaustive key search and table precomputation, at `http://www.esat.kuleuven.ac.be/~borst/downloadable/tm.ps.gz`

• An extension of Hellman's original TMTO attack. This approach allows for an efficient distributed attack.

[32] J. Bowen, Formal methods, *The World Wide Web Virtual Library*, at `http://vl.fmnet.info/`

[33] D. Brumley and D. Boneh, Remote timing attacks are practical, at `http://crypto.stanford.edu/~dabo/papers/ssl-timing.pdf`

• A nice paper describing a side-channel attack on the RSA implementation in OpenSSL.

[34] D. M. Burton, *Elementary Number Theory*, fourth edition, Wm. C. Brown, 1998.

[35] K. W. Campbell and M. J. Wiener, DES is not a group, *CRYPTO 1992*, pp. 512–520, at `http://www3.sympatico.ca/wienerfamily/Michael/MichaelPapers/desgroup.pdf`

• Definitive proof—though late in coming—that triple DES really is more secure than single DES.

[36] P. Capitant, Software tamper-proofing deployed 2-year anniversary report, Macrovision Corporation, at `http://www.cs.sjsu.edu/faculty/stamp/DRM/DRM%20papers/Software_Tamper-Proofing.ppt`

• Some good information on DRM techniques, based on real-world experiences.

[37] J. Carr, Strategies & issues: thwarting insider attacks, *Network Magazine*, September 4, 2002, at `http://www.networkmagazine.com/article/NMG20020826S0011`

[38] L. Carroll, *Alice's Adventures in Wonderland*, at `http://www.sabian.org/alice.htm`

[39] CERT coordination center, at `http://www.cert.org/`

[40] P. Červeň, *Crackproof Your Software: Protect Your Software Against Crackers*, No Starch Press, 2002.

- Easily the best available book for information on anti-disassembly and anti-debugging techniques. A new edition would be valuable since the material is heavily focused on Windows 98.

[41] G. Chapman et al., *The Complete Monty Python's Flying Circus: All the Words*, vols. 1 and 2, Pantheon, 1989.

[42] H. Chang and M. J. Atallah, Protecting software code by guards *Workshop on Security and Privacy in Digital Rights Management 2001*.

- Surprisingly similar to the paper [110], which was presented at the same conference.

[43] Clipper chip, at http://en.wikipedia.org/wiki/Clipper_chip

[44] A. Main, Application Security: building in security during the development stage, at http://www.cloakware.com/downloads/news/Application_Security_Building_in_Security_During_the_Development_Stage.pdf

[45] F. B. Cohen, Experiments with computer viruses, 1984, at http://www.all.net/books/virus/part5.html

- Discussion of early virus experiments by the inventor of the computer virus.

[46] F. B. Cohen, Operating system protection through program evolution, at http://all.net/books/IP/evolve.html

- A fascinating idea, that has implications far beyond operating systems.

[47] F. B. Cohen, *A Short Course on Computer Viruses*, second edition, Wiley, 1994.

- A nice book by the father of the computer virus. However, the material is dated.

[48] C. S. Collberg and C. Thomborson, Watermarking, tamper-proofing and obfuscation—tools for software protection, *IEEE Transactions on Software Engineering*, vol. 28, no. 8, August 2002.

- These authors are the originators of most of the sophisticated methods of software obfuscation.

[49] Compuware Corporation, at http://www.compuware.com/

[50] M. Barrett and C. Thomborson, using NGSCB to mitigate existing software threats, at http://www.cs.quckland.ac.nz/~cthombor/Pubs/cses04NGSCBthreats.pdf

[51] S. A. Craver et al., Reading between the lines: lessons learned from the SDMI challenge, *Proceedings of the 10th USENIX Security Symposium*, Washington, DC, August 13–17, 2001, at http://www.usenix.org/events/sec01/craver.pdf

- One of the best security papers you'll ever read. The authors totally demolish the security of the proposed SDMI system. If you think watermarking is easy, or if you're tempted to ignore Kerckhoffs' Principle, you'll change your mind after reading this.

[52] Cryptographer's Panel, RSA Conference 2002, see `http://home.earthlink.net/~mstamp1/tripreports/RSA2002.html`

[53] Cryptographer's Panel, RSA Conference 2004, see `http://www.cs.sjsu.edu/faculty/stamp/papers/tripreports/RSA04.html`

[54] J. Daemen and V. Rijmen, The Rijndael block cipher, at `http://csrc.nist.gov/encryption/aes/rijndael/Rijndael.pdf`

[55] J. Daugman, How iris recognition works, at `http://www.cl.cam.ac.uk/users/jgd1000/irisrecog.pdf`

[56] D. Davis, Defective sign & encrypt in S/MIME, PKCS#7, MOSS, PEM, PGP, and XML, at `http://world.std.com/~dtd/sign_encrypt/sign_encrypt7.html`

[57] E. X. DeJesus, SAML brings security to XML, *XML Magazine*, at `http://www.fawcette.com/xmlmag/2002_02/magazine/columns/collaboration/edejesus/`

[58] Defcon 11; see `http://home.earthlink.net/~mstamp1/tripreports/defcon11.html`

  • My "trip report" of Defcon 11.

[59] Enigma machine, at `http://eu.wikipedia.org/wiki/Enigma_machine`

[60] Definition of John Anthony Walker, at `http://www.wordiq.com/definition/John_Anthony_Walker`

[61] Definition of Zimmermann Telegram, at `http://www.wordiq.com/definition/Zimmermann_Telegram`

[62] Definition of Purple code, at `http://www.wordiq.com/definition/Purple_code`

[63] D. E. Denning and D. K. Branstad, A taxonomy for key escrow encryption systems, *Communications of the ACM*, vol. 39, no. 3, March 1996, at `http://www.cosc.georgetown.edu/~denning/crypto/Taxonomy.html`

[64] D. E. Denning, Descriptions of key escrow systems, at `http://www.cosc.georgetown.edu/~denning/crypto/Appendix.html`

[65] Y. Desmedt, What happened with knapsack cryptographic schemes?, *Performance Limits in Communication, Theory and Practice*, J. K. Skwirzynski, ed., Kluwer, pp. 113–134, 1988.

[66] J. F. Dhem et al., A practical implementation of the timing attack, at `http://www.cs.jhu.edu/~fabian/courses/CS600.624/Timing-full.pdf`

[67] W. Diffie and M. Hellman, New directions in cryptography, *IEEE Transactions on Information Theory*, vol. IT-22, no. 6, pp. 644–654, November 1976, at `http://www.cs.jhu.edu/~rubin/courses/sp03/papers/diffie.hellman.pdf`

- Diffie and Hellman's classic paper, where they argue (correctly, as it turned out) that public key cryptography is possible, without offering a viable system.

[68] I. Dubrawsky and L. Hayden, Wireless LANs and privacy, at INET2002.org/ CD-ROM/lu65rw2n/papers/t07-c.pdf

[69] I. Dubrawsky, Effects of Internet worms on routing, RSA Conference 2004, see http://www.cs.sjsu.edu/faculty/stamp/papers/ tripreports/RSA04.html

[70] EFF DES cracker project, at http://www.eff.org/Privacy/ Crypto_misc/DESCracker/

[71] P. Earley, Family of spies: The John Walker Jr. spy case, *The Crime Library*, at http://www.crimelibrary.com/spies/walker/

[72] Easy solution to bypass latest CD-audio protection, at http:// www.cdfreaks.com/news/4068
  - The classic "felt-tip pen" attack.

[73] C. Ellison and B. Schneier, Ten risks of PKI: what you're not being told about public key infrastructure, *Computer Security Journal*, vol. 16, no. 1, pp. 1–7, 2000, at http://www.schneier.com/paper-pki.html

[74] G. Ellison, J. Hodges, and S. Landau, Risks presented by single sign-on architectures, October 18, 2002, at http://research.sun.com/liberty/ RPSSOA/

[75] P. England et al., A trusted open platform, *IEEE Computer*, pp. 55–62, July 2003.
  - A general description of NGSCB/TCG at an early stage in its development.

[76] D. B. Everett, Trusted computing platforms, at http://www.netproject. com/presentations/TCPA/david_everett.pdf

[77] Exploit Systems, Inc., at http://www.exploitsystems.com/
  - An unsuccessful—yet clever—approach to making money from the pirates who inhabit peer-to-peer networks.

[78] W. Feller, *An Introduction to Probability Theory and Its Applications*, third edition, Wiley, 1968.
  - The classic source for information on discrete probability.

[79] U. Fiege, A. Fiat, and A. Shamir, Zero knowledge proofs of identity, *Proceedings of the Nineteenth Annual ACM Conference on Theory of Computing*, pp. 210–217, 1987.

[80] S. Fluhrer, I. Mantin, and A. Shamir, Weaknesses in the key scheduling algorithm of RC4, at http://www.drizzle.com/~aboba/IEEE/rc4_ ksaproc.pdf
  - Several attacks on RC4 are discussed, including a devastating attack on the encryption in WEP. This paper suffers from some typos and a lack of detail. See Mantin's thesis [150] for a more readable and complete version.

[81] B. A. Forouzan, *TCP/IP Protocol Suite*, second edition, McGraw Hill, 2003.

- Forouzan has digested the relevant RFCs and provides the important points in a readable form—no mean feat.

[82] S. Forrest, A. Somayaji, and D. H. Ackley, Building diverse computer systems, at `http://www.cs.unm.edu/~forrest/publications/hotos-97.pdf`

[83] S. Forrest, S. A. Hofmeyr, and A. Somayaji, Computer immunology, *Communications of the ACM*, vol. 40, no. 10, pp. 88–96, October 1997.

- A somewhat "far out" view of the role that biological analogies can play in security.

[84] L. Fraim, SCOMP: A solution to the multilevel security problem, *IEEE Computer*, pp. 26–34, July 1983.

- One of the few serious attempts to develop a trusted operating system.

[85] J. Fraleigh, *A First Course in Abstract Algebra*, Addison Wesley, seventh edition, 2002.

[86] GSM cloning, at `http://www.isaac.cs.berkeley.edu/isaac/gsm.htm`

[87] K. Gaj and A. Orlowski, Facts and myths of Enigma: breaking stereotypes, at `http://ece.gmu.edu/courses/ECE543/viewgraphs_F03/EUROCRYPT_2003.pdf`

[88] M. R. Garey and D. S. Johnson, *Computers and Intractability: A Guide to the Theory of NP–Completeness*, W. H. Freeman & Company, 1979.

[89] B. Gates, Keynote address, RSA Conference 2004, see `http://www.cs.sjsu.edu/faculty/stamp/papers/tripreports/RSA04.html`

[90] D. Geer, comments from "Who will kill online privacy first—the lawyers or the techies?", see `http://home.earthlink.net/~mstamp1/tripreports/RSA2002.html`

[91] W. W. Gibbs, Software's chronic crisis, Trends in Computing, *Scientific American*, p. 86, September 1994, at `http://www.cis.gsu.edu/~mmoore/CIS3300/handouts/SciAmSept1994.html`

[92] R. Glenn and S. Kent, RFC 2410—The NULL encryption algorithm and its use with IPsec, at `http://www.faqs.org/rfcs/rfc2410.html`

- Good nerdy humor.

[93] D. B. Glover, *Secret Ciphers of the 1876 Presidential Election*, Aegean Park Press, 1991.

[94] D. Gollmann, *Computer Security*, Wiley, 1999.

- A fairly theoretical treatment of most topics. Includes an excellent discussion of security modeling.

[95] S. W. Golomb, *Shift Register Sequences*, Aegean Park Press, 1982.

[96] S. Goodwin, Internet gambling software flaw discovered by Reliable Software Technologies software security group, at `http://www.cigital.com/news/index.php?pg=art&artid=20`

- A nice description of an attack on an online version of Texas hold 'em poker.

[97] E. Grevstad, CPU-based security: the NX bit, at `http://hardware.earthweb.com/chips/article.php/3358421`

[98] B. Guignard, How secure is PDF?, at `http://www-2.cs.cmu.edu/~dst/Adobe/Gallery/PDFsecurity.pdf`

- A brief explanations of the ElcomSoft utility to remove PDF security. Correctly concludes that "your encrypted PDF files offer about as much strength as dried egg shells!"

[99] E. Guisado, Secure random numbers, at `http://triumvir.org/articles/rng/`

[100] A. Guthrie, "Alice's Restaurant," lyrics at `http://www.arlo.net/lyrics/alices.shtml`

[101] Hacker may be posing as Microsoft, *USA Today*, February 6, 2002, at `http://www.usatoday.com/tech/techinvestor/2001-03-22-microsoft.htm`

- Discusses a Microsoft certificate that went astray.

[102] Hand based biometrics, *Biometric Technology Today*, pp. 9–11, July/August 2003.

[103] N. Hardy, The confused deputy (or why capabilities might have been invented), at `http://www.skyhunter.com/marcs/capabilityIntro/confudep.html`

- This paper is itself confusing, but it's worth understanding.

[104] D. Harkins and D. Carrel, RFC 2409 The Internet key exchange (IKE), at `http://www.faqs.org/rfcs/rfc2409.html`

[105] M. Hellman, A cryptanalytic time-memory tradeoff, *IEEE Transactions on Information Theory*, vol. 26, pp. 401–406, 1980.

[106] History of GSM, at `http://www.cellular.co.za/gsmhistory.htm`

[107] G. Hoglund and G. McGraw, *Exploiting Software*, Addison Wesley, 2004.

- In spite of some good reviews, this book is, in my opinion, much inferior to Kaspersky's book [123].

[108] B. Horne et al., Dynamic self-checking techniques for improved tamper resistance, *Workshop on Security and Privacy in Digital Rights Management 2001*.

- Very similar to the "guards" paper [42]. Interestingly, both papers were presented at the same conference and both are undoubtedly patented.

[109] IDA Pro disassembler, at `http://www.datarescue.com/`

- The best disassembler known to man.

[110] Iridian Technologies, Iris recognition: science behind the technology, at `http://www.iridiantech.com/basics.php?page=1`

[111] D. Isbell, M. Hardin, and J. Underwood, Mars climate team finds likely cause of loss, at http://www.iki.rssi.ru/jplmirror/mars/msp98/news/mco990930.html

[112] A. Jain, L. Hong, and S. Pankanti, Biometric Identification, *Communications of the ACM*, vol. 43, no. 2, pp. 91–98, 2000.

[113] A. Jain, A. Ross, and S. Pankanti, *Proceedings of the 2nd AVBPA Conference*, Washington, DC, March 22–24, pp. 166–171, 1999.

[114] C. J. A. Jansen, *Investigations on Nonlinear Streamcipher Systems: Construction and Evaluation Methods*, PhD thesis, Technical University of Delft, 1989

- An unusual and hard to find manuscript. Some very difficult research problems are discussed.

[115] H. S. Javitz and A. Valdes, The NIDES statistical component description and justification, at http://www1.cs.columbia.edu/ids/library/javitz.pdf

- One of many NIDES papers available online from SRI.

[116] John Gilmore on the EFF DES cracker, at http://www.computer.org/internet/v2n5/w5news-des.htm

[117] John the Ripper password cracker, at http://www.openwall.com/john/

[118] M. E. Kabay, Salami fraud, *Network World Security Newsletter*, July 24, 2002, at http://www.nwfusion.com/newsletters/sec/2002/01467137.html

[119] D. Kahn, *The Codebreakers: The Story of Secret Writing*, revised edition, Scribner, 1996.

- The source for crypto history prior to its original publication date of 1967. Supposedly, it was updated in 1996, but virtually no new information was added.

[120] L. Kahney, OS X trojan horse is a nag, at http://www.wired.com/news/mac/0,2125,63000,00.html?tw=rss.TEK

- Additional discussion of this harmless trojan can be found at [149].

[121] K. Kaspersky, *Hacker Disassembling Uncovered*, A-List, 2003.

- An excellent book for anyone interested in software reverse engineering. Far superior to [107], though it does suffer somewhat from poor writing (as do most "hacker" publications).

[122] C. Kaufman, R. Perlman, and M. Speciner, *Network Security*, second edition, Prentice Hall, 2002.

- Excellent coverage of networking protocols as well as good—though brief—coverage of many relevant crypto topics. Chapter 11 alone is worth the (high) price of the book. The substantive content is consistently first rate—with one major exception. The exception is the coverage of IPSec (two chapters) which is very poor. Another failing is that the book has way too much emphasis on some tedious issues such as where all of the bits go, the exact format of certain messages, etc. This sort of information is the reason why RFCs exist.

[123] J. Kelsey, B. Schneier, and D. Wagner, Related-key cryptanalysis of 3-WAY, Biham-DES, CAST, DES-X, NewDES, RC2, and TEA, *ICICS '97 Proceedings*, Springer-Verlag, November 1997.

[124] Kerckhoffs' law, at `http://en.wikipedia.org/wiki/kerckhoffs'_law`

[125] A. Kerckhoffs, La cryptographie militaire, *Journal des Sciences Militaires*, vol. IX, pp. 5–83, January 1883, pp. 161–191, February 1883.

[126] L. Kesteloot, Byzantine failures in synchronous systems, at `http://www.teamten.com/lawrence/290.paper/node7.html`

[127] P. Kocher, J. Jaffe, and B. Jun, Differential power analysis, *Advances in Cryptology CRYPTO '99*, vol. 1666 of Lecture Notes in Computer Science, M. Wiener, editor, Springer–Verlag, pp. 388–397, 1999, at `http://www.cryptography.com/resources/whitepapers/DPA.html`

   • One of the few papers written by Kocher on side channel attacks. This is curious, since he is clearly the leader in the field.

[128] P. C. Kocher, Timing attacks on implementations of Diffie-Hellman, RSA, DSS, and other systems, at `http://www.cryptography.com/resources/whitepapers/TimingAttacks.pdf`

[129] Kodak research and development, at `http://www.kodak.com/US/en/corp/researchDevelopment/`

[130] F. Koeune, Some interesting references about LLL, at `http://www.dice.ucl.ac.be/~fkoeune/LLL.html`

[131] D. P. Kormann and A. D. Rubin, Risks of the Passport single signon protocol, at `http://avirubin.com/passport.html`

[132] J. Koziol et al., *The Shellcoder's Handbook*, Wiley, 2004.

   • For a long time, there were few books that made any serious attempt to discuss hacking techniques. Of course, hackers knew (or could learn) about such techniques, so this lack of information only hindered the good guys while doing little or nothing to deter attackers. Recently, however, there has been a flood of "hacking" books and this book is easily among the best of the genre.

[133] H. Krawczyk, M. Bellare, and R. Canetti, RFC 2104—HMAC: Keyed-hashing for message authentication, at `http://www.faqs.org/rfcs/rfc2104.html`

[134] D. L. Kreher and D. R. Stinson, *Combinatorial Algorithms*, CRC Press, 1999.

   • The best available mathematical discussion of the lattice reduction attack on the knapsack. However, be forewarned that this book is filled with typos, which is a major problem for an algorithms book.

[135] M. Kuhn, Security—biometric identification, at `http://www.cl.cam.ac.uk/Teaching/2003/Security/guestslides-biometric-4up.pdf`

[136] J. F. Kurose and K. W. Ross, *Computer Networking*, Addison Wesley, 2003.
- A good textbook for an introduction to networking class. But for self-study, I'd recommend Tanenbaum [226].

[137] P. B. Ladkin, Osprey, cont'd, *The Risks Digest*, vol. 21, issue 41, 2001, at `http://catless.ncl.ac.uk/Risks/21.41.html#subj7`

[138] M. K. Lai, Knapsack cryptosystems: the past and the future, March 2001, at `http://www.cecs.uci.edu/~mingl/knapsack.html`

[139] B. W. Lampson, Computer security in the real world, *IEEE Computer*, pp. 37–46, June 2004.

[140] S. Landau, Communications security for the twenty-first century: the Advanced Encryption Standard, *Notices of the AMS*, vol. 47, no. 4, April 2000, pp. 450–459.
- This paper has good detail on the Rijndael algorithm, as well as an overview of the other AES finalists.

[141] S. Landau, Standing the test of time: the Data Encryption Standard, *Notices of the AMS*, vol. 47, no. 3, March 2000, pp. 341–349.
- A good technical description of DES. As the title suggests, this paper should have (finally) put to rest all of the nonsense about a back door in DES.

[142] C. E. Landwehr et al., A taxonomy of computer program security flaws, with examples, *ACM Computing Surveys*, vol. 26, no. 3, pp. 211–254, September 1994, at `http://chacs.nrl.navy.mil/publications/CHACS/1994/1994landwehr-acmcs.pdf`

[143] R. Lemos, Spat over MS 'flaw' gets heated, *ZD Net UK News*, at `http://news.zdnet.co.uk/software/developer/0,39020387,2104559,00.htm`
- The debate over the implementation of Microsoft's buffer overflow prevention technique. It is claimed that the implementation made the problem worse, not better.

[144] C. J. Lennard and T. Patterson, History of fingerprinting, at `http://www.policensw.com/info/fingerprints/finger01.html`

[145] A. K. Lenstra, H. W. Lenstra, Jr., and L. Lovàsz, Factoring polynomials with rational coefficients, *Math. Ann.*, 261, 1982.
- The LLL lattice reduction algorithm.

[146] J. Lettice, Bad publicity, clashes trigger MS Palladium name change, *The Register*, at `http://www.theregister.co.uk/content/4/29039.html`
- What's in a name? That which we call NGSCB by any other name would smell like Palladium.

[147] S. Levy, The open secret, *Wired*, issue 7.04, April 1999, at `http://www.wired.com/wired/archive/7.04/crypto_pr.html`

- So you think Diffie, Hellman, Merkle, Rivest, Shamir, and Adleman invented public key cryptography? Think again.

[148] Liberty alliance project, at `http://www.projectliberty.org/`

[149] A. C. Engst, Mac OS X trojan technique: beware of geeks bearing gifts, Tid-BITS, no. 726, April 12, 2004, at `http://db.tidbits.com/getbits.acgi?tbart=07636`

- A proof-of-concept trojan for the Mac. See [120] for additional context.

[150] I. Mantin, Analysis of the stream cipher RC4, at `http://www.wisdom.weizmann.ac.il/~itsik/RC4/Papers/Mantin1.zip`

- A clearer and more detailed description of the RC4 attacks presented in [80].

[151] J. L. Massey, Design and analysis of block ciphers, *EIDMA Minicourse 8–12 May 2000*.

- Some excellent insights by one of the lesser-known giants of cryptography.

[152] D. Maughan et al., RFC 2408—Internet security association and key management protocol (ISAKMP), at `http://www.faqs.org/rfcs/rfc2408.html`

[153] J. McLean, A comment on the "basic security theorem" of Bell and LaPadula, *Information Processing Letters*, vol. 20, no. 2, February 1985, at `http://chacs.nrl.navy.mil/publications/CHACS/Before1990/1985mclean-ipl.pdf`

- Mclean attacks BLP.

[154] J. McNamara, The complete, unofficial TEMPEST information page, at `http://www.eskimo.com/~joelm/tempest.html`

[155] T. McNichol, Totally random: how two math geeks with a lava lamp and a webcam are about to unleash chaos on the Internet, *Wired*, issue 11.08, August 2003, at `http://www.wired.com/wired/archive/11.08/random.html`

[156] A. Menezes, P. C. van Oorschot, and S. A. Vanstone, *Handbook of Applied Cryptography*, CRC Press, 1997, Chapter 7, at `http://www.cacr.math.uwaterloo.ca/hac/about/chap7.pdf`

- More precise than Schneier's book [203], but badly in need of a second edition.

[157] R. Merkle, Secure communications over insecure channels, *Communications of the ACM*, April 1978, pp. 294–299 (submitted in 1975), at `http://www.itas.fzk.de/mahp/weber/merkle.htm`

- Given its submission date, this paper should be at least as famous as Diffie and Hellman's [67]. However, due to its absurdly late publication date, it's not.

[158] Micosoft.NET Passport: one easy way to sign in online, at `http://www.passport.net`

[159] M. S. Miller, K.-P. Yee, and J. Shapiro, Capability myths demolished, at `http://zesty.ca/capmyths/`

- Capabilities are loved by academics, as this paper illustrates. However, in typical academic fashion, the paper ignores the significant practical challenges that arise when capabilities are actually implemented.

[160] F. Mirza, Block ciphers and cryptanalysis, at `http://fermat.ma.rhbnc.ac.uk/~fauzan/papers/`

- A good paper that uses STEA (simplified TEA) as an example to illustrate certain cryptanalytic attacks.

[161] D. Moore et al., The spread of the Sapphire/Slammer worm, at `http://www.cs.berkeley.edu/~nweaver/sapphire/`

[162] A. Muchnick, Microsoft nearing completion of Death Star, at `http://bbspot.com/news/2002/05/deathstar.html`

- Geeky humor at its best.

[163] NGSCB: Trusted computing base and software authentication, at `http://www.microsoft.com/resources/ngscb/documents/ngscb_tcb.doc`

[164] National Security Agency, at `http://en.wikipedia.org/wiki/NSA`

[165] R. M. Needham and D. J. Wheeler, Tea extensions, at `http://www.cl.cam.ac.uk/ftp/users/djw3/xtea.ps`

- An "extended" version of TEA that eliminates an obscure related key attack.

[166] R. Needham and M. Schroeder, Using encryption for authentication in large networks of computers *Communications of the ACM*, vol. 21, no. 12, pp. 993–999, 1978.

- This is the foundation on which Kerberos was built.

[167] Next-generation secure computing base, at `http://www.microsoft.com/resources/ngscb/default.mspx`

[168] J. R. Nickerson et al., The encoder solution to implementing tamper resistant software, at `http://www.cert.org/research/isw2001/papers/Nickerson-12-09.pdf`

[169] A. M. Odlyzko, The rise and fall of knapsack cryptosystems, at `http://www.research.att.com/~amo/doc/arch/knapsack.survey.pdf`

[170] OllyDbg, at `http://home.t-online.de/home/ollydbg/`

[171] Our Documents—High-resolution PDFs of Zimmermann Telegram (1917), at `http://www.ourdocuments.gov/doc.php?flash=true&doc=60&page=pdf`

[172] P. S. Pagliusi, A contemporary foreword on GSM security, in G. Davida, Y. Frankel, and O. Rees, editors, *Infrastructure Security: International Conference—InfraSec 2002*, Bristol, UK, October 1–3, 2002, Lecture Notes in Computer Science 2437, pp. 129–144, Springer–Verlag, 2002.

- In spite of the title, this is a comprehensive and highly readable description of the major security flaws in GSM.

[173] J. C. Panettieri, Who let the worms out?—the Morris worm, *eWeek*, March 12, 2001, at `http://www.eweek.com/article2/0,1759,1245602,00.asp`

[174] D. B. Parker, Automated crime, at `http://infosecuritymag.techtarget.com/articles/1999/autocrime.shtml`

[175] D. B. Parker, Automated security, at `http://infosecuritymag.techtarget.com/articles/1999/autocrime2.shtml`

- One of the gurus of security discusses the use of metamorphism to enhance security.

[176] Passwords revealed by sweet deal, *BBC News*, April 20, 2004, at `http://news.bbc.co.uk/2/hi/technology/3639679.stm`

- Most users reveal passwords for a candy bar.

[177] C. Peikari and A. Chuvakin, *Security Warrior*, O'Reilly, 2004.

- A reasonably interesting book with some real software hacking examples. However, Kaspersky's book [121] is much more thorough, and much better.

[178] S. Petrovic and A. Fúster-Sabater, Cryptanalysis of the A5/2 algorithm, at `http://eprint.iacr.org/2000/052/`

[179] C. P. Pfleeger and S. L. Pfleeger, *Security in Computing*, third edition, Prentice Hall, 2003.

- Particularly good for OS security and some software issues. However, much of the information is dated—the book is ancient by computing standards, having been originally published in 1989. It's also not an easy read.

[180] M. Pietrek, Peering inside the PE: a tour of the Win32 portable executable file format, at `http://msdn.microsoft.com/library/default.asp`

[181] D. Piper, RFC 2407—The Internet IP security domain of interpretation for ISAKMP, at `http://www.faqs.org/rfcs/rfc2407.html`

[182] A. Pressman, Wipe 'em out, then sue for back pay, at `http://www.internetwright.com/drp/RiskAssess.htm`

- An interesting description of an insider attack. Most interesting of all is the response by the company, which remains typical today.

[183] J. Raley, Ali Baba Bunny—1957, Jenn Raley's Bugs Bunny page, at `http://www.jenn98.com/bugs/1957-1.html`

- Bugs Bunny and Daffy Duck in Ali Baba's cave.

[184] J. R. Rao et al., Partitioning attacks: or how to rapidly clone some GSM cards, *2002 IEEE Symposium on Security and Privacy*, May 12–15, 2002.

[185] C. Ren, M. Weber, and G. McGraw, Microsoft compiler flaw technical note, at `http://www.cigital.com/news/index.php?pg=art&artid=70`

- A discussion of an attack on Microsoft's buffer overflow prevention technique. Microsoft argued that the claimed attack was exaggerated [143].

[186] G. Richarte, Four different tricks to bypass StackShield and StackGuard protection, at `http://downloads.securityfocus.com/library/StackGuard.pdf`

[187] V. Rijmen, The Rijndael page, at `http://www.iaik.tu-graz.ac.at/research/knypto/AES/old/~rijmen/rijndael/`

- Excellent source of information on the AES algorithm, by one of its inventors.

[188] R. L. Rivest et al., The RC6 block cipher, at `http://www.secinf.net/cryptography/The_RC6_Block_Cipher.html`

[189] Robert Morris, at `http://www.rotten.com/library/bio/hackers/robert-morris/`

- The creator of the Morris Worm.

[190] S. Robinson, Up to the challenge: computer scientists crack a set of AI-based puzzles, *SIAM News*, vol. 35, no. 9, November 2002, at `http://www.siam.org/siamnews/11-02/gimpy.htm`

[191] M. J. Rose, Stephen King's 'Plant' uprooted, *Wired*, November 28, 2000, at `http://www.wired.com/news/culture/0,1284,40356,00.html`

[192] M. Rosing, *Implementing Elliptic Curve Cryptography*, Manning Publications, 1998.

- A good elementary introduction to elliptic curve cryptography.

[193] Rsync Open source software project, at `http://samba.anu.edu.au/rsync/`

[194] R. A. Rueppel, *Analysis and Design of Stream Ciphers*, Springer-Verlag, 1986.

- In spite of its publication date, this book is still the best available introduction to many issues related to stream ciphers. Rueppel developed this book when he was Massey's student.

[195] SSL 3.0 specification, at `http://wp.netscape.com/eng/ssl3/`

[196] A real MD5 collision, Educated guesswork: August 2004 archives at `http://www.rtfm.com/movabletype/archives/2004_08.html#001055`

[197] R. Sanchez-Reillo, C. Sanchez-Avila, and Ana Gonzalez-Marcos, Biometric identification through hand geometry measurements, *IEEE Transactions on Pattern Analysis and Machine Intelligence*, vol. 22, no. 10, pp. 1168–1171, 2000.

[198] P. Sayer, 'The Plant' withers for Stephen King, *Info World*, November 29, 2000, at `http://www.infoworld.com/articles/hn/xml/00/11/29/001129hnplant.html`

[199] B. Schneier, Attack trees, *Dr. Dobb's Journal*, December 1999, at `http://www.schneier.com/paper-attacktrees-ddj-ft.html`

- A practical and intuitive approach to "hazard analysis".

[200] B. Schneier, Biometrics: truths and fictions, at `http://www.schneier.com/crypto-gram-9808.html`

[201] B. Schneier, Risks of relying on cryptography, Inside Risks 112, *Communications of the ACM*, vol. 42, no. 10, October 1999, at `http://www.schneier.com/essay-021.html`

- Schneier, in his own inimitable style, emphasizes the point that attackers don't necessarily play by the rules.

[202] B. Schneier, The Blowfish encryption algorithm, at `http://www.schneier.com/blowfish.html`

- Schneier describes his favorite crypto algorithm.

[203] B. Schneier, *Applied Cryptography*, second edition, Wiley, 1996.

- This book has, for better or for worse, become the crypto bible for working security professionals.

[204] A. Shamir and N. van Someren, Playing hide and seek with stored keys, at `http://www.ncipher.com/resources/downloads/files/white_papers/keyhide2.pdf`

- This paper includes a simple and effective statistical test for distinguishing random from non-random.

[205] A. Shamir, A polynomial-time algorithm for breaking the basic Merkle-Hellman cryptosystem, *IEEE Transactions on Information Theory*, vol. IT-30, no. 5, pp. 699–704, September 1984.

- Shamir's clever attack on the original knapsack cryptosystem.

[206] A. Shamir, How to share a secret, *Communications of the ACM*, vol. 22, no. 11, pp. 612–613, November 1979, at `http://szabo.best.vwh.net/secret.html`

[207] C. E. Shannon, Communication theory of secrecy systems, *Bell System Technical Journal*, vol. 28-4, pp. 656–715, 1949, at `http://www.cs.ucla.edu/~jkong/research/security/shannon1949.pdf`

- The paper that started it all. Most of this paper remains surprisingly relevant after more than a half-century.

[208] K. Skachkov, Tamper-resistant software: design and implementation, at `http://www.cs.sjsu.edu/faculty/stamp/students/TRSDIfinal.doc`

- Discusses some of the issues related to tamper-resistant software of Aucsmith [17] variety. A toy implementation is presented.

[209] S. Skorobogatov and R. Anderson, Optical fault induction attacks, *IEEE Symposium on Security and Privacy*, 2002.

[210] E. Skoudis, *Counter Hack*, Prentice Hall, 2002.

- An excellent book that includes plenty of details on the sophisticated hacker's approach to a target. A must read for the system administrators of the world.

[211] R. Slade, Brain, at `http://www.cknow.com/vtutor/vtsladebrain. htm`

[212] Staff Report, U. S. Senate Select Committee on Intelligence, Unclassified summary: involvement of NSA in the development of the Data Encryption Standard, Staff Report, 98th Congress, 2nd Session, April 1978

- Senate report that cleared NSA of any wrongdoing in the design of DES. Needless to say, this did not convince the critics.

[213] M. Stamp and A. Hushyar, Multilevel security models, to appear as a chapter of *The Handbook of Information Security*

- This paper gives an overview of many different security models. It likely contains more than you'll ever want to know about security modeling.

[214] M. Stamp and D. Holankar, Secure streaming media and digital rights manage- ments, *Proceedings of the 2004 Hawaii International Conference on Computer Science*, January 2004, at `http://home.earthlink.net/~mstamp1/ papers/hawaii.pdf`

- A nice protocol for delivering DRM-protected streaming media that includes many of the software protection tricks discussed in this book. A working beta implementation also exists.

[215] M. Stamp and E. J. Sebes, Enterprise digital rights management: Ready for prime-time?, *Business Communications Review*, pp. 52–55, March 2004, at `http://www.bcr.com/bcrmag/2004/03/p52.asp`

- Makes the case that DRM within an enterprise is a much different beast than DRM for e-commerce.

[216] M. Stamp and P. Mishra, Software uniqueness: how and why, *Proceedings of ICCSA 2003*, at `http://home.earthlink.net/~mstamp1/papers/ iccsaPuneet.doc`

- Discusses the potential security benefits of software uniqueness or metamor- phism, and describes a simple system for achieving a reasonable degree of uniqueness.

[217] M. Stamp and P. Sabadra, The MediaSnap digital rights management sys- tem, *Proceedings of ICCSA 2003*, at `http://home.earthlink.net/~ mstamp1/papers/iccsaDRM.doc`

[218] M. Stamp and S. Thaker, Software watermarking via assembly code trans- formations, *Proceeding of ICCSA 2004*, June 2004, at `http://www.cs. sjsu.edu/faculty/stamp/papers/iccsaSmita.doc`

- A simple and intuitive software watermarking scheme. The goal here is to devise a system where automated watermark removal is unlikely to succeed.

[219] M. Stamp, Digital rights management: For better or for worse?, *Extreme- Tech*, May 20, 2003, at `http://www.extremetech.com/article2/ 0,3973,1051610,00.asp`

- Makes the argument that, in spite of its technical shortcomings, DRM can facilitate e-commerce if the business model is appropriate.

[220] M. Stamp, Digital rights management: the technology behind the hype, *Journal of Electronic Commerce Research*, vol. 4, no. 3, 2003, at `http://www.csulb.edu/web/journals/jecr/issues/20033/paper3.pdf`

- Perhaps the most detailed description of a fielded commercial DRM system.

[221] M. Stamp, Risks of digital rights management, Inside Risks 147, *Communications of the ACM*, vol. 45, no. 9, p. 120, September 2002, at `http://www.csl.sri.com/users/neumann/insiderisks.html#147`

- This article highlights some of the obvious difficulties of doing DRM in software.

[222] M. Stamp, Risks of monoculture, Inside Risks 165, *Communications of the ACM*, vol. 47, no. 3, p. 120, March 2004, at `http://www.csl.sri.com/users/neumann/insiderisks04.html#165`

- An intuitive discussion of the potential security benefits of diverse software.

[223] S. Staniford, V. Paxson, and N. Weaver, How to own the Internet in your spare time, at `http://www.cs.berkeley.edu/ ~nweaver/cdc.web/`

- The best article I've seen on the future of malware.

[224] H. L. Stimson and M. Bundy, *On Active Service in Peace and War*, Hippocrene Books, 1971.

[225] A. Stubblefield, J. Ioannidis, and A. D. Rubin, Using the Fluhrer, Mantin and Shamir attack to break WEP, at `http://philby.ucsd.edu/~bsy/ndss/2002/html/2002/papers/stubbl.pdf`

[226] A. S. Tanenbaum, *Computer Networks*, fourth edition, Prentice Hall, 2003.

- Probably the best networking book for self-study or casual reading. The book is comprehensive, yet Tanenbaum has plenty of stories to keep the reader interested and awake.

[227] TechnoLogismiki, Hackman, at `http://www.technologismiki.com/en/index-h.html`

[228] D. Terdiman, Vegas gung-ho on gambling tech, *Wired*, September 19, 2003, at `http://www.wired.com/news/print/0,1294,60499,00.html`

[229] The German Enigma machine, at `http://www.myke.com/enigma.htm`

[230] The Warhol, at `http://www.warhol.org/`

[231] C. Thomborson and M. Barrett, NGSCB: a new tool for securing applications, at `http://www.cs.auckland.ac.nz/~cthombor/Pubs/barrettNZISF120804.pdf`

[232] K. Thompson, Reflections on trusting trust, *Communication of the ACM*, vol. 27, no. 8, pp. 761–763, August 1984, at `http://www.acm.org/classics/sep95/`

- A classic paper that probes the theoretical limits of security in software.

[233] B. C. Tjaden, *Fundamentals of Secure Computing Systems*, Franklin, Beedle & Associates, 2004.

- An introductory information security textbook. Much of the coverage is uninspired, but the chapter on intrusion detection is well worth the (modest) price of the book.

[234] W. A. Trappe and L. C. Washington, *Introduction to Cryptography with Coding Theory*, Prentice Hall, 2002.

- An excellent and mathematically sound introduction to many aspects of cryptography.

[235] Trusted Computing Group, at `http://www.trustedcomputinggroup.org/home`

[236] B. W. Tuchman, *The Zimmermann Telegram*, Ballantine Books, 1985.

- An entertaining historical account by one of the better writers of popular history.

[237] US v. ElcomSoft & Sklyarov FAQ, at `http://www.eff.org/IP/DMCA/US_v_Elcomsoft/us_v_elcomsoft_faq.html`

[238] R. Vamosi, Windows XP SP2 more secure? Not so fast, at `http://reviews.zdnet.co.uk/software/os/0,39024180,39163696,00.htm`

[239] VENONA, at `http://www.nsa.gov/venona/index.cfm`

- VENONA is an interesting topic, both for crypto and for the historical material. Many of those who vigorously denied they had any role in espionage are implicated by VENONA decrypts. Also, of the hundreds of traitors mentioned (by cover name) in the decrypts, the true identities of most remain unknown.

[240] VeriSign, Inc., at `http://www.verisign.com/`

- The leading commerical certificate authority (CA).

[241] J. Viega and G. McGraw, *Building Secure Software*, Addison Wesley, 2002.

- This is a worthwhile book that provides considerable detail on issues related to secure software development. One of the weaknesses of this book is that it provides no evidence of the effectiveness of its suggestions.

[242] VMware is virtual infrastructure, at `http://www.vmware.com/`

[243] L. von Ahn, M. Blum, and J. Langford, Telling humans and computers apart automatically, *Communications of the ACM*, vol. 47, no. 2, pp. 57–60, February 2004, at `http://www.cs.cmu.edu/~biglou/captcha_cacm.pdf`

- A fascinating, informative and entertaining article. This is the place to start your research into CAPTCHAs.

[244] L. von Ahn et al., The CAPTCHA project, at `http://www.captcha.net/`

[245] J. R. Walker, Unsafe at any key size; an analysis of the WEP encapsulation, at `http://www.dis.org/wl/pdf/unsafe.pdf`

- A clever title and a good description of the some of the problems created by WEP's use of IVs. However, the most serious problem is the devastating cryptanalytic attack discussed in [80], which is not mentioned here.

[246] D. J. Wheeler and R. M. Needham, TEA, a tiny encryption algorithm, at `http://www.cix.co.uk/~klockstone/tea.pdf`

- Less than four pages to present TEA in all of its wonderful simplicity.

[247] R. N. Williams, A painless guide to CRC error detection algorithms, at `http://www.ross.net/crc/crcpaper.html`

[248] N. Winkless and I. Browning, *Robots on Your Doorstep*, dilithium Press, 1978.

- While it seems dated today, this classic and off-beat book presents the conventional wisdom of its time in an unconventional way.

[249] W. Wong, Revealing your secrets through the fourth dimension, to appear in *ACM Crossroads*, available at `http://www.cs.sjsu.edu/faculty/stamp/students/wing.html`

- An elementary and highly readable description of the ideas behind RSA timing attacks.

[250] M. Zalewski, Strange attractors and TCP/IP sequence number analysis—one year later, at `http://lcamtuf.coredump.cx/newtcp/`

- Fascinating scatter plots of the distribution of TCP initial SEQ numbers for many different vendor's products. Many are extremely non-random. See Section 9.4 for a discussion of the security flaw this creates.

[251] L. Zeltser Reverse-engineering malware, at `http://www.zeltser.com/sans/gcih-practical/`

- An excellent discussion of malware as well as reverse engineering principles. Highly recommended. See also [252].

[252] L. Zeltser, SANS malware FAQ: reverse engineering srvcp.exe, at `http://www.sans.org/resources/malwarefaq/srvcp.php`

- Much overlap with [251] but this one also includes a link to the malware executable that is reverse engineered.

[253] M. Zorz, Basic security with passwords, at `http://www.net-security.org/article.php?id=117`

INDEX

3DES, *see* triple DES
3GPP, 254, 260
3rd Generation Partnership Project,
    see 3GPP

A3/A5/A8, 34–36, 57, 148, 256–258
access control, xv, 2, 4–5, 153
   and operating system, 328
access control list, *see* ACL
access control matrix, 178
ACK scan, 193, 205
ACL, 179, 203
Address Resolution Protocol, *see* ARP
Adleman, Leonard, 66
Adobe, 308
   eBooks, 314
Advanced Encryption Standard, *see* AES
AES, 45–48, 57, 82, 104, 309
   AddRoundKey, 48
   block size, 46
   ByteSub, 47
   confusion and diffusion, 57
   key length, 46
   key schedule, 48
   MixColumn, 48
   number of rounds, 46
   ShiftRow, 47
   subkey, 48
AFS Software, Inc., 99

AH, 240, 248–249
   and Microsoft, 249
Ali Baba's Cave, 227
Alice's Restaurant, 1
Almes, Guy, 341
Anderson, Ross, 318, 330,
    336, 337
anomaly detection, 286–287
anonymity, 232
anti-debugging, 301
anti-disassembly, 300
Apple II, 66, 134
application layer, 342, 344–345
Aristotle, 33
ARP, 350
   cache poisoning, 350
asymmetric cryptography, 61
ATM
   card, 155
   machine, 211
attack tree, 319
authentication, 2, 153–155, 262
   and TCP, 224–226
   two-factor, 172
authentication header,
    see AH
authorization, 2, 4–5, 154
availability, 2
avalanche effect, 90

Information Security: Principles and Practice, by Mark Stamp
Copyright © 2006 John Wiley & Sons, Inc.